St. Jerome Grammar

7

Based on the series by

by REVEREND PAUL E. CAMPBELL
formerly Superintendent of Schools, Diocese of Pittsburgh

and SISTER MARY DONATUS MACNICKLE
Sisters, Servants of the Immaculate Heart of Mary

Do not miss **MY ENGLISH RECORD** *at the back of your book.*

St. Jerome Library

WWW.STJEROMELIBRARY.ORG

Copyright © 2020AD-2024AD by St. Jerome Library Press
Fairbanks, Indiana

All Rights Reserved. No part of this book may be reproduced or transmitted in any form or by any means, electronic or mechanical, including photocopying, recording, or by any information storage or retrieval system, without written permission from the publisher. The contents of this book are humbly laid before you in complete submission to the review of the Holy See when God in His Divine Providence chooses to send a Holy Pontiff once again to rule His Church.
St. Peter, St. Jerome, pray for us!

Preface

It is no doubt true that the child grows toward maturity and independence of thought as he progresses through the grades; but this growth is not as a rule a sharp and sudden one, nor does the psychology of the child undergo any great change during his years in the elementary school. Methods, general objectives, and, certainly, the fundamental principles that underlie the work of the school remain the same from year to year. The need in every grade is to bring about pupil growth by making good use of the experiences of the child and by providing new and broader experiences.

A child can grow in school only if he is active. He must therefore do something with or about his experiences. The first and most obvious thing that he can do is to tell others of them. We encourage his desire to tell about his experiences. We wish him to express himself naturally and joyfully. If we make him feel that we and all the group discover a value in what he has to say, he will wish more and more to express himself well and successfully. We give him models of written expression that will make him sensitive to the beauty of word and phrase. We teach him to use certain methods and to observe certain rules; and

PREFACE

these he accepts because he finds that our methods and our rules are things that he can easily use or understand, and that they help him.

VOYAGES IN ENGLISH endeavors, insofar as a textbook can accomplish such a purpose, to create a classroom atmosphere conducive to a group spirit rather than to a selfish and individualistic spirit. Every child is made to feel that the entire group is interested in what others have to say. He is taught to listen courteously and to criticize in a kindly and constructive manner.

It is also necessary to supply the child with new experiences. Schools can do this by means of motion pictures, excursions, and other similar activities. A textbook can do so only by encouraging the reading of books and by the models and exercises it contains. VOYAGES IN ENGLISH studiously excludes from its model paragraphs and from the sentences in its exercises whatever is misanthropic, or destructive, or psychologically harmful. The world that it seeks to create for the child is a bright world, a happy world, a hopeful world, and a usefully busy world.

A child can tell of his experiences either orally or in written form. The authors accept it as a fundamental principle that oral expression should precede written expression. Expression, whether oral or written, should provide variety, stimulate the imagination, and inspire creative effort by taking different forms. Children can express themselves by telling the class of something they have read, by taking part in discussions, by class dramatizations of things read in books, by imaginary broadcasts, telecasts, and telephone calls, by writing a paragraph or by writing a letter. It has been the aim of the authors to make use of every form of expression that has been found to be practical and appealing.

The authors believe very wholeheartedly in the child-centered school, but only if that term is properly understood. The child is necessarily the center of the school's activity, for everything that the school undertakes, every activity in which it engages, has for its immediate object the doing of something to or for the child; nor can the school afford to forget, in any of its planning, what the child needs to achieve and what the child is capable of achieving. The school should be child-centered in the sense that it accepts child growth as something to be sought in everything that it does. But this growth need not be undirected; rather it should be planned by those whose broad experience has given them a vision of the heights to which children can rise when guided wisely and lovingly. This direction is something that children need, something that they desire, and something that they willingly accept if nothing has ever occurred to destroy their confidence.

Child growth has not only volume or quantity; it has what we may call direction. The child growth that is sought in VOYAGES IN ENGLISH is growth toward a Christian adulthood that is truly cultured, that accepts social service as a sacred duty, and that can render social service the better because it has been taught to think clearly and to express itself effectively.

Ahead of the child in the elementary school who is to arrive at this destination there does indeed lie a long, a very long, voyage. The authors cannot hope to have taken him many miles on his journey. It will be enough for them if they can feel that they have given him a seaworthy ship and started him on his way. To have done this much—even to have made a sincere attempt at doing it—is not a small thing in a day when for many children there is no sound vessel in which to sail, no known port of call, no provision for the journey, no compass, nor any stars visible through the ragged clouds by which to chart a course.

Contents

PART ONE **CREATIVE ACTIVITIES**

CHAPTER ONE

Preparatory Experiments in Speech

Giving directions, definitions, explanations, 3
Class conversations, 7
Introductions, 10
Formal talks, 13
Choral speaking, 21
   "We Be the King's Men," 23
   "Daybreak," 24
Chapter challenge, 26

CHAPTER TWO

Studying the Paragraph

The parts of a paragraph, 29
   The beginning sentence, 30
   The topic sentence, 34
   Middle sentences, 37
   The ending sentence, 38
Qualities of a good paragraph, 41
   Unity, 41
   Clearness, 43
Longer compositions, 46

Chapter Two, *continued*

Choral speaking, 50
   "Roofs," 51
Chapter challenge, 54

CHAPTER THREE
Writing a Paragraph

Building a class paragraph, 57
Steps in writing the paragraph, 63
   Selecting and limiting the subject, 64
   Building a vocabulary, 65
   Making an outline, 68
   Writing the paragraph, 69
   Christening the paragraph, 75
Keeping a diary, 78
Writing verse, 79
Choral speaking, 81
   "Barbara Frietchie," 82
Chapter challenge, 84

CHAPTER FOUR
Polishing a Paragraph

Polishing words, 87
Polishing sentences, 97
Polishing paragraphs, 106

Writing for the school newspaper, 110
Choral speaking, 113
    "America the Beautiful," 114
Chapter challenge, 117

CHAPTER FIVE

Letters and the Telephone

Social letters, 119
Types of social letters, 129
Business letters, 138
Types of business letters, 139
Conversations by telephone, 143
Choral speaking, 147
    "O Captain! My Captain!" 148
Chapter challenge, 150

CHAPTER SIX

A Good Citizenship Club

Organizing a Good Citizenship Club, 153
    Rules of order, 155
Meetings of the Good Citizenship Club, 158
Choral speaking, 163
    Scene from "The Courtship of Miles Standish," 164
Chapter challenge, 168

CHAPTER SEVEN

Dramatizations

Dramatizing interviews and dialogues, 171
Writing a play, 174
   "The Legend of the Robes," 177
Still-life dramatizations, 180
The radio and modern life, 181
   A classroom broadcast, 183
Choral speaking, 185
   "The Story of the Shepherds," 186
   Presenting the drama, 188
Chapter challenge, 188

CHAPTER EIGHT

Living Life through Books

Sharing books with others, 191
How to judge a book, 194
Writing a book report, 196
Learning to use the library, 199
Choral speaking, 205
   "The West Wind," 206
   "Mother of Mercy," 208
Chapter challenge, 209

PART TWO **GRAMMAR**

CHAPTER ONE

Nouns

Definition, 213
Proper nouns and common nouns, 213
Collective nouns, 214
Abstract nouns, 215
Person, 217
Number, 218
Gender, 221
Nominative case, 223
   Subject, predicate nominative, address, 223
   Nominative in apposition, 224
   Nominative of exclamation, 225
Possessive case, 227
Objective case, 230
   Direct object, object of preposition, 230
   Objective in apposition, 231
   Indirect object, 232
   Adverbial objective, 234
   Retained object, 234
   Objective complement, 235
   Cognate object, 236
Test on nouns, 238

CHAPTER TWO

Pronouns

Personal pronouns, 239
    Compound personal pronouns, 241
Interrogative pronouns, 242
Relative pronouns, 243
    Compound relative pronouns, 249
Adjective pronouns, 250
The correct use of pronouns, 254
Test on pronouns, 268

CHAPTER THREE

Adjectives

Descriptive adjectives, 269
Limiting adjectives, 271
Position of adjectives, 274
Comparison of adjectives, 276
The correct use of adjectives, 279
Words used as nouns and adjectives, 283
Test on adjectives, 284

CHAPTER FOUR

Verbs

Definition, 285
Regular and irregular verbs, 287
Defective verbs, 290
Transitive and intransitive verbs, 290

Cognate verbs, 292
Copulative verbs, 292
Active and passive voice, 295
Simple and compound tenses, 298
Indicative mood, 301
    Potential form of the indicative mood, 301
Imperative mood, 303
Person and number, 304
Conjugation, 304
The correct use of verbs, 309
Uses of *shall* and *will*, 322
Troublesome verbs, 325
Words used as nouns and verbs, 332
Test on verbs, 332

CHAPTER FIVE

Adverbs

Classification of adverbs according to meaning, 334
Simple adverbs, 336
Interrogative adverbs, 336
Conjunctive adverbs, 337
Relative adverbs, 338
Adverbial objectives, 340
Comparison of adverbs, 341
The correct use of adverbs, 343
Test on adverbs, 347

CHAPTER SIX

Prepositions, Conjunctions, Interjections

Prepositions, 348
    The correct use of prepositions, 350
    Words used as adverbs and prepositions, 352
Conjunctions, 353
    Coordinate and correlative conjunctions, 353
    Subordinate conjunctions, 356
    The correct use of conjunctions, 358
Interjections, 361
Test on prepositions, conjunctions, interjections, 363
Test on parts of speech, 364

CHAPTER SEVEN

Phrases

Definition, 366
Phrases introduced by prepositions, participles, infinitives, 366
Adjectival, adverbial, and noun phrases, 367

CHAPTER EIGHT

Sentences

The essential elements of a sentence, 370
    Natural and transposed order, 372
    Compound elements, 373
Classification of sentences according to use, 374
Simple and compound sentences, 375

Complex sentences, 378
  Adjectival clauses, 381
  Adverbial clauses, 384
  Noun clauses, 388
Test on phrases, clauses, and sentences, 398

APPENDIX

Model diagrams, 399
Punctuation, 407
  The period, 407
  The comma, 408
  The semicolon, 412
  The colon, 413
  The exclamation point, 414
  The interrogation point, 415
  Quotation marks, 415
  The apostrophe, 416
  The hyphen, 416
  The dash, 417
Capital letters, 418
Poem for dramatization, 421

Index, 433

TO

CHRIST THE KING

THROUGH

THE IMMACULATE HEART

OF MARY

PART ONE

CREATIVE ACTIVITIES

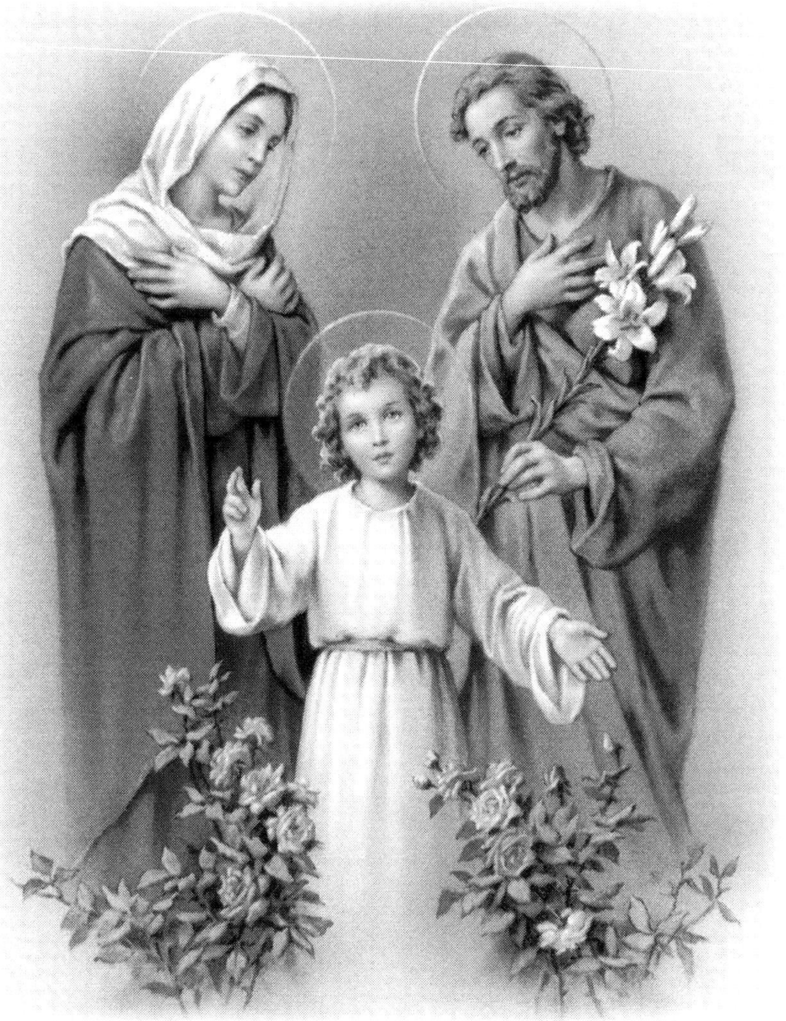

CHAPTER ONE **Preparatory Experiments in Speech**

In which we take part in life situations through speech

School days are part of our lifework. The morning and the afternoon sessions are the business hours; the time after school is for recreation and play. Businessmen never let anything interfere with business. Neither should we. During his leisure hours the businessman shares his pleasures with others in the give-and-take of everyday living. We do the same. If we look upon our experiences in and out of the classroom as a preparation for future participation in the business world, we shall be able to meet our own problems with Christian fortitude and courtesy.

The Importance of Conversation

Now and later we shall come in contact with people, converse with them, give them information, share their experiences, and be called upon to express an opinion. Conversation, therefore, is the basis of all communication.

1. Giving Directions

Perhaps the briefest and simplest kind of conversation is that used in giving directions by question and answer. Examine the model conversation on page 4. Is it marked by a spirit of respect and courtesy on the part of the person asking for directions and the boy?

4 VOYAGES IN ENGLISH, SEVENTH YEAR

MODEL: GIVING STREET DIRECTIONS

As Arthur is walking home from school, a lady driving an automobile addresses him as follows:

LADY. Can you tell me the way to Saint Mark Church?

ARTHUR *(raising his hat and pausing a moment).* Yes, madam. Drive straight ahead on Main Street for three blocks. Turn left on Madison Street and continue until you reach Broadway. Saint Mark's is on the corner of Madison and Broadway.

LADY. Thank you very much.

ARTHUR. You are welcome. I am glad that I could assist you.

Are the directions given by Arthur clear? Could they be followed readily? Note that Arthur paused a little before he gave the directions. He did this in order to be sure that he himself knew the way and to think how he should word the directions so that the lady would be able to follow them easily.

> **DIRECTIONS SHOULD BE:** *1. Accurate*
> *2. Clear*
> *3. Brief*

Unless you really *know*, don't risk giving directions at all. Direct the person making the inquiry to some place where you know he can obtain the correct information.

Questions should be so worded that they are easily understood. "Did Central High win the football game?" is clear. "Did they win?" would be difficult to answer.

CLASS ASSIGNMENT

1. Dramatize the following conversations in your classroom:

1. A gentleman whom you meet outside your school asks, "Where is the nearest drugstore?" Direct him properly.

2. A priest whom you meet at the entrance to the school says, "Please direct me to the principal's office." Answer him courteously.

3. Your uncle, who is visiting your family, wants to know how to reach the business section of the city. Direct him.

4. A girl asks, "What is that tall monument?" Answer her.

2. Reword these questions so that they are clear:

1. Where is the play?
2. Did you like it?
3. Can I reserve a seat?
4. What time does the train leave?

2. Giving Definitions and Explanations

Time and again in school we are called upon to give definitions, longer directions, or explanations. In answering such questions we must be sure that we: (1) *understand the question,* (2) *know the answer,* (3) *word the answer clearly.*

MODEL: GIVING A DEFINITION

TEACHER. What is a comet, Neil?
NEIL. A comet is a heavenly body that passes through the solar system at regular periods. It is known by its long, bright tail.

Neil had studied his lesson and knew what the textbook had said about comets. He tried, however, to answer in his own words. This habit of trying to put into our own words the long explanations given in the textbook will help us answer questions intelligently and correctly.

Our geography, history, English, and other textbooks contain many paragraphs which explain or contain information. If we learn to give definitions in our own words, we shall have no difficulty in selecting important facts from paragraphs and restating them in our own words. What is explained in the following paragraph?

MODEL: AN EXPLANATION

The Assembly was made up of all citizens of Athenian birth. In it every member had a voice in making the laws which governed his state. The Athenians thus had more personal liberty than any other people ever enjoyed. From them we get our idea of a democracy and an assembly. *Demos* is a Greek word meaning "the people." A democracy is therefore a country governed by the people and in which all the people are equal before the law.

CLASS ASSIGNMENT

From the following questions select two or three to be answered in class. Try to make your definitions and explanations clear, accurate, and brief:
1. What is the Declaration of Independence?
2. What is the Constitution of the United States?
3. How does a bill become a law?
4. What is a desert?
5. How did the "iron horse" originate?
6. Why do Catholics go to confession?
7. What is a vocation?
8. Why do Catholics honor our Blessed Mother?
9. How does a pilot know when and where to land?
10. What is vaccination?

3. Class Conversations

Let us now turn our attention from directions, definitions, and explanations to conversation which gives pleasure as well as information. This is the daily exchange of ideas, viewpoints, and courtesies which makes for gracious living. Do we always contribute our share to the conversation at home and in school?

A *class conversation* is one in which we talk as a group upon some selected topic. The pupils, for example, may have felt that they would like to go to the country to see the trees and the wild flowers which they have been studying in science. With the consent of their teacher, they decide to make plans for the excursion. The teacher appoints Frederick to act as leader when they discuss these plans. The whole class enters into the conversation, but it is Frederick's duty to see that all the important matters are covered. He has the following questions in mind before the conversation begins: Where shall we go? When? Where shall we meet? Shall we take our lunch? He then starts the class conversation in the following manner:

MODEL: A GROUP CONVERSATION

FREDERICK. John, have you any suggestions about our trip?

JOHN. The first thing I think we ought to decide, Frederick, is where we should go.

FREDERICK. Does anyone know a good place to go?

DANIEL. Let's hike along Wissahickon Drive in Fairmount Park. It's not far and the scenery is beautiful.

FREDERICK. That's a good suggestion, Daniel, but are we sure of finding wild flowers there?

BLANCHE. Oh, yes, my uncle drove us out there last Sunday and the wild flowers were just beginning to bloom.

FREDERICK. Has anybody any other suggestions? If not, let's decide to hike along the Wissahickon. What do you think is our next question, Beatrice?

BEATRICE. When shall we go?

FREDERICK. What about Saturday morning? John and I have to serve Mass at eight o'clock, but we could be ready to go at nine.

BEATRICE. That will be early enough. I hope it's a pleasant day.

FREDERICK. Of course. Now, where shall we meet?

COURTESY FORBIDS: 1. *Introducing unpleasant topics*
                                    2. *Interrupting a speaker*
                                    3. *Monopolizing a conversation*
                                    4. *Speaking in a loud voice*

HELEN. Would you like to meet at our house? It's nearest for everybody, I think.

FREDERICK. Thank you, Helen. We shall be happy to meet at your house.

HENRY. Who will go on the trip? Shall we ask the other sections of the seventh grade?

MARY. I think it will be better to organize the hike for just this group.

FREDERICK. Does everybody agree? *(Nods of agreement)* Then that's settled. Is there anything else?

PETER. Frederick, shall we take lunch with us?

FREDERICK. That's always part of every hike, Peter. Yes, I think we'll carry our own lunch.

Thus the group continues to converse, arranging details carefully with the leader, until the whole plan is complete. The conversation might end with an expression of pleasure at the thought of the hike or with a simple promise, such as "See you on Saturday, Helen."

Discussions of how to organize something make good topics for group conversations. The class may be divided into groups of from five to ten members each. The teacher may appoint a leader for each group. The leader must study the topic carefully so that he will be able to guide the conversation of his group. In a group conversation there must be both good talkers and good listeners.

CLASS ASSIGNMENT

1. Answer the following questions about the model conversation:

1. Did Frederick introduce the topic immediately?
2. Did he keep to the point?
3. Were the questions which the leader had outlined before the conversation began discussed and settled by the group?
4. Was the leader courteous? Did he listen to suggestions?

> **GOOD TALKERS:**
> 1. *Contribute their share*
> 2. *Help to advance the topic*
> 3. *Answer difficulties*
>
> **GOOD LISTENERS:**
> 1. *Are attentive*
> 2. *Show their interest*
> 3. *Ask questions*

2. Hold a group conversation in your own classroom in which you make plans for an outing of some type.

3. Divide the class into groups of from eight to ten members. Let each group choose a leader and prepare a conversation to be given before the class on one of the following topics:

1. Organizing a baseball team
2. Starting a mission fund
3. Holding a hobby show
4. The value of manners
5. How students should treat school property

4. Introductions

We have many opportunities for practicing the art of conversation in various situations and with different persons. The way we converse with others very often reveals traits of character. Even the way in which we introduce one person to another may be an index of our refinement, training, and consideration for others.

In making introductions we should be gracious and not act in a stilted and self-conscious manner. This end will be accomplished if we are familiar with the following customs observed by people of refinement:

1. A man is introduced to a woman or a boy to a girl. We address the woman first and then introduce the man.

"Mrs. Grandi, may I introduce Mr. John Chapman, our football coach?"

2. A younger person is introduced to an older or more distinguished person. That is, we say the name of the older person first.

"Mother, this is my classmate Jeremiah Carney."

3. A lay person is introduced to a priest or a member of a religious order. The name of the priest or the religious is mentioned first.

"Father Conway, may I present my sister Rose?"

4. When two people of the same sex and about the same age are introduced, the name of either person may be mentioned first.

"Mary Carroll, this is Elizabeth Campbell."

"Elizabeth Campbell, I want you to meet my cousin, Mary Carroll."

In acknowledging an introduction we simply say, "How do you do." We may add the person's name if we wish, as "How do you do, Mr. Graham." When boys and men are introduced to one another they usually shake hands. Girls and women do not. When a gentleman is introduced to a lady she usually smiles and bows. An expression of pleasure, as "I'm happy to know you," is always appropriate.

MODEL: AN INTRODUCTION

When John's mother came to school to see the exhibition of posters for Catholic Book Week, he introduced her to his teacher in the following manner:

JOHN. Sister Peter, may I present my mother?

SISTER. How do you do, Mrs. Conley. I am very glad to meet you. I hope you like John's poster.

MOTHER. John has spoken very often about you, Sister. I am so happy to know you.

CLASS ASSIGNMENT

Practice the following introductions:

1. A classmate visits you. Introduce him to your mother.
2. You take your friend Mary Enley to the school picnic. Introduce Mary to your pastor, whom you meet at the park.
3. Introduce your cousin, Mary Cray, to Rita Owens.
4. Maurice Wilhere, a friend of yours, passes your home while you are sitting on the porch with your twin sister. Introduce Maurice to her.
5. Introduce your father to your principal, Sister David.
6. You have just joined the Boy Scouts. Introduce yourself to another Scout who is sitting next to you at a meeting.

Introducing a Speaker to a Class

Introducing a speaker to a class requires more formal courtesy. The new president of the Good Citizenship Club of our class may want to introduce a missionary priest who is to give an address at one of our club meetings. The president should accompany the guest speaker to the place of honor in the classroom or the auditorium. After the speaker has been seated the president should bow to him and then proceed, facing the class:

MODEL: INTRODUCING A SPEAKER

Members of the Good Citizenship Club, we are certainly fortunate to have with us this morning Father Hubbard, the Glacier Priest. Father is not a stranger to the boys and girls of this class, because we have followed him in imagination on many of his thrilling adventures. Father Hubbard himself will tell us many more stories, I know. Father Hubbard.

The speaker then bows to Father Hubbard.

CLASS ASSIGNMENT

How would you introduce the following persons to your class?
1. A city official who is to talk on safety rules
2. A visiting nurse who is to discuss first aid
3. Dr. Ryan, a dentist, who is to talk on dental hygiene
4. Miss McCall, a librarian, who has been asked to explain the use of the card catalogue
5. A noted author who is to discuss the Catholic press

5. Formal Talks

There are many occasions on which we may be called upon to give a formal talk in our classroom. In such a talk we take our place at the front of the classroom and speak in a formal manner. We must always prepare for a formal talk and know exactly what we wish to say.

MODEL: BRIDGING TIME AND SPACE

The airplane is daily changing our ideas of time and space. This modern means of transportation surpasses all others in its ability to follow the shortest possible route between two places. Ships at sea must often circle large masses of land, and this may necessitate a detour of hundreds of miles. Icebergs, shallows, and dangerous reefs also constitute possible hazards. Ships of the air encounter no such difficulties. On land, the automobile and the train must follow twisting, turning routes through mountainous country because they lack the ability to ascend steep slopes. On level surfaces they must go around swamps and lakes. These problems do not present themselves in travel by air. Given the proper weather conditions for flying, a twentieth-century air liner can go anywhere by the shortest possible route.

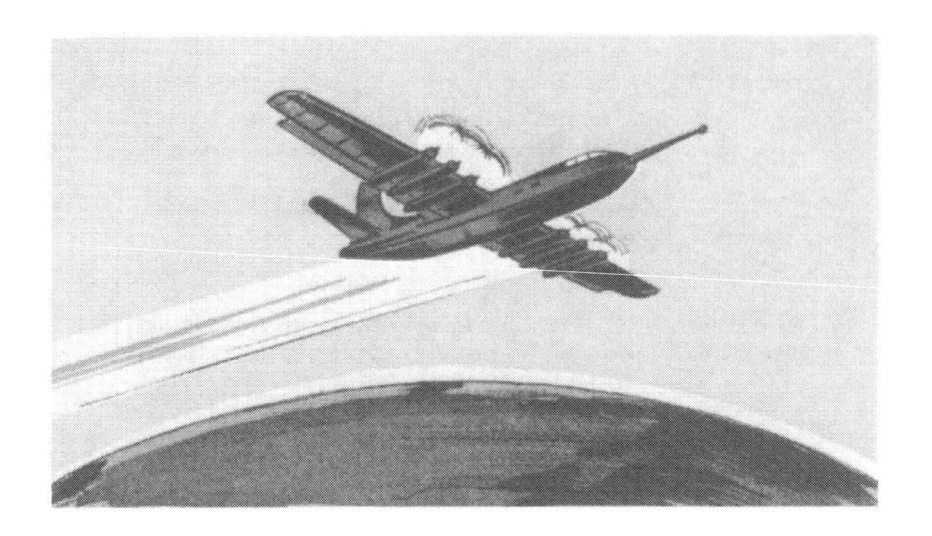

There are many things connected with air travel which might have been used as the topic for a formal talk. Note that this talk told only how the airplane surpasses other means of transportation in shortening the distance between two points. The topic of this talk, therefore, is *shortening distances by airplane.*

What to Talk About

We all enjoy sharing experiences with others. We may share our joys, our hopes, our ambitions, even our sorrows. Personal experiences or ambitions make good subjects for talks to our classmates. Imaginary experiences also provide good material for class talks and tax our imaginations as well. On the other hand, we may prefer to tell someone how to do something or how to make something.

Planning the Talk

After we have selected the subject we must always limit it to a particular topic that can be covered in a short talk. Here is a list of subjects and topics that might be used for formal talks:

Subject	Topic
My favorite saint	An incident in the life of my favorite saint
Penicillin	The discovery of penicillin
A flood	The damage caused by a flood
Tin	The importance of tin
A day in the park	An amusing experience

Having limited the subject to an interesting topic, we make the following plan for the talk:

1. We think of a good beginning sentence that will attract the listener's attention and indicate what we are going to talk about.

2. We organize the middle sentences so that we do not wander from the topic, but keep our thoughts traveling from one action to another.

3. We plan a good and effective ending sentence.

CLASS ASSIGNMENT

1. Limit the following subjects to topics that might be used for formal class talks:

My dog	Competition	Ways of earning money
Indoor amusements	Sports	New inventions
Communication	Corn	A well-known American
Visiting in the country	Aviation	Church windows
Travel experiences	Wild flowers	Advertisements

2. What is the topic of this talk which Regina Haller gave before her class?

SECRETS TO SHARE

This great earth has secrets to share with all who are curious and eager to learn. Marvelous are those already revealed! The stately spruce tree can disclose the origin of the plastic steering wheel on your new car or the rayon bedspread that adorns your bed. Coal tar offers itself as the basis of many exotic perfumes. Insignificant soybeans, too, have many astounding uses to divulge. Be alert and read widely if you wish to share Nature's secrets.

3. Study this talk and answer the questions that follow:

HOW TO PREPARE FOR CONFESSION

A person who wishes to make a good confession must remember certain things. In the first place, he should pray to the Holy Spirit for grace to know and detest his sins. Then he should examine his conscience carefully, recalling how he has offended God in thought, word, deed, or omission since his last confession. After this he should try to make an act of perfect contrition by thinking of God's goodness and of how shamefully he has acted toward his heavenly Father. If he cannot make an act of perfect contrition, he should at least make an act of imperfect contrition by thinking of the punishment of unforgiven sin. Before he enters the confessional he should know what he is going to say and should be prepared to tell the priest exactly what he did and how often he committed each sin. One who prepares in this way will make his confession properly by accusing himself of all his transgressions and by having true contrition for them.

1. Does this talk tell the audience about a personal experience or does it explain how to do something?

2. Does the first sentence introduce the topic of the talk?

3. Do the middle sentences explain the process step by step?

4. Are any important details omitted?

5. Does the ending sentence explain the last step or does it summarize the explanation?

6. What are the requisites of a good confession?

Vocabulary Hints

If we wish one sentence to follow another smoothly, we must pay attention to our *transitional expressions*. Here are some transitional words, phrases, and clauses. Write in your notebook a sentence containing each one. See if you can add others to those given.

WORDS	PHRASES	CLAUSES
finally	despite this	when this has been done
nevertheless	as a result	after this has been finished
thereupon	for this purpose	when the work was completed
furthermore	in the first place	while we were speaking
meanwhile	on the other hand	if you observe these rules
consequently	on the contrary	since delay was dangerous

How to Talk Well

Not only should a speaker have something really worth while to say, but he should say it in the very best possible way. His posture (how he stands when he is talking), his easy, pleasant manner, his friendly tone—all these go to make up his good points as a speaker. Try to improve in these points every time you are called on to speak.

Good posture **Friendly tone** **Pleasant manner**

CLASS ASSIGNMENT

1. Select one of the three talks outlined here and develop it for presentation in your class. You will find a suggested beginning sentence and an ending sentence for each topic and ideas that might be developed in the middle sentences:

1. A Leader of His People

Beginning sentence Out of the chaos into which his newly found freedom had plunged the Negro, there emerged that great leader, Booker T. Washington.
Middle sentences Washington favored industrial education.
He opened Tuskegee Institute.
He lectured to break down racial prejudice.
Ending sentence The glory of liberating the slaves belongs to Abraham Lincoln; to Booker T. Washington belongs the honor of elevating them to social and economic freedom.

2. God's Way

Beginning sentence Strange and devious ways are used by God to attract souls.
Middle sentences Ignatius, the soldier, is wounded in battle.
He reads a book for diversion.
He decides to dedicate his life to God.
Ending sentence Hence we see that even among the trivial things of everyday life God finds means of drawing souls to His service.

3. Antarctic Invasion

Beginning sentence Perhaps the most thrilling conquest made by the airplane is its penetration of the mysterious white silence of the Antarctic.
Middle sentences Early flights
Continuance of explorations despite loss of life
Discoveries
Ending sentence Watch for new scientific wonders which the airplane will help to uncover in this strange world.

> **TESTS OF A PLEASANT SPEAKER:**
> 1. *Do I stand well, head erect, looking at the class?*
> 2. *Is my voice friendly and my articulation clear?*
> 3. *Is my manner pleasant and courteous?*
> 4. *Is my choice of words good?*

2. Prepare a talk describing an experience. Select some event in your own life or use any of the following:

Titles	Topic Sentences
My Turn as Cook	I always look forward to my turn as cook at our house.
An Exciting Fifteen Minutes	There were just fifteen minutes of the game to go.
Lost!	Were you ever lost?
Next!	Everybody knows that awful feeling when the dentist says, "Will you come in?"
An Apt Pupil	Last summer I became a swimming instructor for my little brother Donald.
Dazed by the Footlights	Our Christmas play had reached its climax when I walked onto the stage.

3. Prepare a talk explaining how to do something. Select a topic of your own or use any of the following:

Topics at Home	Topics at School and Church
How to make fudge	How to introduce a new pupil
How to wash an automobile	How to write a book report
How to plan a party	How to display the flag
How to care for a sprained ankle	How to assist at Mass
How to operate a dial telephone	How to genuflect

Relating Anecdotes

Are you able to tell a good story? Can you make your hearers live the incidents that you relate? Public speakers often make use of anecdotes to illustrate a point. An anecdote is an interesting incident, sometimes amusing, connected with the life of some person. The story should be easily understood. We should never have to point out a moral or a lesson to be learned.

Here is an anecdote related by a boy who had been chosen to address the pupils of the seventh and the eighth grades. The pastor of his church was conducting a membership drive for the Junior Holy Name Society. Do you think this anecdote would encourage the boys to love the sacred name of Jesus?

Model: An Anecdote

A venerable old man had the custom all through his life of saying "Praised be Jesus Christ" in moments of great sorrow or joy and whenever he met old friends.

When he lay dying a strange worry came into his mind. "There is only one thing that troubles me," he told the priest who was visiting him, "and that is what I will find to say when I stand before the throne of God."

"There is only one thing you need to remember to say," replied the priest. "Just repeat your familiar greeting, 'Praised be Jesus Christ,' and the whole court of heaven will answer you, 'Forever and ever, Amen!'"

CLASS ASSIGNMENT

1. Your class is organizing a history club. Let each member relate an anecdote to illustrate patriotism.

2. Look up an interesting anecdote concerning the life of some famous person and be prepared to tell it to the class. Anecdotes concerning any of the following characters are interesting:

1. Abraham Lincoln
2. Knute Rockne
3. Saint John Bosco
4. Saint Patrick
5. Saint Augustine
6. Nathan Hale
7. Saint Nicholas
8. Mark Twain
9. Patrick Henry
10. Father De Smet

3. Relate an amusing anecdote you have read in a favorite magazine. Tell why you selected this particular story.

4. Bring to class an anecdote that will inspire your classmates to be generous in the collection for the missions.

6. Choral Speaking

Choral speaking gives us an opportunity of enjoying great poetry by reading it together. We learn to feel the swing of the rhythm, the variations of time and pitch, and the beauty and the music of the words.

Two simple rules apply to all choral speaking:
1. The emotion or feeling must fit the thought and must never be exaggerated.
2. The thought of the poem must become *your own*.

Markings Used in Choral Speaking

In this book we will use certain markings that will help us to phrase the poems we recite together in chorus. These markings are \ for a falling inflection, / for a rising inflection, and // for a pause.

Use a falling inflection (\) of the voice for important or emphatic words:

We be the King's \ men.

Use a rising inflection (/) of the voice when a question is asked:

Are you ill? /

Use a rising (/) and a falling (\) inflection of the voice for words used in pairs and for stressed words used in succession:

We be the King's \ men hale / and hearty. \
We want men, \ women, / and children. \

Tuning-up Exercises

Breathing:

Breathe deeply. Inhale through the nose, inflating the diaphragm, chest wall, and ribs. Then exhale slowly with the sound of *ah*.

Enunciation:

Learn to enunciate—or "speak out"—both vowels and consonants. Vowels should be said with the mouth round. Consonants should be enunciated crisply and accurately.

Exercise for the vowels:

Say the vowels, first in a low pitch, then in a high pitch. Use the piano where possible to establish the high and low pitch.

Say these short sounds with relaxed tongue:

ă as in *hat*. Repeat several times: *patch, lad, stamp.*

    Catch the lad that stamps pads in the pantry.

ĕ as in *pet*. Repeat several times: *red, wet, tell.*

    A wet red thread went through the hedge.

Nonsense Jingles

Nonsense jingles tickle our sense of humor by the ridiculous sayings and actions of absurd people, or amuse us by their coined words or strange dialect.

We Be the King's Men
(An Old Nonsense Jingle)

Heartily, as if marching nearer and nearer	We be the King's \ men hale / and hearty, \ Marching to meet one Buono-party; // If he won't come lest the wind should blow, // We shall have marched for nothing, O! //
Explosively	Right fol lol!
More heartily Nearer still	We be the King's \ men hale / and hearty, \ Marching to meet one Buono-party; // If he be sea-sick say "No, No!" // We shall have marched for nothing, O! //
Explosively	Right fol lol!
Most heartily and nearest	We be the King's \ men hale / and hearty, \ Marching to meet one Buono-party; // Never mind, mates, // we'll be merry though // We shall have marched for nothing, O! //
Explosively	Right fol lol!

Study of the Poem

Let us establish the rhythm—that is, count out the beats in the line. Take the first line:

We' be the King's' men hale' and hear' ty

There are four beats in the line. This rhythm is repeated in every line except the last one, which has three beats and is said with full voice and breath, like the military command of Right!' For'ward! March!' Keep the rhythm steady and even. Try to imitate the sound of marching feet.

A Verse-Speaking Choir

A verse-speaking choir is a group trained to recite poetry in chorus. When the choir recites a poem in unison each word is pronounced as clearly and distinctly as though it were spoken by a single voice. The members must first be sure that they understand the poem and then decide how they wish to interpret it. Then they must practice just as an orchestra or choir does, so that all the voices are blended together harmoniously. Some of the parts of the poem may be assigned to one individual as a solo, or to a group such as the soprano voices or the alto voices.

Just as an orchestra tunes up before beginning to play, so the verse-speaking choir should take some preparatory exercises before reciting.

Lyrics or Singing Poems

Poems that sing, or lyrics, make the best poems for choral speaking, for their rhythm (the beat of the lines) is like the rhythm of music. These poems do not tell a story; they express the author's emotion.

DAYBREAK

By Henry Wadsworth Longfellow

Medium Voices	A wind \ came up out of the sea, / And said, / "O mists, make room for me!" /
Light Voices	It hailed the ships \ and cried, / "Sail on, // Ye mariners, / the night is gone!" //
Heavy Voices	And hurried landward \ far away, Crying, / "Awake! it is the day!" //
Medium Voices	It said unto the forest, / "Shout! // Hang all your leafy banners out!" //
Light Voices	It touched the wood-bird's folded wing, \ And said, / "O bird, awake and sing!" //

Heavy Voices	And o'er the farms, \ "O chanticleer, / Your clarion blow; / the day is near!" //
Medium Voices	It whispered to the fields of corn, / "Bow down, / and hail the coming morn!" //
Light Voices	It shouted through the belfry-tower, / "Awake, O bell! \ proclaim the hour." //
All	It crossed the churchyard \ with a sigh, / And said, / "Not yet! in quiet lie." //

STUDY OF THE POEM

This is a lyric poem; that is, a song sung from the heart of the poet to the hearts of his listeners. The lines are filled with pictures of early morning.

All the earth and all the people awake at daybreak, all except the dead lying in the churchyard. They will not arise until the trumpet of the angel Gabriel calls them on that last daybreak to judgment.

In reading the poem for choral speaking, be careful to mark the time well. Use slow time for things sad, or tending to be sad, like the last stanza, and quick time for things that are glad, or tending to be glad, like the second stanza. As the time changes with gladness or sadness, so does the pitch of the voice—higher pitch for gladness, lower pitch for sadness.

7. Chapter Challenge

Show that you understand the contents of this chapter by filling in the blanks in the following statements:

1. Directions should be (1) ...., (2) ...., (3) ....

2. In answering questions in school we should be sure that: (1) we .... the question; (2) we .... the answer; (3) we .... the answer clearly.

3. A class conversation is one in which we talk as a group upon ....

4. The guide in a group conversation is called a ....

5. In group conversations there must be both good .... and good ....

6. Courtesy forbids (1) introducing .... topics; (2) .... the speaker; (3) .... a conversation; (4) speaking in a .... voice.

7. In introducing a man to a woman we ....

8. A lay person is introduced to a .... by mentioning the name of the .... first.

9. An introduction is acknowledged by saying, ...

10. We must always .... a formal talk.

11. The general thing that we decide to talk about is called the .... The particular aspect of the talk is called the ....

12. The tests of a pleasant speaker are: (1) Do I .... well, head erect, looking at the class? (2) Is my .... friendly and my articulation ....? (3) Is my manner .... and ....? (4) Is my choice of .... good?

13. An .... is an interesting incident connected with the life of some person.

14. Poems that sing are known as ....

15. The lines of the poem .... are filled with pictures of early morning.

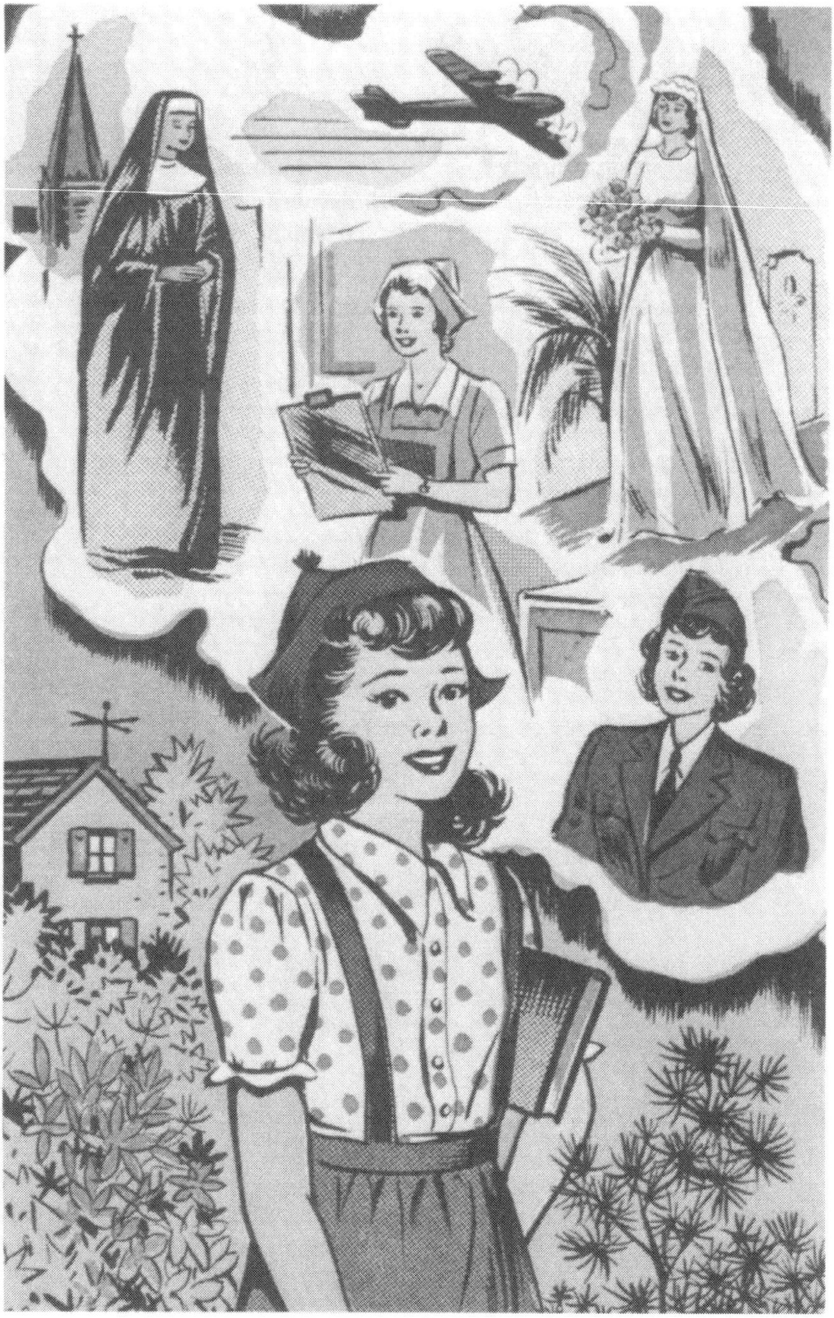

CHAPTER TWO **Studying the Paragraph**

In which we learn how to recognize a paragraph

A paragraph is a group of closely related sentences developing a topic. There is no rule about the length of a paragraph. Some paragraphs are long; others are short. Every sentence in the paragraph, however, must help to develop one main idea or topic. In the following model all the sentences relate to one idea, *indecision concerning the writer's vocation.* Also discuss if these are good vocations to be considered.   MODEL: INDECISION

Sister's words, "Pray to Our Lady of Good Counsel," are echoing in my ears as a panorama of life's vocations passes before my eyes. There is the nun, with flowing robe of blue, who wears our Lady's beads and teaches of God's love. Next, the nurse walks briskly by in uniform so crisp and white. "Brides, too, are beautiful," I think, as wedding bells resound throughout my dreamland church. Fancy then takes me cruising through the clouds. I am a hostess on a great air liner. Grounded again, I become interested in the life of an artist. Surely indecision rules my days. "O Mother, tell me, what am I to do?"

1. The Parts of a Paragraph

Every paragraph is composed of three parts: (1) a beginning sentence, (2) middle sentences, and (3) an ending sentence. The beginning sentence attracts the attention and arouses the interest of the reader. The middle sentences work together to develop the thought of the paragraph. The ending sentence gives the last detail, sums up the paragraph, or makes a personal comment.

MODEL: TOWN CRIER OF THE AIR

Beginning sentence What would busy Americans do without the commentator with his radio digest of the news?
Middle sentences Father no longer scans the headlines as he gulps down his coffee or chokes on his bun. While driving to work he learns, by a mere twist of the dial, all the details of the fire downtown or the most recent happenings in Congress. Mother cheerfully dusts the library as she is informed by radio that the queen of England will visit our land. Even the harmony of the evening family circle is undisturbed by the scramble for the newspaper. Someone simply reminds us, "Don't forget the news at
Ending sentence seven o'clock." With his fingers on the pulse of the world, the newscaster has become a vital part of American life.

The Beginning Sentence

Every paragraph should have a good beginning sentence. This sentence must do what its name implies, begin the paragraph. It should arouse the interest of the reader and encourage him to continue reading. The beginning sentence may reveal the topic of the paragraph or give only a hint of what is to follow.

MODEL: DAILY DRAMA

Beginning sentence Have you ever thought of a prosaic railroad station as a vast theater where real-life drama is daily portrayed? The motley crowd, blending into a kind of traveling democracy, constitutes a di-

Begins the paragraph — *Gives a hint of the contents of the paragraph* — *Attracts attention* — *Arouses curiosity*

versified cast. Each performer has a part to play in the great drama of life. For some this railroad station may be a scene of intense joy, as in the case of dear ones reunited. Tragedy may be the keynote for others as they bid doleful farewells. A number must play the part of jesters that laughter may not die, while others are cast in roles of a more romantic nature. Yes, I think a railroad station may readily be compared to a stage where tragedy, comedy, and romance are ever in the making.

The opening sentence of this paragraph has the qualities of a good beginning sentence. It unlocks the thought of the paragraph by suggesting what follows. Our attention is attracted immediately and we are eager to know how a railroad station represents the stage in a theater.

CLASS ASSIGNMENT

1. Examine the beginning sentences in the following paragraphs. Are they good beginning sentences? Why?

1. A Decorative Meal

Never did I dream, when I became the proud owner of a frisky white goat, that her eating habits would be the cause of disaster for both of us. Though this pet of mine managed on various occasions to tear down the clothesline, I very deftly rescued the clothing, shielded her, and pacified Mother. All my efforts to curb Lady's ferocious appetite for wearing apparel proved unsuccessful. Finally, Mother inadvertently dropped her new flowered hat on one of the benches in our flower garden. Too late I discovered my hungry goat feasting sumptuously on the hat. Alas! Lady lost a home and I lost a goat.

2. FAMILY COOPERATION

The conversion of our basement into a recreation room was from start to finish a family project. Father began by putting up smooth board walls and laying bright new linoleum on the floor. Gay chintz curtains for the high windows and matching slip covers for the old furniture from the attic were Mother's contributions. The boys did their share by making tables and benches for the game corner and a platform for table tennis. My older sister furnished several original paintings to give an artistic touch to the room. I lent moral support to everyone, ran numerous errands, and bore patiently the accusation of being a general nuisance. Good teamwork brought our efforts to a successful close, and family labor is now reaping the rich harvest of family enjoyment.

2. Examine the following beginning sentences and decide whether they conform to the characteristics of beginning sentences mentioned on page 33. What thoughts does each suggest?

1. An interesting book can be a smooth highway to enchanting lands.
2. Circus animals have a great attraction for both young and old.
3. What feelings of dismay enveloped me on the occasion of my teacher's first visit to our home!
4. Gathering curious facts about the countries of the world is my favorite pastime.
5. My candid camera accompanies me on every outdoor trip I take.
6. Knute Rockne, the Notre Dame football coach, was an outstanding example of true sportsmanship.
7. Mark's initiation into the club was a memorable occasion.

> **A GOOD BEGINNING SENTENCE:**
> 1. *Begins the paragraph*
> 2. *Attracts attention*
> 3. *Gives a hint of the contents of the paragraph*
> 4. *Often arouses curiosity*

8. Every precaution has been taken to make the park across from our home a safe place to play.

9. The silence of the cozy little room was suddenly broken by a loud crash.

10. The day I mistook Dr. Walsh for a salesman will live long in my memory.

11. In spite of our efforts, the members of our family fail to impress Paul with the ancient adage that order is heaven's first law.

12. The courageous and heroic martyr who answered the call of God and went to the aid of her beloved France is my favorite saint.

3. For each of the two paragraphs that follow supply an opening sentence that contains all the qualities required in a good beginning sentence:

1. NEW SPEED RECORD

.... When in a moment of weakness I accepted his foolish suggestion, the journey homeward resulted in a cross-country race. Streets were taboo. Only the wide-open spaces and the narrow wooded trails were considered. Hurdling fences, crawling beneath bridges, groping through fields thick with weeds, on and on my brother traveled, followed closely by breathless me. Finally, on reaching our destination, I sank exhausted to the nearest bench, vowing that never, never again would I permit my young brother to entice me into taking a short cut home.

2. ORDER IN DISORDER

.... Whatever is order in my brother's mind spells disorder for the rest of the family. In response to Mother's earnest pleas, he insists that every object in his room is a precious souvenir, and as such has to remain in its coveted spot. Dad, too, seems to resent the array of treasures gracing John's den. Much to his sorrow, even Aunt Helen has a few disparaging remarks to make about his copious collection. Despite all opposition, however, John will probably remain orderly in his disorderly way.

The Topic Sentence

In some paragraphs the beginning sentence does more than give a hint of the content of the paragraph. It may be a brief statement of the *topic*. A sentence that states the central thought of the paragraph is called the *topic sentence*. It is usually followed by other sentences which develop the thought of the topic, give necessary details, and bring the paragraph to its conclusion.

MODEL: SHOES SPEAK

Topic sentence   As I rode on the streetcar yesterday, a survey of my fellow travelers' footwear disclosed to me many interesting personalities. A boy's worn but well-polished shoes told me of personal habits of neatness and care. Dainty, toeless sandals, trimmed with bright bows, indicated that their wearer's love of dancing and parties left no room for more useful slippers. Expensive but mud-spattered brogues, toes upturned, bespoke the sportsman, a lover of the great outdoors. Practical oxfords, dark in color and well used, suggested that their wearer was a sensible, efficient man whose business required tiresome walking. Battered, torn shoes, with knotted laces, revealed the piteous tale of a discouraged person whose condition perhaps was occasioned by extreme want. If these shoes could really talk, I wonder if they would verify my musings?

Although the beginning sentence is very often the topic sentence, this is not always true. One of the middle sentences, or even the ending sentence, may serve as the topic sentence. The important thing to remember is that one of the sentences in the paragraph should clearly reveal the topic of the paragraph.

MODEL: SWINGING INTO THE AIR AGE

Topic sentence — Did Great-grandmother ever play at sailing the skies in the days when airplanes were still a dream? One ride on the old rope swing dangling from Grandfather's apple tree convinced me that this must have been my great-grandmother's favorite girlish pastime. The take-off was accomplished in a series of easy jerks. Gaining momentum with each forward thrust, the swing began to climb. Reaching outward, beyond the tip of the longest branch, it soared higher and higher! A semisomersault gave warning that the top altitude had at last been attained. What sheer delight it was to glide in breathless joy through a world of radiant blue and downy white! As fuel ran low and power lagged, a safe landing came in gradual descent. Banish the thought that life was dull and commonplace in the pre-air age of Great-grandmother's day.

Notice that the beginning sentence gives a hint of the contents of the paragraph. It does not, however, limit the subject to the specific topic treated in the paragraph. The second sentence, *One ride on the old rope swing dangling from Grandfather's apple tree convinced me that this must have been my great-grandmother's favorite girlish pastime,* is the topic sentence. This sentence states the *one main idea* (the joy of a ride on an old rope swing) which the other sentences in the paragraph develop.

CLASS ASSIGNMENT

Which is the topic sentence in each of these paragraphs?

1. PEACE PORTRAYED

Peace, profound and deep, permeates every detail of Millet's masterpiece, "The Angelus." The rustic couple in the foreground confirm our belief that it can be purchased with work and prayer. They have paused, in the calm hush of evening, to address the Lord and Master of the universe, and their reverently bowed heads reflect the quiet joy of busy souls who seek their rest in God. Close by, the wheelbarrow, filled with overflowing sacks, the basket, and the hoe are tokens of contentment in a day well spent. Beyond lie fields that stretch in miles of furrowed rows to promise peaceful days to come. Out of the purple mist veiling the horizon the church steeple, rising heavenward, points eloquently to a land of perfect peace. Over all the setting sun radiates a tranquil benediction. Would that this peace were projected to the canvas of the world today!

2. An Admirable Abode

Everyone takes pride in displaying his personal possessions, and my father is no exception. A visitor to our home never departs without seeing the room which is Dad's combination study and den. The furnishings indicate his dual plan of alternating serious thought with relaxation. Dignified bookshelves line the walls on three sides. A huge desk and a straight-backed chair tell a story of many hours of arduous mental labor. In one corner, however, a comfortable easy chair reposes beside an inviting radio that affords welcome diversion. For my father this abode is indeed a retreat from distractions during business hours and a haven of delight during leisure time.

Middle Sentences

Each of the middle sentences in a paragraph contributes directly to the central thought or topic of the paragraph. They tell the facts one by one, add details, explain the process step by step, or relate actions and events of the story. A sentence which introduces some other thought or idea and does not relate to the topic of the paragraph is called a *misfit*. Do not permit misfit sentences to creep into your paragraphs.

Do all the middle sentences in this paragraph develop the *one main idea?*

Model: Visual Delights

Middle sentences Television has brought to our modern life many delightful advantages. No longer are we dependent upon a play-by-play description of games by football's top teams, for we can actually see our favorite eleven prancing onto the field and fighting yard by yard toward victory. Enacted before our very eyes, eerie mystery stories now seem more realistic than ever. To her childish voice the diminutive performer on the children's program has added a dimpled smile. Convalescents today not only hear the inspiring music and reverent voice of the officiating priest at high Mass, but they witness the ceremonies of the August Sacrifice as well. What a store of visual treats is revealed by a twist of the television dial!

The Ending Sentence

A clear and effective ending sentence satisfies the reader and lets him know that the paragraph is finished. It is the final link connecting the sentences of the paragraph. This sentence may be the last detail, a summing up of details, or a personal comment. Notice the ending sentence in the paragraph entitled "A Floral Tragedy." This ending sentence does not relate the last event. It is a word of advice to the reader, or a personal comment.

MODEL: A FLORAL TRAGEDY

The rush hour is a rather precarious time to carry a bouquet of flowers on a busy subway train. This I learned to my dismay the evening I was instructed to bring home a centerpiece for Mother's bridge party. To begin with, my bouquet was minus its fragile wrappings when I finally found myself standing in the crowded aisle. As fellow passengers jostled toward the exit at each stop, I grew alarmingly aware of the havoc being done to my fragrant bundle. Flowers took root in umbrella spokes, shopping bags were transformed into floral baskets, and dignified businessmen acquired boutonnieres. When at length I alighted from the car, my hands were clutching a bunch of blossomless stems. "Avoid the rush hour" is my advice to all who contemplate transporting flowers via the subway.

Ending sentence

CLASS ASSIGNMENT

1. Examine the ending sentences in the following paragraphs and tell why they are good:

1. Junior Edition

Are all younger sisters meant to be just miniature copies? Everyone I know seems to think so. Mother, I am sure, is convinced of it. Inevitably she forecasts the junior styles for me by asserting that Janet's coat, with a few alterations, will be completely in fashion. Dad, in his sober, matter-of-fact way, seems to be in league with her. He solemnly declares that his older daughter at my age never asked for the things I demand. The neighbors likewise consider me only a replica, for they refer to me merely as "the younger one." Even Sister Alice, disappointed in the second edition, regretfully mourns my inability to measure up to Janet's excellent English grades. If all younger sisters share this common fate, I should be resigned, but how I long to be the original "me" for just one day!

2. Reserved Seat

Although Grandpa is well over seventy, he is still an ardent lover of baseball. Every afternoon finds him in a strategic spot behind home plate. With thousands of other spectators he applauds strenuously when his favorite players come to bat and joins the howling mob in violent disagreement with the umpire's decisions. He watches wistfully as younger folks devour the wares of the ice-cream and soda-pop vendors, but consoles himself that, at his age, such things are not for him. As one of the crowd he

---

A GOOD ENDING SENTENCE:

1. *Ends the paragraph*
2. *Satisfies the reader or the listener*
3. *May give the last fact or detail*
4. *May tell what the writer thinks or feels*

takes his seventh-inning stretch, and then settles back again to watch anxiously the concluding performance of the home team. When the game is over, however, and the warm, weary fans begin the long trek home, Grandpa shifts a little in his chair, relights his pipe, and comfortably awaits the next television program.

2. Examine each of the following sentences and tell whether it meets the standards of a good ending sentence:

1. This spirit of courage displayed by my brother is only one of his outstanding characteristics.
2. In the future I will think twice before racing after fire engines.
3. Alas! Dreams do sometimes come true.
4. From this day forward a dictionary will be my constant companion.
5. Follow these directions carefully, and your success as a tennis player is guaranteed.
6. That one unconscious act of courtesy won for Paul the position coveted by all the applicants.
7. Truly, it is only a strong character that accepts defeat with a smile.
8. That ordeal made me more determined than ever to overcome stage fright.
9. Drenched but happy, the picnickers scrambled out of the water.
10. That experience has taught me to let places which appear mysterious remain mysterious.

3. For each of these paragraphs supply an ending sentence:

1. Meet the Pretzel Man

Each morning and afternoon, rain or shine, you can see old Pete, the pretzel man, at the gate of our school. This venerable but ragged figure, standing beside his antiquated cart, is a familiar picture to every child. His bushy, slate-colored hair is covered with a dilapidated felt hat, from which a bright red feather bobs right and left in cheery greeting. Two keen gray eyes peer humorously over the heavy-rimmed spectacles that rest atop his short, pug nose. Pete's habitual attire consists of a faded blue sweater, nondescript trousers with brown patches at the knees, and high scuffed shoes. ....

2. Sorrow Brings Joy

In the gospel stories we find many illustrations of this truth, "Sorrow reaps for sinners rewards exceedingly great." Repentance earned reconciliation for the prodigal son, while his well-deserved punishment was forgotten. The Samaritan woman received the gift of faith because she humbly acknowledged her guilt. Grief for past sins won a heavenly peace for the sinful Mary Magdalene. Justification in God's sight was the reward given to the publican for his deep sorrow. The penitent thief gained paradise by his contrition. ....

2. Qualities of a Good Paragraph

There are two essential qualities which every acceptable paragraph must possess. These are *unity* and *clearness*. We all know that a paragraph is a group of sentences developing one thought. Let us now see how unity and clearness are attained in paragraphs.

Unity

When all the sentences of a paragraph are related to the topic sentence and stick to the one main idea, we say that the paragraph has *unity*. We have to be particularly careful in writing our middle sentences, so that each one not only contributes something important to the paragraph, but relates to the topic as well. Any sentence which introduces a thought or an idea that does not relate to the topic is a misfit. We may test for unity in a paragraph by summing up the whole thought in a single sentence.

MODEL: A FLIGHT THROUGH SPACE

With a confidence born of experience, the pilot taxied his plane down the runway and gradually lifted the graceful vessel into the ocean of air above. Smoothly through the ether waves, over storm centers and around stratus clouds which are so hazardous to his plane, the pilot guided the silver ship. Slowly at first, but gaining momentum rapidly, it zoomed its way above the fleecy clouds of the atmosphere. The airport tower faded into a mere speck as the altimeter registered the desired altitude. As the landing field loomed into view, the ship of the air zipped downward until its wheels touched the ground. Another successful flight through space had been completed.

CLASS ASSIGNMENT

1. Does this paragraph have unity? Can you sum up the thought of the paragraph in a single sentence?

TIME IMPRESSIONS

With what varied emotions the coming of a certain hour fills the hearts of those who await it! To Gerald, who has an appointment with the dentist, the hour of three seems to be his doom. How different the stroke of three appears to Helen, who is then to make her first appearance at the hairdresser's! The thought of three o'clock carries with it transitory joy to Leo, about to begin his first job of carrying newspapers. Three o'clock brings relief to Jane, who looks forward to the end of a trying day at school. Today, note your feelings at three.

2. Read the following paragraph carefully and then answer the questions which are asked:

Masterful Michael

One of the most striking features about the entrance to our parish church is the stained-glass window of Saint Michael which surmounts the inner doorway. This reproduction of Lucifer's archenemy has captivated my fancy, and I have derived many worthwhile thoughts from the study of it. The brightly colored glass depicts the great archangel driving Satan into the flaming pit of hell and so fills me with a real horror of sin and its punishment. I am made aware, too, of the protecting guidance of this warrior of God as he proves triumphant over the powers of darkness. I thank God for Saint Michael whenever I view him in this magnificent work of art.

1. What is the thought introduced in the beginning sentence?
2. What is the topic sentence?
3. Do the other sentences develop step by step the main idea of the paragraph?
4. Does the paragraph have unity? Why?

Clearness

In addition to unity, every good paragraph possesses clearness. A paragraph has this quality when the sentences follow in natural and logical order. Each sentence leads to the next in an orderly way so that they develop clearly and effectively the one main idea. The paragraph that follows has unity and clearness. The central thought which is introduced in the topic sentence is developed step by step without interruption.

Model: A Pearly Surprise

Having decided to make rice pudding one day, I proceeded to follow the directions in the cookbook. When I came to the amount of rice required, I hesitated dubiously. "One-half cupful," the recipe directed. "That can never be enough for six generous helpings," I reflected, and quickly concluded that the book contained a misprint. Immediately I poured the entire contents of the box into boiling water and further busied myself with the meringue which was to top this masterpiece. Suddenly a series of odd sounds coming from the direction of the stove startled me. Turning quickly, I beheld rice here, there, and everywhere. Never did I realize that this pearly grain could grow to such mammoth proportions. Need I say that my experience at culinary endeavors is most limited and that cooking is an art?

Disorderly Paragraphs

Clearness in a paragraph is destroyed when the sentences are not correctly arranged. Since our aim in paragraph writing is to make clear to the reader our thoughts on the selected topic, particular attention should be given to the order of sentences and the manner in which the topic is developed.

Read the two versions of the paragraph entitled "The Unexpected Reality." The disorderly paragraph appears very ridiculous to us. It does have unity, for the sentences are all about the one main idea, but the arrangement of sentences within the paragraph confuses us. Compare the paragraph on the left with the one that possesses clearness as well as unity.

The Unexpected Reality

Disorderly Paragraph

Into the dreamy stillness of slumberland, like an unwelcome intruder, came Mother's persistent morning call. Instantly I withdrew to the warmth of the blankets. Throwing off the blankets, I hopped out of bed with a start. Regretfully, but with determination, I proceeded to poke one toe out from beneath the covers, but the icy greeting it received banished my courage. Again Mother's voice sent a warning and I made another futile attempt. Before long a glance at the clock cautioned me that the hour was late. Strange to relate, when both feet were on the floor the cold was not so piercing as I had expected, thereby proving that "anticipation is greater than realization."

Clear Paragraph

Into the dreamy stillness of slumberland, like an unwelcome intruder, came Mother's persistent morning call. Regretfully, but with determination, I proceeded to poke one toe out from beneath the covers, but the icy greeting it received banished my courage. Instantly I withdrew to the warmth of the blankets. Again Mother's voice sent a warning and I made another futile attempt. Before long a glance at the clock cautioned me that the hour was late. Throwing off the blankets, I hopped out of bed with a start. Strange to relate, when both feet were on the floor the cold was not so piercing as I had expected, thereby proving that "anticipation is greater than realization."

CLASS ASSIGNMENT

Rearrange the middle sentences in the following paragraph:

A Date Delicacy

The date is a delicious fruit, but its charms are enhanced considerably by stuffing it in the following manner. Next make a creamy fondant by mixing a lump of softened butter about the size of a walnut with enough confectioner's sugar to make a smooth paste. Press the sides of the date together and as a final step roll it in granulated sugar. With a sharp knife first split the date and remove the stone. Place a small amount of this fondant inside the date together with a large nut meat. The result will be a dainty tidbit fit for a king.

3. Longer Compositions

A paragraph describes *one* thing, tells of *one* event, explains *one* process. When a new topic is introduced it is necessary to use a new paragraph. All writing is done in paragraphs. We have only to examine our readers, our histories, or our geographies to see examples of paragraph writing. Each of the paragraphs explains one thing only. A new topic demands a new paragraph.

Did the pupil who wrote the following composition understand writing in paragraphs?

Model: Volumes of Happiness

A stranger examining the contents of our family bookcase would be puzzled, no doubt, by the odd assortment he finds there. Thick books on engineering stand side by side with gaily colored volumes of fairy tales. Detective stories with bloodthirsty titles occupy the same shelf as staid history texts. "Who," he will surely ask, "owns this strange collection?"

A glance through our living-room window some evening will provide an answer to his question. In the easy chair by the lamp he will see Dad puffing contentedly on his pipe as he unravels a mystery that is baffling the professional sleuths. Little Clare will be curled happily in Grandfather's lap while he reads to her of the thrilling adventures of some heroic prince in her beloved Land of Make-Believe. The onlooker will notice George, our college student, stretched out full length before the friendly fire, poring over complicated illustrations and dreaming of the day when he will build his first bridge.

Although this glimpse will account for the variety of our books, it will not even begin to tell the inquiring stranger of the pleasure we have found in them. It can give him only a hint of the peace, contentment, and close companionship that a common interest in good reading has brought to our family.

Read the model composition again, paying particular attention to the ending sentence in the first paragraph and the beginning sentence in the second paragraph. Notice how the writer refers to the question in the first paragraph as he begins the second paragraph. Note, too, that this paragraph answers the question asked. Again in the third paragraph the writer refers to the glimpse through the window and to the "inquiring stranger." Such sentences serve to link one paragraph with another and to give unity to the entire composition.

The Importance of an Outline

An outline is a pattern or plan for a composition or a talk. The outline helps the writer keep his thoughts in order because it shows how the ideas he has gathered on a topic can be related. In making an outline the writer lists first the tentative title of his composition, the subject that he plans to discuss. Then he writes the topic of the first paragraph, with the ideas he wishes to develop in the beginning sentence, the middle sentences, and the ending sentence. If there is more than one paragraph, he writes the topic for each paragraph and makes a list of the details he plans to include in that paragraph. Study this outline which the writer made for the composition "Volumes of Happiness." Is the title in the model on page 46 a better one than the one which the pupil used in his outline?

THE BOOKCASE IN OUR LIVING ROOM

   I. The contents of the bookcase
      A. Types of books
         1. Books on engineering
         2. Fairy tales
         3. Detective stories
         4. History textbooks
      B. Ownership a puzzle
  II. The readers of the books
      A. My father
      B. My grandfather
      C. My baby sister
      D. My older brother
 III. The enjoyment the books bring
      A. Peace
      B. Contentment
      C. Close companionship

RULES FOR MAKING AN OUTLINE

1. Use a roman numeral for the topic of each paragraph and place a period after the numeral. Keep the periods following these numerals under one another.

2. Use a capital letter for each of the important subdivisions within each paragraph. Indent each subhead so that the letter will fall directly under the first letter of the first word of the main heading, and place a period after each letter.

3. If there are any additional details to be added to any subdivision, use arabic numbers. Indent so that the number falls directly under the first letter of the first word of the subhead.

4. Begin the first word of each topic, subhead, and detail with a capital letter. Do not use capital letters for other words in the outline unless they are proper nouns or proper adjectives.

CLASS ASSIGNMENT

The following composition should have been written in two paragraphs. Indicate where the second paragraph should begin:

BOOKWORM OR EARTHWORM

To read or to weed is the problem that confronts me whenever I have five extra minutes. Reading satisfies the wanderlust in me. It affords the opportunity to abandon the monotonous paths of everyday life and to trip excitedly along the mysterious trails in the enchanting land of books. Lost in the magic of the printed page, I cast off my customary clothing and array myself in the raiment of a victorious knight or a football star. No longer shackled by the chains of time and space, I shiver with Washington's valiant men in the biting cold of Valley Forge and I kneel in reverent awe at Bethlehem's crib. Is it any wonder that I am unable to resist the beckoning call of a good book? My interest in weeding is probably the result of my interest in reading. This occupation puts me on a par with those noble characters that I have admired in books. Few tasks are more intriguing to me than that of rescuing struggling plants from the greedy claws of choking weeds. I like the feel of the cold, damp earth as I eject the intruding roots. With the confident swagger of a conquering hero I march triumphantly through our flower garden, leaving grateful shrubs in my wake. Even the squirming worms wriggle their gratitude for my noble deed. Yes, recreation time is always debating time for me. The topic of this secret controversy ever remains the same, to read or to weed?

4. Choral Speaking

If we learn to read poems in chorus, we shall have a pleasant topic for paragraph writing. Poems are compositions in verse. The poet selects a topic and expresses his own feelings. When we recite the poem we try to portray the author's thoughts.

Remember that a verse-speaking choir always practices the tuning-up exercises before attempting to read together the poem to be used for choral speaking.

Tuning-up Exercises

Breathing:
Breathe deeply. Inhale through the nose, inflating the diaphragm, chest wall, and ribs. Then exhale with the sound of *ah*.

Inhale. Hold the breath for ten counts; then exhale with the sound of *ha*, gently and gradually.

Enunciation:

Practice the sound of $\breve{\imath}$ as in *it*. Say in different pitches the words *it, kit, pit, bit*.

That's it—hit the kit with the bit.

Practice the sound of $\breve{o}$ as in *not*. Say in different pitches *cot, dot, lot*.

Cots dot the lot on the spot.

Practice the sound of the consonant *m* by repeating the following syllables firmly and clearly:

ma me mi mo mu moo moi

The Love of Home

We all love our own home. It is the scene of many happy events. Here we have the close companionship of our parents and our brothers and sisters. How many have had the joy of returning home after a long absence?

We will now turn our attention to the study of Joyce Kilmer's poem "Roofs." The author puts into this poem a longing for home and all that home means. It is a good selection to recite in chorus, for it may be read by three groups and a chorus in which all the groups join.

ROOFS

By Joyce Kilmer

Medium Voices

The road is wide / and the stars are out and the breath of the night is sweet, //
And this is the time when wanderlust / should seize upon my feet. //
But I'm glad to turn from the open road / and the starlight on my face, //
And to leave the splendor of out of doors / for a human dwelling place. //

Light Voices

I never have seen a vagabond / who really liked to roam
All up and down / the streets of the world / and not to have a home. //
The tramp that slept in your barn last night / and left at break of day //
Will wander only until he finds another place to stay. //

Heavy Voices

A gypsy-man will sleep in his cart / with the canvas overhead; //
Or else he'll go into his tent / when it is time for bed. //
He'll sit on the grass and take his ease / so long as the sun is high, //
But when it is dark / he wants a roof to keep away the sky. //

Medium Voices

If you call a gypsy a vagabond, / I think you do him wrong, //
For he never goes a-traveling / but he takes his home along. //
And the only reason a road is good, / as every wanderer knows, //
Is just because of the homes, / the homes, / the homes to which it goes. //

Chorus

They say that life is a highway / and its milestones are the years, //
And now and then there's a toll-gate / where you buy your way with tears. //
It's a rough road and a steep road / and it stretches broad and far, //
But at last / it leads to a golden Town where golden Houses are. //

STUDY OF THE POEM

This is a lyric poem; that is, a poem that sings into one's heart by the music of its verse. Read it first in unison. Feel the beat of the lines, one—two—three—four—five—six—seven.

The beauty of the poem lies not only in its music, but in its thought. The poet is saying that the only reason any road is good is because it leads to a home whose roof shelters the loved ones. The stars shining bright on a clear night may lure us to wander on the open road, but the man who loves his home is glad to seek the shelter of its friendly roof. Even the vagabond and the gypsy seek their poor homes when night comes on.

The poem ends with a beautiful comparison. It says that life itself is a highway where joy and sorrow often meet, but the highway leads at last to a home where there will be no more sorrow.

Vocabulary Hints

Explain the meanings of the following words and sentences found in the poem "Roofs":

wanderlust	tramp	milestones
vagabond	gypsy	toll-gate
roam	open road	dwelling place

"And this is the time when wanderlust should seize upon my feet."

"They say that life is a highway and its milestones are the years."

"And now and then there's a toll-gate where you buy your way with tears."

5. Chapter Challenge

1. A paragraph is a group of related ....

2. The parts of a paragraph are: (1) ...., (2) ...., and (3) ....

3. A good .... sentence attracts attention, gives a hint of the contents of the paragraph, and often arouses curiosity.

4. A sentence that states the central thought of the paragraph is called the .... sentence.

5. The beginning sentence is usually the .... sentence, but one of the .... sentences or even the .... sentence may serve as the .... sentence.

6. The .... sentences help to develop the .... of the paragraph.

7. The ending sentence may be (1) the .... detail, (2) a .... of details, or (3) a .... comment.

8. The two essential qualities of a good paragraph are .... and ....
9. A paragraph that develops one idea and one idea only has ....
10. A paragraph has .... when the sentences follow in natural and logical order.
11. If we wish to introduce a new topic, we must
....
12. An .... is a pattern or plan for a composition or a talk.
13. In an .... we use roman numerals for the .... of each paragraph, capital letters for the important .... within each paragraph, and arabic .... for the details to be added to any
....
14. The poem .... by .... tells of man's longing for home and all that home means.

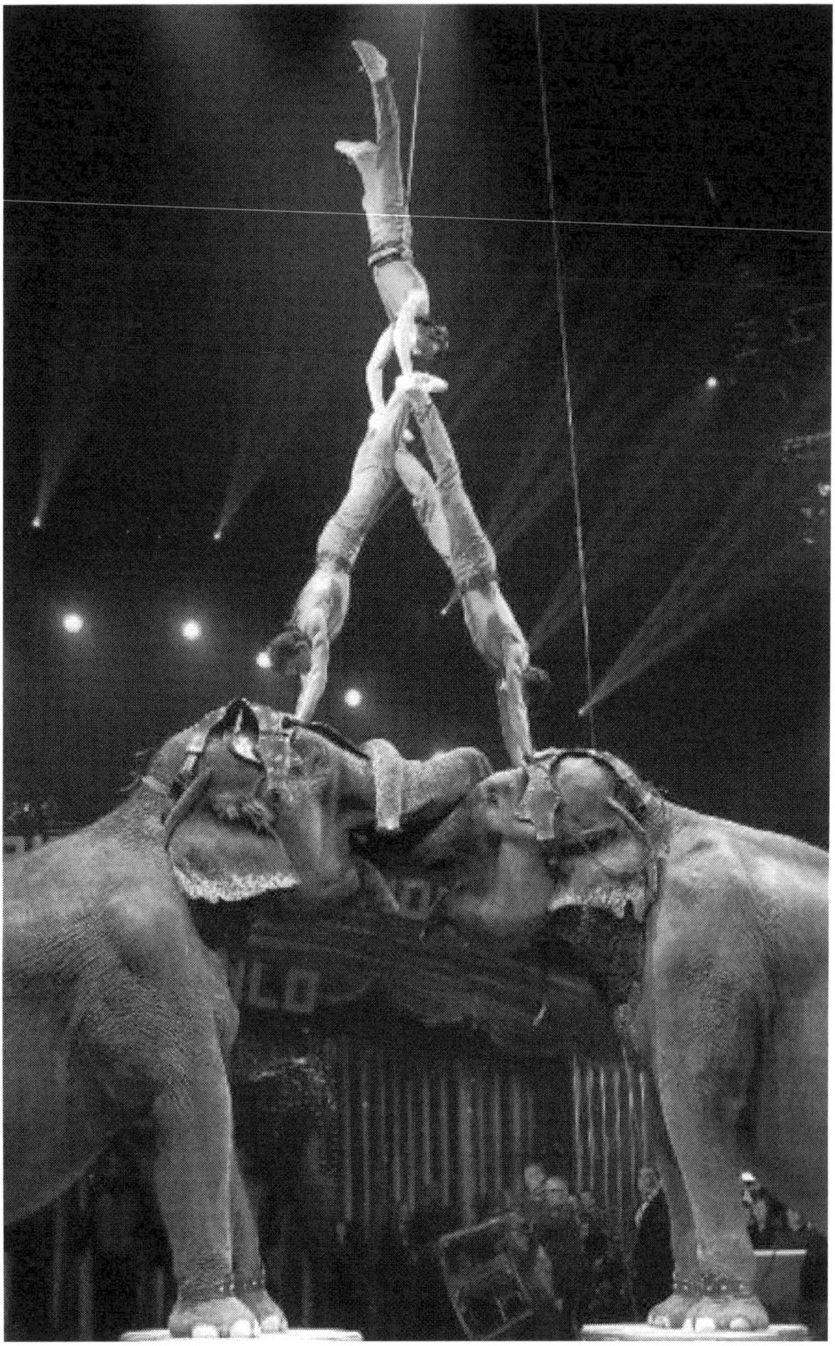

CHAPTER THREE **Writing a Paragraph**

In which we learn how to follow definite steps in writing a paragraph

In Chapter Two we learned that a paragraph is a group of sentences developing one thought. The sentence that tells what the topic of the paragraph is, or what the paragraph is about, is called the *topic sentence*. It is usually found at the beginning of the paragraph. This sentence is followed by others (the *middle sentences* of the paragraph) that develop the thought of the topic sentence and give necessary details. The ending sentence may sum up what has been said, give the last detail, or express the author's feelings concerning the topic. The paragraphs we studied and the experiences we had in writing beginning and ending sentences helped to increase our understanding of the structure of a paragraph.

Now we are to write paragraphs of our own. If the members of the class work together as a group and follow a definite plan, we shall obtain much useful practice in writing paragraphs.

1. Building a Class Paragraph

What shall we write about in our group paragraph? We call this selecting the subject. Nearly everyone likes the circus. For weeks we anticipate its arrival and for days afterward we remember eye-filling spectacles of daring trapeze artists and aerialists, of amusing clowns, and of strange animals from all parts of the world. The circus, therefore, may be the subject of our paragraph.

It is impossible, however, to write in one paragraph everything that might be said about the circus—its history, its arrival, its wonders, its colors, the animals, the crowds attending. We must limit the subject to *one topic*. One seventh-grade class decided to write about the wonders of the circus.

The pupils in this class knew that a good choice of words was essential to successful paragraph writing. Accordingly, they discussed some of the wonders to be seen in the circus and built a vocabulary of words and phrases that would help them to paint vivid word pictures of the circus. They arranged this list in three classifications: (1) people and animals of the circus, (2) descriptive words and actions, and (3) sounds and colors.

People and Animals of the Circus

battalion of clowns	trapeze artists
inimitable mimics	daring acrobats
fun-provoking clowns	nine-foot giant
accomplished horsemen	sheiks and sultans
amazing contortionists	roller-skating bears
graceful jugglers	colossal elephants
skilled musicians	awkward, dancing elephants
imperious ringmaster	trained seals
dainty equestrienne	bicycle-riding monkeys
bearded lady	prancing saddle horses
snake charmer	wild animals in gilded cages

Descriptive Words and Actions

dazzling	pantomiming of clowns
spectacular	waddling of elephants
irresistible	flying perilously through space
superb	strutting of ringmaster
stupendous	coiling the whip
amusing antics	bewildering somersaults
swinging on flying trapeze	feats of aerialists
mixture of merriment, mystery, and magic	balancing on tightrope
	incredible wonders

Sounds and Colors

thundering applause	brilliant colors
peals of laughter	chalk-faced clowns
chuckles of merriment	trappings of purple and gold
blare of band	shimmering silk gowns
rumbling of animal wagons	motley suits of clowns
bewitching sound of music	smooth jet-black seals
echoes through the arena	variegated uniforms

An outline or written plan is also necessary to guide us in organizing the paragraph so that it will have both unity and clearness. The pupils who chose the wonders of the circus as the topic of their class paragraph made the following outline:

TOPIC: WONDERS OF THE CIRCUS

Beginning sentence   A. Transformations wrought by circus wonders
Middle sentences   B. Memorable features
           1. Ringmaster and animals
           2. Daring equestriennes
           3. Pantomiming clowns
           4. Feats of aerialists
           5. Freaks
Ending sentence   C. Summary of impressions

The class then thought about good beginning sentences. As the outline indicated, this sentence was to concern the transformations wrought by circus wonders. A beginning sentence, we recall, should command attention and arouse the interest of our readers. The following were suggested by the class:

1. The fairy godmother of Circusland has again waved her magic wand over an ugly, weed-choked lot in our city.
2. Combine marvels, mirth, mystery, magic, and you have the word *circus*.
3. Into our book of commonplace days the circus annually slips a page of strange and incredible wonders.
4. Forget the hustle and bustle of modern life, and come for a day to a realm of enchantment!
5. Follow the crowds to Circustown, that miniature city of enchanting wonders.

The pupils in the class also suggested ending sentences for the paragraph. These were written on the blackboard

for all to examine. Do these sentences conform to the outline by giving a summary of impressions?
1. Cinderella-like, the old lot seems unaware of its short-lived transformation, and delights in merriment, music, and marvels.
2. Dazzling, incomparable, irresistible—that's the circus!
3. Circus day is, indeed, a page resplendent with merriment and marvels.
4. Long after the circus grounds are silent and dull, the memory of that enchanting spectacle will live on.
5. How brilliant is the trail of wholesome fun and cheer left by these people of Circusland!

Each pupil in the class then selected the beginning sentence which attracted him most, used the vocabulary on the blackboard in writing middle sentences that described the memorable feats mentioned in the outline, and chose the ending sentence that told his impressions of the wonders of the circus. Did the group work—the vocabulary, the outline, the beginning sentences, and the ending sentences—help the writer of this paragraph?

MODEL: PAGING THE CIRCUS

Into our book of commonplace days the circus annually slips a page of strange and incredible wonders. There struts the imperious ringmaster, coiling and cracking his whip, while awkward elephants dance and trained seals juggle rainbow balls. Here we see the little equestrienne, dainty and daring, whose white horse provides a graceful landing after her bewildering somersaults. Shuffling in and out of the rings are the pantomiming clowns, who send peals of laughter echoing through the arena. Overhead, daring aerialists, brilliantly arrayed in silks and spangles, whirl rhythmically through space. No less amazing, if not so spectacular, are the side shows, featuring the bearded lady, the sword swallower, and the nine-foot giant. Circus day is, indeed, a page resplendent with merriment and marvels.

The title is a very important part of the paragraph, for it is always possible to arouse interest with an attractive title. Does the title of the model paragraph, "Paging the Circus," attract the reader's attention? Does it suit the paragraph this pupil wrote?

The following are some of the titles suggested by the class writing a paragraph on wonders of the circus:

Paging the Circus	Colors on Parade
Land of Laughter	World of Wonders
The Big Top	Circus Delights
Canvas City	Featuring the Circus
Circus Wonderland	Circus Fever

THE SENTENCES OF A PARAGRAPH:
  1. *Are closely related*
  2. *Develop one topic*

CLASS ASSIGNMENT

1. Read the following paragraph about the circus and then answer the questions which follow:

CIRCUS FEVER

Every spring I succumb to an attack of circus fever. Its symptoms occur as our town is being invaded with billboards, which flash before my eyes daring feats of skill, dancing elephants, and roller-skating bears. Failing to check the progress of this unique ailment, I am caught in the contagion of the crowd jamming the grounds on circus day. Amid the blare of the band I elbow my way to the Big Tent, whose bulging sides connote the teeming life within. Once inside those canvas walls, I undergo all the various stages of this thrilling disease, ranging from sidesplitting laughter to breath-taking excitement. Perhaps the crisis is reached when a group of pirouetting dancers, poised on milk-white horses, are greeted with thunderous applause. Slowly the fever subsides as I eventually return from this enchanted realm, musing meanwhile that circus fever is one malady from which I would never desire a "speedy recovery."

1. Does the paragraph develop a single topic?
2. Is the beginning sentence the topic sentence?
3. Does every sentence pertain to the idea announced in the topic sentence?
4. Are the sentences in the paragraph written in logical order?
5. Does the ending sentence give the paragraph an effective conclusion?
6. Does the title suggest the story that follows?

2. Write a paragraph of your own, using wonders of the circus as the topic and following the outline on page 60. Select a beginning sentence, an ending sentence, and a title from those suggested.

2. Steps in Writing the Paragraph

The development of a group paragraph showed us the steps to be followed in writing paragraphs. A detailed study of these steps will develop orderly habits of thought and help us to express our ideas freely and accurately.

Selecting and Limiting the Subject

Subjects for paragraphs are as varied and unlimited as our interests. We may, for example, write descriptions of persons, places, or things. We may tell of our experiences, either real or imaginary; of trips we have taken or would like to take; of outings we have enjoyed; of games our team has won or lost; of books we have enjoyed reading.

The topic of our paragraph, however, must not be vague or general. *Houses* would not be a good topic for a paragraph, but if we were to limit this subject to a *haunted house,* we would have a topic for a paragraph.

Compare the following subjects and topics. Can you suggest other ways of limiting the subject?

Subject	Topic	Other Topics
Winter sports	Why I like skiing	
Vacation	Packing my suitcase	
Camp life	Cooking breakfast	
Picnics	A lost lunch	
Letters	A mysterious letter	
Fires	How to build a fire	
Flowers	A florist's window display	
A street	Our street on a windy day	

CLASS ASSIGNMENT

1. Supply the missing subject or the missing topic:

Subject	Topic
1. A city	....
2.	An unexpected drenching
3. Interesting people	....
4. Amusements	....
5.	Friendliness of our kitchen
6.	A view from a mountaintop
7. Canaries	....
8.	My favorite childhood toy
9.	What our flag means to me
10. Fishing	....

2. Limit each of the following subjects to a topic that can be developed in a single paragraph:

1. An inventor
2. Our attic
3. Mary's shrine
4. A horse race
5. Our cafeteria
6. A hornet's nest
7. The gypsy camp
8. A railroad station
9. A creek
10. Our holy father

Building a Vocabulary

The effectiveness of our writing depends to a great extent upon our vocabulary. We should use words that will not only make our meaning clear, but will arouse interest and paint vivid pictures. After we have limited the subject to a topic that can be developed in a paragraph, we should think of picture words and picture phrases to be used in describing or explaining the topic.

If you are describing a house, for example, try to remember some striking feature of its appearance. Form a mental picture of the house that you wish the reader of your paragraph to see. You will also want to make a list of words that can be used in place of *house* so that you will not need to repeat this word endlessly. If the topic is a visit to a haunted house, you will probably wish to tell the reader why you wanted to enter the house, the appearance of the building, the sounds you heard, what you saw, and your own reactions.

Would the following vocabulary developed by one group of pupils help you to write a paragraph on a visit to a haunted house?

Appearance	Condition	Other Words
moss-covered	dilapidated	abode
gloom-enshrouded	rambling	dwelling
ivy-mantled	deserted	edifice
weather-beaten	abandoned	mansion
wind-swept	crumbling	manor

Reasons for Entering	Sounds	Reactions
lured me	weird	terrified
enticed me	eerie	paralyzed with fear
captivated my curiosity	piercing	rooted to the spot
intrigued me	bloodcurdling	gripped with terror

CLASS ASSIGNMENT

1. Read the following paragraph entitled "Mystery Mansion." Did the pupil make use of the vocabulary on this page when he wrote the paragraph? Make a list of the words and the phrases that he used in developing his paragraph.

Mystery Mansion

How we regretted our vain boast to unveil the secrets of "Mystery Mansion"! All the bloodcurdling tales of horror ever associated with it kept recurring to our overwrought imaginations as our moonlight walk brought that spectral edifice into view. Lured by its gloom-enshrouded appearance, we approached with hesitant footsteps the vivid outline of the ancient dwelling. The ivy-mantled abode was surrounded by heavy foliage and neglected shrubbery, whose stinging thorns almost compelled us to forego the adventure. Curiosity conquered our fear as we crawled upon the crumbling porch. Low, eerie moans coming from the direction of the wind-swept balcony caused us to shudder anew. Suddenly a weird scream pierced the night air, and in one horribly confused minute we spontaneously voted to abandon the exploration of the moss-covered manor. Never again will we try to determine the truthfulness of the stories we hear about deserted lodgings.

2. What words in this paragraph appeal to the imagination and paint a vivid picture of the colors in the circus?

A Realm of Color

Riotous colors add a pleasing effect to the skilled performances and clever artistry of the circus. A brilliant blue satin, studded with silver sequins, graces the peerless equestrienne, and the imperious ringmaster flashes a suit of yellow. Smooth, jet-black seals balance themselves on immense rainbow balls. Daring acrobats, dizzily flying through space above a scarlet-netted floor, glisten in their dazzling costumes. Regiments of clowns in motley suits contribute to the color scheme, while awkward elephants waddle to and fro beneath gorgeous trappings of purple and gold. Beautiful dancers in shimmering silk and spangled gowns gracefully trip in and out of multicolored hoops. It is color that enhances the glamorous activity of Circusland.

3. Build a vocabulary that might be used to describe any one of the following. Select words or expressions that will make the picture real or striking:

The ringmaster at the circus	A trailer camp
A graceful juggler	A character in Bookland
A village post office	A trapeze artist
A unique gift	A forest fire
A cottage at the beach	A cantering white horse

Making an Outline

An outline helps the writer to keep his thoughts in order because it shows how the ideas he has gathered on a topic can be related. In making an outline the student lists first the topic of the paragraph, then the ideas he wishes to develop in the beginning sentence, the middle sentences, and the ending sentence.

There are two kinds of outlines, a *sentence outline* and a *topical outline*. A sentence outline states each point in a complete sentence; a topical outline does not use complete sentences. Study the outline made by a pupil who intended to write a paragraph on a bakery shop. What is the topic of her paragraph? What does she expect to mention in the beginning sentence? In the middle sentences? In the ending sentence? Is this outline a sentence outline or a topical outline?

TOPIC: TREASURES OF MRS. DOYLE'S BAKERY
    A. Wonderland of treasures
    B. Location of treasures
        1. On the showcase
        2. Inside the cabinet
        3. On the shelf
        4. In the closets
    C. The guardian of the treasures

CLASS ASSIGNMENT

1. Compare the following paragraph with the outline on page 68. Did the definite plan shown by the outline help this writer? Do you like the title she selected?

A Treasury of Treats

Just open the heavy door of Mrs. Doyle's bakery and you are immediately transported into an old-fashioned wonderland. The sweet aroma of ginger, molasses, and chocolate pervades the air. On top of the showcase is a huge cake; its pink-and-white frosting fairly dances with the word "Welcome." Sugar and currant cookies look happily at one another from their decorative flowered boxes inside this sparkling display cabinet. From a prominent place on the trim, orderly shelf, little peppermint-stick ladies and gentlemen sedately bow in candy greeting. Hidden deep in delicious pastry closets are enough treasures to tempt any boy or girl. Not the least of all the treasures is Mrs. Doyle herself, whose beaming smile and quaint stories of long ago induce you to return again and again to her wonderland.

2. Write an outline for a paragraph on any of the ten topics that are listed here:

1. The family album
2. A stalled automobile
3. A busy delicatessen
4. My first telegram
5. Plans frustrated
6. Fun for a dime
7. Gathering apples
8. A robin's nest
9. A Chinese laundry
10. A crowded train

Writing the Paragraph

The outline indicates the ideas to be developed in the beginning sentence, the middle sentences, and the ending sentence. The beginning sentence, we recall, should attract the reader's attention and arouse his interest. It must at least give a hint of the idea to be developed in the other sentences. The beginning sentence is very often the topic sentence of the paragraph.

The topic sentence announces the main idea of the paragraph; it is the most important sentence in the paragraph. Notice how each of the following topic sentences tells what is to be discussed in the paragraph:

Topic	Topic Sentence
Cleaning the attic	Cleaning our attic is a real adventure for me.
Activity of ants	Ceaseless activity exists in ant-land.
Initiative in a leader	Initiative is a requisite for good leadership.
The pope and prayer	Our late holy father, Pope Pius XII, was above all else a man of prayer.
Dismissal from school	Our school takes great pride in the order which characterizes its dismissal.

The outline tells us the order to be followed in the middle sentences. Only those sentences which develop the topic can be included in the paragraph. If we introduce misfit sentences, our paragraph does not have unity. We must also aim for clearness in our paragraph. If we are relating some experience or telling a story, we must see that the middle sentences lead step by step to the most interesting or exciting part. In a paragraph that describes, our sentences should be arranged in the order of observation. In observing a person, for example, our eyes would probably travel from his head to his feet.

In the first model on page 71 clearness is gained by telling the facts in the order of their occurrence; in the second the writer presents details as they were observed. Do the paragraphs exhibit unity?

Model: Sailing through Space

Fear and anticipation struggled in my heart when I stepped for the first time into the riotously colored roller coaster. As the little car chugged confidently up the first steep incline, my timidity faded. I peeped over the edge of the miniature train to look down upon the park growing rapidly smaller before my eyes. Suddenly, with mounting terror, I found myself ready to swoop into space. Down rushed the car, to the accompaniment of my frantic but delighted screams. Hardly had I gained my breath after this downward plunge when the chariot again ascended, intent on dropping me once more into the yawning abyss. With sudden abruptness the thrilling ride came to an end. Smiling bravely for the benefit of my watching friends, I assured them that this mad rush through time and space was truly the greatest ride on earth.

Model: Sunset at the Shore

The entire landscape seemed bathed in a rose-gold light as the family car approached the ocean at sunset. Everything within the eye's range was flooded with unearthly beauty. Although the sun itself was not visible from our position, this radiance seemed to emanate from the glowing, blue-gold sky above. In mid-air sea gulls, like model planes of pearl, shifted and glided in graceful movement. A white-sailed fishing vessel was peacefully making its way to a distant shore. The tireless rolling waves took on new beauty as they sparkled rhythmically from horizon to shore, depositing treasures on the sandy beach. We gazed in awe, marveling at the many ways God has of revealing His beauty to us.

The concluding sentence of the paragraph must satisfy the reader and let him know that the paragraph is finished. This is sometimes done by relating the last detail or summarizing the facts presented in the paragraph. The ending sentence very often takes the form of a personal comment. Note how various feelings or emotions can be expressed in an ending sentence.

Feeling	Ending Sentence
Admiration	This incident taught me to admire a high-principled person.
Gratitude	Then it was that I realized I owed my success to Mother's patient guidance.
Security	As I heard the sound of Father's footsteps the great fear which had enveloped me disappeared like magic.
Reverence	Haven't you always felt reluctant to leave this hallowed spot where God, our Savior, dwells?
Anticipation	How eagerly we look forward to our own graduation next year!

CLASS ASSIGNMENT

1. Evaluate the following topic sentences. Can you determine the topic of the paragraph for which each was written?

1. Have you ever considered the importance of the motions of the sun?
2. The baking of my first pie proved to be a disappointing venture.
3. Of all the subjects we study I think that composition requires the most originality.
4. The harbor was alive with ships from every part of the world.
5. The center of activity in our home is the small but cheerful kitchen.

2. Find the topic sentence in the following paragraphs. What is the subject of the paragraph? The topic?

1. Winter Warmth

You may elude the icy clutches of winter if you become experienced in building a furnace fire. After the grates have been cleaned, crumple two or three sheets of newspaper, lay them in the center of the firebox, and add a few pieces of kindling or light wood. Cover with a few pieces of coal. It is most important that all these articles be dry, since the least bit of moisture will dampen and kill your fire. Light a match and deftly ignite at least two corners of the paper. Close the furnace door, making certain that the draft is open and oxygen reaches the flames. After a short time the wood and coal should be blazing. When this happens add more coal, give it a chance to ignite, then close the draft so that the coal will not burn too rapidly. If you follow these instructions, you will be assured of a fire that will successfully heat your home.

2. King of Laughter

Grinning from ear to ear, the comically garbed clown captivates the fancy of the circus crowd with his amazing antics. By merely tapping ridiculously long feet to a lively tune, Jo-Jo sends the spectators into an uproar. All eyes focus on this chalk-faced comedian as he adroitly turns numerous cart wheels. The audience merges into one grand "Ah!" when he slowly but expertly balances himself on an immense rainbow ball. Reverberating laughter echoes through the arena at the moment the jester transforms his nose into a flashy red light. Though he takes only a small part in the circus, the clown is its most irresistible character.

3. Here are some details which might be used in developing certain topics. Arrange these details in the order in which they should be taken up in the middle sentences:

Topic	Details
A familiar bird	Head, eyes, tail, breast, beak, wings
A gift package	Ribbon, name card, bow, paper, seals
Preparation of chalice for Mass	Purificator, corporal, burse, veil, pall, chalice, large host, paten
Making my bed	Bottom sheet, pillows, blanket, top sheet, spread
My new party dress	Material, skirt, belt, style, sleeves, color, waist, neckline

4. Read the following paragraph and make a list of the details covered in the middle sentences. Is the paragraph clear?

Dancing Dodo

Of all the spectacular performances at the circus, the antics of Dodo, the elephant, are perhaps the most amusing. Bedecked in a purple-and-gold panoply, he humorously waltzes to and fro to everyone's delight. As the procession forms, Dodo quickly and cleverly joins it, grasping in his trunk the tail of another elephant and waddling from side to side to rhythmical accompaniment. In the ballet this colossal figure enacts a prominent part as he lifts one huge foot, then the other, in perfect time. When the lordly old tusker nonchalantly picks up a cornet and pretends to play it, he creates a hilarious uproar. Amidst the enthusiastic cheers of the audience Dodo steps upon the platform with surprising agility to accept with a gracious bow the plaudits of the crowd. Enjoyed by all, the king of Jungleland is indeed a most entertaining performer.

5. What thoughts or feelings do you think the following ending sentences suggest?

1. Imagine my disappointment when I read the sign over the door, "Closed all day Saturday."

WRITING A PARAGRAPH 75

2. Those weird screams were still echoing in our ears as we fled to the safety of the street.
3. Having followed all the directions carefully, there was no doubt in my mind that I would succeed in the project.
4. I could sit for hours drinking in Grandfather's tales of the sea.
5. My cheers merged with those of the other spectators as the ball soared over the goal post.
6. As the front door closed on the unruly group, Aunt Josephine breathed a sigh of relief.
7. A feeling of satisfaction and contentment was mine as I tucked away a real "gold mine."
8. When I am as old as my grandmother I hope I can still laugh at the world.
9. As the echo of Father Dougherty's admonition faded away, I became conscious of my obligations to my parents.

Christening the Paragraph

Since the title advertises our paragraph, it should attract attention and arouse interest or curiosity. However, it should not reveal the contents of the composition. Let it be a billboard that advertises our product.

Would these titles engage one's attention? Are they thought-provoking?

Topic	Title
My first violin lesson	A Budding Maestro
An airplane ride	Winged Adventure
Tales of an attic	Hidden Treasures
A lucky incident	A Silver Lining
A sunset	Evening Glow
An Irish immigrant	A Shamrock Transplanted
A collector of old coins	A Modern Midas
A lighthouse	Ever Vigilant
The first robin	Spring's Herald
Riding an escalator	Puffless Method

Putting the Paragraph on Paper

Good form requires that certain rules be followed when paragraphs are written in final form to be submitted to the teacher. Many schools have definite regulations concerning the form of written work in all subjects. Here are some rules to be observed in paragraph writing if your school does not require a specific form:

1. Leave a margin of at least one inch at the left of the paper and a half-inch margin at the right.
2. Place the title in the center of the first line.
3. Leave one line between the title and the first line of the paragraph.
4. Indent the first word of the paragraph about an inch from the left-hand margin.
5. Let your handwriting be plain and neat.
6. Observe all the rules for spelling, punctuation, and capitalization.
7. When the paragraph is completed, leave one line blank and write your name on the right-hand side of the next line.
8. Write the date on the same line as your name, on the left-hand side.

CLASS ASSIGNMENT

1. Write an attractive title which will be suitable for the paragraph that follows:

My ambitions have been quite numerous and amazing in variety. At preschool age I longed eagerly to be a fairy princess who would be the lovely and wise ruler of spacious kingdoms. After being admitted to the precincts of the classroom, this childish notion was disdainfully discarded. The life of a teacher was then the only worth-while aspiration. How magnificent it would be to don a Sister's habit and teach the little ones the way to God! It wasn't until I was hospitalized that I decided on an entirely different vocation. The work of a busy nurse, swishing through hospital corridors to bring cheer and comfort to the suffering, became a most appealing profession. This constant changing of careers continued from year to year until I reached seventh grade. To my deep satisfaction I found myself quite content to be just me.

2. Using the topic sentences and the ending sentences provided, develop the two paragraphs outlined here:

1. Topic sentence — Yesterday morning proved hectic in every sense of the word.
   Middle sentences — What happened
   1. Faulty alarm clock
   2. Toast burned
   3. Bus missed
   4. Assignment misplaced
   Ending sentence — But how can I blame my faithful clock when I myself forgot to wind the alarm!

2. Topic sentence — God has provided safeguards to the angelic virtue of purity, which, like sentinels, keep watch over this exquisite jewel.
   Middle sentences — Safeguards to purity
   1. Diligence and temperance
   2. Devotion to our Lady
   3. Frequent reception of Holy Communion
   Ending sentence — Keep your sentinels always on duty and you may trustfully expect the reward which Christ promised when He said, "Blessed are the clean of heart, for they shall see God."

3. Write a paragraph using the vocabulary you built for one of the topics on page 68.

> **STEPS IN WRITING A PARAGRAPH:**
> 1. *Select a subject that interests you.*
> 2. *Limit the subject to a particular topic.*
> 3. *Think of the topic about which you intend to write, and ask yourself questions about it.*
> 4. *Build a vocabulary.*
> 5. *Make an outline.*
> 6. *Write a beginning sentence that attracts attention.*
> 7. *Follow the outline in writing the middle sentences so that the paragraph will have unity and clearness.*
> 8. *Let the ending sentence really end the paragraph.*
> 9. *Give your paragraph an appealing title.*

4. Write an original paragraph based on some subject that interests you. Follow all the steps mentioned above.

3. Keeping a Diary

The easiest story to write is one about ourselves and the things we do day by day. A record of our daily deeds is called a *diary*. We can keep a diary by writing each day a short account of the most important events. Many persons like to keep diaries.

MODEL: DIARY OF MARY ROBERTSON

September 8. School opened today. We assisted at holy Mass at eight o'clock and then went to the school building. Mother Superior introduced us to our new teacher in the seventh grade, Sister Joan. I am glad to be in school again.

September 9. Today I taught Blackie, our dog, a new trick, jumping through a hoop. Now when company comes he can perform for them.

September 10. The first meeting of the Good Citizenship Club was held today. I have been appointed chairman of a committee to decide what a good citizen should do. I hope our committee makes a good report.

September 11. Today, my birthday, I received a gift which I like very much. It is a statue of the Blessed Mother holding in her arms the Infant Jesus. I am so proud to have it for my own!

We can buy at the stationery store a little book which has all the dates listed and a few lines on which to write what has happened each day. It is much more fun, however, to make our own diary. We need only some small sheets of paper and some heavy cardboard for the cover. We can then write the dates as Mary did and can begin with any day we like.

4. Writing Verse

Very often boys and girls like to express their thoughts in verse. Writing poetry is not hard. Poems may be written on many subjects. Here is a poem about a flower, the dainty forget-me-not:

FORGET-ME-NOTS

By the shady stream they grow,
   On its mossy brink;
Forget-me-nots like little girls
   In dresses blue and pink.

I'll pick a little handful,
   Mary dear, for you;
They'll match the color of your eyes,
   They are so very blue!

The pupil who wrote this poem knows something about rhyme, for we notice that the second and the fourth lines end with the same sound. Are his thoughts expressed in an interesting manner?

What rhyming words can you find in this poem about an airplane?

My Plane and I

Like birds we fly
In the morning sky,
My trusty plane and I.

    A small taillight
    Moving bright—
    We wing the starry sky.

Through snow or hail
We cannot fail,
For we carry precious mail!

It is not necessary that our verses rhyme. Many modern poets write poetry that has no rhyme. In writing poetry we simply paint beautiful pictures. Study carefully the lifelike picture the student paints in the line "We wing the starry sky." Notice that the first word of each line of the poem begins with a capital letter.

CLASS ASSIGNMENT

Write a clear word picture in verse of what is suggested to you by one of the following. Your poem need not rhyme:

1. A field of daisies
2. A speedboat
3. A snowstorm
4. Sunset on a lake
5. A boy fishing
6. Spring rain
7. City noises
8. Our band on parade
9. Grandmother
10. A pet

5. Choral Speaking

In this chapter we will use for choral speaking a poem that tells a story. Observe how well the story is told, and how the poet follows the standards we have explained. Reciting in chorus the words of the stanzas will give a sense of rhythm which will help us to write sentences that are musical.

Tuning-up Exercises

Breathing:

Breathe deeply. Inhale through the nose, inflating the diaphragm, chest wall, and ribs. Then exhale with the sound of *ah*.

Inhale. Hold the breath for ten counts; then exhale with the sound of *ha*, gently and gradually.

Enunciation:

Practice saying the sound of $\bar{i}$ as in *night*. Say in high, low, and medium pitch:

Might does not make right in God's sight.

Practice saying the sound of $\bar{o}$ as in *mow*. Say *row, so, no, low* in different pitches.

Mow the rows so no row will be low.

Say firmly and clearly:

gallant get gift gold good goiter
Good girls get gallant grooms.

"Barbara Frietchie" is an excellent poem for choral speaking at any patriotic celebration. It may be recited by various groups, with solos by Barbara Frietchie and Stonewall Jackson.

Barbara Frietchie
By John Greenleaf Whittier

First Group, Up from the meadows ╱ rich with corn, ∥
Medium Voices Clear ╲ in the cool September morn, ∥

The clustered spires of Frederick ╲ stand
Green-walled ╲ by the hills of Maryland. ∥

Second Group, Round about them orchards ╲ sweep, ∥
Light Voices Apple ╱ and peach tree ╲ fruited deep, ∥

Fair as the garden of the Lord ∥
To the eyes of the famished rebel horde, ∥

Third Group, On that pleasant morn of the early fall ∥
Heavy Voices When Lee ╲ marched over the mountain wall; ∥

Over the mountains winding down, ∥
Horse ╱ and foot, ╲ into Frederick town. ∥

First Group, Forty flags ╲ with their silver stars, ∥
Medium Voices Forty flags ╱ with their crimson bars, ∥

Flapped in the morning wind: ╱ the sun
Of noon ╲ looked down, and saw not one. ∥

Second Group, Up rose old Barbara Frietchie ╲ then, ∥
Light Voices Bowed with her fourscore years and ten; ∥

Bravest of all in Frederick town, ∥
She ╲ took up the flag the men ╱ hauled down; ∥

In her attic window ╲ the staff ╱ she set, ∥
To show that one ╲ heart was loyal yet. ∥

WRITING A PARAGRAPH 83

Third Group, Heavy Voices	Up the street came the rebel tread, // Stonewall Jackson riding ahead. //
	Under his slouched hat left \ and right / He glanced: // the old flag \ met his sight. //
Solo	"Halt!"— \ the dust-brown ranks stood fast. //
Solo	"Fire!"— \ out blazed the rifle blast. //
First Group, Medium Voices	It shivered the window, pane \ and sash; // It rent the banner with seam \ and gash. //
	Quick as it fell, from the broken staff // Dame Barbara snatched \ the silken scarf. //
	She leaned far out on the window-sill, // And shook it forth with a royal will. //
Solo	"Shoot, \ if you must, this old gray head, // But spare your country's flag," \ she said. //
Second Group, Light Voices	A shade of sadness, \ a blush of shame, // Over the face of the leader \ came; //
	The nobler nature within him stirred To life \ at that woman's deed and word. //
Solo	"Who touches a hair of yon gray head // Dies like a dog! \ March on!" / he said. //

... UP FROM THE MEADOWS ...

Third Group, Heavy Voices	All day long through Frederick street // Sounded the tread of marching feet: //
First Group, Medium Voices	All day long that free flag \ tossed Over the heads of the rebel host. //
Second Group, Light Voices	Ever its torn folds rose and fell // On the loyal winds \ that loved it well; //
Third Group, Heavy Voices	And through the hill-gaps \ sunset light Shone over it \ with a warm good-night. //
Unison	Barbara Frietchie's work is o'er, // And the rebel rides on his raids no more. //
	Honor to her! \ and let a tear Fall, for her \ sake, on Stonewall's bier. //
	Over Barbara Frietchie's grave, // Flag of Freedom \ and Union, / wave! //
	Peace \ and order / and beauty / draw Round thy symbol of light and law; //
	And ever the stars above \ look down On thy / stars below in Frederick town! //

6. Chapter Challenge

1. After selecting a .... for a paragraph we must limit it to a .... that can be covered in a single paragraph.

2. We build a .... because a good choice of .... is essential for paragraph writing.

3. An .... helps the writer keep his thoughts in order.

4. The .... indicates the ideas to be developed in the .... sentence, the .... sentences, and the .... sentence.

5. The .... is a billboard that .... our paragraph.

6. The steps to be followed in writing a paragraph are: (1) Select a .... that interests you. (2) Limit the .... to a particular .... (3) .... of the .... about which you intend to write, and ask yourself .... about it. (4) Build a .... (5) Make an .... (6) Write a .... sentence that .... (7) Follow the .... in writing .... sentences so that the paragraph will have .... and .... (8) Let the .... sentence really .... the paragraph. (9) Give your paragraph an appealing ....

7. A record of our daily deeds is called a ....

8. Thoughts on many subjects may be expressed in ....

9. Many modern poets write poetry that has no ....

10. ".................. ...." is a narrative poem; that is, it tells a story.

11. The two prominent characters in the narrative poem in this chapter are .... and ....

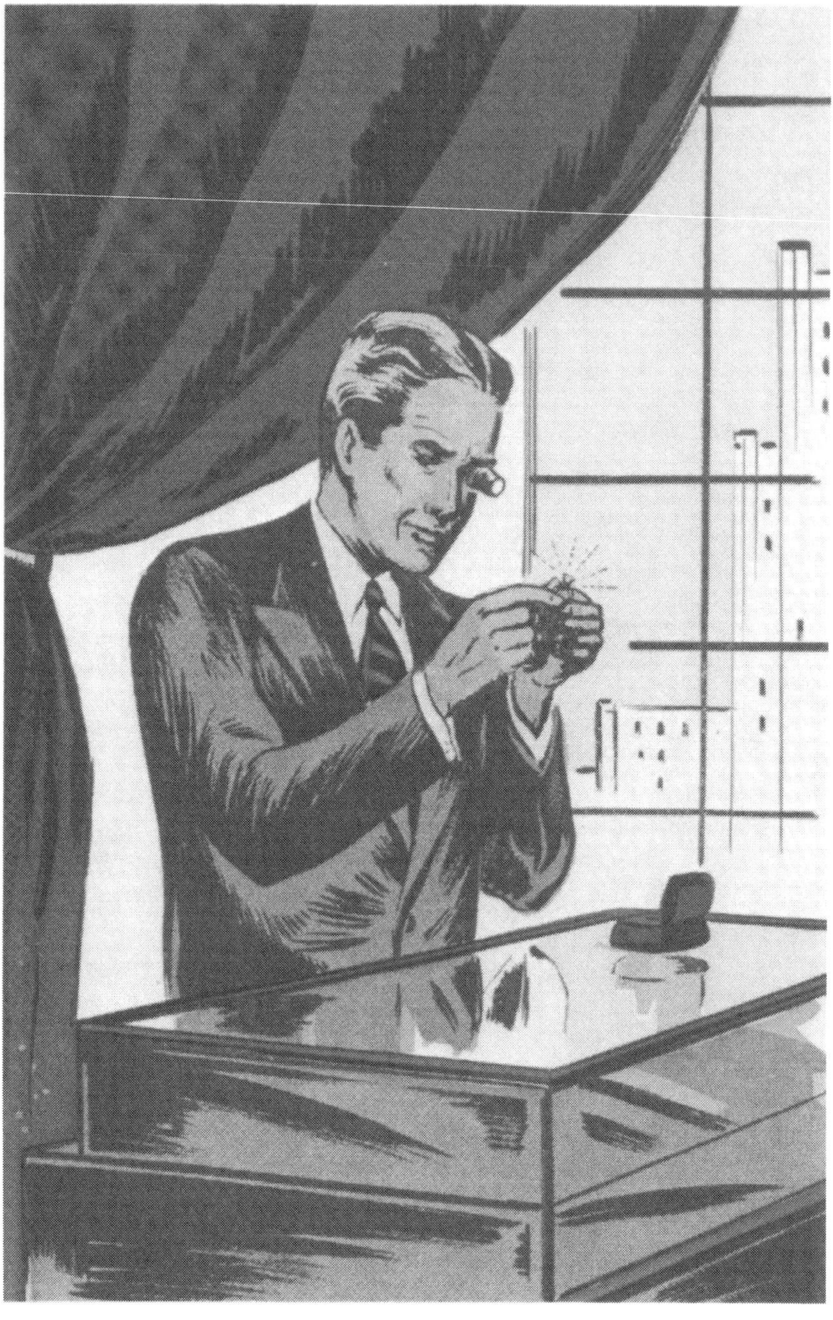

CHAPTER FOUR **Polishing a Paragraph**

In which we learn how to improve our writing

Kimberley—the word calls to our mind sparkling, shining diamonds in a chalice, monstrance, or in some other object of great value. The children of Kimberley, however, rarely see the dazzling wonders of this precious gem. They see diamonds in the rough, mud-stained and having little beauty on the surface. How, then, is the marvelous beauty of the diamond produced? Beauty is brought to the surface by skillful polishing done by patient, trained workers. The greater the number of facets or faces that an accomplished artisan can put on a stone, the more resplendent is its brilliance and the greater is its value.

We too have rough diamonds of thought that come unbidden as we gaze upon something that appeals to us or inspires us. Can we communicate to our friends and comrades these innermost thoughts and clothe them with the beauty of language? With personal effort, plus the guidance received from skillful teachers, we can.

1. Polishing Words

In order to have others enjoy our writing, we should have a large stock of words by means of which we can communicate our thoughts. Do we employ words which add vividness and life, and give individuality to our writing? We must continually strive to add new words to our vocabulary so that we shall be able to polish our sentences by choosing accurate and exact words. We should not be too easily satisfied with what we write, but should labor with patience and perseverance until we feel that we have used words that appeal to the imagination and exactly fit the ideas we wish to convey.

In the sentences which follow, vivid, action-flashing, and picture-making words have been substituted to give life to the sentences on the right:

The boat came toward us.	The *launch drifted* toward us.
A group of excited gypsies shouted loudly as they walked along the new trail.	A *band* of excited gypsies shouted *boisterously* as they *wandered* along the *unfamiliar* trail.
A loud noise was heard through the house.	A *thundering crash resounded* through the house.

Synonyms

Synonyms are words that have the same general meaning. They are not identical in meaning, however, and each of a series of similar words has a shade of meaning not expressed specifically by another. What is the exact meaning of each synonym for *old* in this paragraph?

Where Time Stands Still

In a remote section of our town stands a little *antique* shop, ready to transport you to the Land of Long Ago. As you enter its musty interior, our *venerable* friend the shopkeeper squints a welcoming glance over his *antiquated* square-rimmed spectacles. Among the many relics of bygone days which he is proud to exhibit is a rare book, bearing a rather *ancient* date. Also numbered among the curiosities of the shop are many articles which have now become *obsolete*.

CLASS ASSIGNMENT

1. Select the vivid, picture-forming words in the following sentences:

1. The battered warship limped into the harbor.
2. Rose-tinted clouds suffused the sunset sky.
3. Spring announces its advent with the blossoming of the fruit trees.
4. The roar of the cannon blasted the stillness of the night.
5. The silvery water majestically cascaded down the mountain.
6. Night descended stealthily on the weary travelers journeying homeward across the deserted prairie.
7. Accompanied by a doleful Scottie, the newcomer stood hesitatingly on the porch.
8. The lazy stream meandered through a cool, verdant forest.
9. The quaint village homes seemed to boast that the thrifty tenants were hospitable to wayfarers.
10. Fascinated by the weird hooting of the owl, we stood transfixed to the spot.

2. Can you improve these sentences by substituting picture words for any of the plain words?

1. The old woman walked slowly and sadly into her home.
2. A worn-out automobile broke down at the foot of the hill.
3. Different ways of solving the problem were talked over by the class.
4. The boy, walking along the edge of the lake, fell into the clear water.
5. A real desire to gain knowledge made him study hard.
6. The canyon was cut out of solid rock by a small but wild stream.
7. An American flag, tied to a high pole, was blowing in the breeze.
8. Groups of birds, singing loudly, gathered to get ready for their long journey southward.
9. A small house stood among the trees.
10. The clapping of the people was heard throughout the building.

3. Write original sentences making use of the following groups of synonyms:

1. beautiful, handsome, pretty
2. honest, sincere, honorable
3. ability, skill, talent
4. accomplish, perform, achieve
5. abandon, discard, reject
6. lift, raise, elevate

4. Examine the italicized word in each of the following sentences, and find in the list that follows each sentence one word that has the same general meaning as the italicized word. Select the word that is particularly appropriate for that sentence:

1. The factory will *supply* the commodities necessary for the project.

return   receive   make   furnish   sell

2. Through the marshy land wandered a *sluggish* river.

deep   languid   shallow   wide   narrow

3. Medical science has almost completely *eradicated* several diseases that were common in the United States a century ago.

extended   uprooted   advanced   suppressed   interrupted

4. President Theodore Roosevelt negotiated a treaty with Panama which placed the Canal Zone under the *control* of the United States.

inspection   jurisdiction   claim   independence   examination

5. Mr. Collins *rejected* the plan.

received   accepted   disapproved   mailed   destroyed

6. Because of the extreme *watchfulness* of Dr. William Gorgas in exterminating the causes of disease in the Panama region, the Canal was made possible.

vigilance   carefulness   patience   thoughtfulness   ingenuity

7. Our holy father's encyclical advocates a *fair* wage for all employees.

low   high   just   exorbitant   small

8. The twins were *identical* in appearance but different in character.

petite   gaudy   alike   attractive   untidy

9. In a true proportion the product of the means is *equivalent* to the product of the extremes.

equal   added   attached   similar   joined

10. The dogma of the Immaculate Conception was *promulgated* in 1854.

proclaimed   written   made   spread   charted

11. Our class received a *friendly* invitation to visit the dairy.

personal   neat   attractive   printed   cordial

12. What a *transformation* these new chintz curtains made in our kitchen!

improvement   change   picture   success   result

13. The children were required to submit a *specimen* of their best penmanship.

page   line   duplicate   sample   folder

14. *Actuated* by a sense of duty to his country, the soldier refused to leave his post.

won impelled changed charmed faced

15. The wealthy man will long be remembered for his generous *benefactions* to charity.

donations will words kindness orations

16. How *comical* he appeared in the old-fashioned high silk hat and the full-dress suit!

handsome strange well-dressed droll gracious

17. The terms of surrender at Appomattox Court House were most *liberal*.

kind beautiful sincere unique generous

18. His only *comment* about your work was complimentary.

remark deduction criticism discussion book

19. *Ample* time was given for the speech to be thoroughly prepared.

little free meager abundant extended

20. Though the problem was both lengthy and *complex,* I managed to solve it correctly.

easy severe intricate obscure uninteresting

5. Rewrite the following sentences, using synonyms for each of the italicized words:

1. If you *discharge* each of your duties well, you will succeed.
2. He made it a *custom* to recite the rosary every day.
3. The nurse displayed *efficiency* in caring for the wounded stranger.
4. The hot, moist lowlands of Queensland produce an *abundant* supply of sugar cane.
5. So *charming* a manner was bound to draw many friends to Mary.
6. An *investigation* is being made to determine the cause of the accident.
7. He issued a *candid* statement.

POLISHING A PARAGRAPH

8. After the Mexican War, Mexico *ceded* to the United States a vast expanse of land.

9. A procession of officially *vested* church dignitaries is unsurpassed in pageantry.

10. The Way of the Cross is a *contemplation* on the passion and the death of Christ.

6. Fill in each blank in the paragraph with one of the following synonyms: *comment, observation, remark, utterance.*

Abraham Lincoln gave .... to his views on the preservation of the Union in the famous Gettysburg Address. It is worthy of note that nowhere in this speech do we find any .... derogatory to the South. A careful .... of the situation had previously prompted him to say that the rebellious states were like little sisters who had wandered away from home. Further ...., therefore, seemed unnecessary.

7. Using the synonyms *reluctant, loath, averse, slow, indisposed,* fill in each of the blanks in the following paragraph:

Richard was .... to accept the money from the old lady. He was not .... to wages paid for work well done, but the dire poverty of the woman made him .... to deprive her of any necessity. Feeling that the boy was .... toward her offer, she was .... to force its acceptance.

Painting Word Pictures of People

In painting a word picture of a person we should try to remember some striking feature about his appearance or his actions. It may be his face, hair, eyes, lips, teeth; perhaps his form or figure or the way he moves stands out clearly in our mental picture.

Skill in expressing our mental image depends on our ability to use words that describe the physical features that make one person different from another.

Facial expression is often an index to character. It may be:

cheerful	humorous	animated	honest
comical	open	earnest	eager
sincere	thoughtful	pleasant	happy
agitated	friendly	interested	pensive

Words describing a person's hair are not difficult to find. Your list might include some of the following:

glossy-black	flaxen	braided	wavy
auburn	dark	tangled	curly
bobbed	wiry	unkempt	flowing
lustrous	thick	shaggy	red-brown
short	shining	wind-blown	shoulder-length

Eyes, too, often tell character. Note these words that describe a person's eyes:

keen	downcast	lake-blue	kind
dull	honest	thoughtful	alert
clear	frightened	stern	round
flashing	glowering	twinkling	amusing
laughing	dreamy	mischievous	lifeless

Lips frequently reveal one's thought. What do the following words tell us about the person being described?

determined	smiling	narrow	full
rosebud	set	colorless	generous
trembling	stern	round	white
firm	cold	thin	gentle

A person's form or figure may be described in various ways. Do you use these words in your sentences?

erect	stately	crippled	noble
graceful	solid	burly	tall
frail	slender	deformed	shriveled
stocky	athletic	delicate	broad-shouldered

Do you remember voices distinctly? Glance over this list of adjectives describing voices and add to it:

laughing	mellow	ringing	low
soft	teasing	raucous	enthusiastic
begging	unkind	lighthearted	clear
rasping	gay	noisy	musical
happy	loud	muffled	gentle

Even the clothes one wears often tell those with whom he associates what he is. How we wear our clothes has a great deal to do with our general appearance. Here are words that can be used in describing wearing apparel:

modest	quiet	old-fashioned	comfortable
gaudy	costly	dainty	sophisticated
tidy	torn	extravagant	neat
pretty	striking	plain	modern
simple	tasteful	flashy	expensive

CLASS ASSIGNMENT

1. What expressions in these sentences are used to describe persons? Do they describe facial expression, eyes, lips, teeth, hair, or figure?

    1. Theodore's earnest expression was his best reference for the position.
    2. Scrooge's thin lips tightened.
    3. The sturdy form of the policeman stood midway between the two streets.

4. Erect and slim, the tall figure of the captain was outlined against the sky.

5. The sweet voices of unseen choristers sang the Christmas carols.

6. Old John shuffled lazily into the schoolyard.

7. The honest eyes of Bob Cratchit beamed with gratitude.

8. Sincere, animated, and cheerful, the man's face reflected his happiness.

9. Energetic, brisk, gay, our class marched in time to the music.

10. The dejected slump of the old man's shoulders betrayed his weariness and discouragement.

11. A tall girl with lustrous red-brown hair and a poised, graceful walk greeted me.

2. Did a good command of words help the writer of this paragraph paint a vivid picture of John? Find sentences that describe his hair, his eyes, his cheeks, and his wearing apparel:

Unanimously Elected

All eyes turned toward John, the newly elected president, as he graciously took his place before the class. John was a leader, an intelligent and charming leader. Every inch of his slight, five-foot figure told you that. Glossy black hair, parted in the middle, glistened on his head. Below a wide, thoughtful brow beamed two clear, lake-blue eyes. The ruddy, red complexion of his cheeks had deepened to rose, which was the only hint he gave of any self-consciousness. What a model of perfect grooming John appeared in his crisp white shirt, faultlessly pressed uniform, and highly polished oxfords! A silver medal about his neck assured the class that this officer would seek our Lady's guidance. With a cheerful smile for everybody, the boy silently surveyed his admiring classmates. The students, returning his glance, knew that they had made no mistake in their choice of a leader.

3. Write sentences which will describe a classmate's hair, eyes, nose, mouth, facial expression, and wearing apparel. The vocabularies on pages 94-95 may prove helpful.

2. Polishing Sentences

In the preceding section we polished individual words; that is, we substituted picture words and words that expressed exact meanings for overworked common words. In many instances this improved our sentences a great deal. In some cases, however, a sentence requires more than a change of one or two words. We may have to add to the sentence, combine sentences, or shorten sentences.

Adding Colorful Pictures and Comparisons

Many sentences become clear and attract our interest when the writer adds adjectives that describe some noun. We are likewise pleased when he makes use of phrases that enable us to imagine how some scene appeared to him or how some action was performed. We call this adding colorful pictures and comparisons.

Study the pictures and comparisons suggested by a seventh-grade class to describe an autumn scene. Do these phrases help you to visualize the scene?

Pictures	Comparisons
a clear blue sky flecked with clouds	a sky like a crystal dome, studded with pearls
brisk, invigorating air	air as bracing as a spring tonic
beds of deep-hued flowers	beds of flowers resembling exquisite oriental rugs
hills aflame with color	assume the air of a Spanish fiesta
fragrant odor of ripened grapes	redolent of the sunny slopes of southern France
fields of rusty corn shocks	corn shocks like rows of Arab tents
fields dotted with vivid orange pumpkins	pumpkins gleaming like miniature suns
glistening red apples	apples as radiant as rubies
chattering squirrels gathering nuts	remind us of misers hoarding gold
birds migrating southward	winging their way like squadrons of planes
animals evading hunters	like frightened children fleeing danger
gaily colored leaves, fluttering to the ground	pirouetting like graceful gypsy dancers

Notice how the skillful use of picture words and comparisons helped the writer of this paragraph to report the sounds from a kitchen. Did you ever think that kitchen noises resembled an orchestra?

Model: Culinary Concerto

On the eve of a holiday our kitchen is the source of myriad sounds. In a flight of fancy they might be said to resemble the performance of some strange orchestra peculiar to cuisine departments. As I listen, the singing teakettle harmonizes with the simmering soup pot, while the "tick-tock" of the friendly clock is submerged in the whir of the cake mixer. Again, the sizzling of sputtering fat blends with the crunching of the nutcracker. Suddenly there is heard the deafening crescendo of clattering dishes and clinking kitchenware. Although the sounds are not always melodic, they are like the tuning up of a concert orchestra, a promise of great things to come.

CLASS ASSIGNMENT

Polish the following sentences by adding picture words and comparisons:

1. The wind seems to blow the leaves about.
2. There were corn shocks in the field.
3. Fallen leaves cover the earth.
4. The fresh air of autumn tempts me.
5. Autumn flowers are not in bloom.
6. Busy squirrels are hiding their nuts.
7. We listen to the leaves under our feet as we walk along the road.
8. Colored leaves fall from the trees to the ground.
9. Here and there in the fields are large pumpkins.
10. In autumn streams flow less noisily than before.
11. The animals hide during hunting season.
12. The hills across the valley look beautiful.
13. I gaze longingly at the large bunches of grapes.
14. Children pick shiny red apples from the ground.
15. The bees go from flower to flower.
16. The smell of ripe grapes fills the autumn air.
17. The birds are vacating their nests and flying southward.
18. The farmers are busy gathering winter supplies.

Combining Short Sentences

How monotonous it is to read a paragraph composed of short, choppy sentences! If we want to write sentences that are not tiresome and childish, we will combine some of our short, choppy ones into more grown-up statements. There are many connectives which may be used to link short sentences. These include *when, where, as, who, although, because, which, while, since, after.* Let us not overwork the word *and* when we decide to combine short, choppy sentences.

SHORT SENTENCES	COMBINED SENTENCES
Texas is commonly known as the Lone Star State. It is in the southwestern section of the United States.	*Texas, which is in the southwestern section of the United States, is commonly known as the Lone Star State.*
Cyril and Ambrose played harder than their opponents. They were not so well trained.	*Although Cyril and Ambrose played harder than their opponents, they were not so well trained.*
The poem "Lochinvar" is considered a ballad. This poem was written by Walter Scott.	*The poem "Lochinvar," written by Walter Scott, is considered a ballad.*

CLASS ASSIGNMENT

Combine each group of short sentences into one smooth sentence:

1. The longest inland waterway in the world is the Amazon River system. It drains northern South America.
2. I like to read biographies. I enjoy lives of interesting people.

3. Orchids are beautiful. They are delicate flowers. They grow in abundance in the forests of South America.
4. A light year is a measure of distance. A light year is the distance light travels in a year.
5. The monstrance was on the altar. It was made of gold. It was set with precious stones.
6. The thunder had stopped. I thought the storm was over.
7. The Nile River is in Africa. The Nile River empties into the Mediterranean Sea.
8. Louis Pasteur discovered a treatment for hydrophobia. Hydrophobia is a disease caused by the bite of a mad dog.
9. The principal entered the room. The pupils rose. They greeted her respectfully.
10. Donald dropped back to his own twenty-yard line. He threw the pigskin far down the field.
11. Father Lavelle spoke at the children's Mass this morning. He gave a thought-provoking sermon.
12. Mrs. Andrews was using the vacuum cleaner. She did not hear the telephone ring.
13. Peter is a thoroughly honest boy. I admire him.
14. My grandparents live on a farm. It is a small farm. It is in Ohio.
15. Gold was discovered in the Sacramento Valley in 1848. Miners migrated from every section of the United States to California.
16. I opened our front door. A spicy odor was wafted to me. The odor told me that Grandmother was engaged in making tomato catsup.
17. The ostrich is the most important bird of the Sudan. It is valuable for its feathers.
18. Our class has a club. It is a Good Citizenship Club. It meets every Friday.
19. Saul belonged to the tribe of Benjamin. He became the first king of Israel.
20. Aluminum is light. Aluminum is tough. It is a good conductor of electricity.

Dividing Long, Involved Sentences

If we constantly use long sentences, our writing will likewise be tiresome and monotonous. The paragraph will lack strength and clearness. Some children form the habit of stringing short sentences together with a series of *ands*. Related ideas may be effectively connected by *and*, but we should not ramble on, joining unrelated ideas with the overworked *and*.

LONG, STRINGY SENTENCES

Children should become more familiar with the reference room of a library, which contains valuable sources of information, although the books may not be checked out.

The Feast of the Assumption of our Blessed Mother, which occurs on August fifteenth, is a holyday of obligation and this beautiful feast commemorates the glory of our Lady as Queen of Angels and Saints.

IMPROVED SENTENCES

Children should become more familiar with the reference room of a library. Although the books found in this section may not be checked out, they are valuable sources of information.

The Feast of the Assumption of our Blessed Mother, which occurs on August fifteenth, is a holyday of obligation. This beautiful feast commemorates the glory of our Lady as Queen of Angels and Saints.

CLASS ASSIGNMENT

Improve the following long, stringy sentences by dividing them into shorter sentences:

1. Last year our basketball team played La Salle team, which is an old rival, and we were defeated, but our team still has a good chance to win first place in the league.

2. Last night as we were having dinner the fire alarm sounded and we ran to the window and saw the house across the street on fire.

3. Theresa found it rather difficult to choose an Easter outfit from among the many fashionable models on display, but she

finally selected an attractive tan suit and selected brown accessories.

4. After you go through the park, then you go across Main Street and then you walk along it for five blocks to 2933 where we live.

5. Last year the seventh and the eighth grades of our school went on a trip to West Point to see the military academy, and we sailed up the Hudson River in a huge steamer named the *Alexander Hamilton*.

6. The cold evening wind whistled through every chink of the old mansion and made the house tremble to its very foundation, and a continual rain of fine sand carried by the wind sprinkled the floors.

7. The bus came up the hill and it was packed to capacity and it was going very fast and when it reached the top it came to a sudden stop.

8. Kindness to the poor and neglected characterized the life of Saint Vincent de Paul and he founded the first Confraternity of Charity.

9. My grandfather told us many interesting Indian stories and some were stirring tales of bravery and others were yarns of horror and cruelty.

10. My brother and I play a game of tennis every morning during vacation and his many helpful suggestions have enabled me to improve my technique considerably.

11. The East Indies lie between southern Asia and Australia and this chain of beautiful green islands is rich in natural resources.

12. Ice skating is no longer a sport limited to colder climates and indoor rinks with artificial ice have made this winter sport popular even in our southern states.

13. The travelers could not recall how long it took them to reach their destination and they did say, however, that the roads were muddy and travel was difficult.

14. The dappled horses were hitched to a new carriage and they wore shining harnesses and attracted the attention of all.

15. We organized a club and called it the Northeastern Athletic Society and its purposes are to uphold the ideals of real sportsmanship and to arrange games between classes.

16. War news had made Lincoln's heart heavy the morning he boarded his special train for Gettysburg, and furthermore, he had had little time to write out the address he was to deliver at the dedication of the national cemetery there.

17. The cardinal virtues are prudence, justice, fortitude, and temperance, and they are so called because all the other moral virtues depend upon them.

18. Arrange your paper neatly and keep a one-inch margin to the left and a narrower one to the right and be very sure to center your title on the first line and indent the first word of each paragraph one inch from the margin.

19. I was quite embarrassed on the occasion of my first appearance on the stage and my well-memorized lines completely left my mind.

20. The game was a victory for us and we decided to celebrate and invited the team to a supper in the school hall.

Changing the Order of Words

Variety in sentence structure is another important goal in paragraph writing. Some boys and girls plod along through their paragraphs, expressing their thoughts in the same sentence pattern: subject, predicate; subject, predicate. By occasionally inverting the word order and varying the length of our sentences, we make them pleasing, interesting, meaningful, and not boring to our readers.

NATURAL ORDER	TRANSPOSED ORDER
Success customarily follows persistent effort.	Customarily success follows persistent effort.
The mountains gathered a hood of gray vapors about their summits.	About their summits the mountains gathered a hood of gray vapors.
A fairyland of exquisite beauty surrounded me as I closed my eyes in sleep.	As I closed my eyes in sleep a fairyland of exquisite beauty surrounded me.

CLASS ASSIGNMENT

Vary the structure of each of the following sentences by changing the word order:

1. He plunged into the icy water after he had hesitated for a moment.
2. The boy, blinded by the whirling snow, charged into a tall man.
3. When the hunting season opens my uncle goes to the Canadian woods.
4. Violets and lilies of the valley grew here and there along the path to the wayside shrine.
5. My great-grandmother has even now, in her eightieth year, the grace and beauty of a queen.
6. A gray fog enveloped the city slowly and silently.
7. Columns of pale blue smoke could be seen as we approached the village.
8. The penguins made their way to the water's edge, waddling along in single file.
9. We failed to notice the approaching storm as we stood fascinated by the antics of two playful squirrels.

10. A fountain of molten lava is emitted from its crater when a volcano erupts.

11. When the Scout put his ear to the ground in Indian fashion, he thought he heard a rumbling sound.

12. Sudsy white foam gushed upward like a geyser as angry waves dashed against the rocks.

13. The mission fields of the world look appealingly toward America for zealous priests and sisters.

14. A little blue vigil light gleamed before our Lady's shrine as if in silent homage.

15. The boys were off to the picnic with a gleam of anticipated fun in their eyes.

16. The children sang merrily as the bus rolled toward the picnic grounds.

17. As the sun rose a sudden burst of color flooded the sky.

18. The Lincoln Memorial in Washington stands near the Potomac River.

19. Along the edge of the pond beautiful white swans glided gracefully.

20. To the tune of the victory march the spectators filed out of the stadium.

3. Polishing Paragraphs

The real test of our ability to use words in a clever manner and to improve sentences will be found in the changes that we make in our paragraphs. We must never be satis-

---

SENTENCES ARE POLISHED BY:
1. *Adding colorful pictures and comparisons*
2. *Combining short sentences*
3. *Dividing long, involved sentences*
4. *Changing the order of words*

fied with the first attempt, but should form the habit of examining the paragraphs we write to see where desirable changes may be made. This habit of self-criticism will be a valuable asset in all our studies.

Standards for Judging Paragraphs

We can judge the paragraphs we write by asking ourselves the following questions:

1. Is the subject interesting?
2. Have I kept to the topic of the paragraph in all my sentences?
3. Is the beginning sentence attractive? Will it interest the reader and hold his attention?
4. Are the events or steps in the paragraph told in an orderly manner? Can they be easily followed?
5. Is the ending sentence appropriate? Interesting? Does it satisfy the reader?
6. Is the choice of words good? Have I used picture words and phrases?
7. Are the sentences varied in structure? In length?
8. Have I varied the kinds of sentences, using statements, questions, and exclamations?
9. Is the paragraph free from grammatical errors? From errors in punctuation?
10. Does the paragraph have a title that attracts attention?

An Improved Paragraph

Read the changes made in the paragraph. Do you think that the pupil who wrote and polished this paragraph had formed the habit of self-criticism?

First Draft: Breakfast Minus Coffee

There are things to learn. Only experience can teach us. I found this out to my dismay the first morning when I attempted to prepare the family breakfast. I entered the kitchen and I saw several large grapefruits and they were lying on the table. I started to cut, core, and arrange the grapefruit. The cereal was easily taken care of. I checked the table for butter and ice water just before the family arrived. Feeling very sure, I watched the toaster send out the last piece of toast and I decided to pour the coffee when everyone was seated. Can you picture how I felt when I found out that I did not think of the most important thing on the menu? My lesson was learned. I will never forget that the first step in preparing breakfast is to put on the coffee.

Improved Paragraph: Please Pour the Coffee

There are things to learn which only experience can teach us. This I found out to my dismay the first morning I attempted to prepare the family breakfast. As I entered the kitchen my eyes encountered several large grapefruits lying on the table. Immediately I proceeded to cut, core, and arrange this popular morning fruit artistically. Preparing the cereal presented no difficulty to me. Just before the family arrived I checked the table for butter and ice water. Feeling very confident, I watched the automatic toaster send out the last piece of toast. When everyone was seated I decided to pour the coffee. Can you picture my embarrassment when I discovered that I had forgotten the most important item on the morning's menu? My lesson was learned, however, and now I will never forget that the very first step in preparing breakfast for the family is to put on the coffee.

Did combining the first two sentences improve the paragraph? What was done to improve the third sentence? How was the fourth sentence improved? Find another stringy sentence that was improved. What words were substituted for the word *grapefruit* in the fourth sentence of the improved paragraph? Point out other words that were polished. Has changing the word order improved the seventh sentence? How were the last two sentences in the paragraph improved? Do you think the title "Please Pour the Coffee" is better than "Breakfast Minus Coffee"?

CLASS ASSIGNMENT

1. Compare the first and final drafts of this paragraph and point out the changes that were made:

FIRST DRAFT: AN AUTUMN SCENE

Nature does her best work just before winter comes. Beautiful clouds tumble into fantastic designs and the sky is clear and blue. Trees painted with bright colors assume beauty. The wind blows their gold and crimson leaves into the air and they fall on the bare ground like a shower of confetti. Chrysanthemums, asters, and dahlias contribute to the beauty of the scene. Autumn certainly makes a colorful pathway for Winter's entrance.

IMPROVED PARAGRAPH: PICTURESQUE PATHWAY

Nature reaches the peak of her artistic skill just before Mr. Winter makes his debut. Soft, fleecy clouds tumble into fantastic designs beneath a clear blue sky. Trees painted with radiant hues assume distinctive, breath-taking beauty. Their gold and crimson leaves, twirled in the air as if by invisible fairies, rain upon the dull brown earth a shower of holiday confetti. Gardens everywhere are glorified by gay chrysanthemums, while starlike asters and dignified dahlias contribute to the charming scene. Autumn, the queen of seasons, certainly paves a magnificent pathway for the arrival of stern King Winter.

2. Polish the following paragraph:

The Doctor

The doctor is a very unselfish character and he works untiringly day and night for suffering mankind. He is in his office every day, patiently prescribing remedies for his patients. During the night he often keeps a vigil at the bedside of the dying. This great hero will even risk his life because he exposes himself to germs in bringing relief to others. The true doctor is a faithful servant and exemplifies devotion to duty.

4. Writing for the School Newspaper

Newspapers perform a very important function in the daily lives of adults. They give information concerning events that have taken place in all parts of the world, notify the people of forthcoming events, and, to a certain extent, mold public opinion.

A classroom newspaper may also play an important part in our lives. In this paper we may report important incidents in our private world (news stories), announce important future events (notices), or express an opinion and attempt to persuade others to adopt our views (editorials). In the newspaper we can also include feature articles, paragraphs that show the best work being done in the class. Study these features in *The Aquinas*.

Saint Thomas Aquinas School

THE AQUINAS

Vol. 6, No. 5   May 19--

Oak Park, Illinois

LITTLE GIANTS TRIUMPH

Another laurel has been added to the Aquinas crown with the eighth successive victory of the famous "Little Giants." This latest game was played on Wednesday, May 14, on our own diamond. Cheered on by the entire student body, the victorious seventh grade beat their opponents to the tune of 12-10. Two more contests will decide what team will claim the coveted silver trophy, to be presented by the alumni. The entire school extends sincere congratulations to the team on their latest victory and best wishes for the successful attainment of the desired goal.

GROUP VISITS PLANETARIUM

A representative group of seventh-grade boys and girls visited the Adler Planetarium last Wednesday afternoon. This trip proved interesting as well as educational since it supplemented the work on the stellar and solar systems.

Those children who were delegated to attend this lecture witnessed a very real representation of the Milky Way, and were able to recognize and name many of the constellations about which they had studied.

In their oral reports to the class the children gave an enthusiastic account of what they had seen and heard. Renewed interest in geography has been the result.

BEGIN NOW TO REVIEW

Looming up in the not too distant future is a formidable specter, final examinations. Annually the blithesome, sunny days of May are clouded with thoughts of probable failure to reach the mark required for promotion. This needless worry can be banished if, having made use of opportunities for study during the year, we begin now a gradual review instead of "cramming" on the eve of examination.

MAY PROCESSION HELD

On Sunday afternoon, May 11, the children of Saint Thomas Aquinas School paid honor to their heavenly Mother. At exactly three o'clock the procession began to wend its way from the school to the church. Devoted voices were raised in homage as the strains of "Ave Maria" filled the air.

Led by John Byrnes, the crossbearer, the procession presented a breath-taking spectacle as it progressed through the streets. Each class was preceded by its individual banner.

In church the program was climaxed with the coronation of the Blessed Virgin by the May queen, Joan Welsh. Her court was composed of seventh- and eighth-grade girls attired in pastel gowns.

Father Mellon lauded the children on their sincere display of devotion to the Queen of Heaven, and exhorted them to keep Mary queen of their hearts.

PICNIC PLANNED

Final arrangements are under way for the annual school picnic, which will be held this year on Thursday, May 24, at Lakeview Park.

Busses will leave the school at nine o'clock. In addition to the usual entertainment of skating and amusements, a special program is to feature group races, contests, and a treasure hunt. Committees for the various events have been selected from the seventh and eighth grades, under the supervision of Father Murphy.

At five o'clock the grand award, a chromium-plated bicycle, will be presented to the holder of the lucky ticket.

* BUY YOUR PICNIC TICKETS NOW!

EDITORIALS

OUR HONORED DEAD

In anticipation of Memorial Day, May 30, our thoughts naturally turn to the meaning and origin of this American holiday.

Although originally set aside to commemorate those who gave their lives during the Civil War, Memorial Day now honors the dead of all America's wars, and we should honor them. Yet floral tributes and parades are meaningless if we are not striving to cherish the ideals for which they made the supreme sacrifice. On this day, especially, every American man, woman - yes, and every child - should seriously reflect on his duty to live worthy of so noble a heritage. In the words of Abraham Lincoln, let us resolve that "these dead shall not have died in vain."

MOTHER'S DAY

Our heavenly Mother, it seems, wishes to share one day of her beautiful month with the mothers of the world, and so we have Mother's Day. Although a good Catholic girl or boy will honor his mother every day, nevertheless, on this her special day it is appropriate to present such tokens of our affections as a box of candy, a plant, or other gift which our pennies have purchased. Let us not forget, however, that the gift of gifts for any mother, living or dead, is a spiritual bouquet representing the Masses and Holy Communions we have offered, the rosaries we have recited, and the aspirations we have repeated for her intention. Make Mother's Day mean much in spiritual benefits for the one you love.

MARY'S MESSAGE

While three children were tending flocks
In Fatima one day,
The Blessed Virgin did appear,
These words she had to say:
"If you will tell the troubled world
To pray the rosary,
To gather families each night,
This their reward will be;
The blessings of a lasting peace
I'll give to all mankind,
If they'll but let my rosary
Each one to my heart bind."

MONTHLY FEATURES

OUR LADY'S SHRINE

"Oh, how pretty!" "Look at their beautiful shrine!" These and similar complimentary remarks can frequently be overheard as timid passers-by hesitatingly pause at the front door of our classroom to get a glimpse of the May shrine. We feel that our Lady must be pleased, since this shrine represents the combined efforts of every boy and girl in the room to pay her special homage during this month of Mary. Standing on the blue-and-white draped eminence which we have erected, our Queen of May smiles benevolently on each child, and her extended arms seem to embrace all. In the background is a trellis, painted with roses and maidenhair fern. On the graduated steps beneath her feet are wax plants and beautiful fresh-cut flowers. Yes, May is Mary's month, and each aisle of students vies with the others to make our shrine one of the loveliest in the school.

CONGRATULATIONS

The staff of the Aquinas congratulates William Fallon, a seventh-grade student, on winning the national essay contest conducted by the American Topic Tree. The topic of the essay was "How We Can Preserve Our Precious Heritage of Freedom."

PUPIL COMMENT

What would you like to see in the Aquinas? Here are some comments received last week:

> I'd like to have an honor roll.
> Mary Hoban

> Could we have a comic strip?
> Charles Lee

The AQUINAS

A student newspaper published six times yearly in Oak Park, Illinois at SAINT THOMAS AQUINAS SCHOOL.

Editor in chief   James Badey

Assistant editor   Jane Looby

Business manager
   . . . . Edward Spence

5. Choral Speaking

In the poems we study in choral speaking we shall find many word pictures of persons, places, and things. Reading the descriptions aloud will help us appreciate poetry. This is also a fine exercise for the voice.

Learn to breathe well for effective speaking in chorus or individually in ordinary conversation.

TUNING-UP EXERCISES

Breathing:

Breathe deeply. Inhale through the nose, inflating the diaphragm, chest wall, and ribs. Then exhale slowly with the sound of *ah*.

Inhale deeply, hold breath for ten counts; exhale slowly with sound of *p*, "the steamboat sound."

    p p p p p p p p p

Enunciation:

Pay special attention to the sound of $\bar{a}$ as in *bay*. Repeat quickly, then slowly:

    way say mate date

Then repeat this line several times:

    May weighs the mail every day.

Practice the sound of $\bar{e}$ as in *meet*. Repeat:

    meet Peter team

Our team meets Peter's team this evening.

Say firmly and clearly:

    bay bee bake beak bait beat

Find other words in $\bar{a}$ and $\bar{e}$ sounds. Make up sentences containing these words that you can use for practice.

The following poem describes in pictures the beauties of our own dear country, the United States of America. Thank God for giving us America!

America the Beautiful

By Katharine Lee Bates

First Group, Medium Voices	O beautiful for spacious skies, // For amber waves of grain, // For purple mountain majesties Above the fruited plain! //
Chorus—reverent	America! \ America! // God shed His grace on thee // And crown thy good with brotherhood // From sea to shining sea! //
Second Group, Heavy Voices	O beautiful for pilgrim feet, // Whose stern, impassioned stress // A thoroughfare for freedom beat Across the wilderness! //
Chorus—grave, dignified, and slow	America! \ America! // God mend thine every flaw, // Confirm thy soul in self-control, // Thy liberty in law! //
Third Group, Light Voices	O beautiful for heroes proved In liberating strife, // Who more than self \ their country loved, // And mercy \ more than life! //
Chorus—quicker and inspiring	America! \ America! // May God thy gold refine // Till all success be nobleness, And every gain divine! //
First Group, Medium Voices	O beautiful for patriot dream // That sees beyond the years / Thine alabaster cities gleam // Undimmed by human tears! //

Chorus—slower and farseeing, as if in a prayer	America! \ America! // God shed His grace on thee // And crown thy good with brotherhood // From sea to shining sea! //

Study of the Poem

This is a lyric poem. It does not tell a story, but expresses emotion or feeling. Each stanza proclaims the glories of America. The inspiration to write this poem came to the poet, Katharine Lee Bates, as she stood on Pikes Peak and looked down upon the beauty of her homeland from that great height.

In the first stanza she celebrates the glories of nature in our beloved country, its mountains, its plains of waving grain. In the second she speaks of the freedom that America has always offered to the oppressed. In the third the poet praises the heroes who gave their lives for their country; and in the last stanza she sees the vision of a greater America, a land where all have equal right and justice. The refrain of each stanza emphasizes the thought of the stanza as a kind of accompaniment, the last stanza repeating the prayer of the first even more fervently:

> And crown thy good with brotherhood
> From sea to shining sea!

Vocabulary Hints

Do you know the meanings of all the words in the poem? Be ready to tell what the following words mean:

amber	nobleness	pilgrim	impassioned
flaw	strife	liberating	brotherhood
alabaster	patriot	grace	thoroughfare

For the choral speaking of "America the Beautiful" divide the class into medium, light, and heavy voices; that is, into mezzo-soprano, soprano, and alto voices. Let the different groups read the poem as marked, the chorus (all three groups) saying the refrain. As each stanza is read, let the feeling increase until the last. This should also be true of the refrains, as they mount to a climax of feeling in the beautiful prayer at the end of the poem. Above all, see the pictures clearly in your own mind.

6. Chapter Challenge

1. We polish words by substituting ...., ... words for commonplace words.
2. .... are words that have the same general meaning.
3. Many sentences are improved by adding .... words and ....
4. We should combine ...., ... sentences.
5. Long, involved sentences should be ....
6. Sentences are sometimes improved by .... the order of words.
7. We should form the habit of .... the paragraphs we write.
8. A newspaper article that reports some event is a .... story.
9. Announcements of important future events are called ....
10. An article that attempts to mold public opinion is called an ....
11. The name of the newspaper is ....
12. The author of "America the Beautiful" is ....

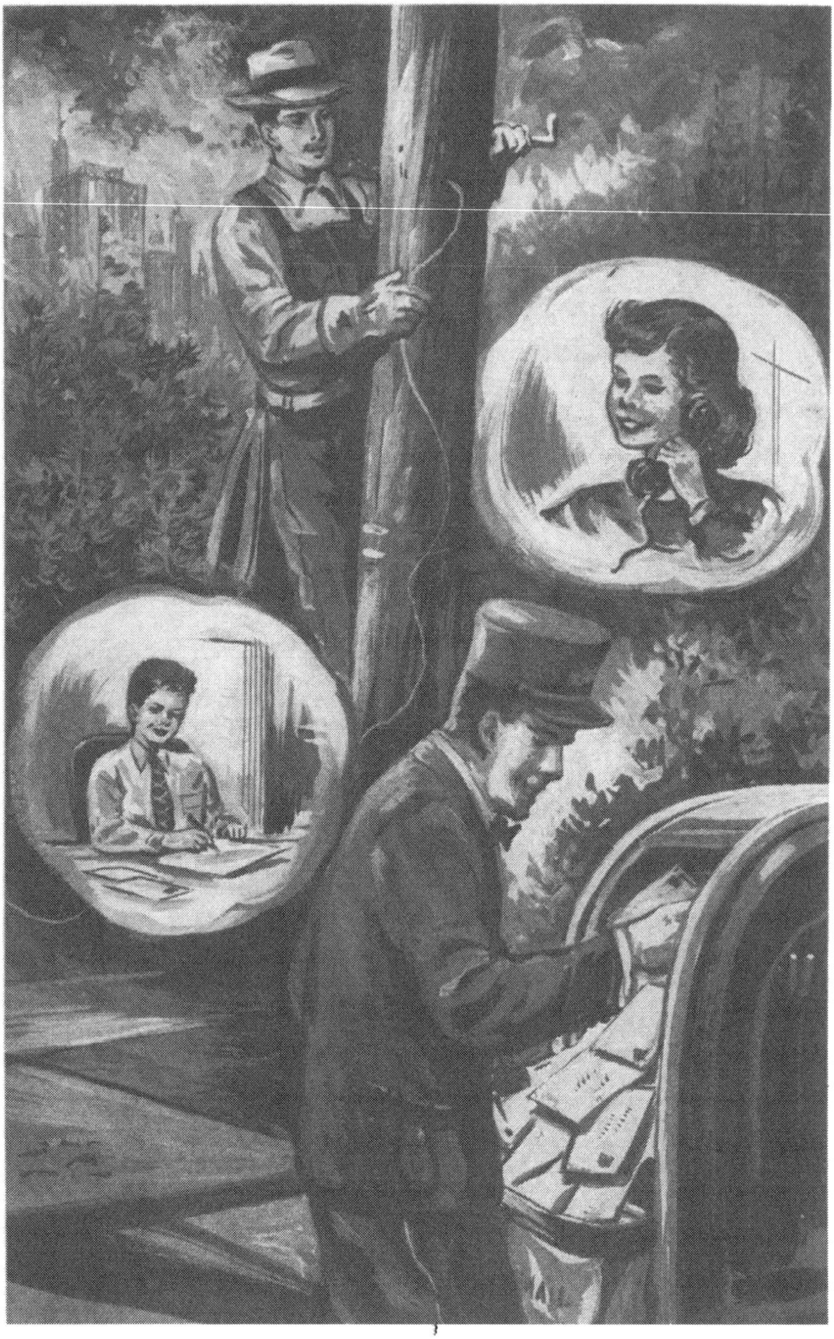

CHAPTER FIVE Letters and the Telephone

In which the Catholic student grows in self-reliance

A letter is really a conversation in writing. Our conversations are *informal* if we are chatting with a friend. They are *formal* if we are talking with someone on a matter of business. Informal letters are called *social* letters; formal letters are called *business* letters. There are many occasions which call for letters of one type or the other.

SOCIAL LETTERS (INFORMAL)	BUSINESS LETTERS (FORMAL)
Friendly letters	Letters of application
Letters of invitation	Letters placing orders
"Thank-you" letters	Letters reporting errors
Letters of sympathy	Letters asking for information
Letters of congratulation	Letters answering inquiries

Letters, whether informal or formal, must always be courteous, for a letter is an expression of our own personality. Every well-bred person avoids rudeness in conversation. We should make it a rule to be doubly courteous in our letters.

1. Social Letters

A social letter contains five parts:

1. THE HEADING. The heading of a letter contains the address of the writer and the date. It is usually written

on three lines. On the first line we write the street address; on the second line the city and the state; on the third line the date. In many social letters, particularly to intimate friends, the date only is written.

The heading is written slightly to the right of the center of the paper and about an inch from the top. If the letter is extremely short, the heading may be lowered. When each line is written directly under the one above it, the heading is said to be in block form. This is the one most commonly used, although each line of the heading may be indented if desired.

MODEL: A HEADING (BLOCK FORM)

101 Montebello Road
Columbus, Ohio
October 2, —

Each word in the heading begins with a capital letter, and abbreviations are avoided. There are two commas in the heading; one separates the city and the state or province, the other separates the day of the month from the year.

2. THE SALUTATION. The salutation is the greeting at the beginning of a letter. The greeting used depends upon the relationship between the writer of the letter and the person to whom it is written. The salutation consists of only one line; it is written at the left-hand margin, below the heading.

MODEL: A SALUTATION

My dear friend Joan,

The first word of the salutation and the name of the person begin with capital letters. Such words as "dear" and "dearest" are not capitalized unless they are the first words. The greeting is followed by a comma.

3. THE BODY OF A LETTER. The body of the letter contains the message. We should write simply and naturally as if we were speaking to our friend. At the same time we should apply all the rules we have learned for paragraph writing and endeavor to make our letters as interesting as possible.

IN THE HEADING OF A LETTER:
1. *There is a comma between the city and the state or province.*
2. *There is a comma between the day of the month and the year.*
3. *All words are spelled out in full.*
4. *All words begin with capital letters.*

The first word of each paragraph should be indented about one inch from the left-hand margin. Whenever we introduce a new topic, we should be certain to discuss that topic in a separate paragraph.

Read and study the model that follows. Why is the letter divided into three paragraphs? Does the writer begin each sentence with a capital letter?

MODEL: BODY OF A LETTER

How delighted I was to receive your letter by air mail! I had been eagerly waiting for the boat to arrive from the United States, for I was confident that you would send a message. I know a great deal about your dear country from your interesting letters.

Now I am going to tell you of a very colorful procession we had here last week. Long ago a severe earthquake occurred in Peru, destroying churches and homes for miles around. In one of these ruined churches was a picture called "Lord of the Miracles." It had been painted by an old Negro. Although the church was completely ruined, the picture was unharmed. Each year the people of Peru gather to venerate this image. Thousands walk in procession, wearing purple dresses and praying that they may be protected, as the picture was, from the destruction of earthquakes.

You must write again and tell me more about your beloved land. Let me know how you celebrate Christmas, which is a most beautiful feast here in Peru. In turn, I promise to relate to you the story of Papa Noel, who brings gifts to the good children here.

Does not the body of this letter, written by a pen pal in Peru, reveal a sincere and friendly individual? She has expressed herself naturally, courteously, and cheerfully.

4. THE COMPLIMENTARY CLOSE. The complimentary close ends the letter. It consists of a concluding word or group of words written before the writer signs his name. The form used for the complimentary close, like the salu-

tation, depends upon the intimacy between the writer and the person to whom the letter is written. The words "hoping to hear from you soon" and other similar expressions should be avoided. The first word of the complimentary close should line up with (be exactly under) the first word of the heading.

MODEL: A COMPLIMENTARY CLOSE

>Your devoted friend,

The first word only of the complimentary close begins with a capital letter. It is followed by a comma.

5. THE SIGNATURE. The signature is the name of the person who is writing the letter. When we are writing to our relatives and close friends we use only our first name. If the person to whom we are writing does not know us well, we use our full name. We write the signature under the first word of the complimentary close.

>Your loving friend,
>Joan

Our name always begins with a capital letter. We do not place any mark of punctuation after the signature.

Review the five parts of a social letter in the model that follows. What are the rules you have learned about each of the parts?

124 VOYAGES IN ENGLISH, SEVENTH YEAR

Heading
        230 East Tenth Street
        St. Paul, Minnesota
        January 29, ——

Salutation   Dear Gertrude,

Body   You will never know how much we girls miss you here at school. Of course we realize that you will return when your grandmother has recovered, but our Good Citizenship Club needs your guiding hand.

    At present we are planning a program for Saint Valentine's Day. We have written for a radio script which we saw advertised in the *Queen's Work*. I do hope it arrives in time to allow a few rehearsals. We have been doing quite a bit of radio work lately, and some of the boys and girls are keenly interested in this type of program. They claim that they are rarely self-conscious because there is no "seen" audience. They also appreciate the fact that there are no costumes or stage properties to worry about. I agree on these advantages, but I always look back with joy to our colonial plays in sixth grade. Didn't you like the swishy feel of those billowy skirts?

    Mother, Dad, and John send best wishes to all in Denver. I hope your grandmother is feeling better and that she will soon be well.

Complimentary Close   Devotedly yours,
Signature   Cecilia

CLASS ASSIGNMENT

1. Arrange each of the following lists of addresses and dates in the proper form for the heading of a letter:

1. St. Louis, Missouri, 2750 South Kingshighway Boulevard, May 10, ——

2. May 7, ——, 100 Princess Street, Winnipeg, Manitoba
3. 8122 Michener Avenue, Philadelphia, Pennsylvania, March 12, —
4. P.O. Box 87, June 14, ——, Detroit, Michigan
5. July 31, ——, 360 Inglewood Drive, Toronto, Ontario

2. Write the heading for a letter, using your own address and the present date.

3. Write the following salutations, using the proper punctuation and capitalization:

1. my dearest mother
2. dear sister virginia marie
3. my dear friend
4. dear mrs copley
5. dear uncle peter
6. right reverend and dear monsignor
7. my darling aunt jane
8. reverend and dear father
9. dearest grandmother

4. Write the salutation of a letter to each of the following:

1. Your grandparents
2. Your Uncle George
3. A classmate
4. A friend
5. Your father
6. Your teacher
7. A priest
8. A cousin
9. A friend's mother
10. Your sister or brother

5. Find the complimentary closings that match the salutations in the first column. Rewrite, capitalizing and punctuating each one correctly:

1. dearest mother and dad
2. dear father walsh
3. my dearest grandmother
4. dear sister regina
5. my dear mr ryan
6. dear dad
7. my darling sister

sincerely yours
your son
your loving sister
your devoted grandchild
your loving daughter
respectfully yours
your pupil

6. Write the complimentary close of a letter to each of the following:

1. Your brother
2. Your teacher
3. Your parents
4. A dear friend

5. The captain of your football team
6. A former neighbor
7. A priest

7. Write a letter to a friend who has moved from your city. You may write about any of the following topics:

1. A baseball game
2. Your new school library
3. Having a tooth extracted
4. Fun in the snow
5. A shopping tour
6. A class excursion
7. The first meal you cooked
8. An unexpected boat ride
9. Your flower garden
10. A book you have read

Writing the Letter

The receiver's first impression of a letter is formed by its appearance. A neatly written letter reflects our own high standards. People of refinement use a good quality of white stationery and black or blue ink. They write legibly, clearly, and neatly. We must examine our letters after they are written, correct any misspelled words or grammatical errors, and rewrite the letter if the original is marred by erasures. Margins are left on both sides of the paper. The one on the left should be slightly larger than the one on the right. If the paper is in folded sheets, the folded edge is at the left of the letter.

When we have finished writing our letter, we should fold the lower half over the upper half and place it in the envelope with the crease at the bottom. If we use a single sheet of paper typewriter size, we should fold the lower half over the upper part until it almost reaches the top, being sure to keep the left and the right edges even. We then fold in thirds, the right side first and the left side over the right. We put the letter into the envelope with the folded edge down.

Addressing the Envelope

The envelope should contain the full name and the address of the person to whom the letter is being sent. Just above the center of the envelope and slightly to the left, we begin to write the name. The form and the punctuation should follow the style of the heading. On the second line we write the street address, on the third the city, the state, and the zip code. It is customary to write our return address in the upper left-hand corner of the envelope.

1130 North Calvert Street
Baltimore, MA 20411

                                      Mrs. Louis Higgins
                                      P.O. Box 204
                                      Tomasville GA 13020

CLASS ASSIGNMENT

1. Copy the following in letter form. Be careful to paragraph the body of the letter properly:

854 Cedar Lane, Salem, Oregon, April 5, —— Dear Ralph, No doubt by this time you feel quite at home in San Francisco. All the boys hope you will be as happy at Visitation School as you were here with us. Our basketball team was awarded a trophy on Thursday night for having won the North Light League championship. The *Times* printed an article about the presentation and a picture of our captain, Gerald Metzinger, receiving the trophy. It is a small gold statuette of a basketball player holding a ball which he is about to toss into an imaginary basket. The prize was immediately placed in the school library and the team made about five unnecessary trips there the next day just to get a good look at it. When you visit Salem I hope you find your way to our house. Mother and Dad miss your calls almost as much as I do. Your pal, Basil.

2. Write the following names and addresses as they should be written on envelopes. Use your own return address:

1. Reverend John Johnson, P.O. Box 340, El Paso, Texas 35024
2. Miss Margaret Hansen, Box 242, Nantucket, MA 35003
3. Mrs. Ellen Peters, 3500 McTavish Street, Montreal, Quebec
4. Mrs. Abigail Jones, 550 South Third Street, St. Paul, Minnesota 55034
5. Miss Rita Augustin, R.F.D. 9, Little Rock, Arkansas 55214
6. Mr. Thomas Dunn, 2214 Taft Avenue, Manila, Philippines

3. Write a letter to a friend in another school, telling him about your Good Citizenship Club.

4. You are on vacation with your cousin. Write a letter to your parents.

5. A friend of yours is in a hospital. Write a letter of cheer to him.

6. Write to a pen pal in another country, describing some place of interest to you.

7. Write a letter to a former teacher, telling her about your work in school.

8. While visiting your grandmother, you made the acquaintance of a boy or a girl your age. Write to him after your return home, reviewing the fun you had together.

9. Write a letter to a friend in which you discuss a topic of mutual interest, such as a baseball game you attended or a museum you visited.

10. Write to your sister who is away at boarding school. Tell her how much you miss her and give her some family news.

2. Kinds of Social Letters

Frequently we write letters for no other purpose than to exchange news. Chatting by mail with our friends is most enjoyable. Certain occasions, however, require us to write special types of social letters. Among these special types are letters of invitation, acceptance, regret, thanks, congratulation, sympathy, or introduction. They differ from the ordinary friendly letter in that they deal with one topic only. Social letters such as these should be brief and specific.

Invitations

Letters of invitation should be cordial and contain accurate information. They must state definitely the occasion, the date, the time, and the place. Do not use figures or abbreviations in writing the day and the hour.

MODEL: A LETTER OF INVITATION

305 Graham Road
Boston, Massachusetts
May 13, ——

Dear Margaret,

My father will not be working Saturday, May nineteenth, and he has offered to take the family on a picnic to Franklin Park. Would you like to join us?

The park boasts of a splendid tennis court and there is also a delightful lake where we can go boating.

We intend to leave at nine o'clock and will gladly stop for you if you decide to accompany us.

Your friend,
Regina LeCompte

Is this letter natural and inviting? Would it make you eager to join Regina at Franklin Park? Does the invitation contain specific information about the day, the date, the time, and the place?

Acceptances

An invitation demands an immediate reply. The answer should contain words of true appreciation. In a letter of acceptance we should repeat the occasion, the place, the date, and the time.

MODEL: A LETTER OF ACCEPTANCE

> 406 Pelham Avenue
> Boston, Massachusetts
> May 14, ——

Dear Regina,

Saturday morning, May nineteenth, cannot come quickly enough for me. Of course I will go with you to Franklin Park. It will be my first opportunity for a match this year, and a rowboat excursion will be an entirely new experience for me. I shall be waiting at our front door at nine o'clock.

Thank you, Regina, for your thoughtful invitation.

> Gratefully yours,
> Margaret Hansen

Regrets

A letter of regret should be just as prompt and courteous as an acceptance. Our cordial reply should give our reasons for declining. We may mention the occasion, the place, and the date, but not necessarily the time.

MODEL: A LETTER OF REGRET

> 406 Pelham Avenue
> Boston, Massachusetts
> May 14, —

Dear Regina,

How disappointed I am that I am unable to accept your invitation! We had already planned to drive to Rhode Island this week end to visit my cousin, Father John, before he leaves for his mission in southern China.

Have a good time at Franklin Park and tell me all about it on Sunday. You know that I would be with you if I could.

I am very grateful to you for having included me in your plans.

> Your devoted friend,
> Margaret Hansen

CLASS ASSIGNMENT

1. Read the following letter of invitation and then answer the questions that follow:

> 12 Divinity Place
> Akron, Ohio
> October 3, — —

Dear Mary Jane,

Would you like to join our Library Club which meets every Friday evening at seven o'clock? The eight girls who now compose the club gather at a member's home to discuss reading likes and dislikes. We use the dues collected to purchase new books and to provide refreshments for the meetings.

I am certain that you would enjoy our club, Mary Jane, and derive genuine profit from it. Won't you come to a meeting at my house on October eighth at seven o'clock?

> Sincerely yours,
> Barbara Dillon

1. Is the invitation a sincere request? Does it offer an inducement for Mary Jane to accept?
2. Does the letter tell the day and the time of the club meetings?
3. Where do the meetings take place?
4. How do the members dispose of the dues?

2. Rewrite the following letter of regret in proper letter form. Paragraph it correctly and use the required punctuation and capitalization:

286 franklin street st louis missouri november 21 —— dearest rose marie nothing but a long-standing family tradition could prevent me from accepting your cordial invitation to spend the thanksgiving holidays with you it has been our custom for many years to visit my grandparents in ohio at this time i shall be thinking of you on thursday morning when you will attend the annual football game you must cheer loud enough for two so that immaculate heart may win please extend hearty holiday greetings to your mother and father your friend anne.

3. Write a letter inviting a friend to any one of the following:
1. A valentine party
2. A school picnic
3. An auto ride through the country
4. A tour of your uncle's dairy
5. Dinner at your home

4. Write a letter of acceptance or regret to any of the above invitations. Be sure that your letter fulfills all the necessary requirements.

"Thank-You" Letters

There is nothing more pleasing than a sincere expression of gratitude for a favor or a gift received. We should be prompt in acknowledging our gratitude to those who have bestowed favors on us. A good way to do this is by a "thank-you" letter. In such a letter we should tell why the gift or favor pleased us.

MODEL: A "THANK-YOU" LETTER

>3850 West 29th Avenue
>Vancouver, British Columbia
>December 28, 19—

Dear Aunt Sarah,

How did you know that I wanted a new fountain pen? I had admired one like the beautiful blue lifetime pen you sent me, but I never thought I would be the proud possessor of one. Each time I use it I'll think of you and your goodness to me.

Thank you, Aunt Sarah, for this attractive and useful gift.

>Your grateful niece,
>Dolores

Another type of "thank-you" letter is a note of gratitude one writes after a visit. Courtesy demands that this letter, sometimes referred to as a "bread-and-butter" letter, should be written promptly. In it we should comment on our visit and tell why we enjoyed it.

MODEL: A "BREAD-AND-BUTTER" LETTER

>8206 Fairfield Avenue
>Hartford, Connecticut
>July 22, 19—

Dear Aunt Catherine,

Since my return home I've monopolized the conversation talking about the delightful time I had at Cedar Grove. That is not to be wondered at, because I never remember having had such a pleasant two weeks.

Uncle Walter's canoe lessons are making me very popular. My speed is better than that of Kenneth Butler, our champ!

Thank you for a perfect vacation. I shall always look back on it as one of the high lights of my twelfth summer.

>Your devoted nephew,
>Arthur

CLASS ASSIGNMENT

1. Write a "bread-and-butter" letter to your grandmother. You may use this beginning sentence: No sooner had the train puffed into North Devon Station than I began excitedly to tell the family of my week end at Valley Ridge.
2. Write a letter to a friend, thanking him or her for a birthday gift that you received.
3. You have been ill for some time. Write a letter to your teacher thanking her and the class for the cards they sent you.
4. George wrote this very interesting letter of gratitude for his uncle's hospitality. Can you correct the mistakes he made in punctuation and capitalization?

1726 Walnut Street
Brooklyn New York
September 3 ——

Dear uncle andrew

Nobody could ever have convinced me that life in the country would be anything but dull and monotonous, it took a week with you on the farm to change my opinion, nothing we do here at home is half so exciting as the fun we managed to pack into those days

In the past seven years i have wanted to be a pilot a lawyer an engineer a doctor and a marine, now i think ill settle down and become a farmer, the enjoyable time you gave me is responsible for that decision

Thank you for making my visit such a pleasant one

your nephew
george

5. Thank your cousin for including you in a camping trip. Let him know why you enjoyed the experience.

Letters of Sympathy

Courtesy and charity oblige us to extend sympathy to one who has suffered some sorrow, such as an illness or the death of a beloved relative. A letter of sympathy should be brief, simple, and kind.

MODEL: A LETTER OF SYMPATHY

2157 Erie Street
Rochester, New York
October 7, 19—

Dear Marietta,

Mother just told me of the death of your dear father. I want you to know that I am very sorry you have lost such a good father and that I shall remember him and you in my prayers.

If there is any way in which I can be of help, do not hesitate to call on me. Should you need our car, Dad will be glad to have you make use of it.

Your loving friend,
Helene

Letters of Congratulation

We share any success or good fortune of a friend by rejoicing with him in a letter of congratulation. If we write a sincere and heartfelt note of congratulation, we add to our friend's joy on the honor, success, or other cause for happiness that has come to him.

MODEL: A LETTER OF CONGRATULATION

>5500 River Avenue
>Red Deer, Alberta
>June 13, — -

Dear Katharine,

It is with a joyful heart that I extend to you my sincere congratulations on your graduation day. You deserve every possible happiness as a reward for your eight years of study. Your friends are very proud of the record you made at Saint Louis School. May great success be yours during the coming days of your high-school career!

>Your devoted friend,
>Mary

CLASS ASSIGNMENT

1. Copy the following in the form of a letter. Use your own name and address:

My dear Grandmother, How sad I am to learn that Grandfather must undergo a serious operation! I shall pray for him every day, Granny, and for you, too, during this trying time.

If there is anything I can do to help you, please let me know. Your loving grandchild, Rose Marie.

2. One of your friends has met with an accident and is in a hospital. Write him a letter of cheer.

3. Write the following in the form of a letter. Use your own address and today's date for the heading: Dear David, So my cousin is a first lieutenant! Congratulations! We are all delighted that your superiors have recognized in you the outstanding qualities needed for such a responsible position. May God bless your work! Your loving cousin, Jane.

4. Write a note of congratulation to a friend who has won first place in an athletic contest.

5. One of the members of your class has been elected to an important office in the Wood Scouts. Write a letter of congratulation from the class.

3. Business Letters

Business letters are marked by clearness, brevity, and simplicity. We should adopt the formal, courteous tone that we would use were we to speak to an official of a business concern. A business letter contains six parts:

1. THE HEADING. This is the same as the heading of a social letter.

2. THE INSIDE ADDRESS. This is the one part of a business letter that is not found in a social letter. The inside address consists of the complete name and address of the person or the firm to whom the letter is written. The inside address is written at the left side of the page above the salutation. The style should be the same as that of the heading, usually in block form.

Sister Mary Francis
Saint Thomas More School
Arlington, Virginia

3. THE SALUTATION. The salutation, or greeting, is more formal than in a social letter. It is usually followed by a colon.

| Gentlemen: | Dear Madam: | Dear Mr. Hughes: |
| Dear Sir: | Ladies: | Dear Miss Mullen: |

4. THE BODY. The body of the letter contains the message, which must be courteous, clear, accurate, and brief. Since a letter represents us before a business firm, we should endeavor to be courteous in our manner, to be clear and accurate in our statements.

5. THE COMPLIMENTARY CLOSE. The complimentary close, like the salutation, is more formal than the closing of a friendly letter. It is followed by a comma.

Yours truly,   Respectfully yours,   Yours sincerely,
Yours very truly,   Yours respectfully,   Very truly yours,

6. THE SIGNATURE. The signature of a business letter contains the full name of the writer. It is not followed by a mark of punctuation.

    Anna Healy   Edward Dormer

Letters Placing Orders

There are many types of business letters, differing from one another in content and purpose. We shall study only those kinds which we may have occasion to write.

In a letter in which we order merchandise, we should state the exact quantity, style, size, and color of the goods. It is advisable also to indicate the manner in which the order is to be shipped and how payment is to be made.

MODEL: A LETTER PLACING AN ORDER

                235 Windermere Avenue
                Wayne, Pennsylvania
                March 12, 19—

Sears, Roebuck and Company
Roosevelt Boulevard
Philadelphia, Pennsylvania

Gentlemen:

    Enclosed you will find a post-office money order for ten dollars ($10.00). Kindly send by parcel post, at your earliest convenience, the following articles:

1 pair gloves, blue, No. 18, size 6	$2.00
1 blouse, blue, No. 815, size 14	5.00
1 purse, blue, No. 725	3.00
	$10.00

                Very truly yours,
                (Miss) Mary E. Cronin

Letters Reporting Errors or Defects

There may be occasions when orders are not filled promptly and correctly, or when the articles received are damaged. We then write a courteous letter to the company calling attention to the error or defect, and asking the firm to make the necessary adjustment.

MODEL: A LETTER REPORTING A DELAY

> 351 Main Street
> Baltimore, Maryland
> December 15, 19—

Newman Book Shop
Westminster, Maryland

Gentlemen:

On November twenty-ninth I placed an order at your shop for *Jacinta, the Flower of Fatima*. The salesman, Mr. Ronald Pilot, promised to have it sent to me within ten days. I have not yet received the book.

Since I intend to give this book as a Christmas gift, it is important that I receive it immediately. Please notify me if you cannot fill my order.

> Very truly yours,
> Teresa Ambrogi

Letters of Request and of Gratitude

We may wish to request a business firm to grant us a favor, such as permission to visit a broadcasting studio or a manufacturing plant. In writing a letter of this type we usually include a stamped, self-addressed envelope for the reply. We should be specific as to the number of persons and the date.

We do not hesitate to write a courteous letter of thanks to express our gratitude after our request is granted.

MODEL: A LETTER OF REQUEST

Incarnation School
Salem, Oregon
April 6, ——

Kleen Dairy Council
Salem, Oregon

Dear Sir:

Our seventh-grade class, which is composed of forty boys and girls, is interested in the invitation you have extended to all schools to visit your dairy. We have been studying about the many delicious and healthful products which a modern dairy supplies and we welcome this opportunity to see a plant in operation.

We shall be happy to make an appointment for the earliest date convenient to you.

Very truly yours,
Jean Madden (Secretary)

MODEL: A LETTER OF GRATITUDE

Incarnation School
Salem, Oregon
April 20, ——

Mr. Joseph Murphy
Kleen Dairy Council
Salem, Oregon

Dear Mr. Murphy:

On behalf of the members of my class, I wish to express our sincere gratitude to you for the courtesy extended to us on the occasion of our recent visit to your plant. The attendant who accompanied us was most friendly and helpful, and we feel that he was a reflection of the spirit of your personnel.

We thank you also for the posters, which are already on display in our classroom.

Respectfully yours,
Jean Madden (Secretary)

CLASS ASSIGNMENT

1. Write a letter to a business firm in your own community ordering one of the following groups of articles:
   1. camera, films, album
   2. knapsack, flashlight, binoculars
   3. notebook, pencils, ink, stationery
   4. ice skates, wool socks, sweater
   5. three books, with correct titles and authors

   Give the shipping directions and method of payment. Use your own home address and signature.

2. Write a letter ordering a subscription to a Catholic magazine. Be sure to include all necessary details, date of the first issue, price of the subscription, how payment is being made.

3. Write the following letter to the office of the Propagation of the Faith in your diocese. Supply the heading, inside address, salutation, complimentary close, and signature:

   Enclosed is a money order for twenty-two dollars and fifty cents ($22.50) which the seventh-grade class at Sacred Heart School wishes to be sent for the support of some foreign mission.

   Our class is very much interested in the work of the missionaries. Besides making the little sacrifices that were necessary to gather this sum, we also pray daily for those who are working in foreign fields.

4. Rewrite the following in letter form. Paragraph the letter and use the correct punctuation and capitalization:

   354 green street, nashville tennessee, march 25, ——
   Nashville Club, 216 quartz avenue, nashville tennessee. gentlemen our seventh-grade baseball team would like to enter the baseball tournament sponsored by your club. please send us an application blank. our pastor father reynolds coaches our team and has given us permission to enter the tournament very truly yours john vermuth (captain).

5. The costumes ordered by the Dramatic Club for the school play have been received by the committee in charge. There is, however, a grave error in the size of two of the costumes. Report

this error to the New York Costume Company and make arrangements to have the correct sizes substituted.

4. Conversations by Telephone

Although telephone conversations lack the joy of a personal visit with a friend and can never be substitutes for cheery and friendly letters, yet they have their place in daily life. When information is wanted at once, the telephone is invaluable. When one wishes to speak personally to the other party in a business or a friendly transaction, the telephone is often a great convenience, provided the matter is not confidential.

There are times when it is not considered good form to use the telephone. For example, in offering sympathy to a friend on the death of a loved one, it is better to pay a personal visit or to write a letter.

Telephone conversations, like letters, may be divided into *social calls* and *business calls*.

In answering the telephone in our own home we should speak politely and distinctly. We should not say simply "Hello," for this necessitates the person's inquiring to whom he is speaking, which is a waste of time. Use any of these forms:

This is Quinn's residence.

Quinn's residence, Grace speaking.

Social Conversations

We use the telephone for many kinds of social conversations. Often we wish merely to visit with our friend. Social calls may include any of the following:

1. An invitation to a friend for any occasion
2. Congratulations on birthdays, anniversaries, etc.
3. A call of sympathy if relatives or friends are ill
4. A "thank you" for favors received
5. A request for information

MODEL: AN INVITATION BY TELEPHONE
(After dialing the number and receiving an answer)

Greeting Hello, Helen. This is Mary.
Message Mother is going to drive David and me to Aronimink Park this afternoon. Will you come with us? We expect to leave about two o'clock. . . . I am so glad! We'll stop for you at two.
Closing Good-by, Helen.

Business Calls

Although we do not have so many reasons for using the telephone for business purposes as we shall have in future years, we wish to become familiar with the correct procedures for such calls. We make business calls when we

> **A GOOD TELEPHONE CONVERSATION INCLUDES:**
> 1. *A greeting*
> 2. *A statement of the purpose of the call—brief, clear, courteous*
> 3. *A conclusion—the last statement, or a simple "Good-by"*

order goods, make appointments with the doctor or the dentist, inquire about train arrivals, or order taxicabs.

MODEL: A BUSINESS TELEPHONE CALL

Greeting May I please speak with the manager?
Message This is John Holt's residence, 2725 Meridian Street. My mother asked me to tell you that the vacuum cleaner we ordered two days ago has not yet been delivered. When will you send it? . . . This afternoon? . . . I'll tell Mother.
Closing Thank you. Good-by.

The importance of the telephone in times of accident and sudden illness cannot be too clearly realized by every Catholic boy and girl. We should train ourselves in school days to think first of telephoning for the priest in times of danger. Even if we do not know the people in an accident we witness, we may render them a great service by calling a priest and a doctor.

MODEL: AN EMERGENCY CALL FOR A PRIEST

Greeting Good afternoon, Father Gordon. This is Charles Burke, 942 Sumner Street.
Message My mother is very ill. The doctor says she should receive the last sacraments as soon as possible. She is conscious and able to swallow. . . . May my brother call for you at the rectory in ten minutes?
Closing Thank you, Father.

CLASS ASSIGNMENT

1. Select a partner to dramatize the following conversation with you:

Mrs. Carr. Mrs. Carr's residence.

Mary Ellen. Grandmother, this is Mary Ellen. I've just removed the wrappings from your birthday gift. I was so surprised and happy to see a candid camera that I just couldn't wait to thank you by letter.

Mrs. Carr. I am glad you like the camera, Mary Ellen. May you have many good times with it!

Mary Ellen. I'll be over to visit you this afternoon, Granny. I want yours to be the first picture I take.

Mrs. Carr. God bless you, child.

Mary Ellen. Thank you! Good-by.

2. Divide the members of the class into groups and dramatize the following telephone conversations:

1. Ask a friend to go on a hike with you.
2. You have been ill and not able to be in school for a week. Call a classmate and ask about the club meeting you have missed.
3. Call your mother and tell her that you will be late in returning home, as your teacher has sent you on an errand.
4. Your cousin is visiting you from out of town. Call a friend and invite him to meet your cousin.
5. A friend of yours has just been elected president of the Altar Boys Club. Call to congratulate him on this honor.
6. One of your classmates has been ill. Call his home to inquire about his health.

3. Dramatize the following telephone conversation:

Clerk. Good morning. Bowman's Dairy Company.

Joan. Good morning. This is Joan Burke, 2540 Regent Street. Please send two quarts of chocolate ice cream. We'd like to have it before six o'clock this evening.

Clerk. Our latest delivery is at five o'clock. Will that be satisfactory?

Joan. Yes, thank you. Good-by.

> **LEARN FROM THE TELEPHONE OPERATOR HOW TO CONVERSE OVER THE TELEPHONE:**
> 1. *She is always courteous.*
> 2. *She has a friendly, cheery voice.*
> 3. *She is never in a hurry.*
> 4. *She is always obliging and tireless in her efforts to serve you.*

4. Call a department store and order a dress you saw advertised in the morning paper.

5. Call a dentist's office and make an appointment to have your teeth cleaned.

6. Notify your family physician that your sister has been taken ill. Describe her symptoms and ask him to come at once.

7. Call the railroad station and inquire if a certain train will arrive at the scheduled time.

8. Place an order at a grocery store for supplies for your family.

9. Call the local newspaper office to report that your paper has not been delivered for two days.

5. Choral Speaking

If you learn to read poems in chorus, you will have a pleasant topic for letter writing. Always practice the tuning-up exercises before attempting to read together the poem that you are to use for choral speaking.

Tuning-up Exercises

Breathing:

Inhale, hold breath for ten counts, exhale slowly, keeping your hands on waistline and feeling the circle of the waist contract.

Enunciation:

Practice ä as in *balm*. Say in different pitches *palm, calm, aunt.*

I heard Aunt laugh under the palm.

Practice *a* as in *staff*. Say *Mass, ask, chance, fast*.

        After Mass grasp the staff fast.

Say briskly and firmly:

        narcotic   nasty   pardon   parenthesis

The following poem, speaks upon the most important spiritual weapon, the Most Holy Rosary. We honor Our Blessed Mother and God so very much by praying it daily, as well as helping ourselves get to Heaven, and praying for others.

The Rosary
by
Joyce Kilmer

Not on the lute, nor harp of many strings

Shall all men praise the Master of all song.

Our life is brief, one saith, and art is long;

And skilled must be the Laureates of kings.

Silent, O lips that utter foolish things!

Rest, awkward fingers striking all notes wrong!

How from your toil shall issue, white and strong,

Music like that God's chosen poet sings?

There is one harp that any hand can play,

And from its strings what harmonies arise!

There is one song that any mouth can say, --

A song that lingers when all singing dies.

When on their beads our Mother's children pray

Immortal music charms the grateful skies.

6. Chapter Challenge

1. Letters are .... in writing.
2. A social letter contains five parts: (1) the ...., (2) the ...., (3) the ...., (4) the ...., and (5) the ....
3. In the .... form one line is written directly under the one above it.
4. In the heading each word begins with .... and .... are avoided.
5. The salutation is the .... at the beginning of a letter.
6. The body of the letter contains the ....
7. The .... consists of a group of words written before the writer signs his name.
8. The .... is the name of the person who wrote the letter.

9. The person who receives a letter obtains his first impression from its ....

10. On the envelope we write the full .... and .... of the person to whom the letter is to be sent. On the first line we write ....; on the second line ....; on the third line ....; and on the fourth line ....

11. It is customary to write .... in the upper left-hand corner of the envelope.

12. In writing an invitation we should mention ...., ..., ..., and ....

13. Our .... or .... should be sent promptly after receiving an invitation.

14. Other types of social letters are ...., ..., and ....

15. The .... is the one part of a business letter that is not found in a social letter.

16. Letters ...., ..., ..., ... are different types of business letters.

17. Social telephone calls include ...., ..., ...

18. When we place an order, call for a doctor, or inquire about the time of a train's departure, we are making ....

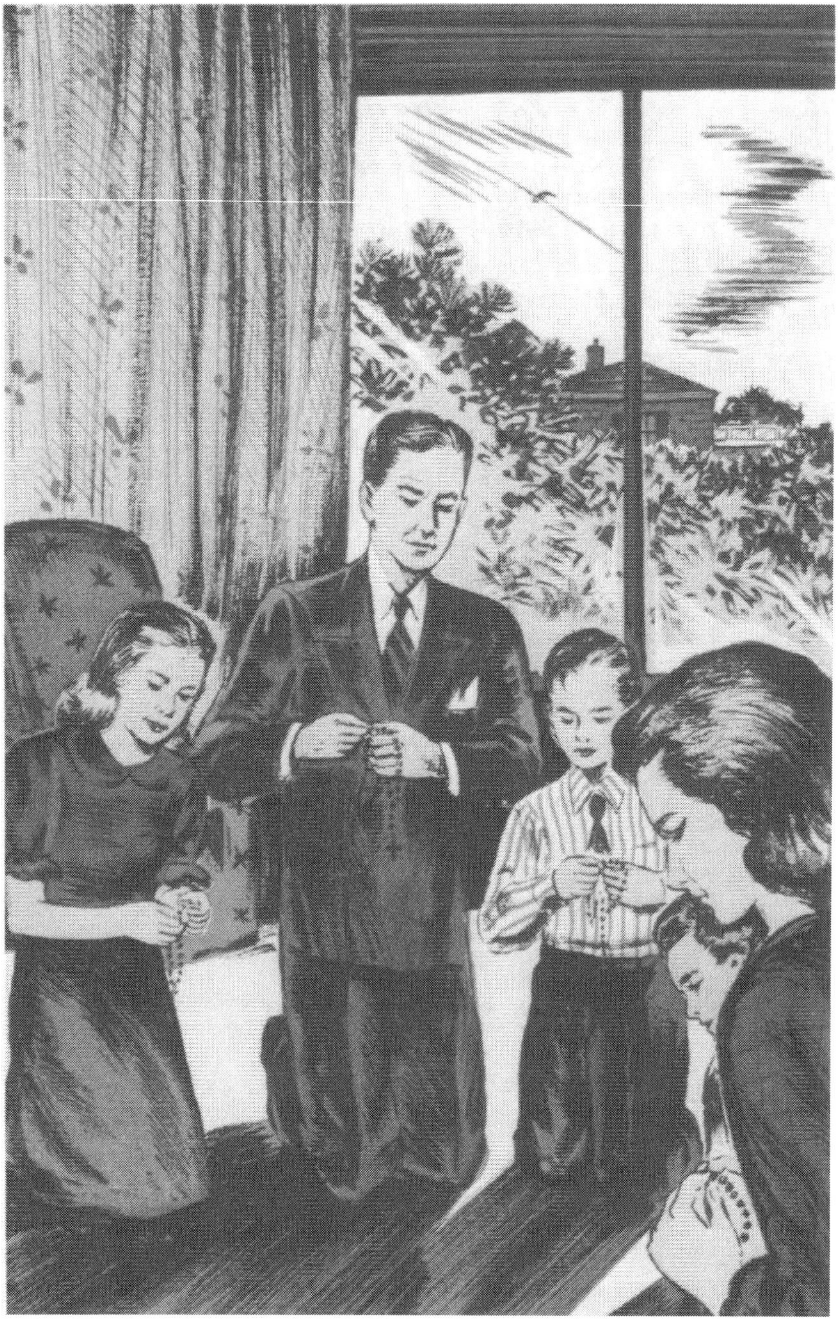

CHAPTER SIX A Good
Citizenship Club

*In which we learn how to form a club
and to conduct meetings*

When a Catholic family says the rosary together at home, the first purpose everyone has in mind is to honor and please God. But we cannot honor and please God as He wishes if our prayers do not make us better citizens. If you are a good Catholic, you will be a good citizen. We say the rosary together, not only to be holy in our *hearts*, but to be holy in our *lives*.

This year we will organize a club which will help us to become better citizens of our school and of our community. Our club can be very simple. We need not have a constitution and we need not observe all the rules of parliamentary procedure that we shall study later. Let us see what we should do to organize a Good Citizenship Club. This classroom club will serve as a model for any other club.

1. Organizing a Good Citizenship Club

Before we begin to organize a club, we should know something about six things that are important in any club. These are the purpose or plan, the officers, the rules of order, the meetings, the committees, and the minutes.

Every club has its own purpose. In a Good Citizenship Club our purpose is to see what we can do to become better citizens of our school and of our community. Every boy and girl is proud to do his share to make his school and his home better. By discussing in our club the duties of a good citizen, we shall have called to our attention things that we did not think of before.

In the beginning we know in a general way what our purpose is. We work out our plans in detail during the meetings of the club.

Officers of the Club

The officers of a club are usually a president, a vice president, a secretary, and a treasurer. The president presides at the meetings of the club. The vice president assists the president and takes his place if he is absent. The secretary writes the minutes, which are a record of what happens at the meetings. He also writes letters in the name of the club if the club has occasion to write to anyone. He keeps reports of committees, programs, and other documents belonging to the club. The treasurer takes care of any money belonging to the club, uses it as directed by the club, and is ready at all times to give a faithful account of what was received and spent.

Rules of Order

In a body such as the United States Senate there are many rules of order which all the members must know. It will be enough for us at present to know the following simple rules:

1. If anyone wishes to speak, he rises and addresses the president, saying "Mr. President" if the president is a boy or "Madame President" if the president is a girl. If he thinks the president may not know his name, he should add it, saying, for example, "Mr. President, Paul Pulaski." Then the president *recognizes* him, or as we say *gives him the floor*, by saying "Paul Pulaski." He is then free to speak from the floor. To say anything in any other way in a club meeting would be bad manners. The only exception is when we second a motion. Then we need not address the chair or rise.

2. If any action is to be taken or if any decision is to be made, someone must make a motion to that effect. He first obtains the floor and then says, for example: "Mr.

MEMBERS:
 1. *Have an interest in all that is done in the meeting*
 2. *Offer suggestions*
 3. *Listen to the suggestions of others*
 4. *Are polite—never interrupt or speak rudely*

President, since our classmate Gertrude Hines has lost her father, I move that the secretary be instructed to write a letter of sympathy in the name of the class." This motion must be *seconded* by someone who says (without rising), "I second the motion."

After the motion has been discussed by members of the club if a discussion is necessary, the president puts the question to a vote. He says: "It has been moved and seconded that the secretary be instructed to write a letter of sympathy to Gertrude Hines, who has lost her father. All in favor of the motion will say *aye. (Those who favor the motion immediately say "Aye.")* Those who are opposed will say *no. (No one says "No.")* The ayes have it.

THE PRESIDENT:
  1. *Calls the meeting to order*
  2. *Gives speakers the floor*
  3. *Calls members to order when necessary*
  4. *Appoints committees*
  5. *Declares the meeting adjourned*

> **ORDER TO BE FOLLOWED IN A CLUB MEETING:**
> 1. *Call to order*
> 2. *Prayer, salute, pledge, or song if customary*
> 3. *Reading of the minutes of the previous meeting*
> 4. *Unfinished business*
> 5. *Business of the day*
> 6. *Program (if any)*
> 7. *Adjournment*

The secretary will write the letter of sympathy to Gertrude Hines as directed."

3. When all the business of the meeting has been attended to, some member says, "I move that we adjourn." This motion is seconded and voted on like any other motion. In some clubs, however, it is understood that the president may declare meetings adjourned when the time assigned for them is up.

The Committees

It is not necessary for every club to have committees. Committees are appointed by the president when there is some special work to be done. For example, our Good Citizenship Club may have decided to have a program in honor of Saint Isaac Jogues. Then the president might say: "I appoint a committee consisting of Catherine Helmer, chairman, John Williams, and Mary Robertson, to report at the next meeting on what we might do to arrange a program in honor of Saint Isaac Jogues."

Minutes of the Meetings

During meetings of the club the secretary keeps a careful record of everything that happens. Afterwards, in a notebook reserved for the purpose, the secretary writes the minutes of the meeting. These tell when and where the meeting was held, who presided, the motions made and whether they were carried or lost, the reports given and the committees appointed, and any other business or discussions that may have taken place. The minutes should be brief, clear, and businesslike.

2. First Meeting of the Good Citizenship Club

The teacher appoints a temporary chairman and a temporary secretary. These take their places at the front of the room and the chairman calls the meeting to order. The meeting then proceeds as follows:

CHAIRMAN. We have decided to have a Good Citizenship Club. The purpose of this first meeting is to elect officers so that we can get started. We ought to have a president, a vice president, a secretary, and a treasurer. Our club may never have any funds, but we ought to have a treasurer in case we should need one. Nominations for president are now open.

CAROLINE WALL *(rising)*. Mr. Chairman.

CHAIRMAN. Caroline Wall.

CAROLINE WALL. I nominate John Halpin.

HARRY SUTPHEN *(rising)*. Mr. Chairman.

CHAIRMAN. Harry Sutphen.

HARRY SUTPHEN. I nominate Mary Robertson.

CHAIRMAN *(after all those who wish to make nominations have done so)*. Will someone move that the nominations be closed?

LUCY SANTO *(rising)*. Mr. Chairman.

CHAIRMAN. Lucy Santo.

LUCY SANTO. I move that the nominations be closed. *(This motion ought not to be made by one who has been nominated. Can you suggest a reason?)*

AUSTIN SMITH *(not rising)*. I second the motion.

If this motion is passed, the chairman says, "The nominations are closed." Then the class proceeds to vote for those who have been nominated. This may be done either by ballots or by calling upon those in favor of each candidate to stand or to raise their hands. The chairman should see that no one votes for more than one candidate. If voting is by ballot, he appoints two students to act as tellers. Everyone writes the name of his choice on a piece of paper and the tellers collect the votes. One teller then reads the votes aloud, and the other teller writes on the board the names and puts after them a mark for each vote received.

Then the chairman says: "As you see, John Halpin has received the most votes and has been elected president. I congratulate the club on having made so good a choice. John, will you please take the chair."

Whoever has been elected says: "I thank you for this honor and will do my best to make a good president. We will now proceed to the election of the vice president." The vice president, the secretary, and the treasurer are elected in the same way as the president. When the secretary is elected, the temporary secretary gives him the notes he has been taking for the minutes.

Then the president says: "Our next meeting will be held Friday at the same hour. Our club is a Good Citizenship Club. The first thing we must do is to decide what we ought to do to be good citizens of our city and school. I know that everyone will have ideas on this subject, but it will help if we have a committee to do some special work and make a report at the next meeting. Mary Robertson will please act as chairman of this committee, and the other members will be Austin Smith and Catherine Helmer. Since this concludes the business of the first meeting, a motion to adjourn is in order."

CLASS ASSIGNMENT

1. Write from memory in brief outline the order to be followed in a club meeting. When you have finished, open your book to page 157 and compare your outline with that given there.

2. Write a letter to Gertrude Hines in the name of the secretary of the Good Citizenship Club. Would this letter be as informal as the model on page 136? Why?

3. Organize a Good Citizenship Club in your own classroom.

3. Second Meeting of the Good Citizenship Club

The second meeting of the Good Citizenship Club proceeds as follows:

PRESIDENT. The meeting will please come to order. Will the secretary read the minutes of the previous meeting?

SECRETARY. The first regular meeting of the Good Citizenship Club was held in Room 12 during oral-expression period on Friday, January 15, with Harry Williams serving as temporary chairman and Margaret Thompson as temporary secretary. The chairman announced that the purpose of the meeting was to get the club started by electing officers. The election resulted as follows: John Halpin, president; Caroline Wall, vice president; Margaret Thompson, secretary; and Harry Sutphen, treasurer. The president appointed a committee consisting of Mary Robertson, chairman, and Austin Smith and Catherine Helmer to make a report on what our club might do. The meeting adjourned at the end of the period to meet at the same hour on Friday, January 22.

Respectfully submitted,
Margaret Thompson

PRESIDENT. Are there any omissions or corrections, or will someone move that the minutes be accepted as read?

ROBERT RICE *(rising)*. Mr. President.

PRESIDENT. Robert Rice.

ROBERT RICE. I move that the minutes be accepted as read.

DOLORES MCNAMARA *(not rising)*. I second the motion.

PRESIDENT. It has been moved and seconded that the minutes be accepted as read. All those in favor will say *aye*. Those opposed will say *no*. The motion is carried. We will now hear the report of the committee.

MARY ROBERTSON *(rising)*. The committee decided that each member would ask older people what a good citizen ought to do. Then we had a meeting and agreed that a good citizen does three things. First, he keeps all the laws and does his duty wherever he is. Second, he tries to be helpful to others. Third, he is always kind and courteous. We ought to act as good citizens at home, at school, and in all the other places we go. The committee recommends (1) that the club begin by trying to improve citizenship in our own classroom, (2) that we open our meetings with a song or a pledge to be chosen by the club, and (3) that we plan to have a program on the anniversary of some great American patriot.

(The president thanks Mary Robertson for her report and invites the members of the club to discuss the suggestions made.)

Here is the program which the committee planned in honor of Saint Isaac Jogues.

PROGRAM FOR Saint Isaac Jogues

OPENING ADDRESS	*The Chairman*
Reading from "Saint in the Wilderness".	*Susan Tere*
St. Isaac Jogues' life story.	*Gerald Smith*
"My Patron's Sacrifice"	*Isaac Foster*
"'Twas in the Moon of Wintertime"	*The Class*

CLASS ASSIGNMENT

1. Use any of the following topics for a discussion in your Good Citizenship Club meetings:
1. How a good citizen treats library books
2. How a good citizen respects property belonging to others
3. How a good citizen cares for his desk in school
4. How a good citizen helps around his home
5. How a good citizen participates in all civic activities

2. Write on the blackboard a list of all the occasions on which we can show courtesy to others. Tell what is discourteous when getting on or off streetcars, riding in elevators, playing a game with another class or school, on an outing with others. What is to be thought of the person who is always late? Of the one who talks and laughs so loud that he disturbs others? Of the person who pushes others out of his way?

3. How can we improve courtesy in our own club? What should be done about the member who wants to talk all the time? About the member who does not take any interest and who never has anything to contribute?

Vocabulary Hints

Study the following synonyms. You may use them in writing minutes, preparing committee reports, or making motions at a meeting of your club.

Make	Habit	Influence	Announce
achieve	custom	encourage	declare
compose	fashion	excite	notify
construct	practice	impel	proclaim
execute	routine	move	reveal
transact	rule	persuade	publish

4. Choral Speaking

Practice in choral speaking will give tone to your voice, so that when you take part in discussions you can be heard plainly and with pleasure. Take these exercises in breathing and enunciation frequently:

Tuning-up Exercises

Breathing:

Breathe deeply. Inhale through the nose, inflating the diaphragm, chest wall, and ribs. Then exhale with the sound of *ah*.

Inhale, hold breath for ten counts, then exhale with sound of *f*.

Enunciation:

Practice the sound of $\bar{u}$ as in *tune*. Say *tutor, due, new* in different pitches, first slowly, then rapidly.

The new tutor teaches new tunes in due time.

Practice the sound of *ŭ* as in *up*. Say *cup, pulp, sup, rough* in different pitches, first slowly, then rapidly.

> Sup the rough pulp in the cup.

We shall now take a scene from a lovely narrative poem, "The Courtship of Miles Standish." The reading of this poem will become much more enjoyable if we prepare for it by studying about the people who are the characters in the poem. They were Pilgrims. In histories and encyclopedias you can find many interesting facts about the customs of the Pilgrims. Topics that you might discuss in class before reading the poem are:

The Coming of the Pilgrims	The Dress of the Pilgrims
The Mayflower Compact	The First Thanksgiving
The Food of the Pilgrims	Leaders of the Pilgrims

In the scene which the poem describes John Alden goes to deliver to Priscilla the message of the captain of Plymouth, Miles Standish. It is springtime, but John Alden's heart is sore and weary. He must ask the hand of Priscilla in marriage, not for himself but for his friend, Captain Miles Standish. Not for a moment does he hesitate. He must be true to his captain even if by doing so he loses the love of Priscilla.

SCENE FROM "THE COURTSHIP OF MILES STANDISH"

Adapted from the poem by Henry Wadsworth Longfellow

Medium So through the Plymouth woods ╱ John Alden ╲ went on his errand ; ∥
Saw the new-built house, ╲ and people ╱ at work in a meadow ; ∥
Heard, ╲ as he drew near the door, ╱ the musical voice of Priscilla. ∥

Then, as he opened \ the door, he beheld the form of the maiden /
Seated beside her wheel, \ and the carded wool like a snowdrift /
Piled at her knee, \ her white hands feeding the ravenous spindle, //
While with her foot on the treadle \ she guided the wheel / in its motion. //

Heavy
So he entered the house; \ and the hum of the wheel \ and the singing /
Suddenly ceased; / for Priscilla, \ aroused by his step on the threshold, /
Rose \ as he entered, / and gave him her hand, \ in signal of welcome,
Saying, /

Solo
"I knew it was you, \ when I heard your step in the passage; //
For I was thinking \ of you, as I sat there singing \ and spinning." //

Medium	Awkward \ and dumb with delight, / that a thought of him \ had been mingled
Thus in the sacred psalm, / that came from the heart of the maiden, /
Silent \ before her he stood, / and gave her the flowers \ for an answer, //
Finding no words \ for his thought. //
Light	Then they sat down \ and talked of the birds \ and the beautiful Spring time; /
Talked of their friends at home, \ and the Mayflower / that sailed on the morrow. //
Solo	"I have been thinking all day," \
Medium	said gently the Puritan maiden, //
Solo	"Dreaming all night, \ and thinking all day, / of the hedgerows of England. //
Kind \ are the people I live with, / and dear to me my religion; //
Still my heart is so sad, \ that I wish myself back in Old England. //
You will say it is wrong, / but I cannot help it : I—" //
Medium	Thereupon answered \ the youth: /
Solo	"Indeed I do not condemn you; //
Stouter hearts than a woman's \ have quailed in this terrible winter. //
Yours \ is tender \ and trusting, / and needs a stronger \ to lean on; //
So I have come to you now, / with an offer \ and proffer of marriage /
Made by a good \ man and true, / Miles Standish \ the Captain of Plymouth!" //
Medium	Mute with amazement \ and sorrow, / Priscilla the Puritan maiden

	Looked into Alden's face, \ her eyes dilated with wonder. //
Solo	"If the great Captain of Plymouth \ is so very eager / to wed me, //
	Why does he not come himself, / and take the trouble to woo me? //
	If I am not worth wooing, \ I surely am not worth the winning!" //
Medium	Then John Alden began explaining \ and smoothing / the matter, //
	Making it worse \ as he went, by saying the Captain was busy,— //
	Had no time \ for such things;—such / things! the words grating harshly
	Fell on the ear of Priscilla; \ and swift as a flash she made answer: //
Solo	"Has he no time \ for such things, as you call it, before / he is married, //
	Would he be likely to find \ it, or make / it, after \ the wedding? //
	This is not right \ nor just; / for surely a woman's affection /
	Is not a thing to be asked \ for, and had / for only the asking. //
	Had he but waited \ awhile, had he only showed / that he loved me, //
	Even this Captain of yours \ —who knows? / —at last might have won me, //
	Old \ and rough / as he is; / but now it never \ can happen." //
Heavy	Still John Alden went on, \ unheeding the words of Priscilla, //
	Urging the suit of his friend, / explaining, \ persuading, / expanding; //

168 VOYAGES IN ENGLISH, SEVENTH YEAR

> He was a man of honor, \ of noble and generous / nature; //
> Any woman in Plymouth, \ nay, any woman in England, //
> Might be happy \ and proud / to be called the wife of Miles Standish! //

Medium
> But as he warmed \ and glowed, / in his simple and eloquent language, //
> Quite forgetful of self, \ and full of the praise of his rival, //
> Archly the maiden smiled, \ and with eyes overrunning with laughter, /
> Said, in a tremulous voice,

Solo
> "Why don't you speak for yourself, \ John?" //

5. Chapter Challenge

1. In a club we learn how to .... for some common purpose.

2. The officers of a club are usually a ...., a ...., a ...., and a ....

3. To obtain the floor in a meeting we ....

4. The presiding officer recognizes us by ....

5. To make a motion we .... the floor and say: ....

6. To second a motion we say, ... It is not necessary to ....

7. After a motion has been made and seconded the president says: ....

8. The .... calls the meeting to order.

9. When all the business has been attended to, or when the time assigned for club activities is ended, the meeting is ....
10. The minutes are taken and read by the ....
11. The .... assists the president and presides when he is absent.
12. Committees are appointed by ....
13. The .... takes care of any money belonging to the club.
14. The minutes should tell (1) .... and .... the meeting was held, (2) who ...., (3) the .... made and whether they were carried or lost, (4) the .... given, and (5) any other .... or .... that may have taken place.
15. The order to be followed in a club meeting is: (1) a call to ....; (2) ...., if customary; (3) reading of the .... of the .... meeting; (4) unfinished ....; (5) .... of the day; (6) ...., if any; (7) ....
16. The characters in "The Courtship of Miles Standish" are .... and ....

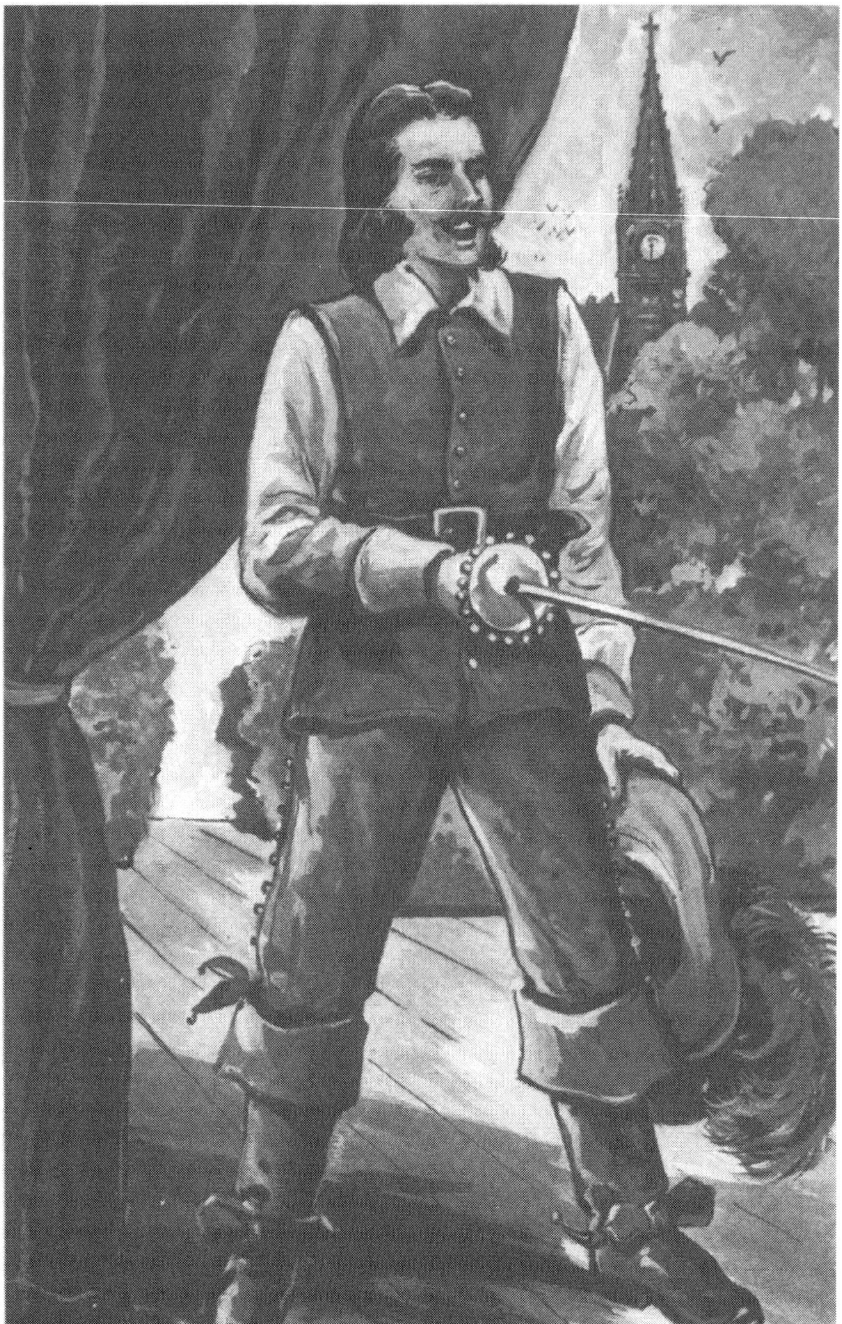

CHAPTER SEVEN Dramatizations

In which we dramatize Catholic life

An interview is a meeting between some distinguished person and a representative of the press (a reporter). A dialogue is a conversation between two persons.

1. Dramatizing Interviews and Dialogues

In dramatizing an interview we imagine that some famous person is present and that we are the reporter in search of information. Then we ask questions about the life and the work of the person we are interviewing.

MODEL: AN INTERVIEW WITH FATHER DE SMET

(One student represents Father De Smet and a second student interviews the famous missionary.)

STUDENT. Father De Smet, we are all happy to see you back in St. Louis after your long trip across the plains. No doubt the Indians were glad to see you.

FATHER DE SMET. Yes, they were very glad indeed. There are many holy persons among them who anxiously await the return of the priest.

STUDENT. But, Father, do you not often find your work hard and disagreeable?

FATHER DE SMET. It is often hard, but I have never found it disagreeable. The Indians are children of God as truly as anyone else. I am very happy to be working among them.

STUDENT. Thank you, Father, for what you have told us. We hope that on your next trip to the Indians you may have the happiness of bringing many more into the Church.

In dramatizing a dialogue two students represent any two characters they wish. The following is an imaginary dialogue between two great leaders in the Civil War.

GENERAL LEE. We have come to Appomattox Court House today to discuss a matter of grave importance.

GENERAL GRANT. Shall we take care of that duty immediately?

GENERAL LEE. In the name of the Confederate army, I am prepared to surrender to you unconditionally.

GENERAL GRANT. Here are the terms I have prepared, General Lee. *(He gives him a paper.)* I think you will find them generous. The soldiers under your command have fought bravely. In defeat you have shown true nobility.

GENERAL LEE. It is for my men and the people of the South that I grieve, General Grant. May I venture to request that the soldiers be permitted to keep their horses?

GENERAL GRANT. Take the horses, General Lee. The men will need them for the spring plowing. Food and clothing will be dispatched as soon as possible. We are brothers, you know.

GENERAL LEE. The South will long remember your generosity, General Grant.

Steps in Preparing an Interview or a Dialogue

There are three introductory steps which should be covered as we begin preparation for an imaginary interview or a dialogue. We should:

1. Learn all we can about the person whom we are interviewing or the persons in the dialogue.

2. Decide upon the *time* and the *place* of the interview or dialogue.

3. Decide upon the *topic* of the interview or dialogue.

We may then prepare the dialogue or interview. When it is presented before the class, we should speak naturally, just as we would speak if we were actually in the presence of the character or as we think the characters in the dialogue would speak.

CLASS ASSIGNMENT

1. Dramatize interviews with famous persons in your classroom, appointing two pupils for each interview. You may use any of the suggested interviews or let each group make its own selection:

   1. With Commander Byrd, about his explorations in the South Polar regions
   2. With Dred Scott, about his struggle for freedom
   3. With Ernest of "The Great Stone Face," about what it meant to him
   4. With Father Damien, about his work in the leper colony on Molokai Island
   5. With Sir Galahad, about his search for the Holy Grail
   6. With Clara Barton, about her experiences on the battlefield
   7. With the mayor of your city, about juvenile delinquency
   8. With your favorite baseball star, about the greatest game he ever played

2. Prepare and dramatize any of the following dialogues:

   1. Between Charles Carroll and John Hancock after they have signed the Declaration of Independence
   2. Between Father Junipera Serra and Governor Portolá concerning the Spanish claims in Upper California

3. Between Lucy and Jacinta after the first apparition of Our Lady of Fatima
4. Between Christ and Saint Peter when our Lord conferred upon him the primacy
5. Between Ellen's father and Lochinvar, when he entered Netherby Hall
6. Between a doctor and a boy who was hurt because he did not observe safety rules when crossing the street

2. Writing a Play

Interviews and dialogues are, in a way, short plays. And it is only a step from writing and acting these to writing and acting plays.

Let's Write a Play!

Would the class like to write a play? Playwriting and play acting are such fun! First of all, we must decide on the subject of our play. Let us base our play on some story with which we are all familiar. We will rewrite the story in the form of a play and then choose pupils to take the parts of the various characters in the play.

Let us look over the list of story poems which we read in seventh grade. The class members may decide which of these they would like to write in the form of a play. Our list will probably contain some of the following poems:

"The Courtship of Miles Standish," by Henry Wadsworth Longfellow
"The Legend of the Robes," by Eleanore C. Donnelly
"Snow-Bound," by John Greenleaf Whittier
"Barbara Frietchie," by John Greenleaf Whittier
"Lochinvar," by Walter Scott
"Lady Clare," by Alfred Tennyson
"Incident of the French Camp," by Robert Browning

In selecting a poem for dramatization, the class should ask the following questions:
1. Will the majority of the class enjoy this play?
2. How many characters or persons are in the story?
3. Would our class really portray these characters well?

Planning the Project

When the play has been selected by the class the next step is to pick out the different events in the story. Since this is a class project, all the members of the class should take part in the discussion. One seventh-grade class which decided to dramatize "The Legend of the Robes," by Eleanore C. Donnelly, held the following discussion:

TEACHER. The poem entitled "The Legend of the Robes" is printed in the appendix of our textbook. At our last meeting we decided that everyone should read this poem before class today. What do you think should be the first scene in a play based on "The Legend of the Robes"?

JOHN. I think the play should begin just where the story poem begins, where Lady Elizabeth and her maid are talking while they sew.

TEACHER. That does seem a good beginning, John. What is the next event, Ruth?

RUTH. The entrance of the Duke, I think, Sister.

TEACHER. Yes, that certainly is the next event. But does this event require a change of scene or does it take place in the room where Lady Elizabeth and her maid are sewing?

MARY. It is the same scene. The Duke comes to the room where they are sewing.

TEACHER. When you read this poem did you discover any event that required a change of scene?

HENRY. Is it the banquet scene?

TEACHER. Yes, that is right, Henry. Now we have two scenes— the first in the room where Lady Elizabeth and her maid are sewing and the second in the banquet hall. Now I think it will help if every pupil in the class writes in his own words the various events in each scene that the author relates. Be sure to include conversations in what you write, for plays are only conversation plus action.

(Each member of the class writes a synopsis of each scene and these are placed on the teacher's desk as they are finished.)

TEACHER. Will Therese, Edna, Blanche, James, William, and Ralph act as a committee to read the synopses? Therese, since I called your name first, you will please act as chairman of this committee. Select the one that you like best and we shall write the first scene at our next meeting.

(At the next meeting of the class, the teacher calls for a report from the committee.)

THERESE. The committee has selected the synopsis written by Edna as the best for Scene 1 of "The Legend of the Robes." We have made copies so that everyone in the class may have one.

Scene 1. The Legend of the Robes

Elizabeth, the wife of Louis of Thuringia, is sewing in her room with her maid Ysentrude. They both smile at the poor robe the great Duchess is wearing.

Soon they hear a step. The Duke enters. He is sad because guests are coming to the castle that very evening, and they will laugh at the poor robes of his wife.

"I know you have given your rich robes to the poor, but these men will blame me."

"Do not worry," says Elizabeth. "Go, welcome your guests, and when the feast is ready I will come down."

When the Duke goes out, the Lady Elizabeth falls on her knees and prays for help: "O dear Lord, I have given all to Thy poor! Make me pleasing in my husband's eyes!"

TEACHER. Now, let us take Edna's synopsis, and make it over into a play. Where is the place of the story, Claire?

CLAIRE *(consulting the synopsis)*. The room of Lady Elizabeth.

TEACHER. In a play we should also tell the name of the country. Do you know where the action takes place, Claire?

CLAIRE. Thuringia.

TEACHER. Now, what is the time of day at which the event takes place?

HUBERT. I think it is near evening.

TEACHER. Why, Hubert?

HUBERT. Because banquets usually take place in the evening.

TEACHER. Yes, that is true. What is the year?

HUBERT. I do not know, Sister. How can I find out, please?

TEACHER. The story, as you know, is about Saint Elizabeth of Hungary, whose feast occurs on November 19. If you consult a book on the lives of the saints, you will find out when she lived.

MONICA. I read that Saint Elizabeth lived from 1207 to 1231.

TEACHER. That is right, and she was married in 1221. Shall we say that this event took place about the year 1225? At the beginning of every scene we write the time and the place in the middle of the paper like this: *(She writes on the blackboard.)*

PLACE: Room of Lady Elizabeth in the castle of Thuringia
TIME: Early one evening in the year 1225

We must now write down the names of the persons in the play, in the order in which they speak. That would be:

> Lady Elizabeth, *Duchess of Thuringia*
> Ysentrude, *her maid*
> Louis, *Duke of Thuringia*

Which characters are in the room when the play begins?

WILLIAM. Lady Elizabeth and her maid are sewing.

TEACHER. Yes, and we put this information under the list of persons in the play, for it is what we call a stage direction. We place stage directions in parentheses to show that they are not part of the conversation in the play.

Here is a copy of the play that the class wrote under the direction of the teacher:

THE LEGEND OF THE ROBES
(Adapted from the poem by Eleanore C. Donnelly)

SCENE 1

PLACE: Room of Lady Elizabeth in the castle of Thuringia
TIME: Early one evening in the year 1225

CHARACTERS

> Lady Elizabeth, *Duchess of Thuringia*
> Ysentrude, *her maid*
> Louis, *Duke of Thuringia*

(Elizabeth and Ysentrude are seated, sewing.)

ELIZABETH. Oh, isn't it a lovely day, Ysentrude?

YSENTRUDE. Very beautiful, my Lady.

ELIZABETH. I'll be so glad when the Duke returns, Ysentrude. He's been away so long. Oh, that must be the Duke now. I hear footsteps in the corridor.

(The Duke enters.)

ELIZABETH. Welcome home, my husband! But you are sad. What is the matter?

DUKE LOUIS. Guests are coming, Elizabeth, and I know you have given all your rich robes to the poor.

ELIZABETH. Do not worry, Louis. Go, welcome your guests, and when the feast is ready I will come down.

(The Duke leaves and Lady Elizabeth falls on her knees.)

ELIZABETH. O dear Lord, you know I have given all to Thy poor. Make me pleasing in my husband's eyes.

(End of Scene 1)

Christening the Play

What would you use for a title of the play? Attractive titles do make all our writings more interesting. Here are some suggestions:

God's Ways	Lady Elizabeth's Faith
The Miracle	Trust in God

CLASS ASSIGNMENT

1. Select different members of the class to take the parts of Elizabeth, Ysentrude, and Duke Louis and act out Scene 1 in your classroom. Perhaps several different groups could do so and the class could then vote for the students who best played the parts assigned them.
2. Write a synopsis of the events that take place in Scene 2 of "The Legend of the Robes." Appoint a committee to select the best paragraph. With this as a model, let the class write Scene 2 in the same way as Scene 1 was written.
3. Write a play based on some story in the Bible. If you select, for example, the story of the Holy Innocents, the scenes would be as follows: (1) Herod decreeing the massacre of the children of Bethlehem; (2) the Holy Family's flight into Egypt; (3) the coming of the soldiers and the grief of the mothers at the massacre.

3. Still-Life Dramatizations

Still-life drama is drama without words. It is done by means of living pictures. These pictures may take the form of scenes from history, literature, or public life. The pictures are usually shown behind large picture frames.

The committee in charge of the program should try to secure pictures of the events as portrayed by artists. Then they should carefully select boys and girls to take part in the scenes. The characters must *look the part*. The picture model should be copied as to grouping, gestures, and facial expressions.

CLASS PROJECT

1. Prepare a program of still-life pictures for the Feast of Saint Joseph. Let the class appoint a committee to decide what pictures can best be presented. See that the pictures tell a story, that they contain action. The following scenes are suggested:

1. The Espousals of Mary and Joseph
2. Mary and Joseph at the Inn in Bethlehem
3. The Nativity
4. The Flight into Egypt
5. Joseph and Jesus in the Carpenter Shop
6. The Finding of the Child Jesus in the Temple
7. The Death of Saint Joseph

2. Another committee should be appointed to make the costumes. Some discarded drapes will serve the purpose. Our Blessed Lady should be dressed in white with a blue mantle. Saint Joseph may wear brown or some dark color.

3. A third committee, composed of boys, should be appointed to make a large picture frame. This can be made from beaverboard or heavy cardboard and painted with gold radiator paint. The frame should be placed in the middle of the stage (the front of the classroom). If the characters group themselves about two feet behind the frame, the picture will have depth.

4. Decide how each scene will be described. During some of the scenes paragraphs may be read; in others appropriate hymns may be sung. A suitable poem may be read by the verse-speaking choir during one of the scenes.

4. The Radio and Modern Life

We all remember the story of Aladdin and his magic lamp. When Aladdin rubbed his lamp a genie appeared and awaited his command. What an awful fairy tale! Yet today we need only turn a dial and information or entertainment is ours to command. It is no fairy tale, but reality! We can go adventuring into worlds of imagination through the magic of radio and television. Space disappears. We can be present at a pope's coronation in Rome or see and hear the president of the United States deliver a message to Congress.

Aladdin used his lamp unwisely. However, we should learn to use the invention of radio and television wisely in order to obtain from both inventions useful instruction and wholesome entertainment. We should not waste our time on worthless programs.

Preparing a Classroom Broadcast

A radio broadcast makes an interesting program for our oral-English period. Our first task is to select some event with which we are all familiar, one that has some action to be described. After the class has agreed upon the subject of the broadcast, all the details should be listed in the order in which they happened. Then we imagine that we are some person present at that time and write a description of the event that would appeal to an unseen radio listener. We add as many details as possible.

Historical events make good subjects for these classroom broadcasts because everyone in the class is familiar with them and can help in writing the broadcast. On March 25, 1634, for example, the first Mass was said in the English colonies in America.

The expedition in charge of Leonard Calvert, the brother of Lord Baltimore, was accompanied by three Jesuit priests, among whom was Father Andrew White, the Apostle of Maryland. Also present were other priests, the colonists, members of the crew of the *Ark* and the *Dove*, Indians, an Indian chief, and Henry Fisher, an interpreter. The place from which this broadcast is made is Saint Clement's Island in the Potomac River. The time is March 25, 1634, the Feast of the Annunciation of Our Blessed Lady. Leonard Calvert is the announcer.

A CLASSROOM RADIO BROADCAST: MARYLAND, FIRST SANCTUARY OF THE FAITH

LEONARD CALVERT. We have just heard holy Mass, celebrated for the first time in this settlement on the shores of North America. The celebrant was the Jesuit priest, Father Andrew White, and the Mass was said in the wigwam of a friendly Indian chief.

All the members of the expedition are assembled on the shores of this beautiful bay, laughing and chatting gaily. *(Sound effects, laughing and talking)* Riding on the waters in the sunlight of early morning are the two ships that by God's providence have brought us safely to this new land. A group of friendly Indians are examining them.

Now the crew of the *Ark* approaches, bearing two great logs hewn from the trees of this new country. Father White blesses the wood; men hammer the logs with steady blows. *(Sound effect of logs being hammered)* Now they raise the logs. It is a great cross, symbol of our faith, reaching to the skies. Reverently the colonists place the cross in the soil of Maryland. The Blackrobe kneels for a moment and kisses the earth newly consecrated to the emblem of Christ's death. Listen, the people are speaking.

MANY VOICES. We pledge allegiance to God—and country!

FATHER WHITE. We take possession of the Province of Maryland, in the name of God and for His honor and glory, and by the authority of His Majesty, King Charles of England.

LEONARD CALVERT. Now the forests of the New World ring with the chant of the Litany of the Holy Cross.

MANY VOICES. Hope of Christians, save us, O holy Cross. Star of the Mariner, save us, O holy Cross.

LEONARD CALVERT. A Jesuit father now approaches the Indians, who are not forgotten in the universal joy.

SOLO VOICE. We come not to war upon you, but to show you the way to heaven.

LEONARD CALVERT. Now Henry Fisher is speaking to the Indian chief, translating the Blackrobe's message. The Indian listens to the message and then answers in his native tongue.

INTERPRETER. The chief gives me this message: "Return with us, O our white brothers, and we will eat of the same food. My followers, too, will hunt for you, and we shall all have things in common."

LEONARD CALVERT. Now we all fall on our knees for the blessing of Father White. *(Sound of many kneeling)*

FATHER WHITE. May the blessing of almighty God, Father, Son, and Holy Ghost, descend upon you and remain forever.
MANY VOICES. Amen.
LEONARD CALVERT. The service is over. White men mingle with the red men in peace and brotherly love. Such is the power of the cross! Our holy faith has at last found sanctuary and freedom in the virgin soil of Maryland.

CLASS ASSIGNMENT

1. Make an oral or written report on an interesting radio or television program.
2. Divide the class into committees of four or five pupils, and let each committee prepare a report concerning the uses of radio by airplanes, ships, the police, the Army, and so forth.
3. Prepare and present a classroom broadcast, using some subject of your own or any of the following:
   1. A trip up the Congo River
   2. Alexander Graham Bell and the telephone
   3. A meeting of Australian ranchers
   4. Esther before King Assuerus
   5. The marriage of the waters (Erie Canal)
   6. Mother Cabrini's first hospital in America
   7. The Webster-Hayne debate
   8. The joining of the East and the West by railroad
   9. Mary Magdalene at the tomb on Easter morning
4. Make a list of the television programs that you consider worth while.

5. Choral Speaking

Your voice will be vastly improved if you practice the tuning-up exercises before you attempt to take part in a dramatization. Listen to the voices of good speakers, actors, and singers, and try to imitate their good qualities: clearness, good enunciation, musical tones.

Tuning-up Exercises

Breathing:

Inhale, hold the breath ten counts, then exhale with sound of *ha*, explosively.

Enunciation:

Practice *ow* as in *how*. Say in different pitches *now, bow, bough*.

How now, bow now, old bough.

Practice *ou* as in *out*. Say in different pitches *out, doubt, pout, bout, rout*.

Without a doubt Mary's mouth pouts.

Say firmly and clearly:

loud   proud   howl   towel

A Choral Drama

The Story of the Shepherds (Luke 2:8-20)

Scene: A hillside in Bethlehem

Time: Christmas Eve nineteen hundred years ago

The Characters: The Shepherds
The Herald Angel
Other Angels

Light Voices

And there were shepherds in the same district / living in the fields and keeping watch over their flock by night. // And behold, / an angel of the Lord \ stood by them and the glory of God shone round about them, // and they feared exceedingly. // And the angel said to them, /

Herald Angel

"Do not be afraid, / for behold, \ I bring you good news of great joy / which shall be to all the people; // for today \ in the town of David / a Savior has been born to you, \ who is Christ the Lord. //

And this \ shall be a sign to you: / you will find an infant wrapped in swaddling clothes \ and lying in a manger." //

Heavy Voices
And suddenly there was with the angel ╱ a multitude of the heavenly host ╱ praising God and saying, ╱

All the Angels
"Glory to God in the highest, ╲ and on earth ╱ peace among men of good will." ⫽

Heavy Voices
And it came to pass, ╱ when the angels had departed from them into heaven, ╲ that the shepherds were saying to one another, ╱

Shepherds
"Let us go over to Bethlehem ╱ and see this thing that has come to pass, ╱ which the Lord has made known to us." ⫽

Light Voices
So they went with haste, ╲ and they found Mary ╱ and Joseph, ╲ and the babe ╱ lying in the manger. ⫽

Heavy Voices
And when they had seen, ╲ they understood what had been told them concerning this child. ⫽ And all who heard ╱ marvelled at the things told them by the shepherds. ⫽

Light Voices

But Mary kept in mind all these things, ∕ pondering them in her heart. ∥

Both Voices

And the shepherds returned, ∖ glorifying ∕ and praising God ∖ for all that they had heard ∕ and seen, ∖ even as it was spoken to them. ∥

Presenting the Drama

The class should be divided into light voices and heavy voices for this drama, and arranged on either side of the stage. As the two groups or choruses tell the story, it may be acted by the principal characters in the center. The scene opens with the shepherds gathered around a little fire warming themselves.

If the drama is given on a stage, the shepherds may take their places in front of the curtain. When the angels appear the curtain may be drawn. If there is a second curtain, it may be drawn at the end, revealing the stable. The shepherds then enter the stable and kneel at the crib. If the drama is given in the classroom, the two groups of light and heavy voices move toward the center of the room, forming a human curtain. They then step aside, revealing the stable.

Try to preserve the utmost simplicity in choral drama, for the voices and the accompanying action, not the setting, are the important things.

6. Chapter Challenge

1. An interview is ....
2. In dramatizing an interview we imagine that we are a .... asking questions of some ....

3. In dramatizing a dialogue .... students represent any .... characters they wish.

4. We say that interviews and dialogues are, in a way, ...

5. When writing a play it is helpful to write first a .... of the events in each scene.

6. At the beginning of each scene in a play we write the ...., the ...., and the ....

7. .... take the place of descriptions in a story. They are placed in .... to show that they are not part of the conversation.

8. .... events make good subjects for classroom broadcasts.

9. Father .... celebrated the first Mass in Maryland.

10. In a .... two groups of voices tell a story acted by the principal characters in the center.

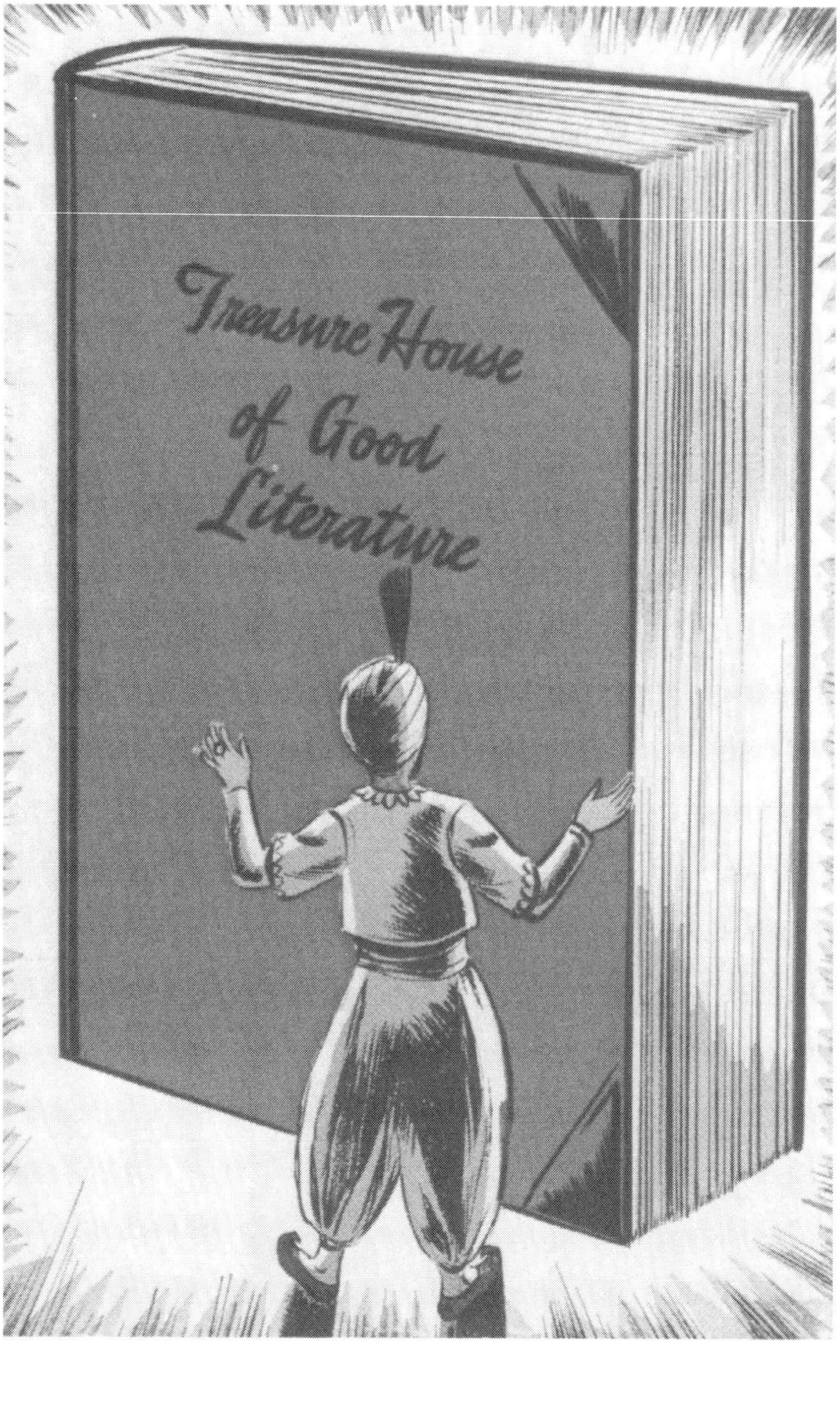
Treasure House of Good Literature

CHAPTER EIGHT Living Life
through Books

> *In which we learn to judge books by Catholic principles and to be at home in libraries*

We remember that when Ali Baba of the *Arabian Nights* wanted to enter the magic cave, he had to say "Open sesame" as a kind of password. Books are the passwords that admit us to a far more wonderful palace than that Ali Baba enjoyed. Books give us access to a whole world of treasures. Here we take part in the adventures of men and women of all times and of all nations. Books can be our guides to the beauties of the great physical world about us. Through literature we learn to appreciate the wisdom of the great and good men and women who have lived in ages gone by.

1. Sharing Books with Others

Have you enjoyed reading a good book recently? Would you like to share it with your classmates? Talking about favorite books in class makes others eager to read the stories we have enjoyed and informs us of interesting books which we would like to read.

Advertising Books

The stories we read in books help us to share the experiences of other young people and to learn lessons of courage and endurance from their brave example. Of course, we do not tell the entire story when advertising a book. We select some striking incident or event to tell.

MODEL BOOK ADVERTISEMENT: BETTY'S RIDE

Gallop! Gallop! Gallop! Betty was riding to Washington's camp on the Brandywine to beg for help for one hundred colonial soldiers besieged by three hundred British in the old Chester meetinghouse. "Halt!" Her heart stood still with fright. There was the thud of horses' hoofs. The Redcoats were almost upon her! She dug her knees into the mare's flanks. She must throw the enemy off the track, but how? You will find out what this brave girl did when you read "Betty's Ride," an exciting story of the Revolution written by Henry Seidel Canby.

CLASS ASSIGNMENT

1. Read the following description of an incident from "Ali Baba and the Forty Thieves," an Arabian Nights tale, and answer the questions that follow:

Marjaneh very cunningly went from jar to jar, whispering "Not yet," until she reached the jar of oil. There she filled her tiny oil pot and a large kettle, which she put on to boil. When the oil was boiling she very quietly poured it into each jar, stifling the cries of the robbers within. What a smile of satisfaction overspread Marjaneh's countenance as she watched the captain of the thieves examine despairingly each deathly silent jar!

1. Does this incident lead you to believe that the story is an interesting one?
2. Does the pupil who related this incident tell you where to find the complete story?
3. How would you improve the advertisement?

2. Select an incident from any one of the following books as a topic for a book advertisement: *Little Women*, by Louisa Alcott; *Adventures of Tom Sawyer*, by Mark Twain; *The Secret Garden*, by Frances Burnett; *Black Stallion*, by Walter Farley; *Lassie Come-Home*, by Eric Knight; *Magic Pen*, by Anne Heagney; *Son of the Land*, by Ivy Bolton; *Daniel Boone: Wilderness Scout*, by Stewart White; *Louis Pasteur*, by Laura N. Wood; *Secret of the Bog*, by Eugenia Stone; *The Good Night at San Gabriel*, by Susanna Clayton Ott; *The Man Who Built the Secret Door*, by Sister Mary Charitas; *Northern Lights*, by Mary Fabyan Windeatt; *Nancy Keeps House*, by Helene Laird; *Fielder from Nowhere*, by Jackson Scholz; *Reaper Man*, by Clara Ingram Judson; *Prince Godfrey, the Knight of the Star of the Nativity*, by Halina Górska; *The Silver Teapot*, by Frances Sanger.

Book Reviews

Another way of arousing interest in a book is by means of a book review. This review may be given orally or it may be written. The main purpose is to inform our classmates of the worth-while features of the book and to tell them of the impression the book made on us. In some cases we may also point out defects in the book or parts that we did not like.

Model Book Review: Larger than the Sky

Are you interested in American heroes? Do their ideals inspire you? Then Covelle Newcomb's *Larger than the Sky* is the book for you. The author realistically relates the struggles of James Gibbons in reaching his desired goal, the priesthood. His endless enthusiasm paved the way for an exciting and colorful life as a priest, a bishop, and finally as a cardinal. This hero fought unceasingly for those who were socially and physically handicapped and numbered them among his friends.

How to Judge a Book

Can we tell when a book is good? We can judge a book by asking ourselves the questions that follow. Test the next book you read by these standards:

1. Did the book hold my interest from the beginning to the end?
2. Do I feel that the persons in the book are *real;* that they act like people I know?
3. Is the place of the action described so vividly that I can almost see it?
4. Do the events in the story seem likely to happen? Are they interesting?
5. Is the book a wholesome book—one that contains nothing against the Catholic faith?

The last is the most important question of all. No matter how well the book may be written, if it does not pass this test, it is not a good book.

CLASS ASSIGNMENT

1. Read this book review and answer the questions that follow:

If you enjoy stories about real, true-to-life boys, the *Adventures of Tom Sawyer* should be your first choice. In amusing and picturesque language the author has related the adventures common to boyhood. You will chuckle to yourself and even laugh aloud occasionally as you read of Tom's pranks and entanglements. The chief charm of the story lies in the fact that many of these episodes find an echo in our own lives.

1. Does this review give you an idea of what the book is about?
2. Does it reveal the plot of the story?
3. Does the reviewer tell you the name of the author?

2. Read the following review of an essay. Would it interest you in literature of this type?

You may have heard much about the popular summer sport of sleeping outdoors. Perhaps you have even secretly wished that you might spend some hot sultry nights in the great open air under a starry sky. Before you attempt it, however, read "Sleeping Outdoors," by Frederick Lewis Allen. In this short essay the author humorously relates the hazards encountered in a night of battling bloodthirsty mosquitoes. You may not agree that this sport is overrated, but you will enjoy the writer's ludicrous description of his first and last experience at sleeping outdoors.

3. Interest your class in one of the following books by writing a review: *All-American*, by John R. Tunis; *Iron Doctor*, by Agnes Hewes; *Secret of Pooduck Island*, by Alfred Noyes; *Royal Banners Fly*, by Anna Kuhn; *Reformed Pirate*, by Frank Stockton; *Mozart, the Wonder Boy*, by Opal Wheeler and Sybil Deucher; *The Secret Door*, by Covelle Newcomb; *For Charlemagne!* by Frank Emerson Andrews; *The Wild Trek*, by James A. Kjelgaard; *The Captain's Daughter*, by Elizabeth Coatsworth.

2. Writing a Book Report

Keeping a record of books that we have read will help us to remember them. The book report or record need not be long, just long enough to give a summary of the story. There are no definite rules to be followed in writing a book report. The essential topics to be covered in the report are: (1) the title of the book; (2) the author; (3) the type; (4) the principal characters; (5) a brief summary, in three or four well-chosen sentences, of the main events of the story; (6) our personal reaction.

The books we read may be stories, biographies, poems, books of travel, or books about nature or inventions. The type of report we write will depend upon the kind of book we have read, but it is a good idea to jot down answers to the following questions as we read:

1. What kind of book is it?
2. Who are the characters in the book?

3. When and where do the events take place?
4. What are the most interesting events in the book?
5. Do I admire the characters?
6. What is my personal reaction?

When we have finished reading the book we should first write a rough draft from the points that we have jotted down. After we have read our first draft, we should improve the book report and copy it neatly before giving it to the teacher.

MODEL BOOK REPORT: OUTLAWS OF RAVENHURST

TITLE: Outlaws of Ravenhurst

AUTHOR: Sister Mary Imelda

TYPE: Fiction

CHARACTERS: Sir Charles Gordon, Lady Margaret (his mother), Sir James (his father), Reverend Stephen Douglas (his uncle).

SUMMARY: *Outlaws of Ravenhurst* is a story of warriors, not ordinary soldiers but fearless men whose swords are crimsoned in battle "for God and our Lady." Sister Imelda has written a story of seventeenth-century Scotland that is packed with excitement.

As our tale unravels we are introduced to Sir Charles Gordon, heir and chief outlaw of Ravenhurst. We relive Gordon's amazement as he listens to his mother's explanation that to be a Catholic in Scotland means death as an outlaw. We witness the cruel beatings inflicted on Gordon because of the lad's refusal to reveal the hiding place of his Uncle Stephen, a hunted priest. We behold the stirring scene in which the outlaws of Ravenhurst save the precious blood of Christ from desecration by the enemies of God. Finally we follow Gordon in his heroic efforts to rescue his loved ones from torments in the dungeon.

MY REACTION: I can still hear Lady Margaret's unflinching command: "The Earl of Ravenhurst must always stand for God and our Blessed Lady, let the cost be what it may!"

Describing Characters in Books

The word pictures we developed in Chapter Four will help us to describe the friends we meet in books. There are many admirable characters in the books we read whom we would like to introduce to our classmates. We may describe either their appearance or the traits of character which we admire most.

MODEL: MY FAVORITE BOOK CHARACTER

Who is the brave young man that daringly moves as a priest in Mexico during the days of Calles' tyrannical reign? Now we see him disguised as a workman carrying a dinner pail; at another time as a university student riding a bicycle through the city streets. Again, he is a stylish young dude or a jaunty-capped chauffeur. Always he is boyishly gay and pleasant, as though he thoroughly enjoys the role he is forced to play. Close scrutiny of this incognito for Christ will disclose the keen, intelligent face, the flashing eyes, the beaming smile, and the merry laughter of Father Miguel Augustin Pro, the martyr-priest of Mexico.

CLASS ASSIGNMENT

1. Read the following description of a favorite book character. Discuss it orally in class:

The most sterling and likable character of the four charming sisters in *Little Women,* by Louisa May Alcott, is, I think, plain, practical Jo. Jo was the tomboy of that harmonious little family; she detested formality and was never more ill at ease than when dressed for a party. She lacked the attractiveness of Meg, the delicate beauty of Beth, the ladylike manners of Amy; but in generosity and self-sacrifice, Jo surpassed them all.

2. Divide the class into groups. Let each group read and prepare a report on one of the following types: fiction, biography, travel, adventure, science.

3. Write a book report on one of the books in your classroom library.

3. Learning to Use the Library

When we enter a library we see a desk called the charging desk. At this desk is the librarian, or one of the assistant librarians if it is a large library. The librarian is there to help us find the books that we want and to charge against us the ones we take away. The part of the library that is responsible for books we take home is called the circulation division.

The reference division has charge of encyclopedias, dictionaries, indexes, magazines, and other books which we are not permitted to take from the library. The reference librarian will also help us find material that we need.

Large libraries may have children's rooms, art rooms, and many other special rooms. In smaller libraries everything may be in one room. We soon learn what is in the library and where to go for what we want. The librarian is a very busy person, and so we try to help ourselves all we can and avoid asking unnecessary questions.

How Books Are Classified

In all large libraries we shall find that books are classified according to the subject with which they deal and are placed on the shelves in that order. Even the grocer follows this same system, for he places all articles of one kind together on his shelves. How much more necessary is it, then, that a library which contains thousands of books should have these books classified and placed in order on the shelves. The next time you visit your school or public library look at the different labels on the shelves. Do you find such classifications as History, Travel, Outdoor Life, Poetry, Plays, Science?

One of the most widely used systems of numbering and classifying books is called the Dewey Decimal Classification System, which divides all books into ten general classes and assigns a block of one hundred numbers to each class. Any book on religion, for example, will have a number between 200 and 299; any book on history will have a number between 900 and 999, and so forth.

The Card Catalogue

The card catalogue is the complete list of all the books in the library. For each book there are usually three cards —an author card, a title card, and a subject card. On the following page are shown the three cards which the library prepared for *The Oregon Trail*. Note that the word *A, An,* or *The* is omitted if it forms the first word of the title. The author's surname (the last name) appears first on the author card. The cards are filed alphabetically in drawers.

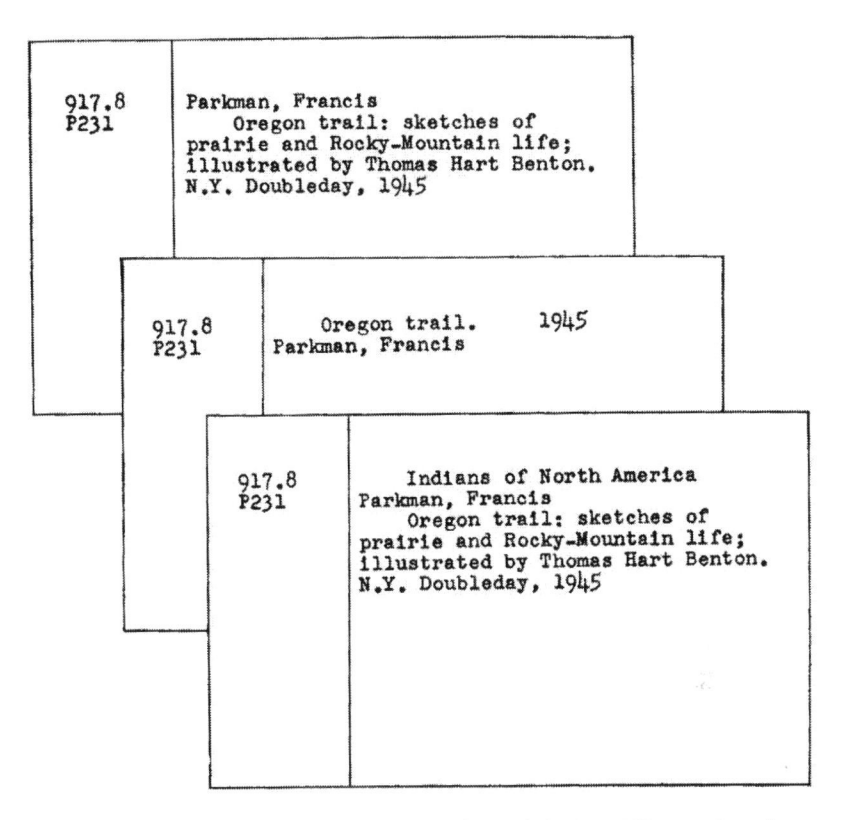

```
917.8    Parkman, Francis
P231         Oregon trail: sketches of
         prairie and Rocky-Mountain life;
         illustrated by Thomas Hart Benton.
         N.Y. Doubleday, 1945
```

```
917.8         Oregon trail.      1945
P231          Parkman, Francis
```

```
917.8         Indians of North America
P231       Parkman, Francis
                Oregon trail: sketches of
           prairie and Rocky-Mountain life;
           illustrated by Thomas Hart Benton.
           N.Y. Doubleday, 1945
```

On the outside of each drawer is a label telling what letters of the alphabet are contained in that particular drawer. In a large library we shall find that the card catalogue occupies many drawers.

If we know the title of a book or the name of the author, the card catalogue will tell us whether or not the library has a copy of that book. If we want material on a certain subject, such as Indians, the card catalogue will tell us what books the library has on that subject.

The Call Number

When we locate the card bearing the title *Oregon Trail* in the card catalogue, we find that it has a certain classification number 917.8 (the numbers 900-999 refer to history), and an author number P231 (the author's name is Parkman). These two numbers make up the *call number* of a book. The call number tells where the book is kept on the shelves. If the library has the open-shelf system, we can go to the shelves containing books numbered 900, find the one with the call number 917.8, P231, and obtain the book immediately. In a large library we must write the call number on a special slip of paper and give it to the librarian at the desk.

Some libraries use a different classification known as Library of Congress System. But whatever system is used in the library we frequent, we have only to write the call number on the slip and give it to the librarian. When we learn to look up the book we need in the card catalogue and call for it by number, the librarian will see that we have begun to grow up and that we are able to take care of ourselves.

Reference Books

Books such as dictionaries, encyclopedias, atlases, almanacs, and indexes are called reference books. We do not study these books nor do we read them for enjoyment; we *refer* to them for information. They are so arranged, in very many cases in alphabetical order, that one can find the information desired quickly. Reference books are usually kept on special shelves in the reading room of a library or on convenient tables. They do not circulate; that is, they cannot be taken from the library.

Even your classroom library will contain some of the more common reference books. The next time you go to the library see how many of the following reference books you can locate:

1. Unabridged dictionaries are arranged exactly like the ordinary desk dictionary, but they contain more detailed information. There are also special dictionaries, such as the *Biographical Dictionary* and the *Geographical Dictionary*.
2. Encyclopedias contain short articles on a great variety of topics, arranged in alphabetical order for convenient reference. Some well-known encyclopedias are the *Catholic Encyclopedia*, the *Encyclopedia Britannica*, the *Encyclopedia Americana*, *World Book Encyclopedia*, and *Compton's Pictured Encyclopedia*.
3. Atlases are collections of maps, larger and more detailed than those found in your geographies.
4. Almanacs, which are published annually, contain brief summaries of events that took place during the preceding year, statistics, and facts. The *World Almanac* and the *Information Please Almanac* are two popular reference books of this type.
5. *Who's Who in America* contains brief biographical sketches of living American men and women. There is also an *American Catholic Who's Who*.
6. Bartlett's *Familiar Quotations* contains quotations from authors of all times. It is useful in finding poems suitable for certain days.
7. Granger's *Index to Poetry and Recitations* contains a list of many poems arranged by titles, authors, first lines, and subjects.
8. The *Reader's Guide to Periodical Literature* indexes many popular magazines. It tells where to find articles on certain subjects.

9. The *Cumulative Book Index* contains the names of books published in the United States.

CLASS ASSIGNMENT

1. Consult the card catalogue in your library and make a list of books on some of the following topics: pilgrims, ships, travel, martyrs, airplanes, puppets, Indians, radio.
2. How many books written by Father Francis J. Finn, S.J., are in your library? Name them.
3. Write the names of the authors and the titles of the books you find in the card catalogue which tell about any one of the following characters: Saint Francis of Assisi, the Little Flower, William T. Sherman, Florence Nightingale, Abraham Lincoln, Robert E. Lee, Julius Caesar.
4. Find three books on United States history in the catalogue. Copy the author's name, the title, and the call number of each book.
5. What books would you consult to obtain information on the following topics?

1. The invention of printing
2. Winners of sporting events during the past year
3. The geography of Finland
4. Recent articles on radio science
5. The author of the poem beginning:

> "Little Jesus, wast Thou shy
> Once, and just so small as I?"

6. The population of Pittsburgh, Pennsylvania
7. The source of the quotation:

> "The quality of mercy is not strained,
> It droppeth as a gentle rain from heaven
> Upon the place beneath."

8. A biography of Charles A. Lindbergh
9. The pronunciation of *hospitable*
10. The life of Saint Ignatius

Catholic Book Week

Once a year pupils in Catholic schools throughout the United States celebrate Catholic Book Week. During this week we talk about good books that can be read by Catholics. We want every member of the class and all our friends to become book-conscious.

There are many ways in which we might celebrate Catholic Book Week. For one thing, we will surely wish to have a display of books and book jackets and to schedule talks about books.

4. Choral Speaking

There is no better way to memorize poetry than to recite it in a verse-speaking choir. In this book we have learned many poems to speak in unison, in groups, or in two parts. Our rendition has always been improved by tuning-up exercises.

Tuning-up Exercises

Breathing:

Here review all the exercises in breathing in this text. See pages 22, 50, 81, 113, 147, 163, 186.

Enunciation:

Practice o͝o as in *look*. Say *took, book, cook, nook, brook.*

Cook took the book.

Practice ō͞o as in *boom*. Say in different pitches *groom, doom, broom, tomb, bloom.*

Boom! The groom met his doom in the tomb.

Now let us turn to a poem written by the poet laureate of England, John Masefield. It may be done as a two-part number, with the heavy voices forming one group and the light voices a second group.

The West Wind

By John Masefield

Heavy Voices

It's a warm \ wind, the west wind, / full of birds' cries; //
I never hear the west wind / but tears are in my eyes. //
For it comes from the west lands, / the old brown hills, //
And April's in the west wind, / and daffodils. //

It's a fine land, the west land, / for hearts as tired as mine, //
Apple orchards blossom there, / and the air's like wine. //
There is cool green grass there, / where men may lie at rest, //
And the thrushes are in song there, / fluting from the nest. //

Light Voices

"Will you not come home, brother? you have been long away, //
It's April, / and blossom time, and white is the spray; //
And bright is the sun, brother, and warm is the rain,— //
Will you not come home, brother, / home to us again? //

"The young corn is green, brother, / where the rabbits run, //
It's blue sky, / and white clouds, and warm rain and sun. //
It's song to a man's soul, brother, / fire to a man's brain, //
To hear the wild bees and see the merry spring again. //

"Larks are singing in the west, brother, / above the green wheat, //
So will ye not come home, brother, / and rest your tired feet? //
I've a balm for bruised hearts, brother, / sleep for aching eyes," //
Says the warm wind, / the west wind, full of birds' cries. //

Heavy Voices

It's the white road westwards is the road I must tread //
To the green grass, / the cool grass, and rest for heart and head, //
To the violets / and the brown brooks / and the thrushes' song, //
In the fine land, / the west land, the land where I belong.

STUDY OF THE POEM

This is a lyric poem, dealing with the love of the poet for his own homeland, the western part of England.

The west wind is the wind that blows over his own shire, as they call the different counties in England. The poem expresses a homesickness for this lovely countryside now that spring is just about to welcome the first signs of summer. Every stanza is a picture. For instance, in the second stanza we can see the apple orchards in blossoming white, feel the air that is strong and fresh, and hear the song of the thrushes. What other pictures can you see in the other stanzas, especially the third and the fourth?

In the last stanza the poet determines to follow the call of the west wind and go back to his homeland, for that is where he belongs. For him it is the finest land to be found in all the world.

This poem is beautiful for its descriptions of the English countryside, but it is also worth memorizing because it represents the longing of every one for his own country, "the land where I belong," as the poet says. There are many poems of the homeland, poems that sing the poet's love for the place dearest to all, home.

Read the poem first in unison. Then divide the class into two divisions, heavy voices and light voices. Try to picture the countryside as you read the poem, and some of this appreciation will come into your voice. The pitch is medium, the time also is medium, neither quick nor slow, though when the beauty of the spring impresses one, he naturally quickens the time and pitch.

Look up the meanings of any words with which you are not familiar. Define the following words:

daffodils	thrushes	fluting
larks	bruised	balm

Tell what these phrases mean to you:

"White is the spray" "Fluting from the nest"
"Fire to a man's brain" "Sleep for aching eyes"

A Poem for May

Here is a lovely Mary poem to learn during May. The author of this poem is Father Faber, a convert to the Catholic faith. Divide the choir into three groups and read the poem slowly and reverently.

MOTHER OF MERCY

By Frederick William Faber

First Group
Medium Voices

Mother of Mercy! // day by day //
My love of thee / grows more \ and more ; //
Thy gifts / are strewn upon my way, //
Like sands \ upon the great seashore. //

Second Group Heavy Voices	Though poverty / and work \ and woe, // The masters / of my life may be, // When times / are worst, who does not know // Darkness / is light, \ with love of thee. //
Third Group Light Voices	But scornful / men have coldly said // Thy love / was leading me from \ God // And yet in this / I did but tread The very path my Savior \ trod. //
First Group Medium Voices or Unison	They know but little of thy worth // Who speak these heartless words to me; // For what did Jesus \ love / on earth // One half so tenderly \ as thee? //

5. Chapter Challenge

1. In a book .... we try to interest other pupils in worth-while books by telling about some striking incident.

2. A book review may be given .... or in ....

3. We keep a record of books read to help us .... them.

4. In judging a book we ask ourselves: (1) Did the book hold my ....? (2) Were the characters in the book ....? (3) Is the .... of the action vividly described? (4) Do the .... in the story seem likely to happen? (5) Is the book a .... book?

5. Two important sections in a library are the .... division and the .... division.

6. Books are classified according to the .... with which they deal.

7. Two widely used systems of numbering and classifying books are the .... System and the .... System.

8. The complete list of all the books in the library is known as the ....

9. The .... tells where a book is kept on the shelves.

10. Dictionaries, encyclopedias, atlases, and almanacs are .... books.

11. Catholic Book Week is celebrated .... a year.

12. "The West Wind" shows a poet's love for his ....

PART TWO

GRAMMAR

CHAPTER ONE Nouns

A noun is a name word.

KINDS OF NOUNS

1. *Proper Nouns and Common Nouns*

There are two main classes of nouns, *proper nouns* and *common nouns*.

A proper noun names a particular person, place, or thing.

A common noun names any one of a class of persons, places, or things.

Proper Nouns	Common Nouns
Joseph	boy
Chicago	city
Washington Monument	monument

All proper nouns begin with capital letters.

EXERCISE 1

Make a list of the nouns in the following sentences. Write *P* after each proper noun and *C* after each common noun:
1. Fresh fruit is shipped to Europe from the Canary Islands.
2. The early settlers of New England lived in towns and villages.
3. "The Pillar of the Cloud" was written by Cardinal Newman.
4. The frequent reading of the Bible should be encouraged in our Catholic families.
5. Indian summer comes late in the fall.
6. The Canon of the Mass follows the Preface.
7. Helen wrote a story about Saint Anthony.
8. Were the Spaniards friendly to the Indians?
9. The first school in the United States was opened by Catholics.
10. The principal money of the Indians was wampum.

11. Tourists from all parts of the United States visit Arlington National Cemetery.
12. Teak is a valuable forest product of India.

2. *Collective Nouns*

A collective noun denotes a group of persons, animals, or things considered as one.

When a bill is introduced in one of the houses of *Congress*, it is referred to a special *committee*. This *group* carefully examines the bill and weighs its good points and its bad points so as to determine whether or not it will be of benefit to the *nation*.

Note that the words *Congress, committee, group,* and *nation* name groups of persons as if they were one. These words, therefore, are collective nouns.

EXERCISE 2

Select the collective nouns in the following sentences:
1. The crew showed great heroism.
2. Our class is going on a picnic next week.
3. Timidly Barbara faced the assembly.
4. The organist played softly as the choir assembled.

5. Joseph Green was appointed chairman of the committee.
6. The flock of sheep was grazing on the hillside.
7. A troop of happy children passed our house.
8. The swarm of bees hovered around the rosebush.
9. The audience appreciated the concert.
10. We saw the jury enter the courtroom.
11. Over the hill marched a company of soldiers.
12. The congregation was most attentive to the sermon.
13. The battalion meets on Monday night.
14. At the last meeting our club elected new officers.
15. Our football team won many games last season.
16. The crowd cheered our band.
17. Over our school roared a squadron of airplanes.
18. The fire brigade rescued the men.

3. *Abstract Nouns*

An abstract noun expresses a quality, a condition, or an action apart from any object or thing.

Good books are the gateway to the world of *culture*. They are guides that help to develop *knowledge, appreciation,* and *love* of *beauty*.

The words *culture, knowledge, appreciation, love,* and *beauty* do not name persons, places, or things. They name qualities and are, therefore, abstract nouns.

Collective and *abstract* nouns are usually included among common nouns.

EXERCISE 3

Make a list of all the abstract nouns in the following sentences:
1. Washington was known for his courage.
2. Perseverance wins success.
3. Mary was admired for her truthfulness.
4. Kindness is a very pleasing virtue.
5. Gold cannot buy happiness.
6. Courtesy is expected of every good Catholic.
7. We should imitate the humility of our Lady.

8. Personal holiness is one of the objects of Catholic Action.
9. Blessed are the merciful, for they shall obtain mercy.
10. Saint Catherine of Alexandria is noted for her intellectual ability.
11. We admire the beauty of God's works.
12. The sincerity of Don Bosco won the affection of the young boys.
13. Knowledge is one of the gifts of the Holy Spirit.
14. Pleasure comes through toil.
15. The Little Flower spent a happy childhood surrounded by a loving family.
16. Faith, hope, and charity are the three theological virtues.
17. The Holy Eucharist gives peace and delight to the soul.
18. Does democracy mean that a person may do anything that he likes?

EXERCISE 4 [Test Your Skill]

Many abstract nouns may be formed from other words by adding such suffixes as *-ty, -ness, -hood, -ship, -ment, -ion, -ure,* and *-ity*. Make an abstract noun from each of the following by adding the proper suffix:

loyal	timid	assert	friend
familiar	agree	arrange	fellow
good	edit	certain	leader
wicked	convict	child	priest
human	fail	express	knight

EXERCISE 5

To what particular class does each of the following nouns belong? Use each noun in a sentence of your own:

club	charity	jury	herd
ambition	band	company	community
brightness	poverty	group	manhood
fleet	piety	squadron	gathering
covey	gratitude	guidance	wisdom

MODIFICATIONS OF NOUNS

1. *Person*

Person is that quality of a noun through which the speaker, the one spoken to, or the one spoken about is indicated.

The first person denotes the speaker.

I, your *teacher*, wish to help you.

The second person denotes the one spoken to.

Children, open your books.

The third person denotes the one spoken about.

The *boy* rose and addressed the *class*.

EXERCISE 6

Give the person of the italicized nouns in these sentences:

1. *John*, you may play the next selection.
2. Religious *toleration* was practiced in the Pennsylvania colony.
3. We, the *members* of the team, desire your support.
4. The new *stadium* will be completed this year.
5. Your work is good, my *child*.

SPOKEN TO   SPEAKER   SPOKEN ABOUT

6. Those *flowers* smell sweet.
7. *Esther*, where is your diary?
8. *Catholics* should be married at Mass.
9. We, your *friends*, promise our assistance.
10. Where did you purchase your book, *Margaret?*
11. *Lord*, have mercy on us.
12. I, the *chairman*, speak for the committee.
13. Return the *books* promptly.
14. The *officers* of the club are your representatives.

2. *Number*

Number is that quality of a noun which denotes whether it refers to one person or thing (singular number) or more than one (plural number).

The most important of the three *books* is the *book* on the table.

METHODS OF FORMING THE PLURAL

There are sixteen well-known rules for forming the plural of various types of nouns. If you wish to use the plural of some noun that does not seem to be included in the rules, consult the dictionary. You will find that a choice of plural forms is given for some words; for example, the plural of *wharf* may be *wharves* or *wharfs*. Study the following rules:

1. Most nouns form the plural by adding *s* to the singular.

Singular, picture; *plural*, pictures

2. For the sake of euphony, nouns ending in *s, x, z, ch*, and *sh* form the plural by adding *es* to the singular.

Singular, box; *plural*, boxes

3. Nouns ending in *y* preceded by a consonant form the plural by changing the *y* to *i* and adding *es*.

Singular, lily; *plural*, lilies

NOTE. Nouns ending in *y* preceded by a vowel form the plural by adding *s* to the singular.

Singular, monkey; *plural*, monkeys

NOUNS 219

4. The following nouns form the plural by changing the *f* or *fe* to *ves*: calf, elf, half, knife, leaf, life, loaf, self, sheaf, shelf, thief, wife, wolf.

5. Nouns ending in *o*:

a. All nouns ending in *o* preceded by a vowel form the plural by adding *s* to the singular.

Singular, trio; *plural*, trios

b. Nouns ending in *o* preceded by a consonant generally form the plural by adding *es* to the singular.

Singular, tomato; *plural*, tomatoes

c. Some nouns ending in *o* preceded by a consonant form the plural by adding *s* to the singular.

Singular, piano; *plural*, pianos

d. Some nouns ending in *o* preceded by a consonant may form the plural by adding *s* or *es* to the singular.

Singular, cargo; *plural*, cargoes or cargos

6. A few nouns form the plural by a change within the singular.

Singular, tooth; *plural*, teeth

7. A few nouns form the plural by the addition of the Old English ending *en*.

Singular, ox; *plural*, oxen

8. A few nouns retain the same form in the plural as in the singular.

SINGULAR	PLURAL	SINGULAR	PLURAL
series	series	sheep	sheep
deer	deer	species	species
swine	swine	salmon	salmon
trout	trout	cod	cod
corps	corps	Chinese	Chinese

9. When a name is preceded by a title, either the name or the title may be pluralized.

SINGULAR	PLURAL
Miss Keegan	The Misses Keegan or The Miss Keegans
Mr. Altman	The Messrs. Altman or The Mr. Altmans

NOTE. The title *Mrs.* is an exception to this rule, as it cannot be pluralized.

Singular, Mrs. Krum; *plural,* The Mrs. Krums

10. Some nouns taken from foreign languages retain their foreign plurals.

SINGULAR	PLURAL	SINGULAR	PLURAL
alumna	alumnae	alumnus	alumni
radius	radii	basis	bases
datum	data	crisis	crises
oasis	oases	bacterium	bacteria

11. Some nouns taken from foreign languages have both a foreign and an English plural. The English form is preferred.

SINGULAR	ENGLISH PLURAL	FOREIGN PLURAL
index	indexes	indices
tableau	tableaus	tableaux
formula	formulas	formulae
memorandum	memorandums	memoranda
vertex	vertexes	vertices

12. Some nouns are used only in the plural.

ashes	goods	scissors
banns	pliers	trousers
clothes	pincers	tweezers

13. Some nouns are plural in form, but singular in meaning and use.

| news | mumps | mathematics |
| measles | aeronautics | civics |

14. Compound nouns usually form the plural by adding *s* to the most important word or words.

SINGULAR	PLURAL
father-in-law	fathers-in-law
proofreader	proofreaders
maid of honor	maids of honor

15. Compound nouns ending in *ful* form the plural by adding *s* to the last syllable.

Singular, cupful; *plural,* cupfuls

NOTE. If more than one cup is filled, two words are used, as: two cups full, three cups full.

16. Numbers, letters, and symbols form the plural by adding 's.

Singular, 6; *plural*, 6's. *Singular*, a; *plural*, a's.

EXERCISE 7

Write the plural of each of the following:

chief	mousetrap	sheep	donkey
notebook	candy	chimney	fife
dwarf	knife	potato	victory
spoonful	Portuguese	remedy	peach
army	trumpet	reply	8
bicycle	man-of-war	sigh	fox
valley	statesman	cliff	sheaf
t	baby	folio	courtesy

EXERCISE 8

Arrange the following nouns in two columns. In the first column put the singular nouns, in the second the plural nouns:

bamboo	pulleys	shelf	stepladder
spectacles	molasses	manservant	passers-by
echoes	goose	Mr. Time	cuff
alumni	bucketful	tomatoes	workmen
roof	series	heiress	news
Iroquois	Japanese	hoof	forget-me-not

3. *Gender*

Gender is that quality of a noun by which sex is distinguished. There are three genders: masculine, feminine, and neuter.

The masculine gender denotes the male sex.

father, son

The feminine gender denotes the female sex.

aunt, mother

The neuter gender denotes objects that have no sex.

desk, sugar

A noun that may be taken as either masculine or feminine is considered masculine gender.

baby, cousin

HOW GENDER IS DISTINGUISHED

Gender may be distinguished in three ways:
1. By using a different word.
   Masculine, brother; *feminine*, sister
2. By using a different ending.
   Masculine, actor; *feminine*, actress
3. By changing part of the word.
   Masculine, salesman; *feminine*, saleswoman

EXERCISE 9

Arrange the following nouns in three columns. In one column write all the masculine nouns, in another feminine nouns, and in the third column copy neuter nouns:

prince	invalid	patron	student
widower	spectator	dictionary	emperor
blackboard	uncle	flag	grandson
queen	money	canoe	directress
clerk	witch	alumni	nephew
hostess	bride	Frances	countess
hero	goose	theater	waitress
Bernardine	radio	duck	aviator

4. *Case*

Case is that quality of a noun which shows its relation to some other word or words in the sentence. There are three cases: nominative, possessive, and objective.

Before a noun can be classified according to case, its use or syntax must be determined.

NOMINATIVE CASE

You have studied in former years the following uses of the nominative case:

Subject. A noun used as the subject of a finite verb is in the nominative case.

Our Lady's *birthday* is celebrated in September.
Morning *prayers* safeguard the day.
The *charity* of the first Christians impressed the pagan world.

Predicate Nominative. A noun used as a predicate nominative or subjective complement is in the nominative case.

The Himalayas are the highest *mountains* in the world.
Faith is God's most precious *gift* to us.
General Lee was appointed *commander in chief* of the Confederate forces.

REMEMBER: Nouns following copulative and passive verbs *take the same case* as the nouns before them *when both words refer to the same thing.*

Address. A noun used in direct address is in the nominative case.

Little *children*, love one another.
To whom shall we go, *Lord?*
Be of good heart, *son*, thy sins are forgiven thee.

EXERCISE 10

Give the syntax of each of the italicized nouns:
1. *Madagascar* is a large *island* off the coast of Africa.
2. *Father*, glorify Thy name.
3. My *brother* is a very ambitious *boy*.
4. *Edward* became the *mascot* of the team.
5. What is the *capital* of Ohio, *Eileen?*
6. You will pardon me, *Miss Elkins*, for the interruption.
7. *Stephen Moylan* was a prosperous Philadelphia *merchant*.
8. You have been very generous with your services, *Michael*.
9. The olive *branch* is a *symbol* of peace.

10. *Patriotism* is *love* of country.
11. No, *Andrew*, I did not forget.
12. In 1608 *Champlain* founded a settlement at Quebec.
13. The *kingdom* of God is the *kingdom* of peace.
14. What book shall I take with me, *Mother?*
15. Good *roads* are necessary for transportation.
16. The *angels* are pure *spirits*.
17. I am sorry, *Joseph*, but I cannot go with you.
18. *Palm Sunday* is the first *day* of Holy Week.
19. The *organ* is considered the most appropriate *instrument* for religious services.
20. *Kentucky* became the fifteenth *state* of the Union in 1792.
21. The *Constitution* of the United States is based on liberty and union.
22. *Master*, we have labored all night and have taken nothing.
23. What is your *question*, Peter?
24. *William*, did you hear the bell?
25. *James Madison* was the fourth *president* of the United States.

We will now take up two additional uses of the nominative case which we have not studied in previous years, the nominative in apposition and the nominative of exclamation.

NOMINATIVE IN APPOSITION

A noun in apposition is in the same case as the noun it explains.

An appositive is a word or a group of words that follows a noun or a pronoun and explains its meaning. An appositive denotes the same person, place, or thing as the noun it explains.

Mary, our *Mother*, intercedes for us.
The leader of the band is my friend *Paul*.

The noun *Mother* explains *Mary* and the noun *Paul* explains *friend*. Such nouns that explain are called appositives. Since *Mary* is the subject of the sentence and in the nominative case, the appositive *Mother* is also in the nominative case. Why is the noun *Paul* in the nominative case?

An appositive with its modifiers is separated from the rest of the sentence by commas if the phrase is *nonrestrictive*. By this we mean that it is merely some added information and that the sentence is clear without the appositive. Thus, *our Mother* is set off by commas because it is added information about Mary and the sentence is clear without this phrase. The noun *Paul*, however, is not set off by commas because it is *restrictive*. By this we mean that this word is necessary in order that we may know the exact person the writer has in mind. If *Paul* were set off by commas, it would indicate that the writer of this sentence had only one friend. Without the comma we know that Paul is simply one of many friends.

NOMINATIVE OF EXCLAMATION

A noun used independently to express a strong emotion is in the nominative case. This is known as the nominative of exclamation.

Happy little *girl!* Her parents have returned.
The *sacraments!* They are steppingstones to heaven.
Praise! Everybody likes praise.

In these sentences all the nouns in italics are used independently to express strong emotion. They are in the nominative case by exclamation. Note that this use differs from the nominative of address, for in the first sentence we are neither speaking to nor addressing the little girl, but are making a statement about her.

The nominative of exclamation is always followed by an exclamation point.

EXERCISE 11

Copy the following sentences, putting one line under each appositive and two lines under the word it explains:
1. Edward, the captain of the team, led the boys to victory.
2. My brother John went to Canada last week.
3. Longfellow, the American poet, wrote "Evangeline."
4. Balboa, the discoverer of the Pacific Ocean, was a Catholic.

5. Thomas Jefferson, our third president, was a Virginian.
6. Raymond, our cheerleader, taught us new cheers.
7. The mill, a battered ruin, stood near the river.
8. Mr. Campbell, the architect, planned our new home.
9. Rose and Kathleen, my cousins, are going to Florida.
10. My sister Josephine is not at home now.
11. Our school nurse, Miss Grady, is in the office.
12. Frisky, our dog, can do many tricks.
13. Mother, here is my classmate Anthony Burns.
14. One of the great saints of the Church is Saint Patrick, the Apostle of Ireland.
15. The writer of that article is Cecilia Mullen, the editor of our school paper.

EXERCISE 12

Select all the nouns in the nominative case and give the syntax of each:

1. Come with me, Edward.
2. Oriental draperies of purple and gold hung in the great hall of the castle.
3. God is our heavenly Father.
4. King Winter dresses all the trees in ermine.
5. Robert, I admire your foresight.
6. David and Thomas play football well.
7. Miss Quinn, the guardian of the children, is ill.
8. Most boys enjoy stories about Indians and pioneer settlers.
9. The happy boy! I rejoice with him.
10. Jane is an honor student in our class.
11. The tall, leafless trees stretched their branches toward the sky.
12. Did you have a pleasant time, Angela?
13. The Sahara, the largest desert in the world, is in Africa.
14. Delicate pink blossoms burst forth on the apple tree.
15. Mr. Mayer became an ardent advocate of Catholic Action.
16. Albert was our best pitcher last year.
17. Prayer! It is a ladder that reaches to God.

18. Mr. Jackson's estate is called Spruce Lawn.
19. Leo, my brother, tells us many delightful experiences of camp life.
20. Religion! What a comfort it is!
21. The Holy Spirit, the Paraclete, will remain with the Church forever.
22. We appreciate your kindness, Mr. Collins.
23. Detroit is the center of the automobile industry.
24. George McNamara was appointed chairman of the literature committee.
25. Who is that old gentleman?

POSSESSIVE CASE

A noun which expresses possession, ownership, or connection is in the possessive case.

Saint Joseph's workshop was in Nazareth.
Mary's days were full of merit.

The sign of the possessive case is the apostrophe and *s*.

METHODS OF FORMING THE POSSESSIVE CASE OF NOUNS

1. To form the possessive singular, add '*s* to the singular form of the noun.

student, student's; Mary, Mary's

2. To form the possessive plural of nouns ending in *s*, add the apostrophe only.

girls, girls'; ladies, ladies'

NOTE. If the plural form of the noun does not end in *s*, add '*s*.

men, men's; children, children's

3. Proper names ending in *s* usually form the possessive case by adding '*s* after words of one syllable and the apostrophe only after words of more than one syllable.

James, James's; Mr. Williams, Mr. Williams'

EXCEPTION. If the proper name is followed by a word beginning with *s*, the apostrophe only is used.

James' sled; Charles' shoes

4. In compound nouns the *'s* is added to the end of the word.

Noun	Singular Possessive	Plural Possessive
commander in chief	commander in chief's	commanders in chief's
sister-in-law	sister-in-law's	sisters-in-law's

EXERCISE 13

Write the possessive singular and the possessive plural forms of the following nouns:

child	pony	lady	mother
playmate	lad	Anthony	queen
Patricia	fox	pupil	uncle
sparrow	doctor	wolf	grandfather
shepherd	fairy	wife	editor in chief
father	passer-by	brother	farmer

EXERCISE 14

Select each noun which is in the possessive case and tell whether it is singular or plural in number:
1. The bird's nest was built in an old oak tree.
2. Leo's dog is a terrier.
3. John's father gave him lessons in woodcraft.
4. Have you read Shakespeare's *As You Like It?*
5. The boys' kites are flying high.
6. The children's drawings are attractive.
7. Saint Paul's letters encouraged the early Christians.
8. Girls' dresses are on sale today.
9. The grocer's truck is painted red.
10. Did Rita's brother give you that picture?
11. I like our baby's new shoes.
12. Is that pen your mother's or your sister's?
13. The teacher praised the students' work.
14. The doctor's report was given yesterday.
15. My sister-in-law's home is surrounded by many beautiful trees.
16. Saint Brendan's boat was built of hides.

SEPARATE OWNERSHIP   **JOINT OWNERSHIP**

17. Smith and Company's store will be closed for the holiday.
18. The Misses Tighe's apartment is on the second floor.
19. We often visit my grandparents' farm.
20. Barbara's hair is the prettiest in the room.

SEPARATE POSSESSION OR OWNERSHIP

If two or more nouns are used together to indicate separate ownership—that is, to show that each person possesses something independently of the other—the *'s* is used after each noun.

Longfellow's and Tennyson's poems were read.

JOINT POSSESSION OR OWNERSHIP

If two or more nouns are used together to indicate joint ownership—that is, to show that one thing is possessed by the group jointly—the *'s* is used after the last noun only.

That is John and Peter's boat.

EXERCISE 15

Indicate possession in the following sentences:
1. Black and Bower store is very large.
2. Helen and Maureen book reports are well written.
3. Mr. Martin and Mr. Faber daughters graduated last week.
4. Women and children shoes are sold here.
5. Edward and William parents are friends.
6. The secretary and treasurer report was read at the meeting.
7. We celebrated Mother and Father wedding anniversary last Thursday.

8. Raphael and Titian paintings are prominent in the world of art.
9. Take Margaret and Joan coats to them.
10. David and Philip room was redecorated.
11. Webster and Thorndike dictionaries are in our library.
12. Montcalm and Wolfe armies met on the Plains of Abraham.
13. Lucy and Irene teacher is from the South.
14. Saint Peter and Saint Paul feasts are celebrated on the same day.
15. Roger and Andrew salaries have been increased.
16. Ferdinand and Isabella reign was one of the most glorious in Spanish history.

OBJECTIVE CASE

You have studied in former years the following uses of the objective case:

Direct Object. A noun used as the direct object of a verb is in the objective case.

Mary and Joseph took the *Child* into Egypt.
Our Savior carried His *cross* to Calvary.
Mary Magdalene anointed the *feet* of Jesus.

Object of a Preposition. A noun used as the object of a preposition is in the objective case.

Jesus was found in the *Temple*.
The little children gathered around *Christ*.
Many pilgrims travel to *Lourdes*.

EXERCISE 16

Give the syntax of each italicized word in the following sentences:

1. She pledged her *loyalty* to the *club*.
2. Snow covered the *mountains*.
3. Mary stood beneath the *cross*.
4. The little girl gathered the *apples*.
5. The aviator sought his *safety* in *flight*.

6. Aunt Catherine made some *cookies* for us.
7. The regiment marched to the *front*.
8. Have you read the *story?*
9. Lent is a time of spiritual *growth*.
10. The Territory of Louisiana was purchased during Jefferson's *administration*.
11. Mary visited her *cousin* in *Boston*.
12. Saint Thomas Aquinas wrote beautiful hymns in *praise* of the *Holy Eucharist*.
13. The legislative department of our *government* makes the *laws*.
14. A small quantity of *salt* is placed in the *mouth* of the *person* at *baptism*.

OBJECTIVE IN APPOSITION

A noun in apposition is in the same case as the noun it explains.

The children knelt before the Infant, the *Babe* in the manger.

When the noun which an appositive explains is in the objective case, the appositive is also in the objective case. In this sentence *Babe* explains *Infant*. Since *Infant* is the object of the preposition *before*, both *Infant* and *Babe* are in the objective case.

EXERCISE 17

Select the appositives in each of the following sentences and name the noun which each explains:

1. The Roman Missal is written in Latin, the official language of the Church.
2. Father called Dr. Smith, our family physician.
3. Rosemary visited New York, the Empire State.
4. Father met Dorothy, my friend, at the station.
5. The Blessed Virgin was visited by Gabriel, an archangel.
6. In the Revolutionary War the Americans were assisted by the Polish patriot, Count Pulaski.
7. We read about Father Flanagan, the founder of Boys Town.
8. My father has just returned from Rome, the Eternal City.

9. Men admire the chivalry of Saint Thomas More, the English martyr.
10. We study about the catacombs, the burial places of the early Christians.
11. Last summer we visited Washington, the capital of the United States.
12. We pray to Saint Thomas Aquinas, the patron of Catholic schools.
13. The letter was addressed to Mr. Woods, the superintendent.
14. Margaret Ann Grier gave a report on Booth Tarkington's delightful story, *Seventeen*.
15. Those skates were given to my little sister Ruth.
16. John Alden was the youngest man on the *Mayflower*, the ship of the Pilgrims.
17. Our class prepared a radio sketch on Henry Stanley, the rescuer of David Livingstone.
18. The prize was awarded to Helen Welsh, my classmate.
19. Two of the Crusades were led by Saint Louis, King Louis IX of France.
20. From the car window she viewed those beautiful mountains, the Alps.
21. We stopped at New Orleans, the metropolis of the South.
22. I left the parcel with Mr. Sullivan, the salesman.
23. He pointed to Jupiter, the largest planet.
24. In winter we see the constellation of Orion, the great hunter.
25. John, write your surname, Donahue, first.

INDIRECT OBJECT

A noun used as the indirect object of a verb is in the objective case.

Some sentences contain two objects—the direct object, the receiver of the action, and another object which tells *to whom* or *for whom* the action is done. The latter object is called the *indirect object*.

Saint Joseph taught the *Child* the carpenter's trade.

The direct object of the verb *taught* is *trade*. *Child* tells to whom the action is directed and is the indirect object. The preposition *to* or *for* can usually be inserted before the indirect object without altering the meaning of the sentence. The indirect object is ordinarily placed between the verb and the direct object. Verbs which may take both direct and indirect objects are: *assign, bring, buy, deny, do, forbid, forgive, get, give, grant, hand, lend, offer, owe, pardon, pay, promise, read, refuse, remit, sell, send, show, sing, teach, tell, wish, write.*

EXERCISE 18

Point out the direct and the indirect objects in each sentence:
1. Michael told his brother an interesting story.
2. Eileen sent Doris an invitation to the party.
3. Vincent wished his friend every success.
4. Uncle Patrick brought the children a box of candy.
5. Father promised Henry a football.
6. Helen showed her brother her new game.
7. Who taught Blackie that new trick?
8. Mother paid Mr. Kelly the money for the bicycle.
9. Will you lend Agnes your camera?
10. Give Loretta the paper, John.

EXERCISE 19

Add an indirect object in each of these sentences:
1. Officer King gave a friendly smile.
2. Sister read an interesting story.
3. Will Martin lend his skates?
4. The agent sold the house.
5. Will you do a favor?
6. Rose Marie sang a song.
7. France sold the Louisiana Territory.
8. Mr. Keenan wrote a long letter.
9. The expressman brought the package this morning.
10. Queen Isabella gave aid.

ADVERBIAL OBJECTIVE

A noun used as an adverbial objective is in the objective case.

The Child Jesus was lost three *days.*

A noun which has the syntax or use of an adverb is called an *adverbial objective* and is in the objective case. Adverbial objectives usually answer the questions *when, where, how long, how much,* and *how far.*

EXERCISE 20

Point out the adverbial objectives in the following sentences:
1. My little niece is two years old.
2. Florida cost five million dollars.
3. The Scouts hiked four miles.
4. The children recite the rosary every day during October.
5. Mother worked three months on this picture.
6. We searched an hour for our dog Pong.
7. This package weighs twelve ounces.
8. The tourists traveled several days through the Sahara.
9. Francis moved to another city last week.
10. This ribbon is three yards long.
11. Father Damien labored a long time on Molokai Island.
12. Raymond walks to school every morning.
13. George weighs ninety-eight pounds.
14. Turn the map this way.

RETAINED OBJECT

A noun used as a retained object is in the objective case.

Saint Peter was given miraculous *power* by Christ.

The object of an active verb which is "retained" when the verb is changed to the passive voice is known as a *retained object.* In the active voice the sentence would read: Christ gave Saint Peter miraculous *power. Power* is the object of the active verb *gave* and of the passive verb *was given.*

EXERCISE 21

Point out the retained objects in the following sentences:
1. The family was left a large estate.
2. Elizabeth was given a hearty welcome.
3. Vincent was offered a position in Milwaukee.
4. Why was Walter refused admittance?
5. Marian has just been given a letter.
6. The class was shown the picture.
7. Timothy was awarded the medal.
8. Leo was paid his wages last night.
9. We have been told that story several times.
10. Mother was given a package.
11. Eugene was denied that privilege.
12. Frederick was asked a difficult question.
13. He was paid the money yesterday.
14. My brother has been promised a watch.
15. Dorothy was allowed more time for study.

OBJECTIVE COMPLEMENT

A noun used as an objective complement is in the objective case.

Certain transitive verbs may take two objects—a direct object and a second object explaining the direct object and completing the meaning of the verb. This second object is called an *objective complement*.

They named the boy *John*.

The direct object is *boy*. The objective complement, *John*, explains *boy* and completes the meaning of the verb. Some of the more common verbs which may take objective complements are *appoint, call, consider, declare, choose, make, name,* and *elect*.

EXERCISE 22

Point out the direct objects and the objective complements:
1. I consider Philip my friend.
2. The school chose Anthony leader.

3. Congress appointed George Washington commander in chief of the continental army.
4. They called the baby Annette.
5. Sister appointed Martin chairman.
6. Father will make John his secretary.
7. The Indians made Captain John Smith a prisoner.
8. The world considers Thomas Edison a great inventor.
9. The Pilgrims chose John Carver governor.
10. William Penn named the city Philadelphia.
11. Pope Pius XII proclaimed Catherine Labouré a saint.
12. God called the light day.
13. The boys elected Francis Loughran captain.
14. The judges declared Vincent winner.
15. Those children make their work play.

COGNATE OBJECT

A noun used as a cognate object is in the objective case.

I have fought a good *fight*.

Nouns that repeat the meaning implied by the verbs of which they are direct objects are called *cognate objects*. Look up the meaning of "cognate" in your dictionary.

EXERCISE 23

Name the cognate objects in the sentences below:
1. Washington prayed a heartfelt prayer at Valley Forge.
2. The old sea captain dreamed happy dreams of far-off lands.
3. My mother thinks happy thoughts of her school days.
4. The boys ran a close race.
5. The child laughed a merry laugh.

EXERCISE 24

Select the nouns in the objective case and give the syntax of each:
1. Andrew gave Michael, the driver of the car, the key.
2. The class elected Josephine president.

3. The Amazon valley has an equatorial type of climate.
4. We sailed from America, our native land.
5. The boys rode on bicycles the whole way.
6. The children named the cat Tabby.
7. The moon shone on the lake like a dull gold coin.
8. In olden days children walked miles to school.
9. John ran a desperate race.
10. Did you give Marita the message?
11. Mildred is sixteen years old today.
12. Edward was taught a lesson by that incident.
13. Nothing remained but the foundation of the house.
14. The cave afforded the hikers shelter.
15. My horse was awarded the blue ribbon.
16. My grandmother lived a long life.
17. The people welcomed Father White, the Apostle of Maryland.
18. Our class gathered leaves of all kinds.
19. Captain O'Hare waited days for news from home.
20. The children filled their baskets with golden daffodils, bright-colored tulips, and sweet-smelling hyacinths.
21. Have you given Peter the box?
22. In early days passengers traveled to the West by stagecoach.
23. Christ fed the multitude bread and fish.
24. Daniel Webster defended the Union in a great debate.
25. That story taught Joan a valuable lesson.
26. Mary and Joseph were refused shelter.
27. Some fine Catholic men have won fame on the gridiron.
28. Magnets do not attract wood, glass, rubber, paper, gold, silver, or cloth.
29. My grandmother lives in a large house on top of a hill.
30. The Temple of Jerusalem was completed by King Solomon, the son of King David.
31. Birds give their babies insects and worms.
32. God took upon Himself, in the person of our Lord Jesus Christ, our poor human nature.
33. The firm built many beautiful buildings.
34. The serfs were given protection against all enemies.

EXERCISE 25 [Test on Nouns]

Read the following selection and then answer the questions which follow:

[1] Harriet Beecher Stowe's famous novel, *Uncle Tom's Cabin*, greatly strengthened public opinion against slavery. [2] While the book gave its readers a somewhat exaggerated picture of the plight of the Negroes, it was a popular narrative and millions of copies were printed. [3] The book traveled many miles, for it was translated into foreign languages and sold to people abroad. [4] This story, class, is often considered an indirect cause of the Civil War.

1. Most of the nouns in the paragraph are in what person?
2. Write the singular number of the noun *Negroes* in the second sentence.
3. Which sentence contains a noun in the feminine gender?
4. From what word was the abstract noun *slavery* formed?
5. Find a collective noun in the paragraph.
6. Name a proper noun in the last sentence that is the name of a thing.
7. Why is the noun *narrative* in the second sentence in the nominative case?
8. Find a noun which is a nominative of address.
9. Which noun in the first sentence is the direct object?
10. In the fourth sentence which noun is the subject?
11. Find an adverbial objective in the third sentence.
12. Name a noun in the possessive case in this paragraph.
13. Find an appositive in the first sentence. In what case is this appositive?
14. Name the objects of the prepositions in the second sentence.
15. Why is *readers* in the second sentence in the objective case?

CHAPTER TWO **Pronouns**

A pronoun is a word used in place of a noun.

The repetition of nouns tends to make sentences monotonous. Hence we use pronouns to take the place of nouns. Which of the following sentences do you prefer?

> Ann's mother took *Ann* to the seashore.
> Ann's mother took *her* to the seashore.

The word to which a pronoun refers is called its antecedent. Thus, *Ann* is the antecedent of *her*.

PERSONAL PRONOUNS

A personal pronoun is a pronoun that denotes by its form the speaker, the person spoken to, or the person or the thing spoken of.

> *I* opened the book.
> Will *you* go with Leo?
> *She* gave *it* to *him*.

The pronouns of the first person (the speaker) are *I, mine, me, we, ours, us*. The pronouns of the second person (the person spoken to) are *you* and *yours*. The pronouns of the third person (the person or the thing spoken of) are *he, she, it, his, hers, its, him, her, they, theirs, them*.

Pronouns change form to denote case and number. Study the declension of the personal pronouns on page 240. The nominative case is used when the pronoun is the subject of a sentence or a predicate nominative. The possessive case is used to denote possession. The objective case is used for a direct object, an indirect object, or the object of a preposition.

> *We* are soldiers of Christ. *(Subject)*
> Mother sang to *her*. *(Object of preposition)*
> These books are *yours*. *(Possession)*

The personal pronouns *I* (first person), *you* (second person), and *he* (third person) are declined as follows:

DECLENSION OF THE PERSONAL PRONOUNS

First Person

Case	Singular	Plural
Nominative	I	we
Possessive	my,[1] mine	our,[1] ours
Objective	me	us

Second Person

Nominative	you	you
Possessive	your,[1] yours	your,[1] yours
Objective	you	you

Third Person

Nominative	he, she, it	they
Possessive	his, her,[1] hers, its	their,[1] theirs
Objective	him, her, it	them

---

[1] The possessive adjectives *my, our,* and so forth, are included in this table for the sake of completeness.

EXERCISE 26

Name the personal pronouns in the following sentences and give the person, the number, the gender, and the case of each:
1. Have I not met you before?
2. We played against them.
3. He is an intelligent student.
4. I shall see you at one o'clock.
5. Shall we carry it, Sister?
6. This tent will shelter us.
7. She gave me a gift.
8. He taught us the lesson.
9. Does she know about it?
10. Return the book to him immediately.
11. The saints and I are members of the same Church.
12. I think that pen is broken.

COMPOUND PERSONAL PRONOUNS

Compound personal pronouns are pronouns made by adding *self* or *selves* to certain forms of the personal pronouns.

FORMS OF THE COMPOUND PERSONAL PRONOUNS

	SINGULAR	PLURAL
First Person	myself	ourselves
Second Person	yourself	yourselves
Third Person	himself, herself, itself	themselves

A compound personal pronoun may be used to give emphasis to a noun or as an object referring to the subject.

An intensive pronoun is used to emphasize a preceding noun or pronoun.

A reflexive pronoun is used as an object referring to and denoting the same person or thing as the subject.

INTENSIVE PRONOUNS	REFLEXIVE PRONOUNS
He *himself* went.	The boy hurt *himself*.
You *yourself* must go.	You must prepare *yourself* daily.
We will do it *ourselves*.	We bought them for *ourselves*.

EXERCISE 27

Select the compound personal pronouns in the following sentences and tell whether they are intensive or reflexive:
1. You yourself are responsible for this.
2. Sit down and make yourselves comfortable.
3. He finished the project himself.
4. The boy helped himself to a large piece of cake.
5. I myself will accompany you.
6. Give yourself more time for study.
7. The teacher herself opened the door.
8. You must prepare yourself for the examination.
9. The Indian himself acted as guide.
10. Mary made herself a dress.
11. Elizabeth wrote every word of the story herself.

INTERROGATIVE PRONOUNS

An interrogative pronoun is a pronoun used in asking a question.

The interrogative pronouns are *who, which,* and *what.* They are used in both direct and indirect questions.

DIRECT QUESTIONS	INDIRECT QUESTIONS
Who lost the package?	He asked *who* lost the package.
Which is yours?	Mother wonders *which* is yours.
What did you see?	They asked us *what* we saw.

Who is used in speaking of persons. *Which* is used in speaking of persons and things, and to denote one of a definite class. *What* is used in speaking of things, and in seeking information.

DECLENSION OF WHO[1]

	SINGULAR	PLURAL
Nominative	who	who
Possessive	whose	whose
Objective	whom	whom

---

[1] The other interrogative pronouns are generally not inflected.

Study the interrogative pronouns in these sentences. Are the sentences direct or indirect questions?

Who lives in that house? *(Nominative)*
From *whom* did you receive the letter? *(Objective)*
Which of the stories do you prefer? *(Objective)*
What is the matter? *(Nominative)*
What did she do? *(Objective)*

EXERCISE 28

Pick out the interrogative pronouns in the following sentences and give the case of each:
1. What is in the basket?
2. Who is speaking?
3. To whom did Lawrence apply for the position?
4. Who is the governor of your state?
5. What were the causes of the Revolutionary War?
6. Which is the oldest city in the United States?
7. He asked with whom she went.
8. Which of the guides accompanied you?
9. What did the speaker say?
10. My father asked which we purchased.
11. Who was selected?
12. What is a ciborium?
13. Who were the evangelists?
14. Whom do you think they met on the road?
15. What are the pyramids?

RELATIVE PRONOUNS

A relative pronoun is a pronoun that does the work of a conjunction by joining to its antecedent the subordinate clause of which it is a part.

The relative pronouns are *who, which, what,* and *that.*

Baptism is a sacrament *which* cleanses us from original sin.

This is a complex sentence. The subordinate clause is joined to the principal clause by the relative pronoun *which.*

PRINCIPAL CLAUSE: Baptism is a sacrament
SUBORDINATE CLAUSE: which cleanses us from original sin.

Which is the subject of the verb in the subordinate clause and its antecedent is *sacrament*. The antecedent of a pronoun is the word in the main clause to which the pronoun refers.

The sentence could also have been written:

Baptism is a sacrament *and it* cleanses us from original sin.

In this sentence we have a conjunction and a pronoun in place of *which*. A relative pronoun does the work of a conjunction and of a pronoun.

Who refers to persons; *which* refers to animals and things; *that* refers to persons, animals, and things; *what* always refers to things. The relative pronoun *who* is declined as on page 242.

When the relative pronoun *what* is equivalent to *that which* or the *thing which*, it is called a double relative.

Give *what* you can to the poor.

In this sentence *what* is equivalent to *that which*. *That* is the antecedent and *which* is the relative pronoun. Hence *what* is called a *double relative*.

EXERCISE 29

Select the relative pronouns in the following sentences and point out the antecedent of each:

1. Children who practice devotion to Mary are sure of their salvation.
2. The altar boy, who serves the priest, makes the responses in the name of the people.
3. Those Christians who die for their faith are called martyrs.
4. Pupils who are industrious will succeed.
5. The student who wrote that story is in our class.
6. St. Augustine, which is the oldest town in the United States, was founded by the Spanish.
7. The dog that did the best trick was awarded a gold ribbon.
8. We are using books which were printed last year.
9. Have you distributed the papers that were on the desk?

10. I have just read the chapter that describes the battle.
11. Violet is a liturgical color that signifies penance.
12. Elephants are huge animals, which are hunted in the jungles of Africa.
13. The children played in the snow, which had fallen during the night.
14. Gold mines are located near Johannesburg, which is a modern city of South Africa.
15. Do you know the names of all the vestments that the priest wears at Mass?
16. The first miracle that our Lord performed was at a marriage feast.
17. The Mass is the same sacrifice that Christ offered on the cross.
18. What you said is true.
19. Imagine the joy with which the colonists received the news of the American victory.
20. The boy to whom you spoke is my cousin.

AGREEMENT OF RELATIVE PRONOUNS

A relative pronoun agrees with its antecedent in person, number, and gender, but its case depends upon its use in the subordinate clause.

We must obey our *pastors, who* have received authority from God.

The relative pronoun *who* is in the third person, plural number, masculine gender to agree with its antecedent, *pastors;* it is in the nominative case (even though *pastors* is in the objective case) because it is the subject of the verb *have received.*

EXERCISE 30 [Relative Pronouns Used as Subjects]

Name the relative pronoun in each sentence and tell its person, number, gender, and case:
1. Father Abram Ryan, who was a chaplain in the Civil War, wrote many inspiring poems.
2. The girl who had written the best report read it to the class.

3. Cyrus McCormick, who invented the reaper, was the son of a Virginia farmer.
4. Saint Thomas Aquinas, who is the patron of Catholic schools, was a learned Dominican teacher.
5. Samuel Slater, who built the first cotton mill in the United States, came from England.
6. The sanctuary lamp, which burns before the tabernacle, reminds us of the presence of Jesus within.
7. Everybody admires a child who is truthful.
8. Mary has a purse that is made of alligator skin.
9. Longfellow wrote the poem "Evangeline," which tells of the exile of the Acadians.
10. Henry Hudson discovered the river that bears his name.
11. Latria is a form of worship that is given to God alone.
12. Easter is the day that commemorates the Resurrection of Christ.
13. Baptism is a sacrament that can be received only once.
14. Green is a liturgical color that signifies hope.
15. Many ships stop at Cape Town, which is the chief seaport of South Africa.

EXERCISE 31 [Relative Pronouns Used as Direct Objects]

Name the relative pronoun in each sentence and tell its person, number, gender, and case:

1. The Church which Christ founded will last forever.
2. The costumes which the dancers wore were very colorful.
3. The bridge that we are crossing is the largest in the state.
4. I have read several books that Father Finn wrote.
5. Everyone admired the dress which Mary's grandmother made.
6. Joseph recited the poem that he had studied.
7. Has Leo accepted the position that your father offered him?
8. We enjoyed the cookies that your sister baked.
9. The Catholic faith is a gift that God has given us.
10. Is this the umbrella that you lost?
11. The cope is a cloak which the priest wears at Benediction.
12. In the field were many pretty flowers which we gathered.

13. Much of the corn which our country produces is fed to animals.
14. Mr. Kane enjoyed the trip that he made.
15. People laughed at the steamboat that Robert Fulton invented.

EXERCISE 32 [Relative Pronouns Used as Objects of Prepositions]

Name the relative pronoun in each sentence and tell its person, number, gender, and case:

1. The man for whom my father works is kind and generous.
2. The country through which we traveled was dotted with prosperous farms.
3. The cotton from which this dress was made came from Texas.
4. The boy for whom I voted is dependable.
5. The wagon into which we climbed was filled with hay.
6. A compass is an instrument by which directions are determined.
7. Confirmation is a sacrament through which we receive the Holy Spirit.
8. The altar is a sacred table upon which Mass is offered.
9. Good Friday is the day on which Christ died.
10. This is the girl of whom I spoke.
11. Is he the man from whom we bought our house?
12. The corporal is a linen cloth upon which the chalice rests during Mass.

EXERCISE 33 [Relative Pronouns Used as Possessive Adjectives]

Point out the possessive forms of the relative pronoun in these sentences and give the person, number, and gender of each:

1. The lady whose purse I found gave me a reward.
2. Joseph, whose brothers plotted against him, became governor of Egypt.
3. Helen Jordan, whose home I visited last summer, has moved to Canada.

4. The children whose voices you now hear are practicing for a Christmas play.
5. The natives of central Africa, whose habits we study, are backward in civilization.
6. On the platform stood a girl whose face radiated happiness.
7. Is he the farmer whose cow won the prize at the state fair?
8. It was Dorothy whose poem you read.
9. Isn't that the man whose house burned?
10. He was a soldier whose courage never wavered.
11. Marco Polo was a young traveler whose father was a rich trader.
12. There goes Joseph Carney, whose father is our coach.
13. Pray often to the saint whose name you bear.
14. I have great admiration for Saint Agnes, whose love of purity won for her a martyr's crown.
15. Information on the protection of our national forests was submitted by Timothy Nabb, whose father is a forest ranger.

EXERCISE 34 [General Exercise on Relative Pronouns]

Select the relative pronouns in the following sentences and explain the case and agreement of each with its antecedent:
1. The man who gave the lecture lives in Holland.
2. Many locomotives that are used in South Africa are manufactured in our country.
3. The Our Father, which Christ taught to His apostles, contains seven petitions to God.
4. Most skins that are used for leather products are imported.
5. At Valley Forge the soldiers had only rude huts which offered little protection from the sleet and snow.
6. Andrew Jackson, who was our seventh president, was a military hero.
7. In Georgia I met a man who knew your father.
8. Samuel Morse, who invented the telegraph, promoted the growth of communication.
9. The monks built schools in which they taught the young.
10. Have you seen the bookrack which my brother made?

11. During December we celebrate the Feast of Saint Stephen, who was the first martyr.
12. I found the pen that I had lost.
13. We sent them the books that they ordered.
14. He showed me the house in which William Penn lived.
15. Are they the boys with whom your brother plays?
16. Saint Bernard composed many beautiful prayers to the Blessed Virgin, to whom he had great devotion.
17. I saw the ship that was launched yesterday.
18. Beside the barn stood a silo in which green corn was stored.

COMPOUND RELATIVE PRONOUNS

Compound relative pronouns are formed by adding *ever* or *soever* to *who, whom, which,* and *what.*

Like *what,* the compound relatives contain their own antecedents.

Whoever (the one who) finds the book will return it.
Take *whatever* (the things which) you need.

EXERCISE 35

Explain the use of each compound relative pronoun:
1. Whoever asks for an interview will be given consideration.
2. Whoever answers the question will be awarded a prize.
3. We may invite whoever seems interested in the work.
4. You should appreciate whatever is done for you.
5. Deliver the package to whoever comes to the door.
6. Give assistance to whoever needs it.
7. Pierre was courteous toward whoever spoke kindly to him.
8. My brother will help whomever you appoint.
9. Janice will welcome whomever you send.
10. You may take whomever you wish.
11. You may purchase whatever you need for the hike.
12. Select whichever you desire.
13. Eleanor made friends with whomever she met.
14. He will be satisfied with whatever you give him.
15. Always do whatever your parents command.

ADJECTIVE PRONOUNS

An adjective pronoun is a pronoun that may also be used as an adjective.

PRONOUNS	ADJECTIVES
These are mine.	*These* books are mine.
Many were present.	*Many* people were present.
Each may go.	*Each* child may go.

Some of the types of adjective pronouns are: (1) demonstrative pronouns, (2) indefinite pronouns, (3) distributive pronouns, and (4) possessive pronouns.

1. *Demonstrative Pronouns*

A demonstrative pronoun is a pronoun that points out a definite person, place, or thing.

The demonstrative pronouns are *this, that, these,* and *those.*

This is my new Scout knife.
That is a statue of Saint Anthony.

This and *these* are used for objects that are near. *That* and *those* are used for distant objects. The demonstratives may be used as pronouns or adjectives.

EXERCISE 36

Select the demonstratives in the following sentences and tell whether they are adjectives or pronouns:
1. This horse is strong.
2. That was a happy day for us.
3. Do you like these?
4. That castle by the sea is very old.
5. Those books are for sale.
6. Is that dog a great Dane?
7. This is an interesting story.
8. Are these your glasses?
9. This is my first attempt.
10. That vine still clings to the wall.

11. That child has a new coat.
12. These are mine; I think those are yours.
13. I lost that book you lent me.
14. That man is a good doctor.
15. That should be avoided.
16. That seems true of people everywhere.
17. This is the exact information I need.
18. These apples taste good.
19. These flowers are very fragrant.
20. I do not like those.
21. Is that tall young girl Mary Lee?
22. This is my opinion.
23. Have you ever seen this before?

2. *Indefinite Pronouns*

An indefinite pronoun is a pronoun that points out no particular person, place, or thing.

Somebody left this message.
Has *everybody* prepared his work?
Everything is in order.
Nothing has been broken.

There are, in all, about thirty indefinite pronouns. The most commonly used are:

all	both	much	several
another	everybody	no one	some
any	everyone	nobody	somebody
anybody	everything	none	someone
anyone	few	one	something
anything	many	same	such

EXERCISE 37

Give the syntax of the indefinite pronouns in the following sentences:
1. Everybody has done his best.
2. Several passed here today, but nobody stopped.

3. Everyone is doing the same work.
4. Many took part in the play.
5. Much of the work has been accomplished.
6. Few seem interested in the new project.
7. I gave some of it to the old man.
8. Nobody answered his call.
9. Both are mine.
10. Some were destroyed by the beetles.
11. Much is being done by the Catholic missionaries.
12. Everybody in that family is a weekly communicant.
13. Anyone may give his opinion.
14. He helped many by his charity.
15. Put everything in order before you leave.
16. Has anybody seen Mildred?
17. Something must be done about the matter.
18. All of us enjoyed the circus.
19. You may invite one of your friends.

3. *Distributive Pronouns*

A distributive pronoun is a pronoun that refers to each person, place, or thing separately.

The distributive pronouns are *each, either,* and *neither.*

Each has his own faults.
Either may go.
Neither of those books is mine.

EXERCISE 38

Give the syntax of the distributive pronouns in the following sentences:
1. Each took a long walk.
2. Neither met the requirements.
3. Either of your plans pleases me.
4. I shall take neither of those books.
5. Each has a special duty.
6. Neither was responsible for the accident.

7. Either of the machines will be sent.
8. Neither had permission.
9. Neither heard of the report.
10. I gave each a picture.
11. I do not remember either of those boys.
12. Will either of these plans interest you?
13. Each told a different story.
14. Neither of them was present at the meeting.

4. *Possessive Pronouns*

A possessive pronoun is a pronoun used to denote possession or ownership by the speaker, the person spoken to, or the person or the thing spoken of.

The pronouns *mine, ours, yours, his, hers, its,* and *theirs* are sometimes called independent possessives because they may be used alone to take the place of nouns. *My, our, your, his, her, its,* and *their* modify nouns. They are sometimes called possessive adjectives to distinguish them from the independent possessives. A possessive adjective indicates ownership, just as a noun in the possessive case indicates ownership.

My book is on the table.   *John's* book is on the table.

When a possessive pronoun or a possessive noun is used independently, the case is determined by its use in the sentence.

John's is on the table.	*Mine* is on the table.	*(Subject)*
Did you see *John's?*	Have you seen *his?*	*(Direct object)*
The book is *John's.*	The book is *theirs.*	*(Predicate nominative)*

In this book we shall call the independent possessives (those that take the place of nouns) possessive pronouns. The possessives that modify nouns will be called possessive adjectives.

Possessive Pronouns	Possessive Adjectives
Mine is new.	*My* hat is new.
Hers is broken.	*Her* pen is broken.
That is *his.*	That is *his* car.
Ours is painted.	*Our* house is painted.
Did you see *theirs?*	Did you see *their* radio?

EXERCISE 39

Select the possessives in the following sentences and determine whether they are pronouns or adjectives:
1. Patricia gave me her watch.
2. They traded theirs for ours.
3. Its nest was destroyed.
4. Jean deposited her money in the school bank.
5. Did you write your exercise?
6. Their plans are better than ours.
7. I think that is his.
8. Her work is superior to yours.
9. Our friends have arrived.
10. He paid the agent his fee.
11. Your examination was a success.
12. The pigeon broke its wing.
13. Jesus met His Mother on the way to Calvary.
14. That card is not mine.
15. The children waved their pennants in the air.

THE CORRECT USE OF PRONOUNS

1. *Drill on the Nominative Case*

SUBJECT OF A VERB

A pronoun used as the subject of a finite verb is in the nominative case.

Elizabeth and (I, me) arrived early.

The correct form is: Elizabeth and *I* arrived early.

EXERCISE 40

Select the correct form of the personal pronoun in each of the following sentences and give the reason:
1. John and (he, him) were invited.
2. (She, her) and (I, me) washed the dishes.
3. Helen and (I, me) will eat lunch together.
4. Mother and (I, me) packed the lunch.

5. Albert and (he, him) raked the leaves yesterday.
6. (He, him) and (I, me) studied our history lesson.
7. Joan and (she, her) were absent from class.
8. Jane and (she, her) picked flowers in the field.
9. (He, him) and (I, me) will play ball in the morning.
10. George and (he, him) came early.
11. Mother and (I, me) attended the ceremony.
12. Were Ruth and (she, her) present?
13. Dr. Smith and (he, him) are in Florida.
14. (She, her) and Marian are writing letters.
15. (He, him) and the captain come here every summer.
16. Margaret and (she, her) are practicing their songs.
17. Therese and (I, me) wore colonial costumes at the party.
18. Did Martin or (he, him) give you the message?

PREDICATE NOMINATIVE

A pronoun used as a predicate nominative or subjective complement is in the nominative case.

It is (he, him).

The correct form is: It is *he*.

EXERCISE 41

Copy the following sentences, selecting the correct form of the personal pronoun in each. Give the reason for your choice:
1. Could it have been (I, me)?
2. It is (they, them) who deserve the credit.
3. Mother imagined it was (he, him).
4. Was that (she, her) at the door?
5. Father thought it was (we, us) who entered the cabin.
6. It was not (he, him) who accompanied us.
7. Was it (they, them) who called?
8. Is it (she, her) at the door?
9. I think it is Leo and (he, him).
10. It was (she, her) who found the lost child.
11. Was it (he, him) who washed the car?
12. It was not (they, them) who did it.
13. Who is calling? It is (she, her).
14. It must be (he, him) who is mistaken.
15. Was it John or (she, her) who ate the fruit?
16. Is it (we, us) whom you suspect?
17. John thought it was Eleanor and (she, her) who made the costumes.
18. It must have been (he, him) whom you saw.

ADDITIONAL DRILLS ON THE NOMINATIVE CASE

EXERCISE 42

Rewrite, omitting the incorrect form of the pronoun:
1. William and (I, me) did the work this morning.
2. It was (they, them) who sent for us.
3. My friend and (I, me) made a snow man.
4. Neither Ralph nor (I, me) went to the meeting.
5. (We, us) went into the garden.
6. Was it (he, him) on the porch?
7. Did you know the visitors were (they, them)?
8. Eleanor and (she, her) are going this afternoon.
9. Mr. Barry and (he, him) did not arrive.

10. (He, him) and (I, me) are brothers.
11. Mother and (I, me) went for a ride.
12. (He, him) and (I, me) have been friends for many years.
13. Who answered the letter? It was (I, me).
14. Father and (we, us) walked through the woods.
15. I knew it was (she, her) when I heard her voice.

EXERCISE 43

Copy and fill in each blank with the correct form of a personal pronoun. Give the reason for your choice:
1. It was .... who made the fudge.
2. Mother and .... will go with you.
3. Thomas and .... have seen that performance twice.
4. Down the street ambled Edward and ....
5. It was .... whom you saw.
6. Father and .... planned a trip to the mountains.
7. Was it .... who decorated the room?
8. My sister and .... are in the canoe.
9. Robert and .... are visiting in Norfolk.
10. Dolores and .... arranged the bookcase.
11. That was ....
12. Here are James and ....
13. In the boat were Thomas, Edwin, and ....
14. Either Rose or .... will sing tonight.
15. Was it .... who closed the window?
16. Sara and .... have an aunt in Miami.
17. .... and .... will assist you.

2. *Drill on the Objective Case*

DIRECT OBJECT

A pronoun used as the direct object of a verb is in the objective case.

God loves (we, us) with an everlasting love.
The correct form is: God loves *us* with an everlasting love.

EXERCISE 44

Copy the following sentences, selecting the correct form of each pronoun. Give the reason for your choice:
1. Father took Peter and (I, me) to the baseball game.
2. Mr. Green drove Francis and (he, him) to the station.
3. Frederick invited Jane and (she, her) to the party.
4. The coach called Albert and (I, me).
5. Will you take Thomas and (she, her) to the concert?
6. They told Ellen and (I, me).
7. Rose saw (he, him).
8. We have heard (they, them) before.
9. We passed Eileen and (she, her) on the old road.
10. Mother dressed Margaret and (she, her) in gypsy costumes.
11. The school nurse directed Anne and (she, her) to the clinic.
12. Maureen thanked Mother and (he, him) for the gift.
13. Did you recognize Dorothy and (I, me)?
14. They surprised our teacher and (we, us).
15. The stems of these flowers will be too long for the vase unless we cut (they, them).

INDIRECT OBJECT

A pronoun used as the indirect object of a verb is in the objective case.

Father bought my brother and (I, me) a new boat.

The correct form is: Father bought my brother and *me* a new boat.

EXERCISE 45

Copy the following sentences, using the correct form of each pronoun. Give the reason for your choice:
1. The dog brought (I, me) the stick.
2. Mother promised (we, us) some fruit.
3. Father wrote Mother and (we, us) an interesting letter.
4. Lend (he, him) your skates.
5. I told Paul and (he, him) the story.

6. The team bought (he, him) a watch.
7. The clerk showed Angela and (she, her) the new magazine.
8. Uncle gave both Edward and (I, me) new football suits.
9. Give Arthur and (I, me) the package you have.
10. The old sailor showed (they, them) his curio.
11. You have rendered my sister and (I, me) a service.
12. Mr. O'Brien gave (she, her) the information she needed.
13. Aunt Marie sent (we, us) a new radio.
14. The mailman brought Jane and (he, him) a pleasant surprise.
15. Will you lend (we, us) your camera?

OBJECT OF A PREPOSITION

A pronoun used as the object of a preposition is in the objective case.

Regina ran toward (we, us).

The correct form is: Regina ran toward *us*.

EXERCISE 46

Copy the following sentences, using the correct form of each pronoun. Give the reason for your choice:
1. The game was won by (they, them).
2. The boys were gathering nuts with Father and (he, him).
3. These paintings were done by (she, her).
4. The dog rushed past my sister and (he, him).
5. Dorothy sits beside (I, me).
6. I rode with the captain and (he, him).
7. Many people think well of (he, him).
8. I have already spoken to (she, her).
9. Is John going with (they, them)?
10. The officer signaled to (they, them).
11. I received a letter from (she, her).
12. The little child ran toward (they, them).
13. This is a secret between Anita and (I, me).
14. Everybody was invited except (I, me).
15. I played tennis with (they, them).

ADDITIONAL DRILLS ON THE OBJECTIVE CASE

EXERCISE 47

Rewrite, omitting the incorrect form:
1. Mary took a picture of (we, us).
2. They expected (he, him).
3. Between you and (I, me), I think she is right.
4. Who will go for (she, her)?
5. Father bought Paul and (he, him) a motion-picture camera.
6. They gave Mother and (we, us) the tickets.
7. Aunt Lucy made (I, me) a new dress.
8. The candy was divided between Jane and (I, me).
9. Who did you say went with (they, them)?
10. The old lady was very kind to (he, him).
11. They refused (he, him) admittance.
12. Thomas took Frederick and (he, him) for a ride.
13. We were playing with (they, them).
14. Sit between (she, her) and (I, me).
15. Father lent (we, us) the canoe.

3. *The Case Used after* Than *and* As

After the conjunctions **than** and **as** there is an omission of words. The pronoun following these conjunctions must be in the same case as the word with which it is compared.

He is older than (I, me).

The correct form is: He is older than *I* (am old).

I know Anne better than (she, her).

The correct form is: I know Anne better than (I know) *her*.

or I know Anne better than *she* (knows her).

EXERCISE 48

Select the correct form of the pronoun:
1. Joseph is stronger than (he, him).
2. Mother gave me as much as (she, her).
3. We like Joseph better than (he, him).

4. Andrew is as tall as (I, me).
5. Jean plays better than (she, her).
6. I gave him as much as (they, them).
7. John is a better player than (I, me).
8. They arrived later than (we, us).
9. No one was so surprised as (I, me).
10. Patricia writes better than (he, him).
11. Mary is as studious as (she, her).
12. He runs faster than (I, me).
13. You are younger than (he, him).
14. I know that he is stronger than (I, me).
15. You are as tall as (I, me).
16. Is he taller than (she, her)?
17. He was as successful as (they, them).
18. No one was more pleased than (I, me).
19. She certainly plays the violin better than (he, him).
20. Paul drives the car as well as (he, him).

EXERCISE 49

Fill in the blanks with the proper forms of the personal pronouns. Give the reason for your choice:

1. We saw .... at the seashore.
2. Mother bought the skates for ....
3. We played tennis with George and ....
4. Margaret knitted .... a jacket.
5. Mr. Benson sold .... the yacht.
6. The paper was read by ....
7. The pictures were taken by Robert and ....
8. Henry rode with ....
9. Eugene told .... and .... about his trip.
10. The visitor sat between .... and ....
11. All the boys in our class have bicycles but ....
12. I have written .... a long letter.
13. This boy has brought .... the message.
14. Helen came with .... to the theater.
15. She stayed with .... at the seashore.

16. Mary went with Edith and ....
17. Did the postman bring .... a letter?
18. The coach is waiting for Thomas and ....

GENERAL EXERCISES ON PERSONAL PRONOUNS

EXERCISE 50

Give the syntax of each pronoun in italics:
1. *They* went on a hike.
2. *We* girls are forming a camera club.
3. Alfred gave *me* the exact address.
4. *She* sang well tonight.
5. The candy was divided among *us* boys.
6. The mailman brought *us* the delightful news.
7. It must have been *they* who called.
8. *They* do not know where he went.
9. The little boy ran toward *him*.
10. Virginia and *I* have studied our parts carefully.
11. Gertrude knew it was *she*.
12. Robert taught *us* boys many new tricks.
13. Uncle George invited *them* on the trip.
14. Therese came with Grace and *me*.
15. Was it *he* who threw the ball?

EXERCISE 51

Pick out the pronouns in the following sentences and tell whether they are in the nominative case or the objective case:
1. You did well today, Albert.
2. He received congratulations from his friends.
3. Give me the ball.
4. My mother said that she might go with us.
5. Who said it?
6. It is the largest tree in the park.
7. They met Donald and me at the airport.
8. Mary Ellen invited her and me to the party.
9. How did you know it was he?

10. Robert said he could play with us tomorrow.
11. Give him the message as soon as he enters.
12. The fisherman told them where he found the canoe.
13. He and I were invited to the meeting.
14. The teacher spoke to him and me.
15. Alice is going with me.
16. The librarian gave me the book.
17. Joseph answered more intelligently than he.
18. We girls are going to the mountains for our vacation.
19. Mary is as accurate as she.
20. Where did you and she go this morning?

4. Drill on Interrogative Pronouns

The interrogative pronoun *who* is used when the sentence requires a pronoun in the nominative case.

The interrogative pronoun *whom* is used when the sentence requires a pronoun in the objective case.

Who taught you your first prayer? *(Subject)*
For *whom* did Christ die on the cross? *(Object of preposition)*

EXERCISE 52

Fill in each of the blanks with *who* or *whom*:
1. .... administers the sacrament of holy orders?
2. .... called me?
3. To .... did you send the book?
4. With .... did Father go?
5. .... was that violinist?
6. .... is your family physician?
7. .... showed it to you?
8. To .... did the Blessed Virgin appear at Fatima?
9. .... is the man that owns the airplane?
10. By .... was the cotton gin invented?
11. With .... are you speaking?
12. .... told you that story?
13. .... did you send to the store?

14. .... bought the house next door?
15. To .... shall I write for the position?
16. .... have you consulted?
17. To .... did you give the toys?
18. .... does he resemble?
19. .... did you call?
20. .... circumnavigated the globe?

5. *Drill on Relative Pronouns*

The relative pronoun *who* is used when the pronoun is the subject of a verb.

The relative pronoun *whom* is used when the pronoun is the object of a verb or of a preposition.

Saint John was the apostle *who* stood with Mary on Calvary.
Saint John was the apostle *whom* Jesus loved best.

EXERCISE 53

Select the correct form of the relative pronoun and give the reason for your choice:
1. The boy (who, whom) we saw is my brother.
2. Jane traveled with the girl (who, whom) lives next door.
3. I sent for the boy to (who, whom) you referred.
4. The young priest (who, whom) was just ordained has been sent to China.
5. Alice is the girl (who, whom) I know.
6. Give the letter to the one to (who, whom) it is addressed.
7. Give the package to (whoever, whomever) is in charge.
8. He is a boy (who, whom) we can trust.
9. We admire pupils (who, whom) study.
10. (Whoever, whomever) perseveres will be rewarded.
11. This is the boy (who, whom) won first prize.
12. They will employ (whoever, whomever) you suggest.
13. The man (who, whom) we notified called immediately.
14. The musicians (who, whom) played at our school live in Troy.
15. The patron (who, whom) we chose is Saint Joseph.

16. It was Washington (who, whom) encouraged the soldiers at Valley Forge.
17. We do not know the boy (who, whom) will be chosen.
18. Is there anyone (who, whom) we can send?
19. I know the man (who, whom) made that address.
20. Alberta is the girl of (who, whom) I spoke.

6. Agreement with Distributive and Indefinite Pronouns

A pronoun or a possessive adjective must agree with its antecedent in person, number, and gender.

The distributive pronouns *each, either, neither,* and the indefinite pronouns *one, anyone, no one, anybody, nobody, everyone, everybody, someone, somebody* are always singular. The pronouns or possessive adjectives referring to these pronouns as antecedents must be singular.

Such indefinite pronouns as *all, both, few, many, several,* and *some* are generally plural. Pronouns and possessive adjectives referring to these pronouns as antecedents must be plural.

Everyone must carry (his, their) own books.
All of the boys carried (his, their) own books.

The correct forms are:

Everyone must carry *his* own books.
All of the boys carried *their* own books.

EXERCISE 54

Select the correct form in each of the following sentences. Give the reason for your choice:
1. Each of those women drives (her, their) own car.
2. Each must do (his, their) best work.
3. They found everything in (its, their) place.
4. If anyone wishes to enter the contest, let (him, them) raise (his, their) hand.
5. Everyone has (his, their) own plans.
6. Both have (his, their) licenses.
7. Neither of the men likes (his, their) appointment.

266 VOYAGES IN ENGLISH, SEVENTH YEAR

8. Somebody lost (his, their) notebook.
9. Everybody should love (his, their) neighbor.
10. Nobody wrote (his, their) paragraph until (he, they) had made an outline.
11. Everyone may go to (his, their) classroom now.
12. One of the books is without (its, their) jacket.
13. Not one of the girls brought (her, their) tennis racket.
14. Each has (his, their) own peculiar style.
15. Someone has lost (his, their) locker key.
16. Many have already purchased (his, their) tickets for the game.
17. Has anybody (his, their) pen with him?
18. Each can do (his, their) best if (he, they) tries.

7. *The Correct Use of* Nothing *and* Anything

When a sentence contains a negative, such as *not* or *never*, use *anything* to express a negation.

Thus we say "I didn't do anything" to show that we did not do anything. If we say "I didn't do nothing," we really mean that we did do something.

I should not have said (nothing, anything) about it.

The correct form is: I should not have said *anything* about it.

The following form is also correct: I should have said *nothing* about it.

EXERCISE 55

Fill in the blanks with *nothing* or *anything*:
1. We never heard .... so interesting before.
2. He did .... to relieve the situation.
3. .... but hardware is sold here.
4. There wasn't .... of great value in the package.
5. Irene did .... but read the whole day.
6. Harry never said .... about his last trip to the mountains.
7. .... but prayer helped him.

8. .... will interfere with my going.
9. Hasn't .... been said about the procession?
10. .... ventured, ... gained.
11. .... that is done hastily is done well.
12. .... you say will convince me.
13. You may not have .... from this counter.
14. .... annoys Joan.
15. Hasn't that boy .... to do?
16. I don't know .... about the picture.

8. *Agreement of Compound Personal Pronouns*

Compound personal pronouns agree with their antecedents in person, number, and gender. They have two distinct uses, as intensive and as reflexive pronouns.

Our Lord *Himself* trained the apostles. *(Intensive)*
We should pray for *ourselves* and for all men. *(Reflexive)*

EXERCISE 56

In each of the following sentences insert the correct compound personal pronoun:
1. We cannot see .... as others see us.
2. He .... told me the story.
3. Marian .... is at fault.
4. James bought .... a new suit.
5. The explorers found .... in a dense thicket.
6. The child hit .... with the hammer.
7. We shall arrange the stage ....
8. None but the pilot .... realized the danger.
9. The girls entertained .... for hours with the puzzle.
10. My father .... told me that story.
11. The committee disagreed among ....
12. The boy muttered to ....
13. The apostles .... preached to the people.
14. Jane made .... comfortable.
15. The lifeguard did it ....

EXERCISE 57 [Test on Pronouns]

Read the following selection and then answer the questions which follow:

[1] Christ worked His first public miracle at a wedding feast to which He and His Mother had been invited. [2] During the celebration the wine failed but no one noticed this except Mary. [3] As she knew that Christ would grant whatever she asked, the Blessed Virgin told Him of the difficulty. [4] Nearby were several of the water jars which were found in all of the Jewish homes. [5] Our Lord instructed the waiters to fill each of these with water. [6] Then He told them to draw out the liquid and carry it to the chief steward, who always tasted the wine himself. [7] Finding it exceptionally good, the steward called the bridegroom. [8] Both were surprised, but neither of them knew what had occurred. [9] Who would have suspected that Christ would work a miracle to solve a problem of theirs?

1. What is the gender of the personal pronoun in the seventh sentence?
2. Which of the pronouns in the third sentence are in the nominative case? Which are in the objective case?
3. Name a personal pronoun that is the object of a preposition.
4. Find a compound personal pronoun in the paragraph. Is it an intensive or a reflexive pronoun?
5. Give the syntax of the indefinite pronoun in the second sentence.
6. Is the demonstrative pronoun in the fifth sentence singular or plural in number?
7. Find an interrogative pronoun in the selection.
8. Give the person, number, gender, and case of the relative pronoun in the first sentence.
9. Find a compound relative pronoun in the selection.
10. Name a distributive pronoun.
11. Which is the only possessive pronoun in the paragraph?

CHAPTER THREE **Adjectives**

An adjective is a word that describes or limits a noun or a pronoun.

CLASSES OF ADJECTIVES

Adjectives are divided into two general classes: *descriptive adjectives* and *limiting adjectives*.

1. Descriptive Adjectives

A descriptive adjective is an adjective that describes a noun or a pronoun.

A proper adjective is an adjective that is formed from a proper noun.

A common adjective is an adjective that expresses the ordinary qualities of a noun or a pronoun.

PROPER ADJECTIVES	COMMON ADJECTIVES
American harbor	*deep* harbor
French flag	*silk* flag

EXERCISE 58

Point out the descriptive adjectives in the following sentences and tell whether they are common or proper:
1. The happy children greeted the kind old gentleman.
2. Elizabeth is a tall, thin, and graceful girl.
3. From my window I could see many twinkling stars in the vast firmament above me.
4. Alice sang a Scottish ballad.
5. American games are more vigorous than Chinese games.
6. The field was dotted with gay yellow daisies.
7. The foamy waves washed the sandy beach.

8. My grandfather speaks several French dialects.
9. In the pale light of early morn the farmer rises.
10. They traveled over the Canadian railroad.
11. Stately elm trees towered over the building.
12. Hawaiian pineapples are shipped to the United States.
13. Paul has brown eyes and firm, close lips.
14. Saint Francis was noted for his ardent zeal.
15. The sky was filled with white, fleecy clouds.

EXERCISE 59

1. Use the following adjectives in sentences of your own: ancient, jolly, sincere, devout, glorious, historic, German, majestic, Italian, stately, Cuban, modern, careful.
2. Use an appropriate adjective with each of these nouns: story, steamer, stairs, snow, brook, breeze, leaves, jewels, cherries, squirrel, ocean, lawyer, beach.
3. Write synonyms for the following adjectives: beautiful, virtuous, rustic, modest, young, violent, short, enthusiastic, delicious, bright, heroic, gentle, immense.
4. Write antonyms for the following adjectives: easy, regular, prompt, restless, faithful, luminous, daring, just, intelligent, progressive, prominent, courteous.

2. Limiting Adjectives

A limiting adjective is an adjective that either points out an object or denotes number.

Limiting adjectives may be subdivided into the following classes: (1) numeral adjectives, (2) pronominal adjectives, and (3) articles.

A numeral adjective is an adjective that denotes exact number.

A pronominal adjective is an adjective that may also be used as a pronoun.

NUMERAL ADJECTIVES	PRONOMINAL ADJECTIVES
six boys	*another* day
third row	*many* people

The articles *the, an,* and *a* are also considered limiting adjectives since they show whether the noun is used definitely or indefinitely. The following rules apply to articles:

1. The definite article *the* may be used with either singular or plural nouns.
2. The indefinite articles *a* and *an* may be used only with singular nouns.
3. The article *an* is used before a vowel sound.
4. The article *a* is used before a consonant sound.

EXERCISE 60

Pick out the limiting adjectives in the following sentences and tell to which class each belongs:
1. There were seven airplanes in the race.
2. You may choose either part.
3. Give John the box.
4. Each child held a large bouquet of white roses.
5. Have you seen the exhibits?
6. We celebrated Margaret's tenth birthday.
7. These rocks are very dangerous.
8. There were several stamps on the package.

9. Christ ascended into heaven on the fortieth day after His Resurrection.
10. My baby sister has three rag dolls.
11. Repeat the five glorious mysteries of the rosary.
12. The first part of the Hail Mary was composed by the angel Gabriel.
13. There are eight beatitudes.
14. This book tells the story of the growth of our country.
15. In colonial times there were few roads.
16. The little boy lost his mittens, but Aunt Lucy gave him that pair of gloves.

FURTHER STUDY OF PRONOMINAL ADJECTIVES

There are certain words like *this, his, each, several,* and *what* which may be used either as pronouns or as adjectives. When they stand alone they are *pronouns;* when they modify nouns they are *adjectives.* The pronominal adjectives may be divided into the following classes:

1. DEMONSTRATIVE ADJECTIVES: *this, that, these, those.*
2. POSSESSIVE ADJECTIVES: *my, our, your, his, her, its, their, whose.*
3. DISTRIBUTIVE ADJECTIVES: *each, every, either, neither.*
4. INDEFINITE ADJECTIVES: *any, all, another, both, few, many, several, some, such.*
5. INTERROGATIVE ADJECTIVES: *which, what.*

A demonstrative adjective is an adjective that points out a definite person, place, or thing.

A possessive adjective is an adjective that denotes ownership.

A distributive adjective is an adjective that refers to each person, place, or thing separately.

An indefinite adjective is an adjective that points out no particular person, place, or thing.

An interrogative adjective is an adjective that is used in asking a question.

EXERCISE 61

Name the class of pronominal adjective to which each of the italicized words belongs:
1. *This* message will delight Mother.
2. *What* number did he call?
3. *Our* team advanced toward the goal line.
4. *Several* boys declined the invitation.
5. Has *your* story been accepted?
6. *These* machines will be very useful.
7. *Whose* umbrella is this?
8. The lawn and hedge require *much* care.
9. Can you give me *some* assistance?
10. *Our* house has just been painted.
11. *Each* task has its own difficulties.
12. *Whose* car arrived first?
13. Return *all* reference books immediately.
14. The robin built *its* nest in *that* old tree.
15. *Which* place did you select?
16. He has contributed *much* money to the cause.
17. *This* dog has saved the life of *its* master.
18. Is *every* package in good condition?
19. *Both* plans deserve careful attention.
20. *Every* child should own a rosary.
21. *Their* jolly laughter re-echoed throughout the building.
22. *Many* varieties of robes were on display.
23. *Every* state, regardless of size, has two votes in the Senate.
24. There were *several* questions that I could not answer.

EXERCISE 62

In the following sentences tell whether the italicized words are pronominal adjectives or adjective pronouns. Name the class to which each belongs:
1. I enjoyed *that* history lesson.
2. Mother is visiting *some* friends in Montreal.
3. *Each* was asked to take part.

4. Who is responsible for *that*?
5. There are *several* new houses on *our* street.
6. The *same* applies to you.
7. *Either* may be chosen.
8. *This* work must be completed today.
9. *Which* boy did you send?
10. *These* are the letters Martin wrote.
11. *All* did *their* best work.
12. Who sent you *those* flowers?
13. *Many* are called but *few* are chosen.
14. I have known *that* for a long time.
15. You are responsible for *this*.
16. *All* directions must be carefully followed.
17. Have you seen *their* new home?
18. Very *few* cars pass along *this* road.
19. *Every* Friday is a day of abstinence.
20. *Another* train will arrive at two o'clock.
21. *Many* colors will be needed for the costumes.
22. Edward does not wish *any*.
23. How *many* days passed between the Resurrection of *our* Lord and *His* Ascension?
24. *Those* letters were addressed to me.
25. *Whose* knife is this?
26. *Few* have read *those* books.
27. The party dresses of *both* girls were made of the *same* material.
28. I am proud of *my* faith.
29. *That* woman is the librarian.
30. *Some* pupils have already arrived.

POSITION OF ADJECTIVES

1. The usual position of the adjective is before the noun. These are called attributive adjectives.

Twinkling stars dotted the *dark* sky.

2. A predicate adjective follows and completes a copulative verb.

The furniture is *old* and *valuable*.
My mother looks *beautiful* tonight.

3. **An adjective that follows the direct object and at the same time completes the thought expressed by a transitive verb is called an objective complement.**

We consider that work *excellent*.

EXERCISE 63

Select the adjectives in the following sentences and tell whether each is an attributive adjective, a predicate adjective, or an objective complement:

1. The child seems very happy.
2. This fruit tastes delicious.
3. Louis is an honest and dependable boy.
4. The music in the distance sounds beautiful.
5. I consider John reliable.
6. That man looks kind.
7. King Solomon was a wise and just ruler.
8. They are enthusiastic over the game.
9. Anne is the smallest girl in our class.
10. My sick friend appears very cheerful.
11. My sister has become a trained nurse.
12. Geraldine's dress is prettier than mine.

EXERCISE 64

Select the adjectives in the following sentences and give the syntax of each:

1. Elephants have a keen sense of smell.
2. An immense crowd surrounded the winner.
3. After two days the weather became clear.
4. Hockey is a favorite sport in our school.
5. A crowd of strange children followed Rip Van Winkle.
6. Michael is very honorable.
7. A light, swift canoe skimmed across the lake.
8. The entire city was decorated with multicolored flags.

9. Dutch children wear wooden shoes.
10. Those peaches are not ripe.
11. Our country has excellent natural resources.
12. As we walked along the quiet road, we noticed a small crystal stream.
13. Many herds of cattle live on the western prairies.
14. His composition was unique.
15. We followed the diagonal path.
16. Longfellow is one of our best-loved poets.
17. A brown leather case has been lost.
18. Lucy dyed her dress black.
19. Little white steamers with black funnels bustled about the lake.
20. The obedient boy makes his parents happy.
21. The two most prominent figures in Washington's Cabinet were Jefferson and Hamilton.
22. Some of our concrete highways follow old Indian trails.
23. My mother received a pair of beautiful brass candlesticks for Christmas.
24. Ella considered the book interesting.
25. We have donated these books to the library.

COMPARISON OF ADJECTIVES

Comparison is the change that adjectives undergo to express different degrees of quality, quantity, or value.

Most adjectives have three degrees of comparison: *positive, comparative,* and *superlative.*

This is a *tall* tree. *(Positive degree)*
This is a *taller* tree. *(Comparative degree)*
This is the *tallest* tree in the forest. *(Superlative degree)*

The positive degree denotes quality.

The comparative degree denotes quality in a greater or a less degree.

The superlative degree denotes quality in the greatest or the least degree.

HOW ADJECTIVES ARE COMPARED

1. Most adjectives of one syllable and some adjectives of two syllables (generally those ending in *ow*, *y*, and *e*) form the comparative degree by adding *er* to the positive, and the superlative degree by adding *est* to the positive.

Positive	Comparative	Superlative
narrow	narrower	narrowest
happy	happier	happiest
humble	humbler	humblest

2. Adjectives of three or more syllables, and some of two syllables, form the comparative and the superlative degrees by prefixing *more* and *most* or *less* and *least* to the positive form of the adjective.

Positive	Comparative	Superlative
studious	more studious	most studious
beautiful	less beautiful	least beautiful

3. Certain adjectives are compared irregularly. Those most frequently used are:

Positive	Comparative	Superlative
little	less	least
bad, ill, evil	worse	worst
good	better	best
many, much	more	most
late	later, latter	latest, last
far	farther	farthest
fore	former	foremost, first
old	older, elder	oldest, eldest
near	nearer	nearest, next
....	*further	furthest
....	*inner	innermost, inmost
....	*outer	outermost, outmost
....	*upper	uppermost, upmost

4. Some adjectives do not admit of comparison, as *dead, perpendicular, eternal, supreme,* etc.

---

* These adjectives have no positive form.

EXERCISE 65

Compare the following adjectives:

smooth	gentle	clever
neat	industrious	worthy
sweet	wise	amiable
eager	lucky	stormy
slow	heavy	sorry
timid	handsome	good
jolly	much	virtuous

EXERCISE 66

Pick out the adjectives capable of being compared and tell the degree of comparison of each:
1. Mount McKinley is the highest point in North America.
2. That is a beautiful portrait.
3. Charles, you gave the best description.
4. Philadelphia is larger than any other city in Pennsylvania.
5. There are fewer people in the audience now.
6. Which is the smallest continent?
7. My father feels better today.
8. Much gold is exported from southern Africa.
9. The roof has small spires at the gable ends.
10. Is the Nile the longest river in Africa?
11. The boys are making a circular flower bed for their mother.
12. He is taller than his sister.

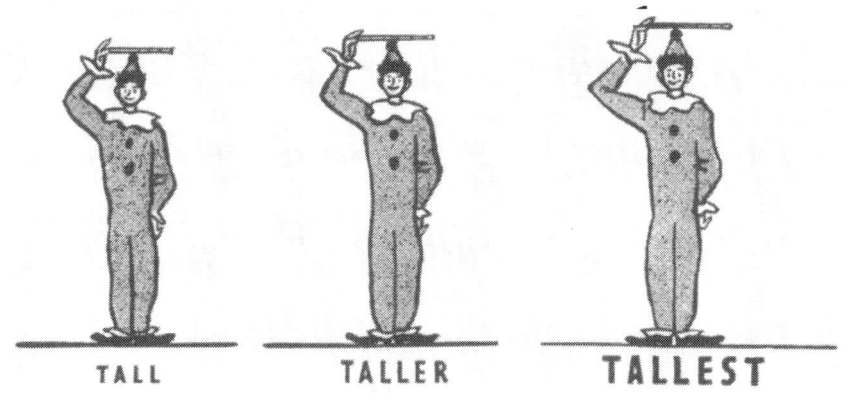

TALL   TALLER   **TALLEST**

13. The Louisiana Purchase was one of the most important events in the history of our country.
14. Children should be courteous at all times.
15. Father Edmund Schreiber gave one of the most interesting illustrated lectures that I have ever heard.

THE CORRECT USE OF ADJECTIVES

1. *Comparative and Superlative Degrees*

The comparative degree of the adjective is used when two are compared. The superlative degree is used when more than two are compared.

Which of the two cities is *larger?*
Which is the *largest* city in the state?

EXERCISE 67

Select the correct degree of the adjective in each of the following sentences:

1. This is the (newer, newest) house on our street.
2. Who is (younger, youngest), you or your sister?
3. Joan is the (more industrious, most industrious) girl of the three.
4. Is Rhode Island the (smaller, smallest) state in the Union?
5. This is the (more beautiful, most beautiful) picture of the collection.
6. This is the (more difficult, most difficult) problem of the two.
7. Is a diamond or a ruby (harder, hardest)?
8. Which continent is (larger, largest), Africa or South America?
9. Paul is the (better, best) writer in the class.
10. Anthony Nolan is the (faster, fastest) runner on the team.
11. Which is the (prettier, prettiest) flower in the basket?
12. The Indian trail is the (longer, longest) route of the two.
13. Joseph's answer is (more accurate, most accurate) than yours.
14. That is the (riper, ripest) peach of all.
15. That is the (more interesting, most interesting) book that I have ever read.

2. Fewer *and* Less

Use *fewer* when number is indicated. Use *less* when quantity is indicated.

In our class there are *fewer* girls than boys.
John earned *less* money this week.

EXERCISE 68

In each of the following sentences fill in the blanks with the correct adjective, *fewer* or *less*:
1. Canada has .... seaports than the United States.
2. I had .... trouble with this problem.
3. Egypt raises .... cotton than the United States.
4. This tree has .... branches than any other near it.
5. James ate .... ice cream and .... pretzels than his brother.
6. Our class has .... absentees than yours.
7. .... boys went to the seashore than ever before.
8. These flowers require .... attention than those.
9. In our school we have .... time for lunch than in yours.
10. I saw .... girls at the party than I had expected.
11. This town has .... people than that.
12. There are .... desks in this room.
13. Mother purchased .... sugar this week.
14. We have .... time for play now because our studies are more difficult.
15. .... children entered the contest this year.
16. That pitcher holds .... water than this one.

3. *Demonstrative Adjectives*

The demonstrative adjectives *this* and *that* agree in number with the nouns they modify. The plural of *this* is *these;* the plural of *that* is *those.*

This and *these* refer to objects that are near at hand. *That* and *those* refer to objects that are farther away.

EXERCISE 69

1. Insert the correct demonstrative adjectives before the following objects that are near at hand:

.... houses	.... kind of paper
.... sort of pen	.... ring
.... news	.... tops
.... kind of weather	.... kinds of stamps
.... types of sentences	.... regiment

2. Insert the correct demonstrative adjectives before the following objects that are far away:

.... kind of candy	.... kinds of oranges
.... cities	.... boxes
.... exercise	.... plants
.... painting	.... order
.... style of coat	.... type of book

EXERCISE 70

Select the correct form of the demonstrative adjective and give the reason for your choice:

1. Father does not like (this, these) kind of cigar.
2. (This, these) brand of tea is from China.
3. (This, these) type will not answer the purpose.
4. (That, those) kinds of lemons are very juicy.
5. (This, these) kind of notebook is more practical than yours.
6. (That, those) varieties of flowers grow in warm regions.
7. (This, these) style of shoe is most comfortable.
8. Do not choose scissors of (that, those) kind.
9. What do you know of (this, these) race of men?
10. (This, these) brand of tobacco grows in Virginia.
11. (This, these) pair of stockings is new.
12. (That, those) kind of drawing is difficult for Catherine.
13. Shall I buy (this, these) kind of glove?
14. (This, these) style of jacket is not suitable for boys of (that, those) age.

15. (That, those) kind of story always interests me.
16. Have you any of (this, these) variety of rose?
17. I have never met (that, those) type of boy before.
18. I always buy (this, these) kind of chocolate.
19. The girls in our class like (this, these) kinds of games.
20. How expensive is (that, those) style of hat?

4. *Repetition of the Article*

The repetition of the article changes the meaning of a sentence.

I know *the* president and secretary.

I know *the* president and *the* secretary.

The first sentence, in which the article is used before the first noun only, tells us that the president and secretary is one individual. The second sentence, in which the article is repeated before the second noun, tells us that the president and the secretary are two different individuals.

EXERCISE 71

Determine whether or not the article should be repeated in the following sentences:
1. The superior and (the) principal meets every new student.
2. The surgeon and (the) neurologist have been called to the hospital.
3. The receptionist and (the) order clerk sits near the window.
4. The captain and (the) manager were present at the banquet.
5. A salesman and (a) lecturer was here on Tuesday.
6. The editor and (the) proofreader have not finished their work.
7. The secretary and (the) treasurer have gone home.
8. The class teacher and (the) adviser has taken a trip.
9. The foreman and (the) supervisor is on his vacation.
10. The library and (the) magazine room is on the first floor.
11. The president and (the) dean decide who shall be accepted.
12. The captain and (the) manager has arranged a new game.
13. An architect and (a) designer is making the plans for our new school building.

14. The adviser and (the) moderator were elected by the class.
15. The head and (the) chief pastor of the Church was appointed by our Lord before His Ascension into heaven.

5. Words Used as Nouns and Adjectives

The use of a word in the sentence determines the part of speech. The same word may frequently be used as a noun or an adjective.

Easter is the greatest feast in the Catholic Church.
Do you like my new *Easter* outfit?

In the first sentence *Easter* is the name of a feast and is therefore a noun; *Easter* in the second sentence describes *outfit* and is an adjective.

EXERCISE 72

Tell whether each italicized word is a noun or an adjective:
1. The young man displayed unusual *executive* ability.
2. The governor is the chief *executive* in the state.
3. My grandfather owns a large *orchard*.
4. The apple is an *orchard* fruit.
5. Brazil is the largest *country* in South America.
6. How we enjoyed our visit to your *country* estate!
7. He keeps valuable papers in a *metal* box.
8. Gold is a precious *metal*.
9. A white picket fence enclosed the *garden*.
10. Ivy covered the *garden* gate.
11. Do you know if Columbus Day is a *bank* holiday?
12. My uncle is a cashier in that *bank*.
13. In *winter* many birds fly south.
14. I always enjoy invigorating *winter* sports.
15. Some *radio* cabinets are made of plastic.
16. I have a portable *radio* in my bedroom.
17. *Light* streamed into the room through the sparkling windows.
18. Father wore his *light* coat this morning.
19. A beautiful tapestry covered the *wall*.
20. In our classroom there is a new *wall* map of Africa.

EXERCISE 73 [Test on Adjectives]

Read this selection very carefully and then answer the questions that follow:

¹ The tableau which brings the Christmas entertainment to a close is always the most impressive feature of our annual party for the Christ Child. ² This familiar picture portrays the Holy Family in the stable at Bethlehem. ³ Several shepherds kneel before the tiny King, while angels in shimmering robes of pastel colors hover in the background.

⁴ As the organ plays softly, one child from each grade approaches the manger and lays a loving gift at the feet of the Infant. ⁵ These offerings represent the presents which the other pupils have brought to the party for the less fortunate children of the parish. ⁶ What better way could we find of saying "Happy Birthday" to the Infant Jesus?

1. Name the descriptive adjectives in the third sentence.
2. Find a proper adjective in the first paragraph.
3. Name a definite and an indefinite article used in the fourth sentence.
4. Name a numeral adjective found in the selection.
5. Find a demonstrative adjective that is singular in number and one that is plural. Do they refer to near or to distant objects?
6. To what class of limiting adjective does *our* belong?
7. Name a distributive adjective found in the second paragraph.
8. Find an indefinite adjective in the first paragraph.
9. Which sentence contains an interrogative adjective?
10. Find two adjectives in the comparative degree in the second paragraph.
11. Find an adjective in the superlative degree in the first paragraph.
12. Can the adjective *annual* in the first sentence be compared?

CHAPTER FOUR Verbs

A verb is a word used to express action, being, or state of being.

We *adore* God by prayer and sacrifice. *(Action)*
The Holy Spirit *is* the Third Person of the Trinity. *(Being)*
The way to heaven *lies* before us. *(State of being)*

The verb is the most important element of a sentence; without it there can be no sentence.

EXERCISE 74

Select the sentences from the following groups of words. Point out the verb in each sentence:
1. Joys of childhood days.
2. Look!
3. George Rogers Clark captured the British strongholds in the Northwest.
4. Fill our hearts with peace.
5. Persons, plants, and animals need air.
6. The task of making an alliance with France.
7. The gold of Indian-summer days.
8. Our school newspaper won the award.
9. When the storm broke we ran for shelter.
10. The Statue of Liberty in New York Bay.
11. The book has just been returned.
12. Do you remember my old friend Theodore?
13. John called his brother.
14. To the south of the United States on the other side of the Equator.
15. Write the comparative and the superlative forms of the adjective *familiar*.
16. What is your answer?

HANG   **JUGGLE**   **CHASE**

VERB PHRASES

A verb phrase is a group of words used to do the work of a single verb.

The third Sunday of Advent *is called* Gaudete Sunday.
Have you *read* the life of Saint Aloysius?
A shrine to Our Lady of Fatima *has been erected* in our school.

In these sentences *is called, have read,* and *has been erected* are verb phrases. The principal verbs are *called, read,* and *erected; is, have,* and *has been* are auxiliary verbs.

Any verb used with the principal verb to form its voice, mood, and tense is called an auxiliary verb.

The common auxiliary verbs are:

be	are	do	has	will	might
am	was	did	had	may	could
is	were	have	shall	can	would

EXERCISE 75

Name the verb phrases in the following sentences:
1. Henry had solved the difficult problem first.
2. The Bible was originally written in Hebrew, Greek, and Aramaic.

3. Did Helen like the play?
4. We must love our enemies.
5. Robert has been sent on an errand by his mother.
6. Have you seen the mission exhibit?
7. The machine was sold at a high price.
8. The "Sistine Madonna" is placed among the first twelve pictures in the world.
9. How long will the Holy Spirit dwell in the Church?
10. We can always resist temptation with God's grace.
11. Do you remember the rules of the game?
12. A spiritual Communion may be made many times a day or at any hour of the day.

KINDS OF VERBS

1. Division according to Form

The principal parts of the verb are the present, the past, and the past participle because all other forms of the verb are determined from these.

According to the manner in which their principal parts are formed, verbs may be either *regular* or *irregular*.

REGULAR VERBS

A regular verb is a verb that forms its past tense and its past participle by adding *d* or *ed* to the present tense.

PRESENT	PAST	PAST PARTICIPLE
walk	walked	walked

IRREGULAR VERBS

An irregular verb is a verb that does not form its past tense and its past participle by adding *d* or *ed* to the present tense.

PRESENT	PAST	PAST PARTICIPLE
choose	chose	chosen

On pages 288-89 are the principal parts of the more common irregular verbs. They should be thoroughly mastered.

Present	Past (These stand alone)	Past Participle (These require a helper)
am (is, be)	was	been
*awake	awoke, awaked	awaked
*beat	beat	beat, beaten
begin	began	begun
bend	bent	bent
bet	bet	bet
bind	bound	bound
bite	bit	bitten
blow	blew	blown
break	broke	broken
bring	brought	brought
*build	built, builded	built, builded
*burn	burned, burnt	burned, burnt
burst	burst	burst
catch	caught	caught
choose	chose	chosen
come	came	come
do	did	done
draw	drew	drawn
*dream	dreamed, dreamt	dreamed, dreamt
drink	drank	drunk
drive	drove	driven
eat	ate	eaten
fall	fell	fallen
find	found	found
fly	flew	flown
forget	forgot	forgotten
freeze	froze	frozen
give	gave	given
go	went	gone
grow	grew	grown
hang	hung	hung
have	had	had
hear	heard	heard
*hide	hid	hidden, hid

* If a verb has more than one form for its past tense or past participle, it is a redundant verb. The asterisk indicates redundant verbs.

Present	Past (These stand alone)	Past Participle (These require a helper)
hold	held	held
hurt	hurt	hurt
keep	kept	kept
*kneel	knelt, kneeled	knelt, kneeled
know	knew	known
lay	laid	laid
leave	left	left
lend	lent	lent
let	let	let
lie (recline)	lay	lain
lose	lost	lost
make	made	made
mean	meant	meant
meet	met	met
read	read	read
ride	rode	ridden
ring	rang	rung
rise	rose	risen
run	ran	run
say	said	said
see	saw	seen
shake	shook	shaken
sing	sang	sung
sink	sank	sunk
sit	sat	sat
speak	spoke	spoken
stand	stood	stood
steal	stole	stolen
stick	stuck	stuck
swim	swam	swum
swing	swung	swung
teach	taught	taught
tear	tore	torn
throw	threw	thrown
wear	wore	worn
win	won	won
wring	wrung	wrung

DEFECTIVE VERBS

Verbs that do not have all the principal parts are known as defective verbs. The defective verbs include *can, may, must, ought, shall, will,* and *beware.*

Present	Past	Past Participle
beware	....	....
can	could	....
may	might	....
must	must	....
ought	ought	....
shall	should	....
will	would	....

2. *Division according to Use*

TRANSITIVE VERBS

A transitive verb is a verb that expresses an action which passes from a doer to a receiver.

Doer	Action	Receiver
The president	saw	the visitor.

Saw is a transitive verb because the action passes from the doer, *president,* to the receiver, *visitor.* To determine the receiver of an action, we ask the question *whom* or *what* after the verb.

The action may pass from the doer to the receiver in two different ways:

The president *saw* the visitor.
The visitor *was seen* by the president.

In both sentences *visitor* is the receiver of the action and *president* is the doer. Since the action passes from the doer to the receiver in each case, the verb *see,* whether in the form of *saw* or *was seen,* is a transitive verb.

The doer is not always expressed when a transitive verb is used in the passive voice.

Men's hats *are sold* here. *(Doer not expressed)*
Men's hats *are sold* by this merchant. *(Doer expressed)*

INTRANSITIVE VERBS

An intransitive verb is a verb that has no receiver of its action.

Intransitive verbs are always in the active voice, since a verb is in the active voice when its subject is the doer of the action.

DOER	ACTION	(NO RECEIVER)
The president	sat at his desk.	....

The action of this verb *sat* begins and ends with the doer. There is no receiver; hence the question *whom* or *what* after the verb will receive no answer.

EXERCISE 76

Select the verbs in the following sentences and tell whether they are transitive or intransitive:

1. Diamonds are mined in South Africa.
2. At last the mail arrived.
3. Have the children finished the assignment?
4. Raymond will come home early.
5. The small child smiled pleasantly.
6. The play begins at eight o'clock.
7. The best composition was written by Margaret O'Leary.
8. Have you sold your stamp collection?
9. A gay banner floated over the ship.
10. Marian received a cedar chest for Christmas.
11. "The Angelus" was painted by Millet.
12. Joseph's report was given to the committee.
13. By her side stood Elizabeth.
14. Bernard polished his father's automobile.
15. We have bought a statue of Saint Anne.
16. Our meeting was postponed.
17. The old car crawled up the hill.
18. Down the stream floated a light canoe.
19. The box has been painted.
20. The maple was planted by our class.

Some verbs are transitive or intransitive, according to their use in the sentence.

The boys *played* a game of ball. *(Transitive)*
The boys *played* here yesterday. *(Intransitive)*

EXERCISE 77

The verbs in the following sentences have been used both transitively and intransitively. Study each verb and tell whether it is transitive or intransitive:

1. The hail beat heavily on the roof.
2. Thomas whistled merrily while he worked.
3. Florence dropped the package.
4. We cracked nuts for the party.
5. The boys beat their drums enthusiastically.
6. Has Francis rung the class bell yet?
7. A strange dog dashed through our yard.
8. Our church bell rings every morning.
9. The glass cracked.
10. Richard whistled a merry tune.
11. He dashed the contents of the fire extinguisher on the blaze.
12. The exhausted runner dropped to the ground.

A cognate verb is a verb whose object repeats the meaning implied by the verb itself.

The athlete *ran* a brilliant *race*.

A cognate verb is usually an intransitive verb that is used transitively. *Cognate* means *related;* the object is related to the verb and has almost the same meaning. Name the cognate verbs in Exercise 23, page 236.

COPULATIVE VERBS

A copulative verb is a linking verb. It links or couples with the subject a noun, a pronoun, or an adjective.

A word or a group of words used to complete the meaning of a copulative verb is called a subjective complement. If the complement is a noun or a pronoun, it is called a *predicate nominative;* if an adjective, it is called a *predicate adjective.*

Subject	Copulative	Complement
Matrimony	is	a sacrament.
It	is	he.
Velvet	feels	smooth.

The verb *be* in its various forms is the most common copulative. Other verbs which may be used as copulative verbs are *appear, become, continue, feel, grow, look, remain, seem, smell, sound,* and *taste.* When these verbs are used as copulatives some part of the verb *be* can be substituted for the original verb.

The velvet *feels* smooth.
The velvet *is* smooth.

EXERCISE 78

Select the copulative verb in each of the following sentences. Tell whether the complement is a noun, a pronoun, or an adjective:
1. The Church is the mystical body of Christ.
2. That is he near the exit.
3. The Canon is the most important part of the Mass.

4. Wind is air in motion.
5. Who is that?
6. A requiem Mass is a Mass for the dead.
7. The Pater Noster is the prayer our Lord Himself taught.
8. I am a soldier of Christ.
9. The chief gases in the air are oxygen and nitrogen.
10. The evangelists are the writers of the four Gospels.
11. Saint Francis Xavier was a famous Jesuit missionary.
12. The room was bright and cheerful.
13. The first martyr was Saint Stephen.
14. The streets were silent and desolate.
15. The people along the Nile River have been farmers for centuries.
16. Christ became obedient unto death.
17. The weather continued cold.
18. The houses seemed mere specks from the airplane.
19. Mary looked beautiful in her new dress.
20. This chair seems comfortable.
21. The orange tasted tart.
22. The Indians became friendly with the white men.
23. Grandmother does not feel well today.
24. Those flowers smell fragrant.
25. You have grown tall.

EXERCISE 79

Classify the verbs in the following sentences as transitive, intransitive, copulative, or cognate:
1. Bernard runs rapidly.
2. Bread is the staff of life.
3. Our class won the penmanship banner.
4. Wonders never cease.
5. That huge building is our college.
6. John Adams became our second president.
7. The apple looks hard and green.
8. Every hill has its valley.
9. The boy deserves a rich reward.

10. Our next holiday is Columbus Day.
11. Virtue is its own reward.
12. Platinum is a metal.
13. The girl smoothed the frill of her collar.
14. The liturgical year begins on the first Sunday of Advent.
15. The children prayed a fervent prayer for peace.
16. On the rug before the fireplace lay a pretty Persian cat.
17. Ethel has gone to the lecture.
18. Alice Cary became a doctor at an early age.
19. In one corner of our yard stands a huge maple tree.
20. The cost of the posters was charged to the school.
21. Elephants are not afraid of other animals.
22. Grandmother has lived a life of happiness and contentment.
23. Leo's friend remained loyal to him.
24. The Communion and the Postcommunion belong to the Proper of the Mass.
25. The Indians danced a ceremonial dance.

ATTRIBUTES OR QUALITIES OF A VERB

1. *Voice*

Voice is that quality of a verb which shows whether the subject is the doer or the receiver of the action.

The active voice denotes the subject as the doer of the action.

The passive voice denotes the subject as the receiver of the action.

John *painted* this picture. *(Active voice)*
This picture *was painted* by John. *(Passive voice)*

In the first sentence *John*, the subject, is the doer of the action, *painted*. The verb, therefore, is in the active voice. In the second sentence the subject, *picture*, is the receiver of the action, *was painted*. This verb, therefore, is in the passive voice.

Only transitive verbs may be used in the passive voice. Intransitive verbs have no receivers of the action.

FORMATION OF THE PASSIVE VOICE

The passive voice is formed by using some tense of the verb *be* as an auxiliary with the past participle of the verb. Therefore the verb *be* (and its tenses), used before a past participle, is generally the sign of the passive voice.

was + painted = passive voice

Two sentences may convey the same idea, the one expressing it by a verb in the *active voice,* and the other by a verb in the *passive voice.* When an active verb is changed to the passive voice, the subject is usually made the object of a preposition; the direct object of the active verb becomes the subject of the passive verb.

Michael opened the door. *(Active voice)*
The door was opened by Michael. *(Passive voice)*

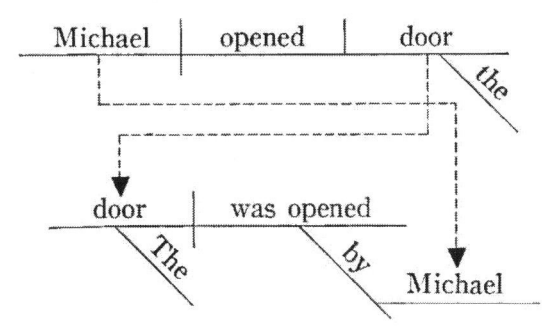

```
Michael │ opened │ door \the
         └────────────────┐
         ┌────────────────┘
         ▼
   door │ was opened
   \The         \by
                 ▼ Michael
```

In both sentences *Michael* performs the action and *door* receives the action. In the first sentence *Michael* is the subject of the verb *opened;* in the second sentence it is the object of the preposition *by.* In the first sentence *door,* the receiver of the action, is the object of the active verb *opened;* in the second sentence it becomes the subject of the passive verb *was opened.*

EXERCISE 80

Rewrite the following sentences, changing the verbs from the active to the passive voice:

1. Our class dramatized *Little Women.*
2. Anita reads many stories of adventure.

3. Miss Nally offered a prize for the best poem.
4. My father has bought a new car.
5. Two boys will collect the ballots.
6. Joseph had finished the work before the bell rang.
7. Each child waved a pennant.
8. Mr. Walker laid the plans before the committee.
9. Who invented the telephone?
10. I plan the meals for our family.
11. Christ cured the blind man.
12. The faithful on earth help the souls in purgatory.
13. Father Louis Hennepin discovered the Falls of Saint Anthony.
14. He threw the paper into the basket.
15. God will punish the wicked.

EXERCISE 81

Rewrite the following sentences, changing the verbs from the passive to the active voice:

1. Jane has been sent to the library by the teacher.
2. The lighthouse was repainted by city employees.
3. The fox has been caught in the trap.
4. The school bell will be rung at nine o'clock.
5. The children were brought some candy by Uncle David.
6. In Catholic schools prayers are recited every day.
7. Maryland was settled by Catholics.
8. That word is often misspelled by Teresa.
9. Virginia was given a pretty picture by her cousin Alice.
10. The lock has been broken before.
11. The Magnificat is sung at Vespers.
12. The rabbit was taken to Australia by the English.
13. Everyone is judged immediately after death.
14. That pen was given to me yesterday.
15. The laws of the United States are made by Congress.

THE RETAINED OBJECT

In studying the objective case we learned that transitive verbs in the passive voice sometimes retain the direct object which they would govern if used in the active voice. This object is called the *retained object.*

Father Smith gave the boys *tickets* to the game. *(Direct object)*

The boys were given *tickets* to the game by Father Smith. *(Retained object)*

Do not confuse the retained object with the predicate nominative. When the noun following the passive verb refers to the same person or thing as the subject, it is a *predicate nominative.*

Mary is called *Queen* of All Saints. *(Predicate nominative)*

My father was given the *grace* of a happy death. *(Retained object)*

EXERCISE 82

Name the retained objects and the predicate nominatives in the following sentences:

1. Leo Carr was elected captain.
2. Singapore is called the gateway to the East.
3. Daniel Murphy was chosen delegate to the convention.
4. The author of that book has been given the award for the outstanding Catholic publication of the year.
5. Mr. Fredericks was appointed chairman.
6. Eileen and her brother have been left a large fortune.
7. Washington was elected president in 1788.
8. He was awarded the silver cup.
9. Each boy was assigned a task.
10. Jesus was called the Nazarene.
11. The colonists were given aid by France.
12. The children were asked many questions.
13. The baby was named Mary Ann.
14. My brother has been offered a commission in the Army.
15. Annapolis, Maryland, was made the site of the United States Naval Academy.

2. *Tense*

Tense is that quality of a verb which denotes the time of the action, the being, or the state of being.

SIMPLE TENSES

Present tense signifies action, being, or state of being in present time.

Past tense signifies action, being, or state of being in past time.

Future tense signifies action, being, or state of being in future time.

Marie *writes* to her sister frequently. *(Present tense)*
Marie *wrote* to her sister yesterday. *(Past tense)*
Marie *will write* to her sister tomorrow. *(Future tense)*

In the passive voice the tense is shown by the *auxiliary verb.*

The letter *is written* now. *(Present tense)*
The letter *was written* yesterday. *(Past tense)*
The letter *will be written* tomorrow. *(Future tense)*

EXERCISE 83

Give the tense and the voice of each verb in the following sentences:

1. Our teacher explained the action of volcanoes.
2. Our reflections were seen in the lake.
3. Joseph receives Holy Communion frequently.
4. They will entertain the committee at their home tomorrow.
5. The children waved the flags proudly.
6. I shall call for you at seven o'clock.
7. The Ohio River flows into the Mississippi River.
8. He will be a mechanical engineer when he completes his education.
9. Sarah will be fifteen years old next week.
10. The picture was admired by all.
11. Catholics played a glorious part in the Revolutionary War.
12. He works diligently.
13. He will succeed in his new work.
14. De Soto discovered the Mississippi River.
15. Last year the library was painted.

COMPOUND TENSES

Present perfect tense signifies action, being, or state of being completed or perfected in present time.

Past perfect tense signifies action, being, or state of being completed or perfected before some definite past time.

Future perfect tense signifies action, being, or state of being that will be completed or perfected before some specified time in the future.

Marie *has written* to her sister today. *(Present perfect tense)*
Marie *had written* to her sister before you called. *(Past perfect tense)*
Marie *will have written* to her sister before night. *(Future perfect tense)*

The present perfect tense is formed by prefixing the auxiliary *have* or *has* to the past participle of the verb.

The past perfect tense is formed by prefixing the auxiliary *had* to the past participle of the verb.

The future perfect tense is formed by prefixing the auxiliary *shall have* or *will have* to the past participle of the verb.

In the passive voice *been* is inserted between the auxiliary and the past participle in the three tenses.

The letter *has been written* today. *(Present perfect tense)*
The letter *had been written* before you called. *(Past perfect tense)*
The letter *will have been written* before night. *(Future perfect tense)*

EXERCISE 84

Give the tense and the voice of each verb:

1. I have just bought a new suit.
2. Gold has been mined in Africa for many years.
3. Mary had gone when I called.
4. My brother has been given an increase in salary.
5. The shepherds found the Infant Jesus exactly as the angel had described.
6. She will have finished the task before noon.
7. The boys had discovered an old cave.
8. The price of sugar has been raised.
9. Have you read the story of Our Lady of Fatima?

10. The lake had frozen during the night.
11. Joseph will have served Mass before he comes to school.
12. Have you entertained Christ as your guest in Holy Communion today?
13. I shall have written the letter before the boat sails.
14. Frances had lived in Mexico for several years.
15. John had left for the camp early in the morning.

3. Mood

Mood or mode is that attribute or quality of a verb that denotes the manner in which the action, the being, or the state of being is expressed.

INDICATIVE MOOD

The indicative mood is used to state a fact, to deny a fact, or to ask a question.

STATES A FACT: My brother *has gone* to school.
DENIES A FACT: He *has* not *gone* to the game.
ASKS A QUESTION: Who *went* with him?

All six tenses are found in the indicative mood. The following sentences use the verb *go* in the six tenses of the indicative:

PRESENT: I *go* to school.
PAST: I *went* to school yesterday.
FUTURE: I *shall go* to school next year.
PRESENT PERFECT: I *have gone* to school for an entire year.
PAST PERFECT: I *had gone* to school before I moved to this city.
FUTURE PERFECT: I *shall have gone* to school before the year is over.

POTENTIAL FORM OF THE INDICATIVE MOOD

The potential form of the indicative mood is used to express permission, possibility, ability, necessity, and obligation.

PERMISSION: You *may go,* John.
POSSIBILITY: It *could happen.*
ABILITY: I *can do* all things in Him who strengthens me.
NECESSITY: Some delicate machines *must be oiled* every hour.
OBLIGATION: Everyone *should pay* his just debts.

The potential form is expressed by the use of the auxiliary verbs *may, might, can, could, must, should,* and *would.* This form is used in the present, the past, the present perfect, and the past perfect tenses, but never in the future tenses. Potential verb phrases are found in both the active and the passive voices. See pages 305-06 and 308-09 for the conjugation of the potential form of the verbs *be* and *choose.*

EXERCISE 85

Select the potential verb phrases in the following sentences and tell what idea is expressed by each:
1. You may use my pencil, James.
2. Eugene should have finished that task earlier.
3. Peter told me that he might leave early.
4. I must leave, for I have an appointment.
5. We should prepare our lessons each day.
6. Where can you buy that kind of pen?
7. Helen, you may give it to whoever comes first.
8. Father, may I play ball with the boys?
9. Each girl must do her best in the game.
10. Paul can lift that box easily.
11. May we be excused early from class?
12. Marie should have asked your permission.
13. Andrew may have taken the key with him.
14. The boy could not find his raincoat.
15. What can't be cured must be endured.
16. Francis could not see the parade from where he stood.
17. This must have been broken before today.
18. He may have left his book at home.
19. We must go now.
20. I could not have completed the work without help.
21. He should have studied harder.
22. Mary thinks that two yards of ribbon may be enough.
23. The speaker could not be heard.
24. I can climb that tree.
25. The clock must be wound daily.

IMPERATIVE MOOD

The imperative mood is used to express a command in the second person. A mild command often takes the form of an entreaty or a request.

COMMAND: Don't *give* up the ship!
ENTREATY: *Give* us this day our daily bread.
REQUEST: *Pray* for me, Father.

The subject of a verb in the imperative mood is always in the second person, either singular or plural, and it is usually not expressed. There is only one tense in the imperative mood, the present tense.

EXERCISE 86

Give the mood, the tense, and the voice of the verbs in the following sentences:
1. Paul, come to the office at once.
2. They have had much experience in that type of work.
3. I was accompanied by a well-informed guide.
4. Dorothy has found her umbrella.
5. The old soldier can recall incidents of the Civil War.
6. Snow could be seen on the distant mountains.
7. The principal was called to the telephone.
8. At what time will he arrive in New York?
9. An encyclopedia contains valuable information.
10. The librarian recommends this book highly.
11. I have read many interesting stories of colonial days.
12. May I borrow your dictionary?
13. My sister can speak Spanish fluently.
14. Mr. Patterson has received a letter from the farmer.
15. Explain the problem, Patrick.
16. Rose should have prepared that assignment yesterday.
17. Mother says that we may go to the beach.
18. Hundreds of water lilies were found in the shallow pond.
19. Bring the map to me.
20. Pray frequently, boys.

4. *Person and Number*

A verb may be in the first, the second, or the third person, and either singular or plural in number. Most verbs do not have a specific inflection or change in form for every person and number. Note the following in the present tense:

	SINGULAR NUMBER	PLURAL NUMBER
FIRST PERSON:	I speak distinctly.	We speak distinctly.
SECOND PERSON:	You speak distinctly.	You speak distinctly.
THIRD PERSON:	He speaks distinctly.	They speak distinctly.

EXERCISE 87

Tell the person and the number of each verb in the following sentences:
1. They have just returned from Cuba.
2. Children, you must study every day.
3. We shall start at dawn tomorrow.
4. She doesn't know where he went.
5. Lend me your fountain pen, George.
6. I am glad you have come.
7. He writes better than his sister.
8. She has not been here since last Thursday.
9. You have torn your dress on that nail.
10. Eugene plays the violin well.
11. Rose Marie had finished the assignment before the other pupils began.
12. Peanuts are exported from the Sudan in large quantities.

CONJUGATION

Conjugation is the orderly arrangement of a verb according to voice, mood, tense, person, and number. It is a tabulated summary of the attributes or qualities of the verb.

CONJUGATION OF THE VERB "BE"

	PRESENT	PAST	PAST PARTICIPLE
PRINCIPAL PARTS:	be	was	been

Indicative Mood

PRESENT TENSE

Singular	*Plural*
1. I am	We are
2. You are	You are
3. He is[1]	They are

PAST TENSE

1. I was	We were
2. You were	You were
3. He was	They were

FUTURE TENSE

1. I shall be	We shall be
2. You will be	You will be
3. He will be	They will be

PRESENT PERFECT TENSE

1. I have been	We have been
2. You have been	You have been
3. He has been	They have been

PAST PERFECT TENSE

1. I had been	We had been
2. You had been	You had been
3. He had been	They had been

FUTURE PERFECT TENSE

1. I shall have been	We shall have been
2. You will have been	You will have been
3. He will have been	They will have been

Potential Form

PRESENT TENSE

1. I may be	We may be
2. You may be	You may be
3. He may be	They may be

---

[1] The subject in the third person singular may also be *she* or *it*.

PAST TENSE

1. I might be	We might be
2. You might be	You might be
3. He might be	They might be

PRESENT PERFECT TENSE

1. I may have been	We may have been
2. You may have been	You may have been
3. He may have been	They may have been

PAST PERFECT TENSE

1. I might have been	We might have been
2. You might have been	You might have been
3. He might have been	They might have been

IMPERATIVE MOOD

PRESENT TENSE

Be (be you)   Be (be you)

CONJUGATION OF THE VERB "CHOOSE"

	PRESENT	PAST	PAST PARTICIPLE
PRINCIPAL PARTS:	choose	chose	chosen

INDICATIVE MOOD
Active Voice

PRESENT TENSE

Singular	*Plural*
1. I choose	We choose
2. You choose	You choose
3. He chooses	They choose

PAST TENSE

1. I chose	We chose
2. You chose	You chose
3. He chose	They chose

FUTURE TENSE

1. I shall choose	We shall choose
2. You will choose	You will choose
3. He will choose	They will choose

PRESENT PERFECT TENSE

1. I have chosen
2. You have chosen
3. He has chosen

We have chosen
You have chosen
They have chosen

PAST PERFECT TENSE

1. I had chosen
2. You had chosen
3. He had chosen

We had chosen
You had chosen
They had chosen

FUTURE PERFECT TENSE

1. I shall have chosen
2. You will have chosen
3. He will have chosen

We shall have chosen
You will have chosen
They will have chosen

Passive Voice

PRESENT TENSE

1. I am chosen
2. You are chosen
3. He is chosen

We are chosen
You are chosen
They are chosen

PAST TENSE

1. I was chosen
2. You were chosen
3. He was chosen

We were chosen
You were chosen
They were chosen

FUTURE TENSE

1. I shall be chosen
2. You will be chosen
3. He will be chosen

We shall be chosen
You will be chosen
They will be chosen

PRESENT PERFECT TENSE

1. I have been chosen
2. You have been chosen
3. He has been chosen

We have been chosen
You have been chosen
They have been chosen

PAST PERFECT TENSE

1. I had been chosen
2. You had been chosen
3. He had been chosen

We had been chosen
You had been chosen
They had been chosen

FUTURE PERFECT TENSE

1. I shall have been chosen
2. You will have been chosen
3. He will have been chosen

We shall have been chosen
You will have been chosen
They will have been chosen

POTENTIAL FORM

Active Voice

PRESENT TENSE

Singular

1. I may choose
2. You may choose
3. He may choose

Plural

We may choose
You may choose
They may choose

PAST TENSE

1. I might choose
2. You might choose
3. He might choose

We might choose
You might choose
They might choose

PRESENT PERFECT TENSE

1. I may have chosen
2. You may have chosen
3. He may have chosen

We may have chosen
You may have chosen
They may have chosen

PAST PERFECT TENSE

1. I might have chosen
2. You might have chosen
3. He might have chosen

We might have chosen
You might have chosen
They might have chosen

Passive Voice

PRESENT TENSE

1. I may be chosen
2. You may be chosen
3. He may be chosen

We may be chosen
You may be chosen
They may be chosen

PAST TENSE

1. I might be chosen
2. You might be chosen
3. He might be chosen

We might be chosen
You might be chosen
They might be chosen

PRESENT PERFECT TENSE

1. I may have been chosen — We may have been chosen
2. You may have been chosen — You may have been chosen
3. He may have been chosen — They may have been chosen

PAST PERFECT TENSE

1. I might have been chosen — We might have been chosen
2. You might have been chosen — You might have been chosen
3. He might have been chosen — They might have been chosen

IMPERATIVE MOOD
Active Voice

Choose (choose you)   Choose (choose you)

Passive Voice

Be chosen (be you chosen)   Be chosen (be you chosen)

SYNOPSIS OF A VERB

A synopsis of a verb is the orderly arrangement of one person and number in all tenses, moods, and both voices, or in a certain designated mood and voice. It is an abbreviated conjugation.

SYNOPSIS OF THE VERB "CHOOSE"
(Indicative mood, third person, singular number)

	Active Voice	Passive Voice
PRESENT TENSE	He chooses	He is chosen
PAST TENSE	He chose	He was chosen
FUTURE TENSE	He will choose	He will be chosen
PRESENT PERFECT TENSE	He has chosen	He has been chosen
PAST PERFECT TENSE	He had chosen	He had been chosen
FUTURE PERFECT TENSE	He will have chosen	He will have been chosen

THE CORRECT USE OF VERBS

1. *Agreement of Verb with Subject*

The verb must always agree with its subject in person and number.

This agreement does not require a specific inflection for every person, number, and tense. In the present tense, for example, there

SUBJECT   **PREDICATE**

is usually no change in the first and the second persons. In the third person of the present tense the singular form ends in *s;* the plural does not.

Observe the inflection of the verbs in the following sentences:

That man works hard.	Those men work hard.
I am cheerful.	We are cheerful.
The reward is his.	The rewards are his.
The boy has gone.	The boys have gone.

A singular subject requires a singular verb; a plural subject requires a plural verb.

Review the conjugation of verbs in the preceding section to be sure that you know perfectly the grammatical changes for all persons and numbers. Note particularly that a finite verb[1] takes the *s* form in the third person singular of the present tense.

EXERCISE 88

Copy the following sentences, using the correct form of the verb in each:

1. God's grace (works, work) in mysterious ways.
2. The men (seems, seem) happy.
3. Around the curve (comes, come) the speeding cars.
4. His friends (has, have) helped him.
5. (Is, are) three sufficient?
6. Many travelers (has, have) followed that route.

---

[1] A finite verb is one that may be used as the principal verb in a clause. *Finite* means "limited."

7. Father, here (is, are) your glasses.
8. Her promises (has, have) been fulfilled.
9. In the orchard (is, are) several kinds of fruit.
10. Here (comes, come) the two boys.
11. Those people (passes, pass) our home every day on their way to work.
12. On the boulevard (is, are) many attractive homes.
13. The storms (has, have) been unusually severe during the entire winter.
14. The votes (is, are) being counted now.
15. The nests (was, were) built in the old tree.
16. The flags (is, are) flying at half-mast because of the death of the president.
17. (Is, are) these apples sweet?
18. Every summer my cousin (visits, visit) me.
19. (Has, have) the invitations been written?
20. The children (helps, help) their mother.

"DOESN'T" AND "DON'T"

If the subject of the sentence is in the third person, *doesn't* is the correct form in the singular; *don't* the correct form in the plural. In the first and the second persons the correct form is *don't*, whether the subject is singular or plural.

My mother (doesn't, don't) like that.

The correct form is: My mother *doesn't* like that.

EXERCISE 89

Rewrite the following sentences, filling in each blank with *doesn't* or *don't:*

1. .... Mary work there now?
2. This house .... look new to me.
3. The problem .... seem difficult.
4. .... she know which books are hers?
5. It .... make any difference to me.
6. Why .... the game begin?

7. This train .... stop at that station.
8. Regina .... understand that work very well.
9. These people .... know where the shrine is located.
10. The noises .... annoy me.
11. The river .... flow into the bay.
12. That .... answer the question that I asked.
13. Raymond .... write very well.
14. .... the Mississippi River rise in Minnesota?
15. Father .... drive our car.
16. .... the bells ring on time?
17. This part of the puzzle .... fit.
18. Those pictures .... appeal to me.
19. .... he know the answer?
20. Why .... she come?
21. John .... know why he did it.
22. It .... seem possible.

"THERE IS" AND "THERE ARE"

There is (was, has been) should be used when the subject, which follows the verb, is singular; *there are (were, have been)* when the subject is plural.

There (was, were) nine eggs in the basket.
The correct form is: There *were* nine eggs in the basket.

EXERCISE 90

Select the correct form of the verb indicated:
1. There (is, are) several boys in the hall.
2. There (is, are) the pilot of this plane.
3. There (has been, have been) many perfect attendance records in this room.
4. There (was, were) many applicants for the position.
5. There (is, are) thirty days in June.
6. There (is, are) the flowers you ordered.
7. There (was, were) no lock on the gate.
8. There (is, are) twelve articles in the Creed.

9. (Is, are) there many people in the audience?
10. There (is, are) my two brothers.
11. There (is, are) an old elm tree near the creek.
12. There (is, are) no difficult problems in this exercise.
13. There (has been, have been) a change in the sport schedule.
14. There (is, are) a man at the door.
15. There (has been, have been) many cold days this month.

"YOU" AS SUBJECT

Use the forms *you are* and *you were* whether the subject is singular or plural. Never use *is* or *was* when the subject is in the second person.

(Was, were) you invited to the party?

The correct form is: *Were* you invited to the party?

EXERCISE 91

Select the correct form in each sentence:
1. (Was, were) you happy when you won the prize?
2. You (is, are) a good friend of mine.
3. (Was, were) you late?
4. (Was, were) you at home when he called?
5. (Was, were) you at the rally, Peter?
6. You (is, are) here on time every day, Jane.
7. (Wasn't, weren't) you with him?
8. You (is, are) too young for the position.
9. You (was, were) there at that time.
10. (Was, were) you excused from the meeting?
11. Where (was, were) you, John?
12. (Is, are) you going by bus or by train?
13. Why (was, were) you absent?
14. You (wasn't, weren't) going to call Jane, (was, were) you?

PHRASES AND PARENTHETICAL EXPRESSIONS

Do not be confused by phrases or parenthetical expressions which may stand between the subject and the verb. A verb agrees with its subject. If the subject is singular, the verb must be singular; if plural, the verb must be plural.

The cost of these plants (has, have) been greatly reduced.

The correct form is: The cost of these plants *has* been greatly reduced.

EXERCISE 92

Rewrite the following sentences, using the correct form in each. Give the reason for your choice:

1. One of the members of our group (was, were) selected.
2. This kind of work (doesn't, don't) appeal to me.
3. A bookcase, together with a supply of books, (was, were) donated to our class.
4. The evergreen, together with the other trees, (was, were) planted yesterday.
5. Her explanation of the charts (was, were) clearly given.
6. Daniel Carroll with his chums (has, have) rented a canoe.
7. One of the boys (has, have) been selected as drum major.
8. Mildred's choice of words (makes, make) her composition interesting.
9. A shipment of oranges (is, are) expected here today.
10. The first game of the season (was, were) played yesterday.
11. Mary, as well as her friends, (is, are) enjoying the play.
12. A guide with a party of ten men and women (is, are) visiting this building.
13. A selection from the Gospels (is, are) read in every Mass.
14. The colors of our flag (is, are) red, white, and blue.
15. The teacher, as well as her pupils, (was, were) at the party.

COMPOUND SUBJECTS CONNECTED BY "AND"

Compound subjects connected by *and* require a plural verb unless the subjects refer to the same person or thing, or express a single idea.

John and James (likes, like) the new canoe.
Waffles and maple syrup (is, are) a favorite breakfast dish.

The correct forms are:
John and James *like* the new canoe.
Waffles and maple syrup *is* a favorite breakfast dish.

EXERCISE 93

Select the correct form of the verb indicated:
1. The chair and the table (was, were) delivered yesterday.
2. The tug and the steamer (was, were) leaving the harbor.
3. (Is, are) your brother and your sister at the entertainment?
4. History and geography (was, were) taught this morning.
5. You and I (has, have) been called.
6. Pride and happiness (was, were) written on his countenance.
7. Books and papers (covers, cover) the library table.
8. Automobiles and airplanes (has, have) made great progress.
9. Edith and Jane (has, have) taken several pictures.
10. Thomas and Robert (weeds, weed) the garden every day.
11. The knives and the forks (has, have) already been placed on the table.
12. Skiing and tobogganing (is, are) winter sports.
13. Anne and Jane (washes, wash) the dishes after each meal.
14. The maple leaves and the oak leaves (turns, turn) beautiful shades in autumn.
15. Jean and Margaret (has, have) their hockey sticks with them.
16. The director and star performer (was, were) Mr. Hanley.
17. Bread and jam (is, are) my favorite lunch.
18. My sister's friend and classmate (was, were) awarded first prize.
19. Cereal and cream (was, were) served first.
20. The new captain and manager (is, are) in our class.

COMPOUND SUBJECTS PRECEDED BY "EACH" AND "EVERY"

Two or more singular subjects connected by *and* but preceded by *each, every, many a,* or *no* require a singular verb.

Each boy and girl (was, were) given a medal.

The correct form is: Each boy and girl *was* given a medal.

EXERCISE 94

Rewrite each of the following sentences, using the correct form of the verb indicated. Give the reason for your choice:
1. Many a box and carton (was, were) made in that old factory.
2. Each teacher and student of our school (wishes, wish) success for the team.
3. Each coat and hat (was, were) in its proper place.
4. Every boy and girl (has, have) been given some candy.
5. Many a man and woman (is, are) excited over the election.
6. (Has, have) every table and chair been painted?
7. Every man and boy (enjoys, enjoy) baseball.
8. Many a toy and trinket (was, were) sold at the circus today.
9. Every boy and girl in this class (seems, seem) very industrious.
10. Many a mail carrier and postal clerk (has, have) benefited by this law.
11. Every shrub and tree (needs, need) rain.
12. Every boy and girl in the club (has, have) been given tickets.
13. (Is, are) each desk and cabinet kept in order?
14. Every sweater and coat (was, were) reduced in price.
15. (Has, have) every pen and pencil been placed in this box?

COMPOUND SUBJECTS CONNECTED BY "OR" AND "NOR"

Singular subjects connected by *or* or *nor* require a singular verb.
Neither the boy nor his sister (is, are) going.

The correct form is: Neither the boy nor his sister *is* going.

Plural subjects connected by *or* or *nor* require a plural verb.
Neither my parents nor my grandparents (is, are) going.

The correct form is: Neither my parents nor my grandparents *are* going.

When two or more subjects of different person or number are connected by *or* or *nor*, the verb agrees with the subject nearest it.
Neither he nor I (am, is, are) going.

The correct form is: Neither he nor I *am* going.

EXERCISE 95

Rewrite each of the following sentences, using the correct form of the verb indicated. Give the reason for your choice:
1. Neither the post card nor the letter (has, have) reached me.
2. Either Mary or Anne (has, have) hidden it.
3. Neither Delaware nor Maryland (mines, mine) coal.
4. Neither Elizabeth nor Jane (has, have) been to the seashore.
5. Neither the radio nor the airplane (was, were) known in pioneer days.
6. Either the farmer or the boy (has, have) the rake.
7. (Was, were) Thomas or Joseph rowing the boat?
8. Neither the textbook nor the workbook (was, were) expensive.
9. Either John or James (has, have) found the lost collie.
10. (Has, have) either your father or your mother returned yet?
11. Neither the boys nor their father (is, are) at home.
12. Neither this book nor those pamphlets (contains, contain) the information you desire.
13. Neither the boys nor the girls in our school (objects, object) to a holiday.
14. Neither my brother nor his friends (is, are) going.
15. (Has, have) neither the desk nor the chairs been delivered?
16. Either they or their friends (has, have) left these gifts.
17. Neither the chalk nor the erasers (was, were) distributed.
18. Either you or I (has, have) made a mistake.

COLLECTIVE NOUNS

A collective noun requires a singular verb if the idea expressed by the subject is thought of as a unit; it requires a plural verb if the idea expressed by the subject denotes separate individuals.

Our class (has, have) prepared a program for Columbus Day.
The team (has, have) attended their classes faithfully.

The correct forms are:
Our class *has* prepared a program for Columbus Day.
The team (members of the team) *have* attended their classes faithfully.

EXERCISE 96

Rewrite each of the following sentences, using the correct form of the verb indicated. Give the reason for your choice:
1. Our orchestra (plays, play) well.
2. A company of soldiers (has, have) encamped in the valley.
3. A French fleet (was, were) entering the harbor.
4. The skating team (was, were) performing on the lake.
5. A bevy of girls (is, are) in the library.
6. The traffic squad of our school (is, are) attending a meeting.
7. A tribe of Indians (was, were) located here at one time.
8. The audience (appreciates, appreciate) your singing.
9. The committee (agrees, agree) on this question.
10. A vast throng (was, were) present at the canonization.
11. Our family (was, were) united for Thanksgiving Day.
12. (Is, are) the class ready for dismissal?
13. The jury (goes, go) into session tomorrow.
14. A herd of sheep (was, were) grazing on the hillside.
15. The council (has, have) gone to their homes.
16. A crowd of children (passes, pass) here every day.
17. (Has, have) the team worn their new uniforms?
18. The group (was, were) awarded prizes.

DISTRIBUTIVE AND INDEFINITE PRONOUNS

The distributive pronouns *each, either, neither,* and the indefinite pronouns *anyone, no one, anybody, nobody, everyone, everybody, someone, somebody* are always singular and require singular verbs.

Each of the boys (has, have) helped with the plan.

The correct form is: Each of the boys *has* helped with the plan.

EXERCISE 97

Copy the following sentences, filling in each blank with the correct form of the verb at the left:

carry   1. Each of the boys .... a Scout knife.
was   2. Each of them .... known.

have	3. Neither of them .... what you need.
like	4. Each of the men .... to play golf.
enjoy	5. Everybody .... a ride in the country during the summer months.
come	6. Nobody .... late in our class.
play	7. Everyone in this group .... a musical instrument.
have	8. Someone .... inquired about you.
have	9. .... anyone seen our new yacht?
is	10. No one .... permitted on these grounds.
live	11. Nobody .... in the house across the street.
was	12. Everyone in our class .... pleased with the election.
write	13. Neither of the girls .... for the school paper.
is	14. Neither of the players .... practicing for the next game.
know	15. Neither of them .... the answer.
was	16. Each of the pupils .... thoroughly prepared for the examination.
have	17. Nobody in the class .... finished the assignment.
attend	18. Neither of those boys .... Saint Luke School at the present time.
ride	19. Each .... a bicycle.
have	20. Somebody .... my watch.

SPECIAL SINGULAR AND PLURAL NOUNS

Some nouns that are plural in form, but usually singular in meaning, require singular verbs. The nouns are: *aeronautics, athletics* (training), *civics, economics, mathematics, measles, molasses, mumps, news, physics.*

Civics (is, are) an interesting subject.

The correct form is: Civics *is* an interesting subject.

Other nouns are usually considered plural and require plural verbs. These nouns are: *ashes, clothes, goods, pliers, proceeds, scales, scissors, shears, spectacles, suspenders, thanks, tongs, trousers, tweezers.*

Grandfather's pliers (has, have) been mislaid.
The correct form is: Grandfather's pliers *have* been mislaid.

EXERCISE 98

Copy the following sentences, filling in the blanks with the correct forms of the verbs at the left:

is	1. Athletics .... beneficial to most boys.
spread	2. News .... rapidly.
is	3. .... your scissors sharp?
need	4. The pliers .... tightening.
hold	5. Aeronautics .... the attention of many young men.
is	6. Mumps .... a child's disease.
is	7. Molasses .... good on hot cakes.
was	8. Grandfather's spectacles .... on the mantel.
have	9. The goods .... been delivered.
develop	10. Mathematics .... good reasoning.
was	11. The proceeds .... given to the hospital.
is	12. The trousers .... made of blue serge.
have	13. Measles .... caused many absences in our primary grades.
is	14. The tongs at our fireplace .... new.
was	15. Civics .... taught the last period.
cause	16. Hot ashes sometimes .... fire.
look	17. Her clothes always .... new.
is	18. .... the tweezers in that drawer?

EXERCISE 99 [Oral Drill]

Read aloud each of the following sentences, choosing the correct verb form. Give a reason for your choice:
1. The men (was, were) pleased with their game.
2. Your suggestion (is, are) acceptable to me.
3. (Doesn't, don't) somebody know the answer?

4. He, as well as his brother, (helps, help) with the work each day.
5. Jane (has, have) found your ring.
6. Why (doesn't, don't) Henry come?
7. The members of the safety patrol (was, were) given certificates for their services.
8. The child, together with her nurse, (is, are) sitting on the porch.
9. Where (has, have) you laid my suitcase?
10. There (goes, go) Thomas and Henry.
11. He (doesn't, don't) understand that work.
12. There (is, are) three departments in our government.
13. (Has, have) the jar of cookies been taken from the shelf?
14. Each of the girls (plays, play) the piano well.
15. A box of flowers (was, were) sent to the sick child.
16. One of the wisest kings (was, were) King Solomon.
17. Why (doesn't, don't) the children hurry?
18. Here (comes, come) the captain and the team.
19. Both of them (is, are) very happy.
20. The jury (is, are) returning to their homes.
21. A crowd of children (was, were) following the fire engines.
22. Every minute of our time (is, are) valuable.
23. Measles (is, are) a common disease among children.
24. There (is, are) many beautiful flowers in this garden.
25. The crew of the liner (has, have) asked for shore leave.
26. Civics (is, are) studied by this class.
27. Neither John nor Edward (has, have) finished the problem.
28. Either Thomas or Jane (is, are) going to the concert.
29. Economics (is, are) a very interesting subject.
30. Either Marie or Ellen (has, have) taken the new car.
31. On that rack (was, were) several coats.
32. The reference books (has, have) lain on the desk for two days.
33. The scissors (has, have) been broken.
34. A book of adventure stories (was, were) selected.
35. The troop (was, were) led by Captain Ford.
36. Mary (has, have) taken that book with her.

37. The proceeds (was, were) used for the hospital.
38. There (is, are) a dozen pens in that box.

2. Uses of Shall and Will

In the future tense of verbs we use *shall* in the first person and *will* in the second and the third persons to express simple futurity or expectation. If we wish to indicate an act of the will, promise, or determination on the part of the speaker, we use *will* in the first person and *shall* in the second and the third persons.

SIMPLE FUTURITY	DETERMINATION
I shall choose the chairman.	Indeed, I will choose the chairman.
You will choose the chairman.	You shall certainly choose the chairman.
He will choose the chairman.	He shall choose the chairman in spite of opposition.

EXERCISE 100

Fill in each blank with the correct form, *shall* or *will*, to express simple futurity:

1. Helen .... be thirteen years old next month.
2. The school bell .... be rung at nine o'clock.
3. We .... miss the bus if we do not hurry.
4. You .... find the package on my desk.
5. Our souls .... never die.
6. I .... return to college in September.
7. The new project .... benefit many people.
8. It is so cold we .... need our coats.
9. The train .... stop at the next station.
10. I .... be happy to see him.

EXERCISE 101

Fill in each blank with the correct form, *shall* or *will*, to express determination or promise on the part of the speaker:

1. We positively .... not go.
2. He .... not leave; my answer is final.
3. Robert .... do as I say.

4. You .... be rewarded for this kind act.
5. I .... take you with me to the mountains.
6. Adam .... not leave this room until he has finished his assignment.
7. "You .... certainly pay for the damage done to my garden," said Mr. Perry.
8. I am determined that he .... come at once.
9. I .... paint the chairs for you.
10. I promise you that I .... be there on time.
11. We .... call for you at four o'clock.
12. "I .... appoint the chairman tomorrow," said Paul.

"SHOULD" AND "WOULD"

The rules for *shall* and *will* also apply to *should* and *would*.

To express simple futurity, use *should* in the first person and *would* in the second and the third persons.

I *should* enjoy helping you.
He *would* enjoy helping you.

To express determination, resolution, or promise on the part of the speaker, use *would* in the first person and *should* in the second and the third persons.

We promised that we *would* go.
We promised that he *should* go.

Should meaning *ought to* is frequently used in all three persons.

We *should* obey all school regulations.
Every pupil *should* obey all school regulations.

Would expressing a wish or customary action is used in all three persons.

I *would* often listen to the old captain's stories.
Would that the boys could hear the old captain's stories.

EXERCISE 102

Select the correct word in each parenthesis:

1. You (should, would) be a loyal student at all times.
2. She (should, would) accept the position if she were well.

3. Our class (should, would) like to have a picnic next week.
4. My mother (should, would) never consent to that.
5. You (should, would) listen attentively to all instructions.
6. We (should, would) support our school in all activities.
7. We (should, would) always pay our just debts.
8. She (should, would) often entertain us while we ate our lunch.
9. He (should, would) not have left the package here.
10. We (should, would) obey all traffic rules.
11. He (should, would) sit by the radio and read.
12. James (should, would) assist you if he had time.

"SHALL" AND "WILL" IN QUESTIONS

Shall is always used to ask a question when the subject is in the first person. In the second and the third persons whichever word is expected in the reply is used in asking the question.

QUESTION	EXPECTED REPLY
Shall we do it?	We shall.
Shall you be able to do it soon?	I shall.
Will you promise to do it soon?	I will.
Will he be able to do it today?	He will.

EXERCISE 103

Copy the following sentences, filling in each blank with *shall* or *will*:

1. When .... we leave?
2. Who .... carry the box?
3. What .... I do about the matter?
4. .... you collect the toys for the poor children?
5. .... you promise to arrive before nine o'clock?
6. What reply .... we give Mr. Artis?
7. .... I distribute the papers now?
8. Jane, when .... you return?
9. Whom .... I invite?
10. Gertrude, ... you lend me your pen?
11. When .... Christ judge us?
12. At what time .... the meeting open?

3. Troublesome Verbs

Every pupil should know the principal parts and the meanings of the following verbs:

Lie, lay, lain

This verb means to *rest* or *recline*. It is always intransitive.

Lay, laid, laid

This verb means to *put* or *place* in position. It is always transitive.

Sit, sat, sat

This verb means to *have* or *keep* a seat. It is always intransitive.

Set, set, set

This verb means to *place* or *fix* in position. It is always transitive.

Rise, rose, risen

This verb means to *ascend*. It is always intransitive.

Raise, raised, raised

This verb means to *lift*. It is always transitive.

Let, let, let
This verb means to *permit* or *allow*.

Leave, left, left
This verb means to *abandon* or *depart from*.

EXERCISE 104

Choose the correct verb form in each of the following sentences:
1. Did you notice who (sat, set) beside you at the show?
2. Leaves of various colors (lay, laid) on the ground.
3. The class will (raise, rise) when the visitor enters.
4. Where did you (lay, lie) the paper?
5. Has the hose (lain, laid) there since yesterday?
6. Vincent (sits, sets) in the first desk.
7. The dog is (laying, lying) in the shade.
8. Please (sit, set) in that chair.
9. Mother (lay, laid) down for an hour.
10. Can you (raise, rise) that window?
11. Will your mother (let, leave) you go with us?
12. Marie (set, sat) the plant on the porch.
13. I must have (left, let) my speller at home.
14. The children became excited when the plane (rose, raised).
15. The exhausted child (lay, laid) on the bed.
16. Mary's gloves are (laying, lying) on the desk.
17. Did Father (sit, set) the alarm clock?
18. We (rise, raise) many vegetables on our farm.
19. He has (laid, lain) the package on the table.
20. I wonder who has (raised, risen) that flag.
21. Mother was (sitting, setting) in the rocking chair when I left.
22. Charles, (lie, lay) the box there.
23. The boys (set, sat) the chairs in rows.
24. The price of coal has been (raised, risen).
25. (Leave, let) me sharpen my pencil.
26. We must (rise, raise) early tomorrow.
27. My sister (leaves, lets) me use her camera.
28. Why are the children (laying, lying) there?

29. (Lie, lay) the map on the desk.
30. (Leave, let) me go with you, Mother.
31. The broken glass has (laid, lain) there all day.
32. Cotton is (raised, risen) in the South.
33. The dog has (laid, lain) in the cool shade for some time.
34. The snow (lay, laid) on the ground for two days.
35. We must (leave, let) our skates in the playroom.
36. Who is that (laying, lying) in the hammock?
37. (Let, leave) us sit here on the bank of the stream.
38. Father is (laying, lying) the rug.
39. (Sit, set) the vase on this table, Marie.
40. Children, please do not (rise, raise) your hands.
41. James, I found your coat (laying, lying) on the floor.
42. During the night the river (raised, rose).
43. Much cotton is (risen, raised) in Texas.
44. Where will the guest (sit, set)?
45. Edward, do not (leave, let) your toys on the floor.
46. That singer has (risen, raised) to fame in a very short time.
47. Thomas (left, let) for camp early this morning.
48. The hospital is (rising, raising) money for a new building.
49. The sun (raised, rose) high above the clouds.
50. Did you (rise, raise) when the teacher spoke to you?

EXERCISE 105 [Checking-up Exercise]

Test your knowledge of irregular verbs by filling in the blanks with the past tense or the past participle of the verbs at the left:

drive   1. Thomas .... the car very rapidly.
swim   2. The boys .... in this pool yesterday.
choose 3. We have .... James as the president of our Good Citizenship Club.
go   4. Who .... to the market with Mother?
write   5. Leo .... his work very neatly.
sing   6. Alice has .... for us each evening.
speak   7. Father .... to me about the work.
rise   8. The moon .... high in the heavens.
see   9. Happiness could be .... on all sides.

give
begin
blow
catch
know
come

speak
take
freeze
do
eat
fall
tear
draw
grow
make
see
shake
forget
tell

10. Mother has .... me a new bicycle.
11. They have .... their work.
12. The wind .... the sails of the small boat.
13. David .... three trout in this stream.
14. We have .... his plans for some time.
15. Twenty children .... to Sheila's birthday party.
16. I have .... to him several times.
17. The tourist .... pictures of the scene.
18. Has the lake .... ?
19. The dog has .... this trick many times.
20. Have the children .... the candy?
21. The tree .... close to the barn.
22. The child has .... her dress.
23. They have .... book-cover designs.
24. My brother has .... very tall.
25. The girls have .... beautiful rugs.
26. We have .... that picture before.
27. The windows were .... by the wind.
28. Michael .... his lunch.
29. John must have .... them.

VERBS 329

fly	30. The birds have .... to a warmer region.
leave	31. Where have you .... the camera?
meet	32. Mother .... me at the theater.
find	33. I .... my ring on the desk.
be	34. My father has never .... across the Atlantic.
make	35. Margaret .... dessert for dinner.
lend	36. William .... him his bicycle.
hear	37. Not a voice could be .... above the clatter.
lose	38. The child had .... his pencil.
lay	39. They .... their reports on the desk.
bring	40. Have you .... your lunch?
speed	41. The car .... over the race track.
come	42. Down the mountainside .... the happy group.
ride	43. For several hours we .... over beautiful country roads.
stand	44. On the top of the hill an old mansion once ....
sit	45. He had .... in that place before.
rise	46. As I spoke to the boy, he ....
lie	47. John has .... down to rest.
say	48. Joseph .... that he would be glad to go.
sell	49. The druggist .... her a can of tooth powder.
hold	50. The dying man .... his crucifix.

EXERCISE 106   [Checking-up Exercise]

Supply the verb form called for in each sentence:

purchase	1. Louisiana .... from France. *(Past tense, passive voice, indicative mood)*
plan	2. The boys .... a one-act play. *(Past perfect tense, active voice, indicative mood)*
scatter	3. The child's toys .... about the lawn. *(Past tense, passive voice, indicative mood)*
close	4. .... the door, John. *(Present tense, active voice, imperative mood)*

call	5. We .... for you early tomorrow. *(Future tense, active voice, indicative mood)*
dress	6. Marita .... in a colonial costume. *(Past tense, passive voice, indicative mood)*
freeze	7. The ice cream .... in various molds. *(Present tense, passive voice, indicative mood)*
finish	8. Eleanor .... her work in two hours. *(Future tense, active voice, indicative mood)*
admire	9. I .... a boy of courage. *(Present tense, active voice, indicative mood)*
study	10. Civics .... in our grade. *(Present tense, passive voice, indicative mood)*
come	11. James .... when he is ready. *(Future tense, active voice, indicative mood)*
raise	12. The farmer .... potatoes on his farm last year. *(Past tense, active voice, indicative mood)*
talk	13. Mr. Adams .... with you this evening. *(Future tense, active voice, indicative mood)*
lose	14. The book .... *(Present perfect tense, passive voice, indicative mood)*
live	15. Albert .... there for five years. *(Past perfect tense, active voice, indicative mood)*
discuss	16. The members of the committee .... the measure. *(Past tense, active voice, indicative mood)*
serve	17. That old soldier .... in the Civil War. *(Past tense, active voice, indicative mood)*
make	18. The gates .... of iron. *(Past perfect tense, passive voice, indicative mood)*
explain	19. Regina, ... the problem to the class. *(Present tense, active voice, imperative mood)*
be	20. Geography .... an interesting subject. *(Present tense, indicative mood)*
reach	21. The children .... school before the shower. *(Past perfect tense, active voice, indicative mood)*

prepare 22. Mother .... lunch for my father and brothers. *(Present perfect tense, active voice, indicative mood)*

write 23. .... the letter now. *(Present tense, active voice, imperative mood)*

lie 24. The old tree .... there for a long time. *(Present perfect tense, active voice, indicative mood)*

take 25. Jane .... very good care of her clothes. *(Present tense, active voice, indicative mood)*

row 26. Robert .... the boat. *(Future tense, active voice, indicative mood)*

invent 27. The telephone .... by Alexander G. Bell. *(Past tense, passive voice, indicative mood)*

be 28. .... kind at all times. *(Present tense, imperative mood)*

tell 29. Edward .... me that he was going to South America. *(Past tense, active voice, indicative mood)*

build 30. High up in the tree the bird .... a nest. *(Past perfect tense, active voice, indicative mood)*

bring 31. .... your bicycle into the house. *(Present tense, active voice, imperative mood)*

weed 32. We .... the garden this afternoon. *(Future tense, active voice, indicative mood)*

give 33. The party .... for Jane and me. *(Present perfect tense, passive voice, indicative mood)*

guide 34. .... by the instructions in the cookbook. *(Present tense, passive voice, imperative mood)*

fall 35. Those pears .... from the tree by tomorrow. *(Future perfect tense, active voice, indicative mood)*

stand 36. The city of Pittsburgh .... on the site of Fort Duquesne. *(Present tense, active voice, indicative mood)*

332 VOYAGES IN ENGLISH, SEVENTH YEAR

4. *Words Used as Nouns and Verbs*

A noun is a name word. A verb generally expresses action or being.

> An angel appeared to Saint Joseph in a *dream*. *(Noun)*
> During his boyhood he would often *dream* of his future. *(Verb)*

EXERCISE 107

Tell whether each word printed in italics is a verb or a noun:

1. Every morning I *ride* to school on the bus.
2. Father took us for a *ride* in the park.
3. This clock *chimes* the hour.
4. The *chimes* in the church tower pealed forth joyously.
5. Play a *march*, Peter.
6. The band will *march* first.
7. *Ship* the goods immediately.
8. A large *ship* has entered the harbor.
9. You must *nail* the top on this box.
10. Mary caught her coat on a *nail*.
11. Those girls *dance* on skates.
12. Miss Gantz taught us a Mexican *dance*.
13. Joseph accidentally spilled a can of *paint* on the floor.
14. Will you *paint* the benches for me tomorrow?
15. A *debate* is scheduled for our next club meeting.
16. This week the teams will *debate* a religious subject.
17. The first *draft* of my composition must be polished.
18. My mother will *draft* a pattern before she makes the dress.
19. In his *travels* he has visited many lands.
20. My father *travels* by airplane whenever possible.

EXERCISE 108 [Test on Verbs]

Read this selection very carefully and then answer the questions that follow:

[1] On that eventful day when the Wright brothers flew successfully their heavier-than-air machine, an agelong ambition of the human race became a reality. [2] For hundreds of years man had

dreamed of flight. ³ Long ago the artist Da Vinci had designed an "artificial bird" and tested wings and propellers. ⁴ During the eighteenth and nineteenth centuries extensive experiments were made with balloons and dirigibles. ⁵ Gliders were later developed and improved. ⁶ Aviation, however, took a giant step when Orville and Wilbur Wright powered their glider with a gasoline engine and demonstrated its practicability. ⁷ Their ingenuity and perseverance laid a firm foundation for the many improvements which modern science has made and will make in the future.

1. Name a verb phrase in the last sentence.
2. Is the verb *flew* in the first sentence regular or irregular?
3. Find an irregular verb in the sixth sentence.
4. Is *had designed* in the third sentence transitive or intransitive?
5. Find a copulative verb in the first sentence.
6. Name the subjective complement in the first sentence. Is it a noun or an adjective?
7. Is the verb in the second sentence in the active or the passive voice?
8. The verb in the second sentence is in what tense?
9. Select two verbs in the passive voice.
10. Write the present tense of the verb *flew*.
11. Write the future perfect tense of the verb *took* in the sixth sentence.
12. Find a verb in the future tense.
13. In what mood are the verbs in the selection?
14. The verb *has made* in the last sentence agrees with its subject *science* in what person and number?
15. Does the verb *powered* in the sixth sentence denote action, being, or state of being?

CHAPTER FIVE Adverbs

An adverb is a word that modifies a verb, an adjective, or another adverb.

Jane sang *sweetly*.
Jane sang *very* beautiful songs.
Jane sang *unusually well*.

CLASSIFICATION OF ADVERBS

1. *According to Meaning*

Adverbs may indicate *time, place, degree, manner, affirmation,* or *negation*.

Adverbs of time answer the question *when* or *how often*.

Please come *early*.

Adverbs of place answer the question *where*.

He has gone *inside*.

Adverbs of degree answer the question *how much* or *how little*.

The work is *half* finished.

Adverbs of manner answer the question *how* or *in what manner*.

John solved the problems *rapidly*.

Adverbs of affirmation and negation tell whether a fact is, was, will be, or has been *true* or *false*.

No, I will *not* go.

EXERCISE 109

Select the adverbs in the following sentences and tell whether they indicate time, place, degree, manner, affirmation, or negation:

1. The children talked gaily.
2. The town was unusually quiet.
3. He glanced anxiously at the paper.

4. She looked everywhere for her pocketbook.
5. Suddenly the gong rang.
6. The pioneers faced danger courageously.
7. I will plant the pansies here.
8. The song of the lark was heard frequently.
9. We have stood here long enough.
10. The baptismal font is blessed with very beautiful and sacred ceremonies.
11. It is always morning somewhere in the world.
12. The paschal candle usually stands at the Gospel side of the sanctuary.
13. The torch glowed steadily.
14. Ruth laughed merrily.
15. We shall undoubtedly receive an answer from him.
16. Yes, she gave her consent readily.
17. Do not walk so fast.
18. No, John has not returned.
19. Keep God always in your heart.
20. She is an exceedingly talented musician.

EXERCISE 110

1. Use the following adverbs of time in sentences: already, daily, again, always, late, before, now.
2. Use the following adverbs of place in sentences: away, here, above, below, outside, down, within.
3. Use the following adverbs of degree in sentences: almost, much, very, enough, too, little, somewhat.
4. Use the following adverbs of manner in sentences: badly, well, slowly, wisely, quickly, gently, easily.
5. Use the following adverbs of affirmation or negation in sentences: yes, not, perhaps, indeed, no, undoubtedly, doubtless, never, certainly.

EXERCISE 111

1. Select appropriate adverbs to modify the following words:

ripe	runs	happily	laughed
well	rapidly	satisfactory	soft
marched	turned	interesting	tripped
heavily	worked	tall	sang

2. Write synonyms for the following adverbs:

continually	carefully	lovingly	quickly
bravely	apart	well	quite
almost	seldom	easily	seriously

2. *According to Use*

SIMPLE ADVERBS

A simple adverb is an adverb used merely as a modifier.
We should receive Holy Communion *frequently*.

INTERROGATIVE ADVERBS

An interrogative adverb is an adverb used in asking questions. The interrogative adverbs are *how, when, where,* and *why*.
When did you arrive?

EXERCISE 112

Point out the simple and the interrogative adverbs in the following sentences:
1. Suddenly a strange sound was heard.
2. How did Jesus remove the doubt of Saint Thomas?
3. Where was the treaty of peace signed after the War of 1812?
4. When did Christ institute the sacrament of holy orders?
5. We should never be ashamed of the Catholic faith.
6. She bore her sorrow gallantly.
7. Do your work quietly and carefully.
8. We should pray daily for strength in time of temptation.
9. Mr. Casey looked at him shrewdly.
10. She has often spoken of that matter.
11. Why did Christ suffer and die?
12. Machinery has made farm work much easier.
13. God is everywhere.
14. The room was artistically arranged.
15. They looked here, there, and everywhere for the lost ring.
16. I have recently received an increase in salary.
17. Never refuse the grace that God offers you.
18. When was the steamboat invented?
19. The boy spoke clearly and distinctly.
20. Now and then could be seen the light from the distant hill.

CONJUNCTIVE ADVERBS

A conjunctive adverb is a word that does the work of an adverb and a conjunction. The principal conjunctive adverbs are *after, until, as, when, before, where, since,* and *while*.

We visited the catacombs *while* we were in Rome.

While explains the time of the action and is therefore an adverb; it also connects the clause *while we were in Rome* with the verb *visited* and is therefore a conjunction.

NOTE. Conjunctive adverbs usually modify two verbs at the same time. In the model *while* modifies the verb *were*, and the subordinate clause introduced by *while* modifies *visited*.

EXERCISE 113

Give the syntax of each conjunctive adverb in the following sentences:
1. I have not seen Paul since he moved to Westville.
2. After the storm was over a beautiful rainbow appeared in the sky.
3. When Jesus was twelve years old He went to Jerusalem.
4. You will never miss the water until the well runs dry.
5. Elizabeth prepared the work as she was told.
6. While you are growing you need good nourishing food.
7. When I reached home I was very tired.
8. The altar must be solemnly consecrated by the bishop before it is used.
9. The boy speaks as he thinks.
10. He waited until the boat arrived.
11. When the shortstop fumbled the ball he made a costly error.
12. The boys had made many attempts before they succeeded.
13. I was very happy when I received my wrist watch.
14. While James Madison was president the second war for independence was fought.
15. When Theodore Roosevelt was a child he was very delicate.
16. Children should always come when they are called.
17. The saints intercede for us in heaven while we celebrate their memory on earth.
18. As he walked along the riverbank he watched the ships pass by.
19. Before the steamboat was invented travel by water was very slow.
20. After I examine my conscience I make a fervent act of contrition.

RELATIVE ADVERBS

A relative adverb is a word that does the work of an adverb and a relative pronoun. The principal relative adverbs are *when, where,* and *why.*

The home *where* obedience is observed is a happy one.

Since *where* tells us the place of the action, it is an adverb. It also does the work of a relative pronoun because it joins the subordinate clause, *where obedience is observed*, to the noun *home*, which is the antecedent of *where*.

NOTE. A relative adverb usually follows a noun of time or place, and it may be replaced by a prepositional phrase containing a relative pronoun.

The home *in which* obedience is observed is a happy one.

EXERCISE 114

Give the syntax of each relative adverb in these sentences:
1. The particular judgment will take place at the moment when each person dies.
2. I can give you no reason why I am late.
3. Last week they visited Denver, where they had not been for five years.
4. The exact time when the boat arrived is not known.
5. Philadelphia is the city where the first flag was made.
6. We visited the place where the battle was fought.
7. Need I state the reason why I asked your assistance?
8. The library is a building where I spend many pleasant hours.
9. I do not know the reason why the letter was delayed.
10. The factory where my father works is now very busy.
11. I found my books in the desk where I had left them.
12. Do you know the reason why Quebec was made the capital of New France?
13. Mr. Murphy lives in the house where he was born.
14. The garage where we keep our car has just been repaired.
15. Not far away was a field where cows were grazing.
16. The time when he will return is uncertain.
17. The doctor turned to the bed where the sick child lay.
18. I know of no reason why that task cannot be done now.
19. We do not know the hour when God will call us.
20. The spot where Benedict Arnold betrayed his country is on the Hudson.

EXERCISE 115

Select the conjunctive and the relative adverbs in the following sentences and give the syntax of each:
1. We stand while the priest reads the Gospel.
2. I saw him as he rounded the corner.
3. June is the month when we honor the Sacred Heart.
4. He gave no reason why he was late.
5. We shall leave after we finish our compositions.
6. When spring comes the birds return.
7. After gold was discovered in California, a wild rush westward commenced.
8. May I use your racket while you go to the library?
9. This is the city where the Declaration of Independence was signed.
10. The little dog waited patiently until his master had finished.
11. When my father goes on business trips, he travels by airplane.
12. I have not seen him since he moved to the country.
13. The place where George Washington lived is called Mount Vernon.
14. We will finish the work before we leave.
15. When the bishop confirms us, he gives us a slight blow on the cheek.
16. He did not remember the place where he left the book.
17. He will not make the announcement until you arrive.
18. The day when vacation begins is a happy one.
19. The Indians roved over the great plains where the buffaloes were abundant.
20. A modern home has been built on the site where the old farmhouse stood.

ADVERBIAL OBJECTIVES

An adverbial objective is a noun that expresses time, distance, measure, weight, value, or direction, and performs the function of an adverb.

Men guarded the Blessed Sacrament all *night*.

In this sentence *night*, a noun, tells how long the men guarded the Blessed Sacrament. This word indicating time, therefore, is a noun that has a characteristic of an adverb. It is called an *adverbial objective*. In the model *night* modifies the verb *guarded* and the adjective *all* modifies the adverbial objective *night*.

EXERCISE 116

Select the adverbial objectives in the following sentences. Tell whether they express time, distance, measure, weight, value, or direction:

1. The display lasted three days.
2. Turn your chair this way, Ethel.
3. Uncle Richard has been waiting hours for you.
4. The aged priest traveled thirty-five miles on his mission of mercy.
5. The girls left this afternoon.
6. My home is six blocks from the school.
7. The shoes cost eight dollars.
8. He remained in Honolulu four years.
9. Patricia has been absent only one day this term.
10. The lake is eighteen feet deep at this spot.
11. The catacombs were built centuries ago.
12. The airplane had fallen one hundred miles beyond.
13. In our parish we have devotions in honor of Saint Martin every Tuesday.
14. The treatments were given every week.
15. The marble block weighs two tons.

COMPARISON OF ADVERBS

Many adverbs are compared. Like adjectives, they have three degrees of comparison: positive, comparative, and superlative.

1. *Regular Comparison*

Some adverbs form the comparative degree by adding *er* to the positive, and the superlative degree by adding *est* to the positive.

POSITIVE	COMPARATIVE	SUPERLATIVE
soon	sooner	soonest
often	oftener	oftenest

Other adverbs, particularly those ending in *ly*, form the comparative degree by prefixing *more* or *less* to the positive, and the superlative degree by prefixing *most* or *least* to the positive.

POSITIVE	COMPARATIVE	SUPERLATIVE
easily	more easily	most easily
rapidly	less rapidly	least rapidly

2. *Irregular Comparison*

Some adverbs are compared irregularly. In this case it is necessary to learn the comparative and the superlative degrees.

POSITIVE	COMPARATIVE	SUPERLATIVE
badly	worse	worst
far	farther	farthest
forth	further	furthest
little	less	least
much	more	most
well	better	best

Many adverbs denoting time and place *(here, now, then, when, where, again, always, down, above)* and adverbs expressing absoluteness or completeness *(round, eternally, universally, never, perfectly, forever)* cannot be compared.

EXERCISE 117

Select the adverbs in the following sentences and tell the degree of comparison of those which can be compared:
1. Robert always writes well.
2. The yellow roadster traveled fastest.
3. I can study best early in the morning.
4. Who drives more carefully, your father or your brother?
5. Edward came late.
6. The corn has been badly damaged by the storm.

7. They listened devoutly to the sermon.
8. Yes, I will do the work immediately.
9. The children laughed merrily.
10. Act courageously.
11. William played his part better than Joseph.
12. Of all the girls in the group, Helen walked most briskly.
13. She felt the disappointment keenly.
14. Whom do you admire more, Washington or Lincoln?
15. Charles can run faster than his brother.
16. The snow had been falling rapidly all morning.
17. Saint Peter ranks highest in the list of apostles.
18. The altar was beautifully decorated for the feast.

EXERCISE 118

In this exercise one degree of the adverb is given. Write out the complete comparison of each adverb by filling in the blanks:

Positive	Comparative	Superlative
....	worse	....
slowly	....	....
....	....	most earnestly
....	less swiftly	....
clearly	....	....
....	less	....
....	....	earliest
....	farther	....
....	....	most fervently

THE CORRECT USE OF ADVERBS

1. *Distinguishing between Adjectives and Adverbs*

Adjectives modify nouns and pronouns. Adverbs modify verbs, adjectives, and other adverbs.

You may sometimes be uncertain as to whether a word is a predicate adjective or an adverb; that is, whether it modifies the subject or modifies the verb, an adjective, or another adverb.

Predicate adjectives are used only with copulative verbs. The verb *be* in its various forms is the most common copulative. Other verbs which may be used as copulative verbs are *appear, become, continue, feel, grow, look, remain, seem, smell, sound,* and *taste.* Study each sentence and ask yourself whether you are trying to tell something about the subject, the verb, or an adjective.

Estelle looked *happy*. (Equivalent to Estelle *was* happy; an adjective)
Estelle looked *intently* at the book. (Tells how she *looked;* an adverb)
Estelle looked *unusually* cheerful. (Tells how *cheerful;* an adverb)

EXERCISE 119

Select the correct word in each parenthesis:
1. Father smiled (happy, happily).
2. He rode (swift, swiftly) down the street.
3. Edgar came (prompt, promptly).
4. The captain appeared (brave, bravely).
5. The machine swerved (sudden, suddenly).
6. It is (extreme, extremely) cold today.
7. The dogs seem (fierce, fiercely).
8. This pie tastes (delicious, deliciously).
9. The sky looks (unusual, unusually) bright today.
10. Doesn't this cloth feel (rough, roughly)?
11. He walked (light, lightly) across the floor.
12. The robin sang (sweet, sweetly).
13. The apple tastes (bitter, bitterly).
14. The sea looks (calm, calmly).
15. His voice sounds (hoarse, hoarsely).
16. The sky looks (clear, clearly).
17. Robert's plan sounds more (attractive, attractively).
18. She paints very (beautiful, beautifully).
19. John answered the questions in the test (correct, correctly).
20. The catcher's glove cost (considerable, considerably) more than I had expected.
21. The concert will (sure, surely) please you.
22. My brother swims very (good, well).
23. The bells rang (quiet, quietly).

24. My mother feels (sad, sadly) over the misunderstanding.
25. The violet smells (fragrant, fragrantly).
26. The music sounded (soft, softly) and (sweet, sweetly).
27. The fog seems very (dense, densely).
28. I had (scarce, scarcely) arrived at the stadium when the game began.

2. Farther *and* Further

Farther refers to *distance*. *Further* denotes an *addition*. Both words may be used either as adjectives or as adverbs.

James lives *farther* from school than Leo.
We camped on the *farther* shore.
The teacher explained the directions *further*.
You need *further* proof.

EXERCISE 120

Select the correct word in each sentence:
1. We had walked (farther, further) than we intended.
2. My home is (farther, further) down this lane.
3. Rose stated that she would say nothing (farther, further) about the matter.
4. Esther had no (farther, further) use for those books.
5. Mr. Reilly moved (farther, further) away.
6. The girls continued the discussion (farther, further).
7. Upon (farther, further) search Gerald found his birthday gift.
8. Michael's car is (farther, further) down the road.
9. My uncle's store is first; ours is (farther, further) down the street.
10. (Farther, further) work on the project is unnecessary.
11. From the (farther, further) side of the stream we could see the cabin.
12. Andrew walked (farther, further) than Eugene.
13. (Farther, further) aid was given to the colonies.
14. What (farther, further) proof has Edward for that statement?
15. Sister made no (farther, further) comment.

3. Uses of There

There may be an adverb denoting place, or it may be an expletive used to introduce a sentence.

There is my home. *(Adverb)*
There is no one at home. *(Expletive)*

The expletive *there* is not a necessary part of the sentence; it merely introduces the sentence and allows the subject to follow the predicate verb. The two sentences above can be written:

My home is *there.*
No one is at home.

In the case of the adverb, *there* cannot be removed from the sentence. The expletive disappears when the sentence is rewritten.

EXERCISE 121

In each sentence tell whether *there* is an adverb or an expletive:

1. There is the city hall.
2. There is a change in the weather.
3. There was absolute silence after the speech.
4. There is new shrubbery on the grounds.
5. There is the professor entering now.
6. There is only one answer to that question.
7. There were few who understood the case.
8. There is nothing lost by the attempt.
9. There go the Scouts.
10. There stood my friend Robert.
11. There is frost on the ground today.
12. There, on the side lawn, is the silver spruce.
13. There is a silver spruce on the side lawn.
14. There were many people at the seashore.
15. There is our old homestead.
16. There was no sound but the ticking of the clock.
17. There is Mr. Dormer of whom I spoke.
18. There lie Leo's skates.
19. There are many boys in our class.
20. There is the book that I lost.

EXERCISE 122 [Test on Adverbs]

Read this selection very carefully and then answer the questions that follow:

[1] Automobile accidents are caused very frequently by the ignorance of pedestrians. [2] More often they are the result of carelessness. [3] These are two important reasons why safety rules should be most conscientiously observed.

[4] Cross the streets only at designated intersections. [5] Watch the traffic signals carefully. [6] Always look up and down before you step off the curb. [7] Never walk behind a bus or a streetcar after you have alighted. [8] If these regulations are followed faithfully, fewer accidents will undoubtedly occur.

1. Name an adverb of time in the first sentence.
2. Point out two adverbs of place in the sixth sentence.
3. What kind of adverb is *very* in the first sentence?
4. What kind of adverb is *carefully* in the fifth sentence?
5. Find an adverb of negation in the second paragraph.
6. What kind of adverb is *undoubtedly* in the last sentence?
7. Select a relative adverb in the first paragraph.
8. What clause is introduced by the relative adverb? What noun does this clause modify?
9. Name two conjunctive adverbs in the second paragraph.
10. Do conjunctive adverbs introduce adjectival or adverbial clauses?
11. Find an adverb in the superlative degree. Write the positive and the comparative forms of this adverb.
12. What degree of comparison is the adverb *more often* in the second sentence?
13. Can the adverb *always* in the sixth sentence be compared?
14. What part of speech does the adverb *faithfully* in the last sentence modify?
15. Find an adverb that modifies another adverb.

CHAPTER SIX **Prepositions, Conjunctions, Interjections**

A preposition is a word or a group of words that shows the relation between a substantive and some other word in the sentence.

The girl stood *at* the window.   The girl stood *beside* the statue.
The girl stood *in* the doorway.   The girl stood *behind* the chair.

In each of these sentences the place where the girl stood is expressed by a phrase consisting of a preposition and a noun which is the object of the preposition. The preposition serves to connect the noun and the verb *stood*.

The most commonly used prepositions are:

about	at	down	near	throughout
above	before	during	of	to
across	behind	except	off	toward
after	beside	for	on	under
against	between	from	over	until
among	beyond	in	past	up
around	by	into	through	with

The following groups of words are considered one preposition when used with nouns or pronouns:

according to	for the sake of	instead of
as for	in addition to	on account of
because of	in place of	outside of
by means of	in regard to	with respect to

Note the groups of words used as one preposition in the following sentences:

Take this book *in place of* that one.
Bake the cake *according to* the directions.
She receives a commission *instead of* a salary.

1. The Object of a Preposition

The object of a preposition is a noun, a pronoun, or a group of words used as a noun.

The horse ambled through the *park*. *(Noun)*
Come with *me*. *(Pronoun)*
We took the stool from *under the desk*. *(Phrase)*
Dorothy was grateful to *whoever assisted her*. *(Clause)*

A preposition usually precedes its object.

EXERCISE 123

Point out the prepositions in the following sentences and name the object of each:

1. The boys shouted with delight.
2. Take John instead of Michael.
3. The girl with the golden curls played the part of the princess.
4. "Doxology" means an expression of praise to God.
5. The dew glistened like millions of diamonds.
6. During the evening George told the boys of his experiences.
7. Each speaker discussed a need of the city.
8. Do you know the story of Joan of Arc?
9. Give the paper to whoever comes to the door.
10. The children have gone with him.

11. All replied except Mother.
12. The child smiled at whoever spoke to her.
13. Listen to what he is saying.
14. The life of Saint Bernadette was read to our class.
15. On the other side of the mountain lay rich, fertile soil.
16. A house without books is like a room without windows.
17. You profess your faith in Christ by your reverence in His presence and by the fervor of your Communions.
18. From under the bench crept the small child.

2. *The Correct Use of Prepositions*

"BETWEEN" AND "AMONG"

Between is used in speaking of two persons or objects. *Among* is used in speaking of more than two.

Mr. Cooke divided his fortune *between* his two sons.
Mr. Murray divided his fortune *among* his five children.

"BESIDE" AND "BESIDES"

Beside means *at the side of*. *Besides* means *in addition to*.

The boy sat *beside* his father.
Joan must prepare the dinner *besides* her other work.

"FROM"

Use *from*, not *off of*, to indicate the person from whom something is obtained.

The boys secured the posters *from* the salesman.

"BEHIND"

Use *behind*, not *in back of*, to indicate location at the rear of.

There is a beautiful spruce *behind* our school.

"DIFFERENT FROM"

Use *from*, not *than*, after the adjective *different*.

Your medal is *different from* mine.

"DIFFER FROM" AND "DIFFER WITH"

Differ with denotes disagreement of opinion. *Differ from* denotes differences between persons or things.

My father *differs with* me about the rules of the game.
The flower beds *differ from* each other in shape.

"WITHIN"

Use *within*, not *inside of*, to indicate the time within which something will occur.

You will hear from me *within* a short time.

"ANGRY WITH" AND "ANGRY AT"

Use *angry with* a person; *angry at* a thing.

Mr. Weber was *angry with* the gardener.
They were *angry at* the announcement.

"NEED OF"

Use *need of*, not *need for*.

Albert will have no further *need of* a tutor.

"AT" AND "TO"

At denotes presence in. *To* denotes motion toward.

My father was *at* the president's reception.
The geography class went *to* the dairy.

"IN" AND "INTO"

In denotes position within. *Into* denotes motion or change of position.

Marie and Jane met *in* the planetarium.
The visitor came *into* the school.

EXERCISE 124

Select the correct preposition in each of the following sentences:
1. Philip was not (at, to) the office today.
2. The mechanic climbed (in, into) the plane.

3. I was not (at, to) the lecture.
4. Eileen is different (from, than) her sister Elise.
5. The playground is (behind, in back of) the gymnasium.
6. The rumor of a holiday spread (between, among) the pupils.
7. The grocer will be here (inside of, within) an hour.
8. The little dog fell (in, into) the pond.
9. I borrowed the book (from, off of) Mildred.
10. The manager was angry (with, at) the designer.
11. The triplets differ (from, with) one another in size.
12. Is John's bicycle different (from, than) Robert's?
13. (Inside of, within) a few days Aunt Marie will return.
14. Divide the candy (between, among) the five boys.
15. This road runs (beside, besides) the canal for several miles.
16. Do you think the child has need (of, for) a nurse?
17. The boys climbed (in, into) the old wagon.
18. The boys went (at, to) the circus.
19. Place the chair (beside, besides) the table.
20. The little sparrow flew (in, into) the nest.
21. The barn is (in back of, behind) the farmhouse.
22. My sister did not sit (beside, besides) me.
23. There are no secrets (between, among) those two boys.
24. I differ (from, with) you regarding that matter.
25. He was angry (with, at) the decision.

3. *Words Used as Adverbs and Prepositions*

An adverb tells *how, when,* or *where.* A preposition shows the relation between its object and some other word in the sentence.

Traffic moves swiftly *on* our modern superhighways. *(Preposition)*
We must move *on.* *(Adverb)*

EXERCISE 125

Tell whether each word in italics is an adverb or a preposition:
1. Children were playing *in* the park.
2. Come *in,* Marie.
3. I have never met your cousin *before.*

4. We should pray *before* every important action.
5. Put the heavy box *down,* Alfred.
6. The children coasted *down* the hill.
7. The parade is now passing *by.*
8. The sewing machine was invented *by* Elias Howe.
9. You must do this work *over.*
10. Cain became a wanderer *over* the earth.
11. Joan will carry the project *through.*
12. *Through* which door did he enter?
13. Almost the entire village was snowed *under.*
14. The ships of Columbus sailed *under* the Spanish flag.
15. The beauties of nature which God has created are all *about* us.
16. The injured boy can move *about* with the aid of a cane.
17. He is *but* twelve years old.
18. Everybody has left *but* Josephine.
19. The wheels turned *round* and *round.*
20. The hoops *round* the barrel are not heavy enough.

CONJUNCTIONS

A conjunction is a word used to connect words, phrases, or clauses in a sentence.

The day was dark *and* dreary. *(Connects words)*
Oranges grow in California *and* in Florida. *(Connects phrases)*
I will go with you *if* I can assist you. *(Connects clauses)*

1. *Kinds of Conjunctions*

There are two kinds of conjunctions, coordinate conjunctions and subordinate conjunctions.

COORDINATE CONJUNCTIONS

A coordinate conjunction is a conjunction that connects words, phrases, or clauses of equal rank.

Next Tuesday will be a holiday, *and* the children will go on a hike.

The most common coordinate conjunctions are *and, or, nor, but,* and *yet.*

354 VOYAGES IN ENGLISH, SEVENTH YEAR

EXERCISE 126

Select the coordinate conjunctions in the following sentences and tell whether they connect words, phrases, or clauses:
1. The doctor sat and watched the boy.
2. Charles and his father are in the car.
3. I do not know the address, nor can I find it in the directory.
4. Will they spend their vacation at Wildwood or at Ocean City?
5. We marched up and down.
6. I called for Sarah, but she was not at home.
7. He has left the office, and we do not know the hour of his return.
8. A brown-and-white dog lay on the porch.
9. We must leave soon or we shall be late for school.
10. He is a boy in poor circumstances but with exceptional ability.
11. The leaves rustled and the wind howled angrily.
12. The early settlers suffered hardships, but they soon adapted themselves to new conditions.
13. The day came to an end and the visitors started homeward.
14. Bright and clear appeared the tiny stars in the heavens.
15. The class was fond of reading, but books were scarce.
16. What is incense, and where is it obtained?
17. Is this yours or mine?
18. The horns blew and the children scrambled into the busses.

19. When and why are blessed ashes used?
20. Pansies and violets grow in our garden.
21. We should make acts of faith, hope, and charity every day.
22. Automobiles and busses lined the streets.
23. Baptism and penance are sacraments of the dead.
24. Over the hill and through the woods tramped the Scouts.

The words *however, moreover, nevertheless, also, therefore, consequently,* and so forth, are also used to link the independent clause in which they occur to the preceding clause. A clause introduced by one of these connectives is grammatically independent of, but logically dependent upon, what has gone before.

My marks were poor; therefore my parents were disappointed.
The beggar looked hungry; consequently we gave him money for lunch.

CORRELATIVE CONJUNCTIONS

Correlative conjunctions are coordinate conjunctions used in pairs.

The most frequently used correlative conjunctions are:

neither . . . nor   not only . . . but also
either . . . or   both . . . and

EXERCISE 127

Select the correlative conjunctions in the following sentences:
1. I admire both his courage and his sincerity.
2. Either Robert or his brother will be selected for the part.
3. Give me either a pencil or a pen.
4. They could locate neither the president nor his secretary.
5. My brother enjoys both tennis and hockey.
6. Either you or she may go.
7. Both Washington and Oregon are noted for lumber.
8. Neither Martha nor Frances could swim.
9. George had not only the principal part but also the most difficult one.
10. Saint Ignatius was both a soldier and a saint.
11. Neither the telephone nor the doorbell rang all day.

12. Patrick was both the boy's friend and classmate.
13. We traveled not only in Italy, but also in France.
14. Our class studies not only history, but also civics.
15. He was doubtful about both the time and the place of the game.
16. She could find neither the gloves nor her purse.
17. Was either Marie or Ruth at the concert?
18. Julia contributed both time and money to the campaign.

SUBORDINATE CONJUNCTIONS

A subordinate conjunction is a conjunction that connects clauses of unequal rank.

You must study hard *if* you want success.
I will go *because* you ask me.

A subordinate clause is one that depends upon some other part of the sentence. Conjunctions that connect subordinate clauses with principal or independent clauses are called subordinate conjunctions. The most common subordinate conjunctions are:

as	if	so	then
because	provided	than	though
for	since	that	unless

The conjunctive adverbs—words that do the work of an adverb and a conjunction—are likewise considered subordinate conjunctions.

Groups of words may also be used as subordinate conjunctions. These are:

| as well as | in order that | provided that |
| as if | inasmuch as | so that |

EXERCISE 128

In each of the following sentences name the principal clause, the subordinate clause, and the subordinate conjunction:

1. Since you desire it, we will begin at once.
2. Our principal seems pleased because the school was awarded the cup.

3. Miss Baker was a good nurse, for she had much experience.
4. Rosalie practices every day that she may improve her playing.
5. Although I have known him for years, I did not recognize him.
6. Chicago is always cool if the wind blows from the east.
7. The boys became impatient because they had been waiting a long time.
8. Since we have a free day, we will gather nuts this afternoon in the woods.
9. The morning passed quickly because we were busy.
10. Joan was overjoyed, for she had completed the assignment without a single error.
11. We take daily exercise that we may strengthen our muscles.
12. The boys arose at dawn that they might start early.
13. Unless you go now, you will not be admitted.
14. If I could have my wish, I would take a trip around the world.
15. Since the highway is closed, you must use the detour.
16. The St. Lawrence River was so called because it was discovered on the saint's feast day.
17. Blessed are the peacemakers, for they shall be called the children of God.
18. We study civics that we may become better citizens.
19. The man worked hard in order that he might support his family.
20. We honor the saints because they are the chosen friends of God.
21. My brother will take us to the park when he returns.
22. The boys sang while they worked.

OTHER CONNECTIVES

Although the work of a conjunction is to connect, this does not mean that all connectives are conjunctions. *Relative adverbs* and *relative pronouns* are also used to connect clauses of unequal rank.

Since it is raining, the picnic will be postponed. *(Conjunction)*
Wednesday is the day *when* we shall have the picnic. *(Relative adverb)*
We shall have our picnic in the grove *that* adjoins the school grounds. *(Relative pronoun)*

EXERCISE 129

Name the connectives in the following sentences and tell whether each is a conjunction, a relative adverb, or a relative pronoun:

1. Although the day was cold, the stadium was overcrowded.
2. We hurried to the door that we might see the parade.
3. You are stronger than he.
4. The boy who won the scholarship has always been a good student.
5. After I moved to the country I did not see many of my former friends.
6. You must come early because you have not reserved a place.
7. I have neither galoshes nor an umbrella.
8. Wait at the door for Timothy and me.
9. That is the building where the contest will be held.
10. Mr. Donnelly travels by train, but I travel by bus.
11. Neither Paul nor Charles attended the game that decided the championship.
12. Both study and play are essential for children.
13. I did the best I could, yet I did not feel satisfied.
14. The boys collected autumn leaves and the girls used them for decorations.
15. My mother purchased a coat which I like very much.
16. I hurried, but I missed the train.
17. He spoke distinctly, yet I did not understand him.
18. At home or in school she is always kind and courteous.
19. Did you open the door and the windows when you returned from your shopping trip?
20. I like both your hat and your purse.

2. *The Correct Use of Conjunctions*

"THAN" AND "AS"

The conjunctions *than* and *as* are used to compare one thing with another, and there is usually an omission of words after each. The substantive which follows *than* or *as* must be in the same case as the word with which it is compared. Particular care must be taken when the substantive is a personal pronoun.

He is taller than *I* (am tall).

EXERCISE 130

Select the correct form of the pronoun in each of the following sentences:
1. John is not so capable as (he, him).
2. My sister is older than (I, me).
3. I see her as often as (he, him).
4. Gerald Murphy has more endurance than (I, me).
5. We were not so cautious as (they, them).
6. They arrived earlier than (we, us).
7. My father is more lenient than (he, him).
8. Paul gets better grades than (she, her).
9. The others have done as much as (we, us).
10. I know her as well as (he, him).
11. Ethel is just as happy as (we, us).
12. Jean can type faster than (he, him).
13. Does he play as well as (she, her)?

"UNLESS" AND "WITHOUT"

Unless is a conjunction and introduces a *clause*. *Without* is a preposition and introduces a *phrase*.

Do not go *unless I accompany you*. (Clause)
Do not go *without me*. (Phrase)

EXERCISE 131

Fill in the blanks with *unless* or *without*:
1. .... they come soon, the work will cease.
2. He cannot drive his car .... a license.
3. The girls will be disappointed .... they hear from you.
4. .... the boys come, the work will not be finished.
5. .... you help, Elizabeth cannot make the costume.

6. .... all do their best, victory will not be ours.
7. Do not take the dress .... the hat.
8. He cannot do it .... your assistance.
9. .... you come with me, I shall not enjoy the trip.
10. .... ice the food will spoil.
11. We shall have no candy .... you make some fudge.
12. Those apples will decay .... we sort them.
13. .... you call early, I shall not be able to go.
14. Edward cannot see well .... his glasses.

"LIKE," "AS," AND "AS IF"

As and *as if* are conjunctions and are used to introduce *clauses*.
Like is a preposition and is used to introduce a *phrase*.

He drives *as* an expert drives. *(Clause)*
He looks *like* his father. *(Phrase)*

EXERCISE 132

Insert the correct term, *like, as,* or *as if,* in each of the following sentences:

1. The oak tree shook before the wind .... it were about to fall.
2. Her pen is .... mine.
3. Our car runs .... it were new.
4. Do .... I do.
5. He panted .... he were exhausted.
6. You look .... you needed a rest.
7. Lace .... this comes from Mexico.
8. That is just .... you.
9. Arthur smiled .... he were well pleased.
10. This stone glitters .... a diamond.
11. I did the work .... I was told.
12. He looks .... his brother.
13. She enjoys the games .... I do.
14. They persecuted the apostles .... they had persecuted the Master.

"EITHER ... OR" AND "NEITHER ... NOR"

Correlative conjunctions are used in pairs. *Or* follows *either* and *nor* follows *neither*.

Either you *or* I must go.
Neither the president *nor* the vice president was at the meeting.

EXERCISE 133

Insert the correct conjunction in each blank space:
1. Neither the boy .... his brother could be found.
2. Neither a borrower .... a lender be.
3. Either you .... Joseph must come with me.
4. The child wore neither shoes .... stockings.
5. Either you .... she is to blame.
6. Give the picture either to Samuel .... to Robert.
7. The old man could neither read .... write.
8. Neither the house .... the barn was saved.
9. You may have either one .... the other.
10. These rugs were made either in Persia .... in Turkey.
11. We heard neither the beginning .... the end of the story.
12. Either my father .... Eugene will drive the car.

INTERJECTIONS

An interjection is a word that expresses some strong or sudden emotion.

Hark! I hear a strange sound.

An interjection is grammatically distinct from the rest of the sentence. Interjections may express *delight, disgust, contempt, pain, assent, joy, impatience, surprise, sorrow,* and so forth. They are generally set off from the rest of the sentence by exclamation points. An entire sentence, however, may be exclamatory. If the sentence is exclamatory, the interjection is followed by a comma and the exclamation point is put at the end of the sentence.

Ah, how refreshing is the cool water!

The most common interjections are:

Ah!	Good!	Hush!	Oh!
Alas!	Hark!	Indeed!	Pshaw!
Beware!	Hello!	Listen!	Sh!
Bravo!	Hurrah!	Lo!	What!

"O" AND "OH"

The interjection *O* is used only before a noun in direct address. It is not directly followed by an exclamation point. *Oh* is used to express surprise, sorrow, or joy. It is followed by an exclamation point unless the emotion continues throughout the sentence. In this case *Oh* is followed by a comma, and the exclamation point is put at the end of the sentence.

O Marie! I am glad to see you. *(Direct address)*
Oh! John has arrived. *(Emotion does not continue)*
Oh, how excited I am! *(Emotion continues)*

EXERCISE 134

Tell what emotions are expressed in the following sentences:

1. Alas! The boat is sinking.
2. O Janet! Have you seen my new car?
3. Hurrah, how happy we are today!
4. What! Has everybody left?
5. Ah, a pleasant sight is that!
6. Hurrah! The boys found the cabin in the woods.
7. Indeed! Is the sunset always so beautiful here?
8. Lo! The angel appeared.
9. Pshaw! I missed the streetcar.
10. Oh, what a surprise this is!
11. Bravo! You are a noble boy.
12. Oh! What will happen to the little child?
13. Good! It shall be accepted.
14. Nonsense! We will have none of it.
15. Hark, how loud the fire bells are ringing!
16. Good! The ball went into the basket.

PREPOSITIONS, CONJUNCTIONS, INTERJECTIONS 363

EXERCISE 135 [Test on Prepositions, Conjunctions, and Interjections]

Read this selection very carefully and then answer the questions that follow:

[1] Courtesy is a quality which should be an outstanding characteristic of all Catholic boys and girls. [2] It is a Christian virtue, for it fulfills a duty both of justice and of charity. [3] Alas! It is misunderstood by many who consider it merely a veneer of good manners instead of the outward expression of a loving kindness which comes from within the heart. [4] True courtesy is not reserved for our friends, but it is extended to whomever we meet. [5] In games it shows itself as sportsmanship, and in work it is cooperation. [6] In all our contacts with others it is a quality which makes smoother and more pleasant the road which we travel with our fellow men.

1. How many prepositions are there in the sixth sentence? Name them.
2. Point out a group of words used as a single preposition.
3. Find a preposition that has a compound object.
4. Name a preposition that has a phrase for its object.
5. Find a preposition which governs a clause.
6. Which sentences begin with prepositions?
7. In the first sentence find a conjunction connecting two words.
8. The conjunction in the first sentence is what kind of conjunction?
9. *Both . . . and* in the second sentence belong to what class of conjunction?
10. Are words, phrases, or clauses connected by *both . . . and* in the second sentence?
11. Find a coordinate conjunction connecting two clauses.
12. Is the word *for* in the second sentence a conjunction or a preposition?
13. What part of speech is *for* in the fourth sentence?
14. Point out an interjection.
15. What emotion does the interjection express?

EXERCISE 136 [Review of Parts of Speech]

Test your knowledge of parts of speech by telling the part of speech of each italicized word:
1. The cast will give a *benefit* performance this evening.
2. Many *rubber* tires are manufactured in Akron, Ohio.
3. Is your mother in the *kitchen?*
4. The fort was captured in a *surprise* attack.
5. *That* is the corner where we turn right.
6. In pioneer days heavy wagons jogged *over* unpaved roads.
7. A trip to the country, Mary, will *benefit* you greatly.
8. Charles Goodyear vulcanized *rubber.*
9. The *principal* of our school visits each classroom daily.
10. Send the package by *express.*
11. Many *kitchen* utensils are made of aluminum.
12. Your sudden return will *surprise* Mother.
13. We bless ourselves reverently *that* we may gain the indulgence.
14. Boston is the capital and the *principal* seaport of Massachusetts.
15. The farmer rises *early.*
16. *Saddle* the horse at once.
17. Philip strapped a warm blanket under the *saddle.*
18. Turn the box *over,* boys.
19. We should always *express* gratitude for favors received.
20. The *early* bird catches the worm.

EXERCISE 137 [Test on Parts of Speech]

Read this selection very carefully and then answer the questions that follow:

[1] The young man who is called by God to the work of the foreign missions must prepare himself for a life of hardship and sacrifice. [2] He must leave family, friends, and home, and go to a distant land where countless difficulties await him. [3] The language will be different; the customs, strange. [4] Often he will find his prospective converts either alarmingly hostile or discouragingly indifferent. [5] Long years of patient sowing may yield apparently little fruit.

⁶ Will the missionary be discouraged by all these trials and regret the choice that he has made? ⁷ Ah, no! ⁸ He will be supported by a strong faith and sustained by the knowledge that his is the glorious work of spreading the kingdom of Christ on earth.

1. Find a proper noun in the selection.
2. To what class of nouns do the words *hardship* and *sacrifice* in the first sentence belong?
3. In what case is the compound personal pronoun in the first sentence?
4. Find a relative pronoun in the sixth sentence. What is its antecedent?
5. In what case is the relative pronoun in the sixth sentence?
6. Name the personal pronouns in the second sentence.
7. Find two descriptive adjectives in the third sentence. How are these adjectives used?
8. What demonstrative adjective is found in the selection?
9. Name three adjectives in the fifth sentence. Compare each adjective.
10. What kind of adjective is *all* in the sixth sentence?
11. Give the voice of the verb in the subordinate clause of the first sentence.
12. Is the verb *has made* in the sixth sentence transitive or intransitive?
13. Find a copulative verb in the last sentence.
14. What is the tense of the verb *will be supported* in the last sentence?
15. Find an adverb of time in the fourth sentence.
16. What kind of adverb is *where* in the second sentence?
17. What words does the conjunction in the sixth sentence connect?
18. Name any correlative conjunctions in the selection.
19. Which word is the object of the preposition in the second sentence?
20. The word *ah* in the seventh sentence is what part of speech?[1]

---

[1] This is an elliptical sentence. (Ah, no, he will not be discouraged!)

CHAPTER SEVEN Phrases

A phrase is a group of related words used as a single part of speech.

We all crave variety. We know that variety in writing may be obtained by the use of colorful adjectives and adverbs. We will now learn how to use groups of words to obtain variety in sentence structure. Note the following sentences:

Egyptian cotton is sent to the United States.
Cotton *from Egypt* is sent to the United States.
The decision of the umpire was given *fairly*.
The decision of the umpire was given *with fairness*.

In the first two sentences we have described cotton by the adjective *Egyptian* and by the phrase *from Egypt*. There is no difference in the meaning of the two sentences. Again, as in the third and fourth sentences, we may tell how a decision is given in two different ways, both of which convey the same thought to our mind. We can say that it was given *fairly*, or we can vary the construction by saying that it was given *with fairness*. These groups of words which take the place of single parts of speech are known as phrases.

KINDS OF PHRASES

1. *Division according to Form*

Phrases may be introduced by prepositions, participles, or infinitives. The introductory word determines the classification of a phrase according to form.

A prepositional phrase is a phrase introduced by a preposition.

A participial phrase is a phrase introduced by a participle.

An infinitive phrase is a phrase introduced by an infinitive

The Naval Academy is *in Annapolis*. *(Prepositional phrase)*
The girl *reading the poem* is a member of our class. *(Participial phrase)*
To play tennis is great fun. *(Infinitive phrase)*
Most of the phrases that we study will be prepositional phrases.

2. Division according to Use

Phrases may be used as adjectives, as adverbs, or as nouns.

An adjectival phrase is a phrase used as an adjective.

An adverbial phrase is a phrase used as an adverb.

A noun phrase is a phrase used as a noun.

A flock *of birds* flew away. *(Adjectival phrase)*
The starry flag floated *in the breeze*. *(Adverbial phrase)*
The sign read *"To the left."* *(Noun phrase)*

EXERCISE 138

Select the phrases in this exercise and classify each according to its use in the sentence:

1. The boys had a canoe race on the river.
2. The members of the basketball team are interested in the new recreation center.

3. William Jones is an enthusiastic student of nature.
4. Henry divided his marbles between him and me.
5. At the Christmas party each child put a small package on the tree.
6. "To the home plate!" he shouted.
7. Throughout the dark night the captain watched for a signal.
8. The moonlight fell in pools on the quiet lake.
9. In this part of your book you will find stories of adventure.
10. What part of Asia lies in the Temperate Zone?
11. The boy worked with remarkable skill.
12. A flock of birds flew from the trees.
13. The children played outdoors in the sunshine.
14. We have a library in our room.
15. "In step!" was the command given.
16. The canoe drifted across the smooth lake.
17. White sailboats darted here and there on the river.
18. The beautiful garden was dotted with beds of brilliantly colored flowers.
19. On the shelf of the old maple cupboard were two antique urns.
20. The boy from the nearby farm sauntered down the road.

EXERCISE 139

1. Add modifying phrases to the following nouns:

boat	star	explorer	lake
flowers	scientist	castle	town
villages	sunshine	people	forest

What kinds of phrases are these? Why?

2. Add modifying phrases to these verbs:

speaks	plunged	skipped	were playing
knelt	was carved	lies	clustered
lives	is benefited	have flown	blossom

What kinds of phrases are these? Why?

3. Make phrases your tools and use them as the artist does his brushes to add color, variety, and harmony to the word pictures you are trying to paint. Here are some colorful groups

of words which you may find helpful in your composition work. Use them in sentences:

gold of Indian-summer days	the bluebirds' nest in the little low tree
joy of the winding road	
the blue of October weather	radiant with joy
rainbow balloons on strings	white with daisies
poured into the room	world of dreams
coverlet of snow	gems of the lake country
spirit of the holiday	flows into the silvery sea
cluster of pine cones	are decked in fairest flowers

4. Substitute colorful phrases for the following words and use them in sentences:

skillfully	blooming	beautiful	ambitious
fearfully	roadside	romantic	mysterious
silently	successful	courageous	victorious

CHAPTER EIGHT Sentences

A sentence is a group of words expressing a complete thought.

EXERCISE 140

Decide which of the following groups of words are sentences:
1. Much of Africa is still undeveloped.
2. Truthfulness is the basis of a good character.
3. Come here.
4. The story of Evangeline.
5. Washington surprised the Hessians at Trenton.
6. When the ship reached port.
7. Go.
8. Philadelphia is about one hundred miles from the ocean.
9. The man who gave the address.
10. Do you like this locality?
11. Helen's dress is very pretty.
12. A good architect is always in demand.
13. Has your state a seal?
14. The church has beautiful bronze doors.

THE ESSENTIAL ELEMENTS OF A SENTENCE

Every sentence has a *subject* and a *predicate*. The subject may or may not be expressed. The predicate is always expressed.

(You) Give us this day our daily bread.

1. *The Subject*

The subject is that part of the sentence which names a person, a place, or a thing about which a statement is made.

The subject with all its modifiers is called the *complete subject*.

2. *The Predicate*

The predicate is that part of the sentence which tells something about the subject.

The predicate with all its modifiers and complements is called the *complete predicate*.

COMPLETE SUBJECT   COMPLETE PREDICATE
Good Catholic children   pray every day.

EXERCISE 141

In each of the following sentences select the simple and the complete predicate and the simple and the complete subject:
1. The canoe came swiftly over the rapids.
2. My sister lived in Detroit for five years.
3. What is a requiem Mass?
4. Among the pines the little birds chirped happily.
5. I have not been absent from school this month.
6. After a long ramble we finally arrived at the lighthouse.
7. Politeness is benevolence in small things.
8. Has Gertrude returned the collection of stamps?
9. The stellar system includes millions of stars.

10. Tell us about your strange adventure.
11. The Sunday after Pentecost is Trinity Sunday.
12. In spring the trees are clothed in softest green.
13. All nature has awakened from its wintry sleep.
14. On the first day of creation God made light.
15. The joyful mysteries of the rosary are recited on Mondays and Thursdays.

NATURAL AND TRANSPOSED ORDER IN SENTENCES

Whenever the complete predicate follows the complete subject, a sentence is in the natural order.

Whenever the complete predicate or part of the predicate is placed before the subject, a sentence is in the transposed order.

NATURAL ORDER: The bright autumn leaves fluttered to the ground.
Who found John's medal?
TRANSPOSED ORDER: Down fluttered the bright autumn leaves.
Did you find John's medal?

EXERCISE 142

Decide which of the following sentences are in the natural order and which are in the transposed order. Name the subject and the predicate of each:

1. The class enjoyed the story about the pioneers.
2. The gardener trimmed the rosebushes.
3. In New York City there are many skyscrapers.
4. The old woman dropped all her parcels.
5. From morn till night the captain sang softly and contentedly at his work.
6. Have you seen Joseph since the last football game?
7. Our Lord looked longingly at Saint Peter.
8. Up started the frightened animal.
9. About midnight a strange ship appeared on the horizon.
10. Along the cliff dashed the rider on a coal-black horse.
11. In the forest sang many birds.

12. Cleanliness is next to godliness.
13. In the old trunk you will find many treasures.
14. We shall never forget that ride through the mountains.
15. When was America discovered?
16. Just within the gates were standing many eager spectators.
17. With God's grace we can accomplish any difficult assignment.
18. On the day of the carnival an enthusiastic crowd assembled.
19. Between the two cities stretches a broad highway.
20. Before the throne of God angels constantly bow in adoration.

COMPOUND ELEMENTS OF A SENTENCE

If the subject of a sentence consists of more than one noun or pronoun, it is said to be a *compound subject*.

If the predicate consists of more than one verb, it is said to be a *compound predicate*.

A sentence may have a compound subject, a compound predicate, or a compound subject and a compound predicate.

Mary and *Joseph* worked for the prize. *(Compound subject)*
The little girl *sang* and *danced*. *(Compound predicate)*
The *boys* and the *girls ran* and *jumped*. *(Compound subject and compound predicate)*

EXERCISE 143

Point out the compound elements in the following sentences:
1. Father Damien labored and died among the lepers.
2. Daisies and violets are spring flowers.
3. My father wrote the letter, signed it, and handed it to me.
4. We visited Mercy Hospital on Sunday afternoon and brought flowers to our sick friend.
5. Apples, bananas, and peaches were being sold on the street.
6. Mary swept the floor, dusted, and arranged the furniture.
7. Columbus landed, knelt, kissed the earth, and thanked God for his safe journey.
8. Anne and her brother won the tennis match.
9. Men, women, and children enjoy the city parks.
10. The boy or his parents signed and returned the paper.

CLASSIFICATION OF SENTENCES

Sentences may be classified according to *use* and according to *form*. Study the following classification according to use.

1. *Division according to Use*

A *declarative sentence* is a sentence that states a fact.

An *interrogative sentence* is a sentence that asks a question.

An *imperative sentence* is a sentence that expresses a command.

An *exclamatory sentence* is a sentence that expresses strong or sudden emotion.

> Delicate flowers grow among the rocks. *(Declarative)*
> What is your favorite sport? *(Interrogative)*
> Run quickly, Louis. *(Imperative)*
> How bright the sun is today! *(Exclamatory)*

END PUNCTUATION

When we are speaking, the inflection of our voice tells the listener whether we are stating a fact, asking a question, giving a command, or expressing surprise. In writing, however, we must use punctuation marks to tell the reader what kind of sentence we are using.

Declarative and *imperative* sentences are followed by periods.

An *interrogative* sentence ends with a question mark.

An *exclamatory* sentence is followed by an exclamation point.

EXERCISE 144

Classify the following sentences as declarative, interrogative, imperative, or exclamatory. Punctuate each sentence:

1. How long is that table
2. Bring the box to me, John

3. Who discovered Antarctica
4. Rangers protect our great forests
5. What a peaceful place this is
6. How can I lock this case
7. Please pass the cake
8. How beautifully they sing
9. The altar should be covered with three linen cloths
10. They looked longingly toward the shore
11. God sees us and watches over us
12. Place your papers under the book in the desk

EXERCISE 145

Copy the following paragraph in correct form. Use a capital letter at the beginning of each sentence and add the correct punctuation marks where they are needed:

suddenly there was a sound like an approaching storm almost instantly every animal in the corral was on its feet the alarm was given and all hands turned out not yet knowing what caused the general commotion the roar we heard was like that of a heavy railroad train passing at no great distance on a still night as by instinct all seemed to know suddenly that it was a buffalo stampede the tents were emptied of their inmates the weak parts of the corral were guarded the frightened cattle looked after and everyone in the camp was on the alert to watch what was coming

2. *Division according to Form*

Classified according to form, sentences may be simple, compound, or complex.

SIMPLE SENTENCES

A simple sentence is a sentence containing one subject and one predicate, either or both of which may be compound.

Saint Isaac Jogues was martyred by the Mohawks.

This sentence contains one subject, *Saint Isaac Jogues,* and one predicate, *was martyred.*

EXERCISE 146

Name the subject and the predicate in each sentence:
1. Agnes plays the violin.
2. Our school is very proud of its band.
3. Suddenly they realized the danger.
4. The president of the company resigned today.
5. You and I shall wait for the postman.
6. Meet me at the corner at five o'clock.
7. James and Leo are going with us to the park.
8. On the top of the hill we saw the tall oak.
9. Miriam wrote the letter and mailed it immediately.
10. A good book is the best companion.
11. Birds of a feather flock together.
12. In an imperative sentence the subject is not always expressed.

COMPOUND SENTENCES

A compound sentence is a sentence that contains two or more independent clauses.

A clause is a part of a sentence containing a subject and a predicate.

Clauses that make independent statements are called *independent* or *coordinate clauses;* clauses that depend upon some other part of the sentence are *dependent* or *subordinate clauses*.

The camel is the ship of the desert, and the reindeer is the camel of the snowland.

This sentence contains two complete thoughts.

The camel is the ship of the desert. The reindeer is the camel of the snowland.

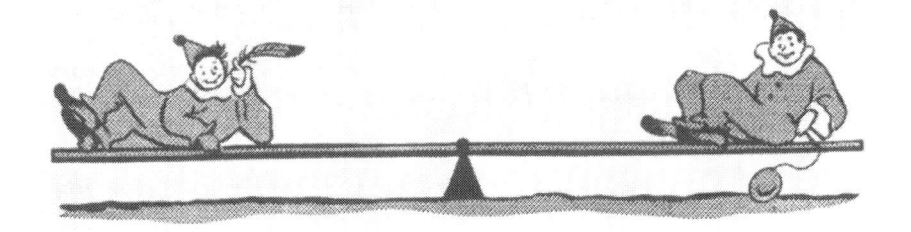

Each thought (clause) is independent and forms a simple sentence in itself. Any such combination of simple sentences is called a *compound sentence*. Each complete thought is called an *independent* or *coordinate clause*.

The clauses of a compound sentence are connected by *coordinate conjunctions*. The most important coordinate conjunctions are *and, but, or, nor,* and *yet*.

PUNCTUATION OF COMPOUND SENTENCES

1. The clauses of a compound sentence connected by the simple conjunctions *and, but,* and *or* are generally separated by a comma.

Fort Christina was surrendered to the Dutch in 1655, and New Sweden became a part of New Netherland.

2. If the clauses are short and closely related, the comma may be omitted.

The rain descended and the floods came.

3. Sometimes the clauses of a compound sentence have no connecting word. The connection is then indicated by a semicolon.

Speech is silver; silence is golden.

4. The semicolon is also used to separate the clauses of a compound sentence connected by *nevertheless, moreover, therefore, however, thus, then,* because these words have very little connective force. A comma is frequently used after these words.

The early settlers suffered hardships; however, they soon adapted themselves to their new surroundings.

EXERCISE 147

Analyze by diagram or otherwise the following sentences. Explain the punctuation:

1. Ice had already formed on the pond, and many skaters had gathered.
2. I heard the screams, but I did not know the cause.
3. Send the book at once; spare no expense.
4. The legislative department makes the laws, and the executive department enforces them.

5. Man proposes but God disposes.
6. We must obey the rules or we shall be dismissed.
7. The book is a success; the writer should be congratulated.
8. Mr. Carr did not succeed in a day; he worked hard for years.
9. We brought some toys, and Teresa hung them on the Christmas tree.
10. Thomas had heard stories about the explorer; moreover, he had seen his pictures.
11. Philip tried hard, but he could not solve the problem.
12. I will not leave you orphans; I will come to you.
13. James will make a fire, and Edward will prepare the meal.
14. Knowledge is a treasure, but practice is the key to it.
15. George Washington was strong; he excelled in athletic activities.
16. Help me now; later your aid will be valueless.
17. Wealth may seek us, but wisdom must be sought.
18. They divided My garments among them, and upon My vesture they cast lots.
19. The coast line of Africa is regular; there are few good harbors.
20. General Grant led the Union army, and General Lee commanded the Confederate forces.

COMPLEX SENTENCES

A complex sentence is a sentence that contains one principal clause and one or more subordinate clauses.

Count Pulaski, who was a great military officer, became the father of the American cavalry.

In this sentence the principal idea is *Count Pulaski became the father of the American cavalry.* These words, therefore, form a part of the sentence called the principal or independent clause. But there is also a clause of lesser importance, *who was a great military officer.* It is called a subordinate or dependent clause. The independent clause forms a complete sentence in itself, but the dependent or subordinate clause is not complete without the principal clause. The entire sentence is complex, for it contains a principal clause and a subordinate clause.

EXERCISE 148

Select the principal and the subordinate clauses in each of the following complex sentences:
1. Saint Alphonsus Liguori, who was the founder of the Redemptorists, wrote many books.
2. Pasteur, who was a Frenchman, gave the world the theory of pasteurization.
3. Alaska, which is rich in minerals, became the forty-ninth state of the Union in 1958.
4. He is never alone who is accompanied by noble thoughts.
5. Lafayette was a young French Catholic who aided the American cause during the Revolutionary War.
6. They are rich who have true friends.
7. The North Pole points toward Polaris, which is often called the North Star.
8. Mary gave Ann the picture that hangs in her bedroom.
9. The flowers that we gathered are for our Lady's shrine.
10. The plans that were proposed by Mr. Mayer have been accepted.
11. We knelt before the tomb where the body of Saint Frances Cabrini is enshrined.
12. When the Magi saw a strange star in the heavens, they prepared for the long journey.

13. If you arrive early, wait for me at the main entrance.
14. Choose a book as you choose a friend.
15. Stevenson went to the Samoan Islands that he might improve his health.

EXERCISE 149

Use the following groups of words as subordinate clauses in complex sentences:

when he was called
before you came
what you did yesterday
which is one of the important canals of the world
until our friends came
although I had never met him before
who lives next door
which is on the table
when night came on
that he will succeed
as the long-awaited day approached
since you are the oldest
if you wish success
where the snowdrifts are deepest

EXERCISE 150

Complete the subordinate clauses in the following complex sentences:

1. The spectators cheered the player who ....
2. Daniel Boone, who ...., settled in Kentucky.
3. Frances is the girl who ....
4. The earth dresses herself in green when ....
5. There are several proofs that ....
6. If ...., you may not go to the party.
7. The teacher explained the problem that ....
8. The little stream dashed along madly as if ....
9. Maryland is the place where ....

10. When ...., we may go sledding.
11. There was great excitement in the little town because ....
12. Open the box which ....
13. Night had just fallen when ....
14. She told the story which ....
15. Leo visited his sister Mary, who ....

TYPES OF SUBORDINATE CLAUSES

Subordinate clauses may be used as adjectives, adverbs, or nouns; and as such are known as *adjectival, adverbial,* or *noun clauses.*

Thomas purchased the book *which you recommended.* (*Adjectival clause*)

If you want knowledge, you must toil. (*Adverbial clause*)

Anne sincerely hoped *that you would return.* (*Noun clause*)

1. Adjectival Clauses

An adjectival clause is a subordinate clause used as an adjective.

The teacher read us an *interesting* story.
The teacher read us a story *of great interest.*
The teacher read us a story *which was very interesting.*

In the first sentence *interesting* modifies the noun *story* and is therefore an *adjective.* In the second sentence *of great interest* modifies the noun *story* and is therefore an *adjectival phrase.* The noun *story* in the third sentence is modified by what group of words? It is modified by the words *which was very interesting.* This group of words contains the subject *which* and the predicate *was.* What do we call a part of a sentence which contains a subject and a predicate? We call it a clause. Since this clause is used as an adjective, it is an *adjectival clause.*

Adjectival clauses are usually introduced by *relative pronouns* or *relative adverbs.*

The relative pronouns are *who, which, what,* and *that.*

The most frequently used relative adverbs are *when, where,* and *why.*

Test for a relative adverb: A relative adverb usually follows a noun of time or place; it may be replaced by a prepositional phrase containing a relative pronoun.

This is the city *where* the treaty was signed.

Where is an adverb of place. In this sentence *where* also does the work of a *relative pronoun* because it connects the adjectival clause with the noun *city,* which is its antecedent. It may be replaced by the prepositional phrase *in which:*

This is the city *in which* the treaty was signed.

EXERCISE 151

Point out the adjectival clauses in the following sentences and tell what word each clause modifies:

1. I am going to my father's office, which is in the Pittsfield Building.
2. June is the month when I was born.
3. The mountains which you see in the distance are the Sierras.
4. This is the crossing where the accident happened.
5. Grace is a supernatural gift which God bestows upon us.
6. My sister Elizabeth, who attends Rosary College, is the assistant librarian.
7. The president welcomed all who attended the meeting.
8. We do not know the day when the test will be given.
9. Jerome is visiting Uncle Cyril, who lives in San Francisco.
10. The gardener cut away the branches that bore no fruit.

EXERCISE 152

Rewrite the following sentences, changing the italicized adjectives to adjectival phrases and adjectival clauses:

1. A *stone* wall surrounded the cottage.
2. The *first* boy will recite the poem.
3. She performed a *kind* act.
4. Mary is a *courteous* child.

5. A *loyal* Scout is obedient.
6. A *friendly* smile was on the boy's face.
7. Thomas is an *ambitious* boy.
8. Uncle John gave me a *Mexican* doll.
9. *Valuable* minerals have been discovered there.
10. Mary has a *plastic* umbrella.

EXERCISE 153

Use the following adjectival clauses in sentences of your own:

whom I trust	where John found it
that held some treasures	which was invented by Fulton
that I forgot	when I visited the Alps
to whom I gave the key	who arrived yesterday
whom I met in Paris	where the box is hidden

RESTRICTIVE AND NONRESTRICTIVE CLAUSES

A clause that helps to point out or identify a certain person or object and is a necessary part of the sentence is called a *restrictive clause*.

A clause that merely adds to the information about the word it modifies and is not necessary to the sense of the sentence is a *nonrestrictive clause*.

A nonrestrictive phrase or clause is separated from the rest of the sentence by commas. No punctuation is required in the case of restrictive clauses.

The man who lives next door is ill. *(Restrictive clause)*
John Riley, who lives next door, is ill. *(Nonrestrictive clause)*

EXERCISE 154

Point out the restrictive and the nonrestrictive clauses in the following sentences and tell what noun or pronoun each clause modifies:

1. He who loves a book will never want a faithful friend.
2. The altar is the sacred table on which the Mass is offered.
3. I often pray to Saint Michael, who is my patron.

4. The girl who just left the room is my sister.
5. We visited Arlington National Cemetery, where the Unknown Soldier is buried.
6. The planets are heavenly bodies that revolve around the sun.
7. They gave no reason why they were late.
8. The man who invented the cotton gin was Eli Whitney.
9. This is the man whose horse won the prize.
10. Martin's paper is the one which was selected.
11. The heart is the pumping engine which controls the circulation of the blood.
12. We purchased wooden figures which the natives had carved.
13. Christmas is the time when we pay special homage to the Infant.
14. John Barry, who was an officer in the American Navy, is buried in Philadelphia.
15. The girl whose ring was lost offered a substantial reward.
16. The Great Barrier Reef, which is of coral formation, is in Australia.
17. Robert Morris, who was a wealthy merchant, came to the aid of Washington.
18. The Church which Christ founded will endure forever.
19. There are seven women martyrs whose names are mentioned in the Canon of the Mass.
20. Ponce de León, who discovered Florida, was a Spanish adventurer.

2. *Adverbial Clauses*

An adverbial clause is a subordinate clause used as an adverb.

The boy came *quickly.*
The boy came *with haste.*
The boy came *when he was called.*

In the first sentence the adverb *quickly* modifies the verb *came.* In the second sentence the verb *came* is modified by an adverbial phrase, *with haste.* The verb *came* in the third sentence is modified by the words *when he was called*. This group of words contains a subject, *he*, and a predicate, *was called*. We call a part of a sentence which contains a subject and a predicate a clause. Since this clause is used as an adverb, it is an *adverbial clause*.

Adverbial clauses are usually introduced by *conjunctive adverbs* or *subordinate conjunctions*.

The principal conjunctive adverbs are:

| after | as | before | since |
| until | when | where | while |

The principal subordinate conjunctions are:

as	because	for	if
that	then	than	provided
since	so	though	unless

REMEMBER: An adverbial clause, like an adverb, may modify a verb, an adverb, or an adjective. It may tell time, place, degree, or manner.

Every introductory adverbial clause may be separated from the rest of the sentence by a comma. In certain adverbial clauses a comma is necessary to make the meaning clear.

When you are rude, your friends are pained. *(Comma may be used)*
When he rose suddenly, all were surprised. *(Comma is necessary)*

The first sentence may be written either with or without the comma after the introductory adverbial clause, *When you are rude*. In the second sentence the comma must be used to tell the reader that he rose suddenly. If the comma were not used, we would not know whether the person rose suddenly or whether all were suddenly surprised.

EXERCISE 155

Point out the adverbial clauses in the following sentences and tell which word each clause modifies:

1. Before the year had passed, he was a successful announcer.
2. When you receive Holy Communion you are a tabernacle of the Most High.

3. Thomas was a splendid athlete when he was younger.
4. I noticed the envelope on the floor as I entered the room.
5. Watch your position as you take your place before the audience.
6. After she had submitted her paper, Mary hurried home.
7. Continue the work until I return.
8. After the room had become quiet we could hear the music.
9. That problem is easier than the ones I have solved.
10. My parents visited several national parks while they were in the West.
11. The boy slept because he was tired.
12. Strike while the iron is hot.
13. We may go there, where I have had many happy vacations.
14. Whenever I lose something I pray to Saint Anthony.
15. This rope is stronger than that one is.
16. After He arose from the dead, our Lord appeared to Mary Magdalene.
17. We can resist temptation, for God has given us free will.
18. Here, where we stand, the battle took place.
19. While she was visiting in Mexico, Mother purchased many lovely gifts.
20. Now, when all are present, we shall say the rosary.

EXERCISE 156

Rewrite the following sentences, changing the italicized adverbs to adverbial phrases and adverbial clauses:
1. The girl spoke *courteously* to the old woman.
2. Mr. Edwards walks *fast*.
3. The pastor is entering the room *now*.
4. We heard that song *before*.
5. The children *joyfully* welcome their parents.
6. The baby laughed *gleefully*.
7. The boys came to church *early*.
8. Mark obeyed his instructions *exactly*.
9. He answers all his letters *promptly*.
10. John never comes *late*.

EXERCISE 157

Use the following adverbial clauses in sentences of your own:

since he lost his memory
after you write the letter to your grandmother
before he returned
when the pioneers moved westward
because he tried
after the Suez Canal was constructed
if you wish good health
after the Revolutionary War ended

EXERCISE 158

Combine the following simple sentences to form complex sentences. Be sure to use commas where they are necessary. Tell whether the subordinate clause is an adjectival clause or an adverbial clause:

1. The flag was raised. We stood at attention.
2. Aunt Mary lives in Quebec. She really likes living there.
3. Wellington is the capital of New Zealand. It has a first-class harbor.
4. Fort Duquesne was the key to the region west of the Alleghenies. It was held by the French.
5. These boys are in the Y class. They are good students.
6. Three altar cloths are used. They represent the linen cloths in which our Lord's body was wrapped.
7. The Indians lived in wigwams. They made the wigwams from the skins of animals.
8. We must hurry. We shall miss the boat.
9. The policeman has a busy time. He directs traffic on the boulevard.
10. The bishop consecrates the altar. He places relics in it.
11. We visited Ireland. We saw a magnificent castle there.
12. Will you lend me your book? I have finished this one.
13. Joseph has returned home. He spent the winter in New York.
14. John succeeds. He is industrious.
15. My sister told me a story. It was very interesting.

16. John Reed is very popular. He is the captain of the team.
17. Visitors entered the room. The pupils were studying.

3. Noun Clauses

A noun clause is a subordinate clause used as a noun.

Mary's *gratitude* is a sign of her noble heart.
That Mary is grateful is a sign of her noble heart.

Compare the two sentences above. In the first sentence the noun *gratitude* is the subject. In the second sentence a group of words, *that Mary is grateful,* is the subject. This group of words is a clause; it has a subject and a predicate of its own. Since the clause takes the place of a noun, it is a *noun clause.*

A sentence that contains a noun clause is a complex sentence. The entire sentence is considered the principal or independent clause; the noun clause is the subordinate or dependent clause.

That Mary is grateful is a sign of her noble heart. *(Principal clause)*
That Mary is grateful. *(Subordinate clause)*

Noun clauses have the same uses as nouns. A noun clause may be used as the subject of a verb, the object of a verb, the predicate nominative, the object of a preposition, or in apposition.

NOUN CLAUSES USED AS SUBJECTS

The subject is that part of the sentence which names a person, a place, or a thing about which a statement is made.

That you may succeed is my wish.

What is my wish? *That you may succeed.* The noun clause *that you may succeed* is, therefore, the subject of the sentence.

That you may succeed is my wish. *(Principal clause)*
That you may succeed. *(Noun clause used as subject)*

EXERCISE 159

Name the subject clause in each of the following sentences:
1. When he wrote the play is not generally known.
2. What caused the accident is a mystery.

3. That James is an excellent student cannot be denied.
4. What people do does not concern me.
5. What Joseph said is true.
6. That Alberta had won the prize seemed impossible.
7. How they would reach the island puzzled the two boys.
8. That your lessons are well prepared is evident.

EXERCISE 160

Supply noun clauses as subjects of the following predicates:
1. .... needs no proof.
2. .... was long remembered.
3. .... is the question.
4. .... is certain.
5. .... has been decided.
6. .... surprised me.
7. .... is a beautiful spot.
8. .... was soon discovered.

NOUN CLAUSES USED AS DIRECT OBJECTS

A transitive verb expresses an action that passes from a doer to a receiver. In the active voice the doer is the subject and the receiver is the direct object of the verb.

I wish that you may succeed.

I wish what? I wish *that you may succeed*. The noun clause *that you may succeed* is the direct object of the verb *wish*.

I wish that you may succeed. *(Principal clause)*
that you may succeed. *(Noun clause used as object)*

EXERCISE 161

Name the object clause in each of the following sentences:
1. Remember that the work must be completed.
2. Marian wished that she might go to the theater.
3. Mr. Doyle said that we might use his car.
4. Will you show me what you found?
5. The boys discovered where the treasure was buried.

6. I know why you gave that answer.
7. He promised that he would do better.

EXERCISE 162

Supply noun clauses used as direct objects in the following:
1. We believe ....
2. The boys thought ....
3. Anne Gray desired ....
4. Mary whispered ....
5. Mother observed ....
6. Lawrence understands ....
7. The paper announced ....
8. Albert wondered ....

NOUN CLAUSES USED AS PREDICATE NOMINATIVES

The predicate nominative follows a linking verb and completes its meaning.

My wish is that you may succeed.

The verb *is* in this sentence is a copulative verb. It links or couples with the subject the clause *that you may succeed*. This clause, which explains my wish, is the predicate nominative.

My wish is that you may succeed. *(Principal clause)*
that you may succeed. *(Noun clause used as predicate nominative)*

EXERCISE 163

Name the clause used as a predicate nominative in each of the following sentences:
1. My first thought was that a mistake had been made.
2. The truth is that he crossed the line.
3. The general opinion is that you are courageous.
4. The orders were that they should begin at once.
5. The decision is that John will be awarded the prize.
6. The question is "What shall we do next?"
7. The rumor is that we are leaving tomorrow.
8. The truth is that the family cannot afford a television set.

EXERCISE 164

Supply noun clauses used as predicate nominatives in each of the following:
1. My belief is ....
2. The saying is ....
3. His desire was ....
4. Mary's excuse is ....
5. My plan was ....
6. The fact is ....
7. His hope is ....
8. Philip's reason was ....

NOUN CLAUSES USED AS OBJECTS OF PREPOSITIONS

A preposition shows the relation between its object and some other word in a sentence. The object of a preposition may be a noun or a group of words used as a noun.

I have no thought but *that you may succeed*.

In this sentence the preposition *but* shows the relationship between the word *thought* and the clause *that you may succeed*. The noun clause *that you may succeed* is, therefore, the object of the preposition *but*.

I have no thought but that you may succeed. *(Principal clause)*
that you may succeed. *(Noun clause used as object of a preposition)*

EXERCISE 165

Name the noun clauses used as objects of prepositions in the following sentences:
1. I was thinking of what you said.
2. We could hear the speaker from where we sat.
3. I am pleased with what you have written.
4. Everything depends upon who is chosen.
5. The boys boasted of what they had accomplished during their short vacation.
6. Mary and Jane chatted about where they might spend their vacations.

7. The Scouts were amused by what had happened.
8. The medal will be awarded to whoever does the best work.

EXERCISE 166

Supply noun clauses used as objects of the prepositions in the following:
1. Our Holy Father gave his blessing from ....
2. The boys have no idea of ....
3. John is counting on ....
4. Pauline wrote a story about ....
5. I have no other reason except ....
6. Have you heard about ....
7. The result depends upon ....
8. Give the package to ....

NOUN CLAUSES USED IN APPOSITION

An appositive is a word or a group of words that follows a noun and gives additional information about the noun. Clauses that explain nouns or pronouns and give additional information are noun clauses used in apposition.

My wish, that you may succeed, is sincere.
It is my wish that you may succeed.

In both these sentences the noun clause *that you may succeed* explains my wish. In the first sentence the noun clause is in apposition with the noun *wish;* in the second sentence the clause explains and is in apposition with the expletive *it*.

NOTE. Do not confuse an appositive clause with an adjectival clause introduced by *that*. When *that* introduces an adjectival clause, it is a *relative pronoun*. When *that* introduces a noun clause, it is a *conjunction;* it cannot be used as a substantive in the subordinate clause.

John caught the ball *that the boy had thrown*. *(Adjectival clause)*
The fact *that he was honest* could not be denied. *(Noun clause in apposition)*

In the first sentence *that* is a relative pronoun, object of the verb *had thrown*. In the second sentence *that* is a conjunction; it introduces the clause *that he was honest*.

EXERCISE 167

Name the appositive clause in each of the following sentences:
1. The hope that we would win the game encouraged us.
2. The notice that we were to assemble aroused our curiosity.
3. It is true that my father is going to Europe in the spring.
4. James heard the news that his brother had won the prize.
5. It is doubtful whether Rose Marie will come.
6. The report that the package had arrived was a mistake.
7. Mother expressed the wish that we would return early.
8. It is generally known that Lincoln was a poor boy.

EXERCISE 168

Supply noun clauses in apposition with the italicized words:
1. The boys cherished the *hope* ....
2. The *news* .... caused much happiness.
3. Do you believe the *report* .... ?
4. *It* is true ....
5. The teacher asked the *question* ....
6. The *rumor* .... spread throughout the camp.
7. The *saying* .... is familiar to all of us.
8. Who can explain the *statement* .... ?

EXERCISE 169

Use the following noun clauses in sentences of your own. Tell how each clause is used:

that she was sincere	what you bought
how the boys played ball	that the plans were canceled
what she prized most	that you would come
that the children arrived	who stole the purse
why Thomas won	that Mr. Milan was elected

EXERCISE 170

Select the noun clauses in the following sentences and tell how each is used:
1. It is my earnest hope that you will succeed.
2. Father asked whom we saw.
3. Paul profited by what he had learned.
4. What Francis did pleased his parents.
5. The Church teaches that we must be holy.
6. We have heard the expression, "Haste makes waste."
7. It is said that Saint Thomas More went to death with a smile.
8. My hope was that I would visit Dublin.
9. When the event would take place was our next consideration.
10. That they enjoyed the picnic cannot be denied.
11. Eleanor realized that she was needed.
12. Everywhere there were signs that we would have a good harvest.
13. That is what Father expected.
14. I did not know that Robert had won the prize.
15. I understand that you must leave before the end of the month.
16. Elizabeth asked when the plane landed.
17. Mary told the story to whoever would listen.
18. There is a rumor that we shall play Thursday.
19. Edward was pleased with what you gave him.
20. Remember that the work must be completed.
21. That they were welcome was evident.
22. James made a promise that he would do the work.
23. We could hear the music from where we stood.
24. I do not know from whom he received the offer.
25. How we shall get the paper is a puzzle to me.
26. My dog makes friends with whoever is kind to him.
27. None of us knew what the professor wanted.
28. The fact that you were willing encouraged me.
29. Edward's desire is that you will be happy.
30. Tell Martin that he may come early.
31. Peter denied that he knew the man.
32. Whether he will go is uncertain.

EXERCISE 171

Give the syntax of the subordinate clause in each of the following sentences:
1. The boy who lives next door has a new bicycle.
2. Did you notice that John Dawson's father has a new uniform?
3. When the flowers arrived I placed them before our Lady's shrine.
4. It could not be denied that Alice excelled in her studies.
5. The child rushed to the spot where his mother was.
6. This is the man whose book won the Pulitzer prize.
7. Mother wishes that we lived in the country.
8. The children work hard because they desire success.
9. When Mary's uncle came from the South he brought her a very strange pet.
10. My father took me to the mountains that I might regain my health.
11. I remember the day when the cornerstone of that school was laid.
12. We thought that you had gone to Boston.
13. Many of the first English settlers in Virginia were young nobles who were not fit for hard work.
14. March is the month when we honor Saint Joseph.
15. Charles Carroll, who was a cousin of Bishop John Carroll, was a signer of the Declaration of Independence.
16. You did not give the reason why the package was delayed.
17. Father Andrew White, who was the pioneer priest of Maryland, made friends with the Indians.
18. This is the field where the final game was played.

EXERCISE 172

Combine these simple sentences to form complex sentences:
1. Africa has for a long time been called the Dark Continent. Little was known about Africa until recently.
2. Father Joseph Greaton, S.J., was the first resident priest in Philadelphia. He was sent to the Quaker City in 1731.

3. The birds flew south. They were seeking a winter home.
4. The Louisiana Territory vastly increased the area of the United States. It was purchased in 1803.
5. Milk is a perfect food. It contains three chief food elements.
6. Saint Francis Xavier is called the Apostle of the Indies. He was a noted Jesuit.
7. You should sweep and dust frequently. Dirt is a germ collector.
8. The maniple is a vestment. The priest wears it on his left arm.
9. We visited Venice. We rode in gondolas on the Grand Canal.
10. Frederick Watts painted "Sir Galahad." A copy of the picture hangs in our room.
11. Nitrate is obtained from the Atacama Desert. The desert is located in northern Chile.
12. The streams so joyful in the spring run slowly in autumn. They mourn the passing of the year.
13. Thomas Fitzsimmons was one of the financiers of the Revolution. He was a personal friend of Robert Morris.
14. Ocean currents are streams of water. The currents influence the climate of the land near the seashore.

EXERCISE 173

Combine the following simple sentences to form compound sentences:

1. The golden sun was mirrored in the peaceful brook. A beautiful rainbow spread across the sky.
2. Saint Anne was the mother of the Blessed Virgin. Saint Joachim was her father.
3. Be mission-minded. Help the missions.
4. Matthew came directly home from school. Richard went to the ball field.
5. The orchestra assembled early. The program did not begin until eight o'clock.
6. The Second Continental Congress met in May 1775. The Congress appointed George Washington commander in chief of the continental army.

7. Mr. O'Brien works in Arizona. His home is in Virginia.
8. Joseph Martin became president of his class. David Wilson became secretary.
9. Rowing exercises the muscles of the upper part of the body. Swimming exercises all the muscles of the body.
10. The crests of the rugged mountains were flaked with snow. The dauntless Alpine climber continued his ascent.
11. Mr. Murphy took me to the circus. He bought popcorn and candy for me.
12. Arthur swam across the lake. He returned in his father's fishing boat.

EXERCISE 174 [Check on Knowledge of Sentences]

Tell whether the following sentences are simple, compound, or complex:

1. Do you know who that girl is?
2. Saint Christopher, the patron of travelers, once carried the Christ Child.
3. A library was provided for the children, and they used it frequently.
4. In the town where I live is a new airport.
5. The radio, which is a modern invention, is an effective means of advertising.
6. The ship brought a cargo of coffee that had been grown in Brazil.
7. It is true that he did not consider the expense.
8. We saw that he did not answer when he was called.
9. Have the children arrived or shall we cancel the engagement?
10. The messenger came and delivered the letter.
11. Andrew Jackson, the hero of New Orleans, later became president.
12. The legislature passed the bill, but the governor vetoed it.
13. Crowds of people passed the crippled man; many spoke kindly to him.
14. We looked in Dr. Bradley's office, but he was not there.
15. Although John was tired, he completed the work.

16. Baptism is the first sacrament that we receive.
17. Do you know when the concert begins?
18. All that glitters is not gold.
19. Mary rejoiced because her brother was improving.
20. As day dawned, the beautiful sun peeped over the horizon.

EXERCISE 175 [Test on Phrases, Clauses, and Sentences]

Read this selection very carefully and then answer the questions that follow:

[1] Have you ever wondered which part of God's world mirrors most faithfully the majesty of the Creator? [2] If you have, look for your answer in the matchless beauty of a starlit sky. [3] Countless tiny points of light pierce the inky blackness and shed a soft radiance on the darkened earth. [4] How true are the words which David spoke so many years ago! [5] The heavens show forth the glory of God, and the firmament declareth the work of His hands.

1. Name one or more adjectival phrases in the first sentence.
2. Find an adverbial phrase in the third sentence.
3. What does the adverbial phrase in the third sentence modify?
4. Is the subordinate clause in the fourth sentence an adjectival or an adverbial clause?
5. Find an adverbial clause in the selection.
6. How is the noun clause in the first sentence used?
7. Are the clauses in the fifth sentence in natural or in transposed order?
8. Which sentences in the paragraph are declarative?
9. Are there any interrogative, imperative, or exclamatory sentences? List them.
10. Is the third sentence simple, compound, or complex?
11. Find a compound sentence.
12. Are there any complex sentences? If so, name them.
13. Is the subordinate clause in the fourth sentence restrictive or nonrestrictive?
14. Which sentence contains a compound predicate?
15. What is the subject of the principal clause in the second sentence?

Model Diagrams

By means of diagrams we show in a graphic manner the relationships that exist among the various words that make up a sentence. As we have seen, there are simple, compound, and complex sentences. Since sentences of all types may contain modifiers, no one form of diagram will serve for every kind of sentence. The diagrams given here are those that should help us in our work. When asked to diagram a sentence, look here for one of the same kind and see how the diagram is made.

The diagraming of sentences should serve a double purpose. First, it should make it easier for us to understand the complete meaning of every sentence we read. Secondly, it should help us to write effectively and to avoid the use of faulty sentences. If we keep these purposes before our mind, diagraming will improve our English. It will not become a mechanical exercise which does not help us to read more intelligently nor to write more correctly.

SIMPLE SENTENCES

NOMINATIVE CASE

Subject: Our Lady's *birthday* is celebrated in September.

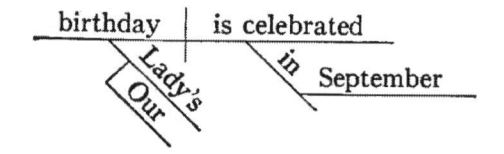

```
   birthday  |  is celebrated
     \ \        \
      \ \        \ in
    Our Lady's    September
```

Predicate Nominative: Mary is our *model.*

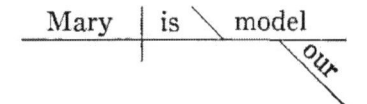

```
   Mary  |  is  \  model
                   \ our
```

Address: Little *children,* love your parents.

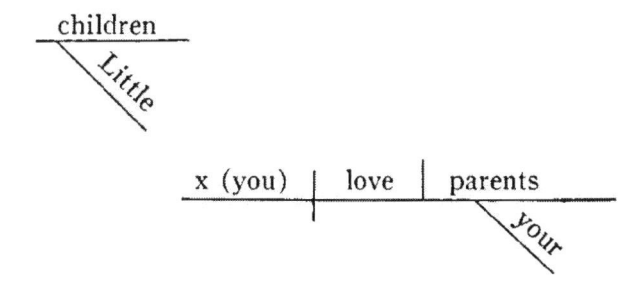

```
      children
       \ Little

   x (you)  |  love  |  parents
                         \ your
```

Apposition: Mary, our *Mother,* intercedes for us.

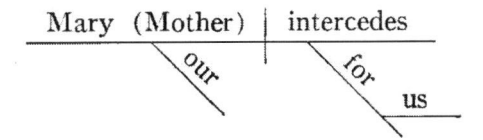

```
   Mary (Mother)  |  intercedes
         \ our         \ for
                          us
```

Exclamation: The *sacraments!* They are steppingstones to heaven.

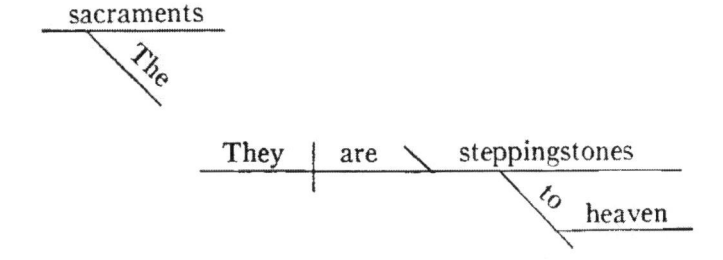

```
   sacraments
      \ The

   They  |  are  \  steppingstones
                     \ to
                        heaven
```

OBJECTIVE CASE

Direct Object: Mary and Joseph took the *Child* into Egypt.

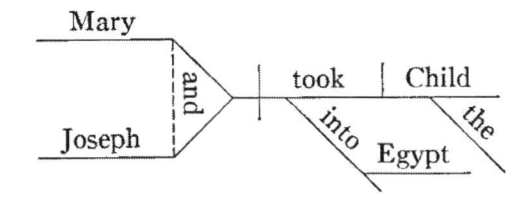

```
        Mary
    _____\
            \ a       took  |  Child
             } n  _____
            / d       \        \
    _____/          \ into   \ the
     Joseph             \        \
                         Egypt
```

Object of a Preposition: Jesus was found in the *Temple* of *Jerusalem*.

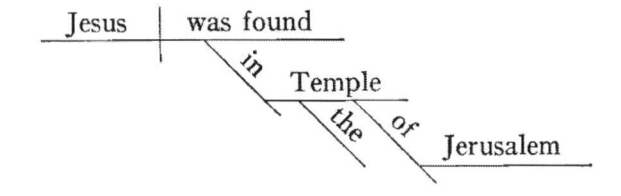

```
    Jesus  |  was found
    _____|_____
              \
               \ in
                \  Temple
                 _____
                    \  \ of
                     \the \
                          \ Jerusalem
```

Indirect Object: Saint Joseph taught the *Child* the carpenter's trade.

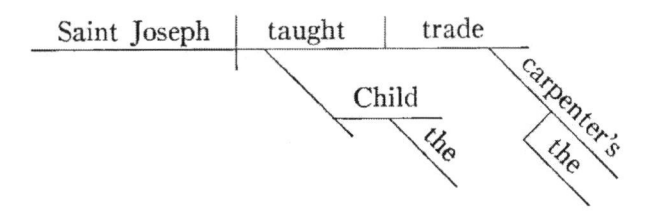

```
    Saint Joseph  |  taught  |  trade
    _____|_____|_____
                       \          \ carpenter's
                        \ Child    \
                         \          \ the
                          \ the
```

Apposition: We love the Infant, the *Babe* in the manger.

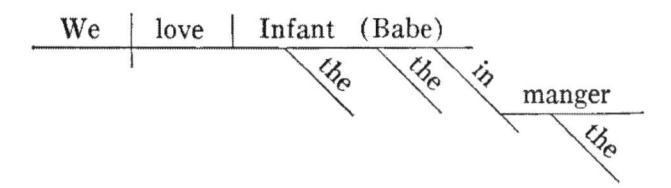

```
    We  |  love  |  Infant  (Babe)
    ____|_____|_____
                     \   \    \ in
                      \the \the \  manger
                                  _____
                                     \ the
```

Adverbial Objective: They walked three *miles.*

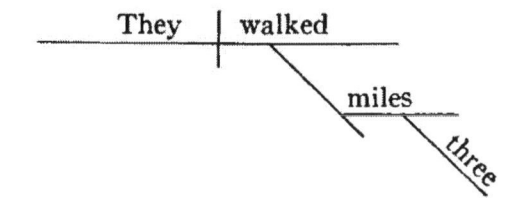

```
    They  |  walked
          |      \
          |       miles
          |         \
          |          three
```

Retained Object: The pupils were given a long *assignment.*

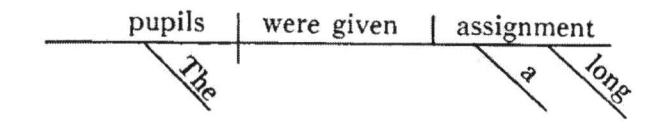

```
   pupils  |  were given  |  assignment
       \                      \      \
        The                    a      long
```

Objective Complement: They named the boy *John.*

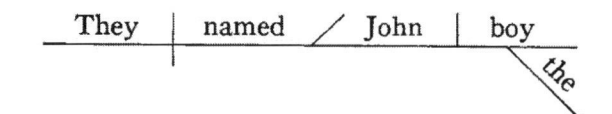

```
   They  |  named  /  John  |  boy
                                 \
                                  the
```

COMPOUND ELEMENTS

Compound Subject: *Mary* and *Helen* worked for the prize.

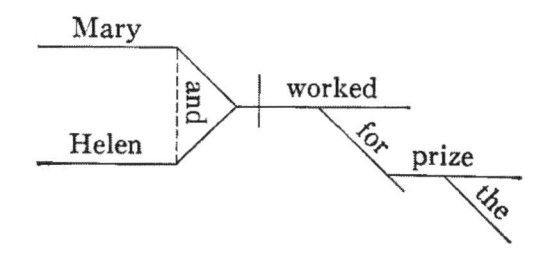

```
     Mary
         \
          and  |  worked
         /         \
     Helen          for
                      \
                       prize
                          \
                           the
```

Compound Predicate: The little girl *sang* and *danced*.

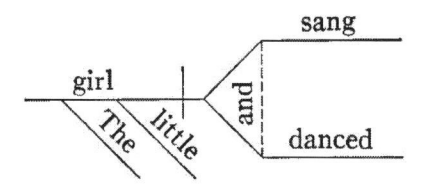

```
                       sang
        girl    |  ⎧
         ⧵    ⧸  ⎨and
       The little ⎩
                       danced
```

Compound Subject and Compound Predicate: The *boys* and the *girls ran* and *jumped*.

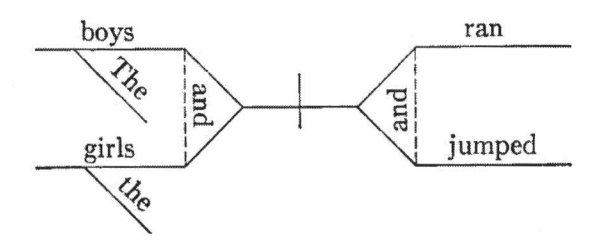

```
     boys                              ran
        ⧵    ⎫                     ⎧
      The    ⎬and        |      and⎨
     girls   ⎭                     ⎩
        ⧸                              jumped
      the
```

COMPOUND SENTENCE

The camel is the ship of the desert, and the reindeer is the camel of the snowland.

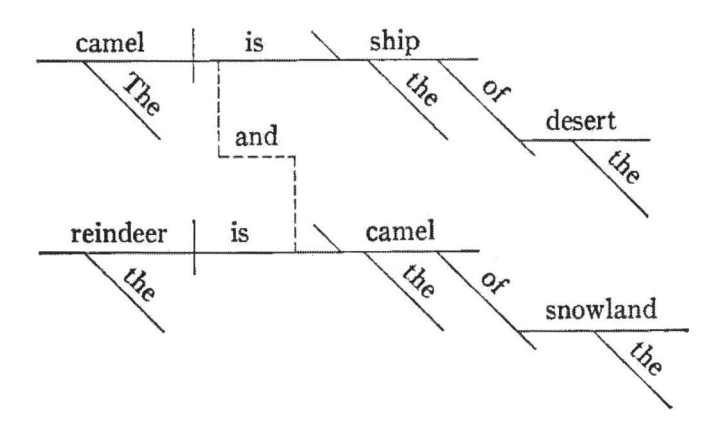

```
   camel   |  is   ⧵  ship
      ⧵            the ⧵ of
     The                    desert
              and                ⧵
              |                  the
              |
  reindeer  |  is   ⧵  camel
      ⧵                the ⧵ of
     the                      snowland
                                  ⧵
                                  the
```

COMPLEX SENTENCES

ADJECTIVAL CLAUSES

The teacher read us a story which was very interesting.

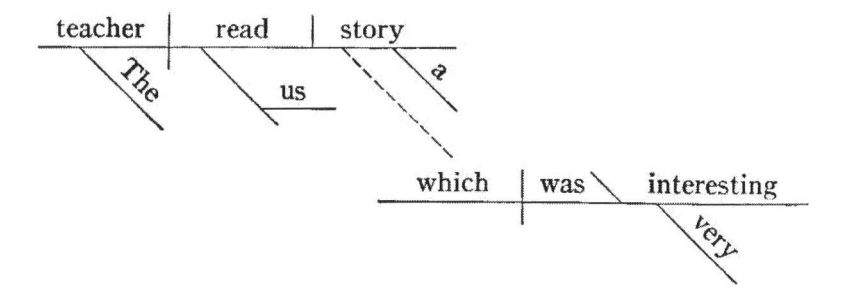

This is the city where the treaty was signed.

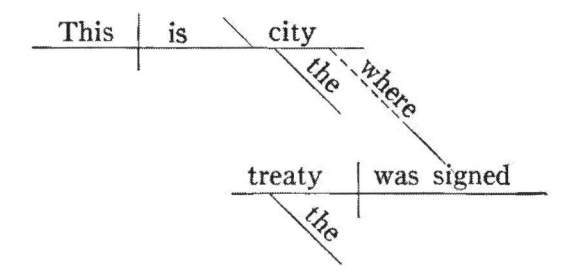

ADVERBIAL CLAUSES

The boy came when he was called.

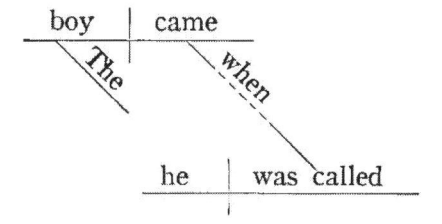

Because the weather was stormy, the Scouts postponed the hike.

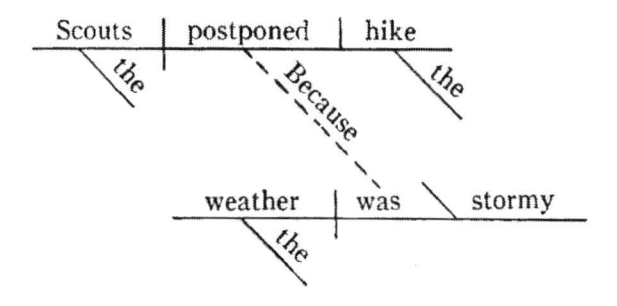

NOUN CLAUSES

Subject: That you may succeed is my wish.

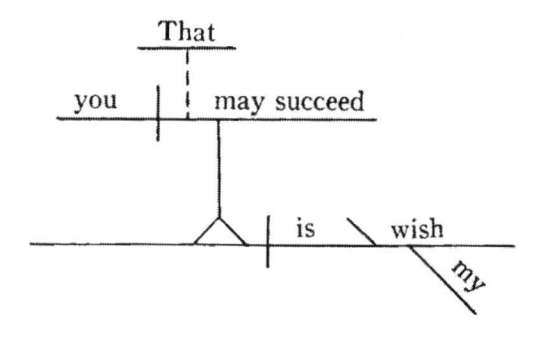

Direct Object: I wish that you may succeed.

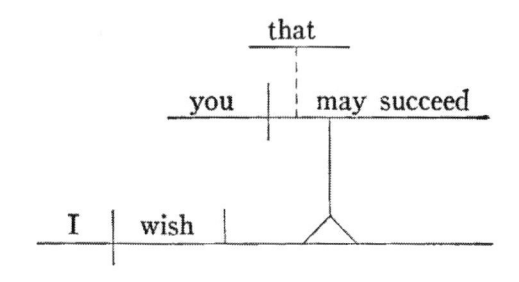

Predicate Nominative: My wish is that you may succeed.

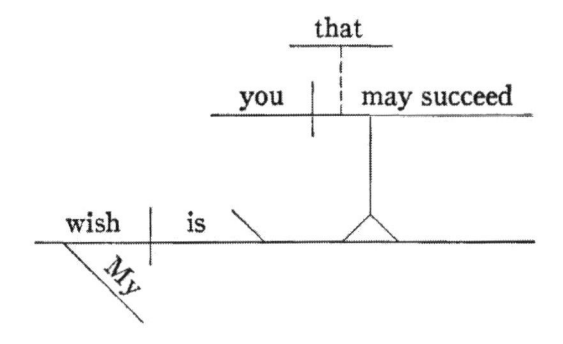

```
                        that
                         |
              you    |   may succeed
                         |
   wish  |  is  \
   \My\        \
                \___/\___
```

Object of a Preposition: I have no thought but that you may succeed.

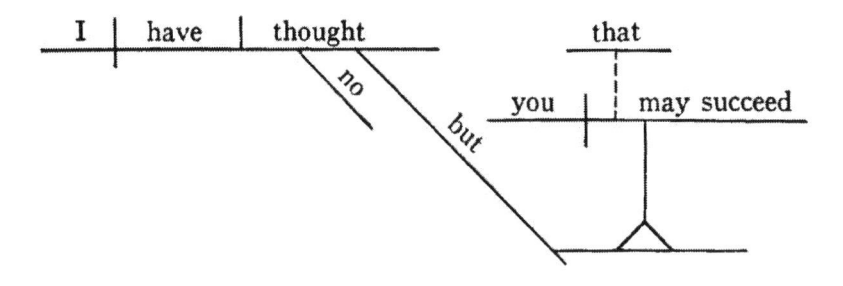

```
  I  |  have  |  thought              that
                   \                    |
                   no\        you  |    may succeed
                      \but                |
                       _____/\____
```

Apposition: My wish, that you may succeed, is sincere.

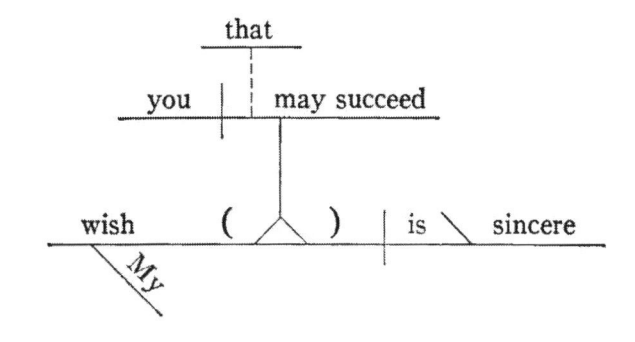

```
              that
               |
     you  |    may succeed
               |
   wish   ( /\ )  |  is  \  sincere
   \My\
```

Punctuation

The purpose of punctuation is to make clear the meaning of what is written. In speaking, the inflection of our voice enables the listener to understand our thoughts. In writing, there are different kinds of punctuation marks—the period, comma, semicolon, colon, exclamation point, interrogation point, quotation marks, apostrophe, hyphen, and dash—which enable the reader to interpret our thoughts. The same marks must be used for similar constructions at all times. The following rules are the ones which we shall need in our own writing.

THE PERIOD

Use a period:
1. At the end of a declarative or an imperative sentence.
   The Feast of the Assumption is celebrated on August fifteenth.
   Close the door, Albert.
2. After an abbreviation or an initial.
   M.D.   George R. Clarke

EXERCISE I

Supply periods where they are needed:
1. Thomas just made a touchdown
2. A silver ladder of light
3. Reverend Connell R Clinton, J C D, delivered the commencement address
4. As we walked through the park
5. The woods were carpeted with leaves
6. We visited the shrine of Saint Anne

7. For their early spring housecleaning
8. The butterflies flitted and danced from flower to flower
9. In this garden the flowers are unusually fragrant
10. The boys are preparing for their trip to the Poconos
11. Me is the abbreviation for the state of Maine
12. If these trees stand as sentinels in the dark
13. A member of the Knights of Columbus will address us tonight
14. In a secluded spot down in the meadow
15. The children were delightfully surprised when the teacher gave the signal for early dismissal
16. Come here, Therese
17. The merry song of the birds tells us of the approach of spring
18. Bring me that book, David
19. The package was addressed to Mr and Mrs Francis J Cook
20. What do the letters Ph D after a name mean?

THE COMMA

Use a comma:

1. To separate words or groups of words in a series.

    Peter, James, and John witnessed the Transfiguration.
    We should love God with our whole heart, with our whole soul, and with our whole mind.
    The teacher kept account of what the class did, what the class said, and what the class read.

2. To set off a short direct quotation and the parts of a divided quotation, unless an interrogation point or an exclamation point is required.

    "Australia is the smallest continent," explained the teacher.
    "I will spend my heaven," promised the Little Flower, "in doing good upon earth."
    "Have you ever read *Percy Wynne?*" asked the boy.
    "What a pretty picture!" exclaimed Marcia.

3. To separate independent elements and words of direct address.

    Yes, we shall attend the play.
    Father, forgive them.

4. To set off the parts of dates, addresses, or geographical names.
   We moved to Savannah, Georgia, on December 10, 1950.
5. To separate nonrestrictive phrases and clauses from the rest of the sentence.
   The sail, torn by the wind, was mended by the old fisherman.
   Saint Stephen, who was the first martyr, was stoned to death.

NOTE. A nonrestrictive phrase or clause is one that may be omitted from the sentence without changing its meaning. Some phrases or clauses cannot be omitted without changing the meaning of the sentence. These are called *restrictive* phrases or clauses and are not set off by commas.

   The hospital built by Dr. Nabb is located on Front Street.

A restrictive clause changes the meaning of the sentence by *restricting* or *limiting* the meaning of some word in the sentence, usually the subject or the direct object. If we say, "Students in Catholic schools, who are specially favored by God, should be grateful for what they receive," we are speaking of *all* students in Catholic schools, and we mean that all are specially favored by God and that all should be grateful. If we omitted the commas, we would not be speaking of *all* students in Catholic schools, but of those only who are specially favored by God. We would imply, therefore, that some students in the Catholic schools are *not* specially favored by God.

Tell why commas must be used in this sentence.
   Lead, which is heavier than water, sinks rapidly.

6. After long introductory phrases and clauses and when needed to make the meaning clear.
   While Christ was hanging upon the cross, His Mother stood near.
   After eating, the horse left the pasture.
7. To set off an appositive that is not part of the name or that is not restrictive.
   Saint Agnes, the patroness of youth, was a Roman maiden.
   Peter the Hermit made a pilgrimage to the Holy Land.
8. To set off a parenthetical expression; that is, a word or a group of words inserted in the sentence as a comment or an

explanatory remark, and one that is not necessary to the thought of the sentence.

This is, I tell you, a pleasant task.

Some of the common parenthetical expressions are:

of course	I admit	in fact	as you know
indeed	it is true	in truth	no doubt
I assure you	in general	however	notwithstanding

9. To separate the clauses of a compound sentence connected by the conjunctions *and, but, or, nor, yet*. If the clauses are short and closely connected, the comma may be omitted.

    We waited at the station, yet the train did not come.
    Matthew called and I answered immediately.

10. After the salutation in a social letter and after the complimentary close in all letters.

    Dear Francis,   Sincerely yours,   Very truly yours,

EXERCISE 2

Give reasons for the use of the commas in each of the following sentences:

1. The captain of the team, a very brilliant young man, is a member of our parish.
2. Poets, musicians, and artists come to this resort every summer.
3. Marian said, "I know nothing about the affair."
4. Francis went on a cruise, but Joseph could not go.
5. Donald, as you know, is a very generous boy.
6. The special classes will be held on Tuesday, Thursday, and Friday.
7. George Washington died on December 14, 1799.
8. A sudden gust of wind, a loud banging of doors, and the rattling of the cabin windows foretold the approach of a storm.
9. Yes, Margaret answered my letter.
10. My father, who had been to Boston, returned at eleven o'clock last night.

11. The windowpane was broken, but the boys offered to pay for it.
12. Instead of all, selfish souls give God only a little.

EXERCISE 3

Insert the punctuation marks needed in the following sentences:
1. John Carroll was appointed the first bishop in the United States on November 6 1789
2. Beyond the lake along the edge of the woods was the wheat field
3. After the sun goes down it will be cooler
4. The doctrine of the Immaculate Conception was promulgated on December 8 1854
5. The children brought sugar butter and molasses for the taffy
6. After he had eaten John went fishing
7. James as well as his friends was invited
8. John Rolfe a Virginia colonist married Pocahontas
9. Speak now or forever keep your peace
10. This man as we all know is a great leader of Catholic Action
11. Saint Catherine Labouré was born May 2 1806
12. Dorothy do you wish some candy
13. Wolves have remarkably keen sight hearing and scent
14. On the fourth day they reached Havana Cuba their destination
15. When you come to our house for the club meeting bring your little brother with you
16. Yes our ship sails at noon
17. The sacred vessels are the chalice the paten the ciborium the ostensorium and the pyx
18. Mrs Clarke our neighbor has an attractive winning forceful personality
19. John you careless boy put your books where they belong
20. Children enjoy sports in spring in summer in autumn and in winter
21. I ran quickly to the window but she had disappeared
22. Mr Ragan may I present my friend Martin Ryan

23. The little girls played in the water on the beach and on the boardwalk each morning during vacation
24. My sister now lives at 417 Market Street Norfolk Virginia
25. Have you ever traveled in the West Miss Greene
26. The Catholic Church owes a debt of gratitude to the religious orders which serve without hope of an earthly reward
27. Cork which is lighter than water floats easily
28. Let Saint Joseph be your model
29. The Declaration of Independence which was adopted in 1776 proclaimed our independence of Great Britain
30. It was I assure you a difficult task
31. Sin which offends God is to be deplored
32. Saint Patrick the patron of Ireland overcame the Druids.

THE SEMICOLON

Use a semicolon:

1. To separate the clauses of a compound sentence when they are not separated by a coordinate conjunction.

   The beach was deserted; the bathers had gone for lunch.

2. To separate the clauses of a compound sentence that are connected by *nevertheless, moreover, therefore, then,* or *thus,* since these words have very little connective force.

   William was here early; nevertheless, I did not see him.

3. Before *as* and *namely* when these words introduce an example or an illustration.

   There are three things necessary to make a sin mortal; namely, a grievous matter, sufficient reflection, and full consent of the will.

EXERCISE 4

Insert semicolons where needed in the following sentences:

1. My brother is very strong he excels in athletics.
2. Our group will take these benches the ones in front are for the upper classes.
3. Gertrude is a very popular girl moreover, she is an excellent student.

4. He was a kind-hearted man we all loved him.
5. I have never seen the magazine therefore I will not subscribe to it.
6. None knew the entire story none cared to hear it.
7. Margaret forgot to feed her dog therefore it was hungry.
8. There are four last things to be remembered namely, death, judgment, heaven, and hell.
9. Father has tried the motor he knows it works.
10. He doesn't like chemistry nevertheless, he does not wish to give up science entirely.
11. William played the violin Helen, the piano.
12. All groups joined in the work it was soon completed.
13. Many words have the same form in the singular and the plural as sheep, trout, and deer.
14. Take pride in your work be satisfied with nothing but the best.
15. Three of the holydays are feasts of our Lord namely, Christmas, the Circumcision, and the Ascension.
16. We were provided with many stringed instruments namely, violins, violas, and cellos.
17. Always read with good light have it come from over your left shoulder.
18. One brother lives in Texas another, in Maine.
19. Go to the gymnasium at once do not delay.
20. I had no lunch therefore I am hungry.

THE COLON

Use a colon:
1. After the salutation of a business letter.
        Dear Mr. Clarke: Gentlemen:
2. Before a list or enumeration of items.
    For this cake I need the following: butter, eggs, sugar, and flour.
3. Before a long direct quotation.
    The lawyer spoke as follows: "My client is trustworthy, honest, and sincere. He is deserving of your consideration."

EXERCISE 5

Explain the use of the colon in each of these sentences:
1. The following supplies are needed: chalk, eraser, paper, and ink.
2. The parts of speech are as follows: noun, pronoun, verb, adjective, adverb, conjunction, preposition, and interjection.
3. Jesus spoke to them, saying: "Go, therefore, and make disciples of all nations, baptizing them in the name of the Father, and of the Son, and of the Holy Spirit, teaching them to observe all that I have commanded you; and behold, I am with you all days, even unto the consummation of the world."
4. We purchased the following: balls, bats, gloves, and shoes.
5. Arrange the following words in alphabetical order: declare, diamond, dream, daring, decide.
6. Dear Sirs:

THE EXCLAMATION POINT

Use an exclamation point:
1. After an exclamatory sentence.
    What a beautiful landscape lies before us!
2. After an exclamatory word, phrase, or clause.
    "Order in the court!" shouted the judge.

EXERCISE 6

Explain the use of the exclamation point in each of the following sentences:
1. How beautiful is the sunset!
2. Hurrah! The task is done at last.
3. What a surprise it was!
4. Splendid! I knew you could do it.
5. Who would believe that story!
6. O Elizabeth! I am glad to see you.
7. Hush! The baby is sleeping.
8. You are lucky!

THE INTERROGATION POINT

Use an interrogation point:

1. At the end of every question.

 How many square rods are there in an acre?

QUOTATION MARKS

Use quotation marks:

1. Before and after every direct quotation and every part of a divided quotation.

 Our Lord said: "I am come that they may have life, and may have it more abundantly."

 "Dearly beloved," said Saint John, "love one another."

NOTE. Sometimes a quotation includes another quotation. The included quotation is known as a *quotation within a quotation* and is marked with single quotation marks.

 Joseph asked, "Was it Lincoln who said, 'With malice towards none; with charity for all'?"

2. To enclose titles of stories, poems, magazine articles, newspaper articles, and works of art.

 John Greenleaf Whittier is the author of "Snow-Bound."

NOTE. Titles of books, magazines, and newspapers are usually printed in italics although some writers quote them.

 The Oregon Trail is a story of pioneer days.
 "The Oregon Trail" is a story of pioneer days.

EXERCISE 7

Punctuate the following sentences:

1. How happy you look exclaimed Marie
2. You may Mary promised have my skates today
3. Please give me the book requested the librarian
4. Mr Martin announced I have nothing to say except that I am proud of my boy
5. Have you ever seen the original picture Sir Galahad asked Walter

6. William answered The driver shouted Watch the signal before you turn
7. Not wishing to be delayed I asked When do we leave
8. Remember the motto All that glitters is not gold reminded Mother
9. It is now no longer I that live but Christ lives in me says Saint Paul
10. When I told him the boy replied I am pleased
11. All that I am and all that I hope to be I owe to my angel mother was said by Abraham Lincoln
12. The teacher said Explain the proverb Honesty is the best policy
13. May I see your new book asked the girl
14. Our class dramatized The Legend of the Robes said Alice
15. There are many dangerous curves in this road warned the policeman

THE APOSTROPHE

Use an apostrophe:

1. To show possession.
    The children's library is open today.
2. With *s* to show the plural of letters, figures, and signs.
          a's   8's   ?'s
3. To show the omission of a letter, letters, or figures.
        wouldn't   we'll   spirit of '76

THE HYPHEN

Use a hyphen:

1. To divide a word at the end of a line whenever one or more syllables are carried to the next line.
2. In compound numbers from twenty-one to ninety-nine.
    He is thirty-two years old.
3. To separate the parts of some compound words.
        self-made   cross-examination   mother-in-law

THE DASH

Use a dash:

1. To indicate a sudden change of thought.

   John came early—an unusual thing for him.

EXERCISE 8

Copy the following sentences and insert the proper punctuation:

1. The Lord is my shepherd I shall not want
2. He recognized every tree bush and hedge and hailed them as he would old friends
3. Were you present yesterday
4. What a happy little girl youll be
5. The car was old moreover it was defective
6. Who won the race he asked
7. Three cheers for our team
8. Pope Leo XIII died in the twenty fifth year of his reign
9. The following accessories are needed typewriter filing cabinet mimeograph machine adding machine
10. I have just finished reading Uncle Toms Cabin
11. Sister said Our school motto Enter to Learn should be put into practice
12. Look There goes the ball said Thomas
13. There are many old fashioned buildings on this street
14. The teacher it seems was very busy
15. Did you go with him Joan
16. She is a member of the class of 50
17. Alaska the largest state in the Union lies northwest of Canada
18. The valley was green but the mountains were covered with snow
19. Ill teach you said Peter
20. If you will do your best I am sure you will succeed
21. My parents have lived twenty four years in this parish
22. The moss covered stone hid the violets
23. How is your sister in law

24. The estate consists of forty one acres
25. He was young too young to enjoy the beauty of the trip
26. He is very careless about crossing his *t*s
27. Chicago had a light snowfall on June 15 a very unusual occurrence for that city
28. The three members of our baseball team who are failing in their studies will I think be asked to turn in their uniforms
29. Cotton which is one of the principal products of the South is used for many different purposes
30. The recipe calls for three fourths cup of flour
31. We have been unable replied Mother to finish the work
32. Hurrah for our team shouted the happy children

CAPITAL LETTERS

Use a capital letter for:

1. The first word in a sentence.

   The trees cast inky pools on the silvery lawn.

2. The first word of every line of poetry.

   Ring out the old, ring in the new,
   Ring, happy bells, across the snow!

3. The first word of a direct quotation.

   Rosemary answered, "My new afghan is made of many colors."

4. Proper nouns and proper adjectives. These include particular persons or groups of persons, religious denominations, political parties, institutions, buildings, cities, states, streets, months of the year, days of the week, holydays, and holidays.

   Michael, June, Valentine Day, Republican party, Catholic. American colleges

5. Titles of honor and respect when preceding the name.

    Queen Victoria   Cardinal Newman

NOTE. Do not capitalize any title not followed by a proper noun unless it is used in direct address as a substitute for the name.

   The cardinal gave his blessing.
   Please give us your blessing, Your Eminence.

6. *North, south, east,* and *west* when they refer to sections of a country.

   She lived in the South.
7. All names referring to God, the Bible, or parts of the Bible.

   For God so loved the world as to give His only-begotten Son.
8. The principal words in the titles of books, plays, poems, and pictures.

   Tennyson wrote "The Charge of the Light Brigade."
9. The pronoun *I* and the interjection *O*.

   O Lord, I am not worthy.
10. Abbreviations when capitals would be used if the words were written in full.

    U.S.A.   Dr.   Ave.   Jan.

Do not capitalize:

1. The seasons of the year.

   winter   spring   summer   fall
2. The articles *a, an, the,* conjunctions, or prepositions in titles, unless one of these is the first word.

   We dramatized "The Man without a Country."
3. The names of studies, unless they are derived from proper nouns.

   history   arithmetic   Spanish
4. The words *high school, college,* and *university,* unless they are parts of the names of particular institutions.

   My brother goes to college in Boston.
   My brother goes to Boston College.
5. Abbreviations for the time of day.

   a.m.   p.m.

EXERCISE 9

Explain the uses of the capital letters in the following sentences:
1. Thomas did not go to Texas.
2. He speaks English, French, and Italian.

3. Mr. Webster has moved to the West.
4. Last Saturday my friend and I went to the American Museum of Natural History.
5. Does your sister attend Immaculata College?
6. There are three persons in God: God the Father, God the Son, and God the Holy Spirit.
7. Many Japanese are engaged in fishing.
8. The headquarters of the Catholic Foreign Mission Society are at Maryknoll, New York.
9. The book was *David Copperfield* and I enjoyed reading it.
10. Mrs. Livingston replied, "Please call Dr. David at once."
11. Early next morning, Monday, they started on their trip to the South.
12. Jesus Christ was born in Bethlehem.
13. The American people are industrious and energetic.
14. The Catholic Church is the interpreter of the Bible.
15. James does not like English, but he is interested in geography.
16. The quality of mercy is not strained;
    It droppeth as the gentle rain from heaven
    Upon the place beneath.
17. Pope Pius XII blessed the pilgrims.

POEM FOR DRAMATIZATION

The Legend of the Robes
By Eleanore C. Donnelly

Elizabeth, (by God's dear grace the spouse
Of Louis of Thuringia,) sat one day
In the fair quiet of her latticed room,
With Ysentrude—of all her maids best loved—
To bear her company.
     The pure spring light
Crept through the ancient casement, and illumed
The noble beauty of the lady's face,
The chaste decorum of her simple robe,
Scarce richer than the beggar's russet cloak,
On which, with persevering love, she wrought;
Singing the while, with summer in her voice,
Sweet snatches of an old Hungarian hymn,
To which maid Ysentrude held meek refrain,
With sweeping lashes and low-drooping veil.
A step pulsed through the hall,—a manly step,—
And, in the doorway, framed (a picture fair),
Duke Louis stood, and smiled upon his spouse,
A tender smile, yet troubled.
      Up she rose,
The fond Elizabeth, and coming, basked
In the mild lustre of his anxious eye;
The Christ-like pity on her girlish lip
Melting and mixing in her smile of joy;
While throbbing heart sent up its purest rose
To tremble through the olive of her cheek,
And bid him welcome there.
      "What ill has chanced,
Dear love, to thee or thine, that this calm face
So sad a mask should wear?" the lady asked.

"O spouse Elizabeth! we are undone!
Four envoys from thy father's court, below,
Come to crave audience with thy gentle self,
Who must respect their plea. What wilt thou do?
Thy love of God, and of His precious poor,
Has so inflamed thy generous soul with zeal,
That gems and silken robes are quite forsworn,
And all the pomp of ducal dignity
Sunk in obscure retreat. *I* do not chide
Thee, love, fair-blushing, like the morning sky!
Thy rosy charms, to *me*, can deck thee out
In raiment comelier than a queen's attire.
But if thou givest audience to these men,
Clad, as thou art, in this poor woolen robe,
They, knowing not the motive of thy deeds,
(That charity which gives, forgetting self,)
Will straightway swell with scandal and depart,
Burning to bruit what gossips burn to hear,
That Louis of Thuringia keeps his bride
In robes no better than a peasant dame's!"
 With ear attentive to his tender words,
With kindling eye uplifted to his own,
Elizabeth was mute; but now her hand
Fell lightly as a snow-flake on his arm,
And through the silence came her silver voice:
 "Fret not thy soul, my Louis, with these cares,
But trust in God. Our noble guests are worn
And weary with long travel; do thou go
And bid them welcome to Thuringia's halls
Most generous. And when the feast is spread,
I shall attend you there!"
      Her glorious smile,
Her pure uplifted brow, o'erawed him,
And he went away communing with her words.
—Then knelt the Lady 'Lisa where she stood,
Her little hands enclasped, her holy face

Brilliant with some strange lustre, as she prayed:
"O Lord! my Crucified! for Thy pure love
I have despoiled myself of royal robes,
And put away the vanity of gems!
Listen, O Best Belovèd! in Thy strength,
(Pure as the fleece and generous as the light!)
Behold me in my poverty and need,
And make me pleasing in my husband's eyes!"
  Circled with veilèd maidens, down she went,
Transfigured with the passion of her prayer;
Her soft, slow step is herald to her coming,
And silence chains the lords who grace the feast.
  What 'mazement leaps to light their sluggish eyes,
What wonder parts their heavy-bearded lips!
While Louis folds his arms upon his chest,
Lifts his proud head, and smiles upon his bride.
  Her robe of silken sheen flowed o'er her feet
Sweeping the marble floor in waves of light;
Clasped at her throat, the yielding mantle sprung
To fold her graceful shoulders with its folds
Of velvet, azure as the summer's sky.
And, from her head (confined with diamond pins
Which lit her locks as stars the midnight gloom),
A fleecy veil fell, shimmering like spray,
Over her blushing cheeks, her pure, clear eyes!
"Sweet wife!" Duke Louis said, the while her hand
Lay, like a pearl, within his manly palm:
"Sweet wife!" ('twas but a whisper, yet she heard,)
"Thy face, methinks, doth sparkle like the sun,
And thy rich raiment—?"
                      Lady 'Lisa bowed
Her forehead, like a lily touched with sleep,
And while the color varied in her cheeks,
"Great is our God," she said, "and wondrous are His ways!"

Index

Abstract nouns, 215
Active voice, 295
Adjectival clauses, 381-83, 392, 404
Adjectival phrases, 367
Adjective pronouns, 250-53
Adjectives, 269-83
  classes of, 269-72
  common, 269
  comparison of, 276-77, 279
  correct use of, 279-83
  demonstrative, 272, 280
  descriptive, 269
  distributive, 272
  indefinite, 272
  interrogative, 272
  limiting, 271-72
  numeral, 271
  position of, 274-75
  possessive, 253, 265, 272
  predicate, 274-75, 293, 344
  proper, 269, 418
  test on, 284
Adverbial clauses, 381, 384-85, 404
Adverbial objective, 234, 340-41, 402
Adverbial phrases, 367
Adverbs, 334-47
  classification of, 334-41
  comparison of, 341-42
  conjunctive, 337, 356, 385
  correct use of, 343-46
  interrogative, 336
  of affirmation, 334
  of degree, 334
  of manner, 334
  of negation, 334
  of place, 334
  of time, 334
  relative, 338-39, 357, 381-82
  simple, 336
  test on, 347
Affirmation, adverbs of, 334
Agreement
  of pronouns, 245, 265, 267
  of verbs, 309-20

"America the Beautiful," 114-15
Among, correct use of, 350
Anecdotes, 19-20
Angry at, correct use of, 351
Angry with, correct use of, 351
Antecedent, 239, 244, 245, 265, 267
Anything, correct use of, 266
Apostrophe, uses of, 221, 227-29, 416
Apposition, 224-25, 231, 392-93, 400, 401, 406, 409
Articles, 271, 282
As, correct use of, 260, 358-59, 360
As if, correct use of, 360
At, correct use of, 351
Attributive adjectives, 274
Auxiliary verbs, 286, 299, 300, 302

"Barbara Frietchie," 82-84
Bates, Katharine Lee, 114
Be, conjugation of, 304-06
Beginning sentence, 30-33, 60, 69
Behind, correct use of, 350
Beside, correct use of, 350
Besides, correct use of, 350
Between, correct use of, 350
Body of letters, 121-22, 138
Books, 191-205
  advertisements of, 191-92
  classification of, 200
  reference, 199, 202-04
  reports of, 196-98
  reviews of, 193-94
  standards for judging, 194
Broadcasts, classroom, 182-85
Business letters, 119, 138-41
Business telephone calls, 144-45

Calendar, liturgical and civil, 424-32
Capital letters
  in letters, 120-21, 123
  in outlines, 48, 49
  in poetry, 80, 418
  uses of, 418-19
Card catalogue, 200-01

Case
  nominative, 222-25, 239, 254-55, 263, 264, 399-400
  objective, 230-36, 239, 257-59, 263, 264, 340-41, 401-02
  possessive, 227-29, 239, 253
Catholic Book Week, 205
Choral drama, 186-88
Choral speaking, 21-26, 50-53, 81-84, 113-16, 147-50, 163-68, 185-88, 205-09
Class conversations, 7-9
Class discussions, 7-9, 175-76
Class paragraphs, 57-62
Clauses, 376-93, 404-06, 409
  adjectival, 381-83, 392, 404
  adverbial, 381, 384-85, 404
  coordinate, 376-77
  introductory, 385, 409
  nonrestrictive, 383, 409
  noun, 381, 388-93, 405-06
  principal, 243-44, 356, 378, 388
  restrictive, 383, 409
  subordinate, 243-44, 356, 376, 378, 381-93
Clearness in paragraphs, 43-45, 70
Clubs, 153-62
Cognate object, 236
Cognate verbs, 292
Collective nouns, 214, 317
Colon, uses of, 138, 413
Comma, uses of, 120-21, 123, 138-39, 225, 377, 383, 385, 408-10
Committees, 153, 157
Common adjectives, 269
Common nouns, 213
Comparison
  of adjectives, 276-77, 279
  of adverbs, 341-42
  polishing sentences by, 97-99
Complex sentences, 243-44, 375, 378-93, 404-06
Compositions, 46-49. *See also* Paragraphs
Compound personal pronouns, 241, 267
Compound predicate, 373, 403
Compound relative pronouns, 249

Compound sentences, 376-77, 403, 410, 412
Compound subjects, 314-16, 373, 402
Compound tenses, 300
Conjugation, 304-09
Conjunctions, 353-61, 377, 385, 392
  correct use of, 358-61
  kinds of, 353-57, 377, 385
  test on, 363
Conjunctive adverbs, 337, 356, 385
Conversations, 3-20, 143-45, 146
Coordinate clauses, 376-77
Coordinate conjunctions, 353-55, 377, 412
Copulative verbs, 292-93, 344, 390
Correlative conjunctions, 355
Courtesy, 3-4, 7, 8, 10-12, 119, 134, 135, 138, 140, 144, 145, 155
"Courtship of Miles Standish," 164-68

Dash, use of, 417
"Daybreak," 24-25
Declarative sentences, 374, 407
Declension of pronouns, 240, 242
Defective verbs, 290
Degree
  adverbs of, 334
  of adjectives, 276-77, 279
  of adverbs, 341-42
Demonstrative adjectives, 272, 280
Demonstrative pronouns, 250
Dependent clauses. *See* Subordinate clauses
Descriptive adjectives, 269
Dewey Decimal Classification, 200
Diagrams, model, 399-406
Dialogues, 171-73
Diary, 78-79
Differ from, correct use of, 351
Differ with, correct use of, 351
Different from, correct use of, 350
Direct address, 223, 400, 408, 418
Direct object, 230, 257, 389, 401, 405
Direct questions, 242-43
Direct quotations, 408, 413, 415, 418
Directions, 3-5
Discussions, class, 7-9, 175-76
Disorderly paragraphs, 44-45

Distributive adjectives, 272
Distributive pronouns, 252, 265, 318
Doesn't, correct use of, 311
Donnelly, Eleanore C., 175, 178, 421
Don't, correct use of, 311
Double relative pronouns, 244
Dramatizations, 171-88

Each, compound subjects preceded by, 315
Editorials, 110
Either . . . or, correct use of, 361
Ending sentence, 38-39, 60-61, 72
Envelopes, 127
Every, compound subjects preceded by, 315
Exclamation, nominative of, 225, 400
Exclamation point, uses of, 225, 361-62, 374, 414
Exclamatory sentences, 361, 374, 414
Explanations, 5-7
Expletives, 346, 392

Faber, Frederick William, 208
Farther, correct use of, 345
Fewer, correct use of, 280
Formal talks, 13-17
From, correct use of, 350
Further, correct use of, 345

Gender, 221-22
Good Citizenship Club, 153-62
Group conversations, 7-9
Group paragraphs, 57-62

Heading of letters, 119-21, 138
Hyphen, uses of, 416

Imperative mood, 303
Imperative sentences, 374, 407
In, correct use of, 351
Indefinite adjectives, 272
Indefinite pronouns, 251, 265, 318
Independent clauses, 356, 376-77, 378, 388
Indicative mood, 301-02
Indirect object, 232-33, 258, 401
Indirect questions, 242-43

Infinitive phrases, 366-67
Inside address, 138
Intensive pronouns, 241, 267
Interjections, 361-63
Interrogation point, uses of, 374, 415
Interrogative adjectives, 272
Interrogative adverbs, 336
Interrogative pronouns, 242-43, 263
Interrogative sentences, 374. *See also* Questions
Interviews, 171-72
Into, correct use of, 351
Intransitive verbs, 291-92
Introductions, 10-13
Introductory clauses and phrases, 385, 409
Irregular verbs, 287-89

Kilmer, Joyce, 51

Lay, correct use of, 325
Leave, correct use of, 326
"Legend of the Robes," 175-79, 421-23
Less, correct use of, 280
Let, correct use of, 326
Letters, 119-41
 business, 119, 138-41
 kinds of, 129-37, 139-41
 parts of, 119-24, 138-39
 social, 119-37
Library, 199-204
Lie, correct use of, 325
Like, correct use of, 360
Limiting adjectives, 271-72
Lincoln, Abraham, 148-50, 162
Longfellow, Henry W., 24, 164
Luke, Saint, 186

Manner, adverbs of, 334
Many a, compound subjects preceded by, 315
Masefield, John, 206
Meetings, club, 153, 157-62
Middle sentences, 29, 30, 37-38, 61, 70
Misfit sentences, 37, 70
Model diagrams, 399-406
Mood, 301-03
"Mother of Mercy," 208-09

Natural order in sentences, 105, 372
Need of, correct use of, 351
Negation
 adverbs of, 334
 sentences expressing, 266
Neither . . . nor, correct use of, 361
News stories, 110
Newspaper, school, 110-12
No, compound subjects preceded by, 315
Nominative case, 222-25, 239, 254-55, 263, 264, 399-400
 in apposition, 224-25, 400
 of address, 223, 400
 of exclamation, 225, 400
 predicate nominative, 223, 255, 293, 298, 390, 400, 406
 subject, 223, 254, 399
Nonrestrictive clauses, 383, 409
Nonrestrictive phrases, 225, 409
Nothing, correct use of, 266
Noun clauses, 381, 388-93, 405-06
Noun phrases, 367
Nouns, 213-36
 abstract, 215
 case of, 222-36
 collective, 214, 317
 common, 213
 gender of, 221-22
 kinds of, 213-15
 modifications of, 217-36
 number of, 218-21, 319-20
 person of, 217
 proper, 213, 418
 test on, 238
Number, singular and plural, 218-21, 304, 319-20
Numeral adjectives, 271

O, correct use of, 362
"O Captain! My Captain!" 148-49
Objective case, 230-36, 239, 257-59, 263, 264, 340-41, 401-02
 adverbial objective, 234, 340-41, 402
 cognate object, 236
 direct object, 230, 257, 389, 401, 405
 in apposition, 231, 401
 indirect object, 232-33, 258, 401

 object of preposition, 230, 259, 349, 391, 401, 406
 objective complement, 235, 275, 402
 retained object, 234, 297-98, 402
Oh, correct use of, 362
Order, natural and transposed, 105, 372
Outlines for compositions and paragraphs, 47-49, 60, 68-70
Ownership, joint and separate, 229

Paragraphs
 in letters, 122
 in longer compositions, 46-47
 parts of, 29-38
 polishing, 87-109
 qualities of good, 41-45
 standards for judging, 107
 steps in writing, 63-78
 study of, 29-50
 writing of, 57-78
Parenthetical expressions, 313-14, 409-10
Participial phrases, 366-67
Passive voice, 295-96, 297-98, 299, 300
Period, uses of, 374, 407
Person, 217, 239-41, 304
Personal appearance, words describing, 93-95
Personal pronouns, 239-41, 254-60, 265, 267
Phrases, 366-69
 introductory, 409
 kinds of, 366-67
 transitional, 17
 verb, 286
Picture words, 58-59, 65-66, 88, 93-95, 97-99
Place, adverbs of, 334
Plays, writing of, 174-79
Plural, methods of forming, 218-21
Poems
 capital letters in, 80, 418
 dramatizing, 174-79
 for choral speaking, 23-25, 51-52, 82-84, 114-15, 148-49, 164-68, 186-88, 206-09
 writing, 79-80

INDEX 437

Possessive adjectives, 253, 265, 272
Possessive case, 227-29, 239, 253
Possessive pronouns, 253
Potential form, 301-02
Predicate, 371-73, 403
Predicate adjectives, 274-75, 293, 344
Predicate nominative, 223, 255, 293, 298, 390, 400, 406
Prepositional phrases, 366-67
Prepositions, 348-52, 366
  correct use of, 350-51
  object of, 230, 259, 349, 391, 401, 406
  test on, 363
Principal clauses, 243-44, 356, 378, 388
Principal parts, 287-89, 304, 306
Programs, club, 162, 180, 183-85
Pronominal adjectives, 271-72
Pronouns, 239-68
  adjective, 250-53
  agreement of, 245, 265, 267
  antecedent of, 239, 244, 245, 265, 267
  case of, 239, 254-64
  correct use of, 254-67
  demonstrative, 250
  distributive, 252, 265, 318
  indefinite, 251, 265, 318
  intensive, 241, 267
  interrogative, 242-43, 263
  kinds of, 239-53
  personal, 239-41, 254-60, 265, 267
  possessive, 253
  reflexive, 241, 267
  relative, 243-45, 249, 264, 357, 381, 392
  test on, 268
Proper adjectives, 269, 418
Proper nouns, 213, 418
Punctuation, 407-17
  of letters, 120-21, 123, 127, 138
  uses of colon, 138, 413
  uses of comma, 120-21, 123, 138-39, 225, 377, 383, 385, 408-10
  uses of exclamation point, 225, 361-62, 374, 414
  uses of interrogation point, 374, 415
  uses of period, 374, 407
  uses of semicolon, 377, 412

Questions
  direct and indirect, 242-43
  punctuation of, 374, 415
  use of *shall* and *will* in, 324
Quotation marks, uses of, 415
Quotations, direct, 408, 413, 415, 418

Radio, 181-85
Raise, correct use of, 325
Reference books, 199, 202-04
Reflexive pronouns, 241, 267
Regular verbs, 287
Relative adverbs, 338-39, 357, 381-82
Relative pronouns, 243-45, 249, 264, 357, 381, 392
Restrictive clauses, 383, 409
Restrictive phrases, 225, 409
Retained object, 234, 297-98, 402
Rise, correct use of, 325
"Roofs," 51-52

Salutation of letters, 121, 138, 410, 413
Semicolon, uses of, 377, 412
Sentences, 370-98
  beginning, 30-33, 60, 69
  classification of, 374-78
  complex, 243-44, 375, 378-93, 404-06
  compound, 376-77, 403, 410, 412
  declarative, 374, 407
  elements of, 370-73
  ending, 38-39, 60-61, 72
  exclamatory, 361, 374, 414
  imperative, 374, 407
  interrogative, 374
  middle, 29, 30, 37-38, 61, 70
  misfit, 37, 70
  order in, 105, 372
  polishing, 97-105, 106
  punctuation of, 374, 377, 383, 385
  simple, 375, 399-403
  topic, 34-36, 57, 69-70
Set, correct use of, 325
Shall, correct use of, 322, 324
Should, correct use of, 323
Signature of letters, 123, 138
Simple adverbs, 336
Simple sentences, 375, 399-403
Simple tenses, 299

Sit, correct use of, 325
Speakers
  introduction of, 12-13
  rules for, 17, 19
Speech, experiments in, 3-27
Still-life dramatizations, 180
"Story of the Shepherds," 186-88
Subject
  agreement of verbs with, 309-20
  for formal talks, 14-15
  of a paragraph, 57-58, 64
  of a sentence, 223, 254, 370, 372, 373, 388, 399, 405
Subjective complement, 223, 255, 292-93. *See also* Predicate nominative
Subordinate clauses, 243-44, 356, 376, 378, 381-93
Subordinate conjunctions, 356, 385
Synonyms, 89, 163
Synopsis
  of plays, 177
  of verbs, 309

Talks, formal, 13-17
Telephone, uses of, 143-47
Tense, 298-300, 322-23
Than, correct use of pronouns after, 260, 358-59
That, uses of, 392-93
There, uses of, 346
There are, correct use of, 312
There is, correct use of, 312
Time, adverbs of, 334
Titles
  for paragraphs and compositions, 48, 62, 75
  for plays, 179
To, correct use of, 351
Topic
  of formal talks, 14-15
  of paragraphs, 29, 30, 46, 47-48, 58, 60, 64
Topic sentence, 34-36, 57, 69-70
Transitional expressions, 17
Transitive verbs, 290, 292
Transposed order, 105, 372
Tuning-up exercises, 22, 50-51, 81, 113, 147-48, 163-64, 186, 206

Unity in paragraphs, 41-42, 70
Unless, correct use of, 359

Verb phrases, 286
Verbs, 285-332
  agreement of with subject, 309-20
  attributes or qualities of, 295-304
  auxiliary, 286, 299, 300, 302
  cognate, 292
  conjugation of, 304-09
  copulative, 292-93, 344, 390
  correct use of, 309-26
  defective, 290
  intransitive, 291-92
  irregular, 287-89
  kinds of, 287-93
  mood of, 301-03
  number of, 304
  person of, 304
  principal parts of, 287-89, 304, 306
  regular, 287
  tense of, 298-300, 322-23
  test on, 332-33
  transitive, 290, 292
  troublesome, 325-26
  voice of, 295-98
Verse, writing, 79-80
Verse-speaking choir, 23-24
Vocabulary, building of, 58-59, 65-66
Vocabulary hints, 17, 54, 116, 163
Voice, 295-98

"We Be the King's Men," 23
"West Wind," 206-07
Whitman, Walt, 148
Whittier, John Greenleaf, 82
Who, declension of, 242
Will, correct use of, 322, 324
Within, correct use of, 351
Without, correct use of, 359
Words
  order of, 104-05, 372
  picture, 58-59, 65-66, 88, 93-95, 97-99
  polishing, 87-95
Would, correct use of, 323

You, correct use of verb with, 313

MY ENGLISH RECORD

for Voyages in English, Grade 7

SEPTEMBER-OCTOBER

Extra Duty
Learning through Listening

As one of the most "talked-to" persons in the world, you have a challenge to learn through listening. If you try to look upon each speaker as a thinker who has something to say, soon you will begin to seek a personal, significant meaning in each message. The following exercise is designed to measure your "listening power quotient" (LPQ).

Copy the following questions into your notebook. Read them thoughtfully; then answer *yes* or *no* to each question.

1. Could you repeat the local weather report that you heard on today's newscast?
2. Could you give an accurate account of a major world event broadcast today?
3. Do you listen so attentively to your mother that, when she assigns a task to you, it is not necessary to repeat any of her instructions?
4. Do you follow your teacher's directions without asking unnecessary questions?
5. Can you repeat four intelligent contributions made by your classmates in school today during the social studies period?
6. As your teacher presented new work, did you formulate mental questions about points you did not fully understand?
7. Can you, without hesitation, discuss some new topic; or at least state the major points you learned in class today?

8 When one of your classmates found it necessary to ask a question concerning new work, did you listen attentively?
9 Did you concentrate on the answers given by the teacher to these questions?
10 Did you listen carefully to home assignments so that you could do them without consulting other classmates about directions, subject matter, or page numbers?

Your *Yes* scores will indicate your LPQ. From time to time, recheck this list to see if your listening attitude has improved.

SELF-CHECK 1

A Answer each of the following questions.
1 In choral speaking what voice inflection indicates a question?
2 What voice inflection indicates the stressing of certain words?
3 When are both rising and falling inflections used?
4 What is the rhyme scheme used in the poem "We Be the King's Men"?
5 What term signifies the beat of a line of poetry?
6 What type of poem expresses the personal thoughts or feelings of an author?

B Using the given list of club officers and members, indicate which officer or member would perform each of the duties listed.

President   Secretary   Any member
Vice president   Treasurer   Committee

1 Presides at meetings when the president is absent
2 Gives account of the money received and spent
3 Calls meeting to order
4 Votes on suggestions submitted
5 Moves to adjourn a meeting
6 Gives a club member the floor
7 Reads the minutes
8 Seconds a motion
9 Concentrates on special assignment from the president
10 Appoints committees
11 Addresses the chair
12 Submits suggestions

C Rearrange the following situations to the order in which they should occur at a club meeting.
1 Clare Holbert reads the minutes of the previous meeting.
2 John Burke calls the meeting to order.
3 Club members recite prayers, salute the flag, and sing "America the Beautiful."
4 A special group presents a "Speak Up for Christianity" program, urging club members to use their leisure time profitably.
5 Helen Harkins moves that the meeting be adjourned.
6 Club members discuss plans for a school newspaper.
7 James Barnes seconds the motion for adjournment.

D Choose the term that completes each of the following statements correctly.
1 Directions should be accurate, clear, and (lengthy, brief).
2 In giving definitions and explanations you should first make certain that you (know the answer, understand the question).
3 In an introduction the name of a (lay person, priest or religious) should be mentioned first.
4 (A formal, An informal) talk requires more preparation on the part of the speaker.
5 To have one sentence follow another smoothly, a speaker should use (transitional, prepositional) phrases.

E Classify each letter by writing S beside a social letter and B beside a business letter.
1 Letter of sympathy
2 Letter of application
3 Letter placing order
4 Letter of congratulation
5 Letter requesting information
6 Letter of invitation
7 Letter answering inquiries
8 Letter reporting errors

F Using the following information, address an envelope. Punctuate and capitalize correctly.
ADDRESS OF WRITER: 543 zachary lane, minneapolis, minnesota
ADDRESS OF RECEIVER: miss mary kealey, 2217 chestnut hill drive, trenton 6 new jersey

G Read the following paragraph; then answer the listed questions. The italicized words are explained in the seventh question.

Books do not constitute the sole source of information about life in past ages. Fossils, stony traces of plant and animal life that flourished thousands of years ago, present a record older than books. Some fossils are merely footprints of animals, made in mud that was covered by layers of rock-forming material. Other fossils include animal skeletons and bones found in rocks. Tree sap *encasing* the *skeletal* remains of insects often hardened into amber, thus preserving the insect shape intact. Sometimes the body outline of an animal was preserved because the soft tissues decayed, leaving a cavity or natural mold which filled with mud that turned into stone. Mineral deposits in water *petrified* the bone structures of dead fish to form their fossils. In the same manner, tissues of ancient plants, especially leaves and ferns, were pressed into rocks through the *preservative* action of soil minerals. Because of their *antiquity*, fossils of *primitive* animal and plant life have been called the earliest of Time's storytellers.

1. What is the subject of the paragraph?
2. What is the topic?
3. Write an appropriate title for the paragraph.
4. Is the beginning sentence also the topic sentence? Explain your answer.
5. Is there a misfit sentence in the paragraph?
6. Does the ending sentence in this paragraph give the last detail, a summary of the facts, or a personal comment?
7. Can you give the meaning of each italicized word in the paragraph? Check with the dictionary.

H Based on the information acquired through the reading of the paragraph in Section G, answer the following questions without rereading. How well did you "listen" to your reading?

1. What does the word *fossil* mean?
2. How many types of fossils can you name?
3. Explain at least three ways in which fossils are formed.

SELF-CHECK 2

A Find three sentence fragments in the following word groups. Add elements necessary to form complete thoughts, making the first revised sentence exclamatory, the second interrogative, and the third imperative.
1 Excessive rainfall frequently causes river floods
2 An incalculable amount of damage each year
3 Livestock are killed and crops are uprooted
4 Besides the destruction of property and life, floods
5 Essential factors in flood control

B Identify each sentence in natural order and in transposed order. List all the proper nouns and give the case of each.
1 Atop Philadelphia's City Hall stands a statue of William Penn.
2 Under the lava of Mt. Vesuvius slept the city of Pompeii.
3 Covered wagons rumbled over the Cumberland Road.
4 Marco Polo traveled to the court of Kublai Khan.
5 Down the Hudson steamed the *Clermont*.

C Punctuate each sentence. Justify the mark you select.
1 Much of the world is still unexplored but that area grows smaller daily.
2 By land by sea and by air man seeks out the unknown parts of the globe.
3 Space the farthest frontier of the universe now lures the modern pioneer.
4 Blastoff This word has become the challenge of the space age.
5 Space flights were first made by Americas astronauts in 1961.

D Complete each statement by selecting the correct word.
1 (Nothing, Anything) will overcome Joseph's obstacle.
2 The librarian recommended this book to Mary and (me, I).
3 The Catholic Charities succeeded in (raising, rising) large sums of money to help the needy.
4 There (is, are) many methods of flood control.
5 Do you think the temperature indicator on the new machine was (set, sat) properly?

E In each sentence underline the simple subject once and the simple predicate twice. Diagram Sentences 3 and 4.
1. From ancient times fur has been a symbol of wealth.
2. The exchange of fur for other commodities marked the earliest known form of trade.
3. Fur traders often preceded settlers into unexplored regions.
4. Fearless trappers, like the French voyagers, traveled down the St. Lawrence River.
5. Trappers established trading posts that later became great cities, such as Pittsburgh and Quebec.

F In the five sentences below underscore each verb; indicate whether it is transitive, intransitive, or copulative. Make a list of nouns and state the case of each. Justify all your answers.
1. An isthmus is a narrow strip of land between two larger portions of land.
2. The Isthmus of Suez joins Africa and Asia.
3. The Isthmus of Panama, in Central America, separates the Atlantic and the Pacific oceans.
4. The Isthmuses of Suez and Panama once greatly hampered ocean travel.
5. The Panama Canal! Everyone considers it an incredible engineering feat.

G Find one example of each of the following verb types in the sentences that follow. Consider only the italicized verbs.

| redundant verb | verb phrase | irregular verb |
| defective verb | regular verb | copulative verb |

1. A French company *built* the Suez Canal.
2. The composer Verdi *wrote* an opera for the ceremony celebrating the completion of the canal.
3. The Suez Canal, opened to traffic in 1869, *connects* the Mediterranean Sea with the Red Sea.
4. Egypt *has gained* control of the Suez Canal.
5. All ships that sail through the canal *ought* to pay a toll.
6. A lock in a canal *is* a kind of elevator.

H Combine each of the following groups of simple sentences into one compound sentence. Punctuate correctly.
1. Many individuals were cited for their service in building the Panama Canal. Foremost among them was the physician Dr. William Gorgas.
2. Scientists discovered that yellow fever is carried by a special kind of mosquito. Dr. Gorgas accepted the task of combating the disease.
3. No one who has traveled through the Panama Canal can forget this fascinating experience. No one can deny that the locks demonstrate man's engineering ingenuity.

I By using appositives combine each of the following pairs of sentences into one sentence. Punctuate correctly.
1. The construction of canals shortened the distances between many cities. Canals are man-made waterways.
2. In 1881 Ferdinand de Lesseps started a canal across the Isthmus of Panama. De Lesseps was a French engineer.
3. The Panama Canal was opened during President Wilson's administration. The Panama Canal is the link between the Atlantic and Pacific oceans.

J Indicate joint or separate possession in each of the following phrases.
1. Lewis and Clark expedition
2. Riley and Whittier poems
3. WoodScouts and Sky Scouts exhibit
4. Rodgers and Hammerstein musical
5. Chile and Peru exports
6. Bradford and Brown store

NOVEMBER-DECEMBER

Extra Duty
Proofreading

With practice proofreading becomes an automatic self-check of everything you write, whether it is a sentence, a paragraph, a letter, or a long composition. Students commonly use their knowledge of proofreading to check answers for essay-type tests and examinations.

After reading an examination question carefully, the first step is to recall what you know about the subject. Then you must select important facts and organize the information that you wish to include. These three steps are essential: you must understand the question, know the answer, and present your information in logical order. Ask yourself questions such as these:

1 Do I understand the question?
2 What are the important facts about this subject?
3 In what order shall the facts be presented?

Frequently it helps to jot down on a piece of scratch paper all the ideas that occur to you before deciding upon the order of presentation. Since you are concentrating on ideas, your sentence structure, spelling, and punctuation may not be perfect. Therefore form the habit of proofreading all written work. These questions will help.

1 Have I used complete sentences?
2 Have I varied the sentence structure?
3 Have I watched verb agreement?
4 Have I checked the spelling of any word of which I am in doubt?
5 Have I punctuated my answer correctly?

Let us see how others proofread their written work. Assume that the question on an examination paper reads:

What are vitamins? Give the sources of and state the value of three important vitamins.

The student recalls that vitamins are chemicals; they are in foods we eat and they prevent disease; many people refer to vitamins by letter; vitamin C is found in citrus fruits; vitamin B is not just one substance; we studied about vitamin B_1, B_2, and B_{12}; vitamin D is added to milk; B_{12} comes from liver; vitamin C is really ascorbic acid; riboflavin is B_2, and thiamin is B_1.

As the three vitamins to be discussed this student selected thiamin, riboflavin, and ascorbic acid. Note the changes that he made after proofreading the answer.

Vitamins are chemical substances found in foods, which we must have in order to keep well. Three important vitamins are thiamin, riboflavin, and ascorbic acid. The first of these, thiamin or B_1 vitamin as it is commonly called, aids digestion and is important to the proper functioning of the nervous system. Better known as vitamin B_2, riboflavin contributes to our well being by promoting growth and by keeping the skin and muscles in a healthy condition. The chief sources of vitamin B_1 and B_2 are milk, eggs, lima beans, nuts, and yeast. The third vitamin, ascorbic acid, is the much-discussed vitamin C. Citrus fruits, vegetables green, tomatoes, and cabbage contain vitamin C. Its main work is to keep in good condition the bones, teeth, and gums, and to help the body resists infection.

To give yourself practice in proofreading read the answer given here to an essay-type question. Decide first whether the student understands the question, presents important facts, and arranges his ideas in good order. Correct any errors in his answer. Here you find the question and the answer.

How would you explain the term "Gift of the Nile"?

By the term Gift of the nile is meant the rich deposit of alluvial soil left by the waters of the Nile river. This is caused by the heavy sumner rains in ethiopia The nile overflows it's banks. It recedes from the high level usually during September. This rich deposit left annually have enabled the Egyptians to rise abundnat crops. Cotton is among these. Egypt exports cotton the.

SELF-CHECK 3

A Complete the following statements.
1 When sentences follow in a natural and orderly way a paragraph has _____.
2 The _____ indicates the order that is to be followed in the middle sentences.
3 Misfit sentences destroy _____ in a paragraph.
4 In a paragraph that _____ sentences should be arranged in the order of observation.
5 A sentence that states the one main idea of a paragraph is called the _____.

B Prepare an outline that would serve for a paragraph on one of the subjects listed on page 64 of this textbook.

        SUBJECT _____
        TOPIC _____
Topic sentence _____
Middle sentences
    1 _____
    2 _____
    3 _____
Ending sentence _____

C Using the outline you prepared for Section B, write an original paragraph.

D Indicate your knowledge of library procedures and practice by matching the purpose or aim with the word that signifies the term or department.

Purpose or Aim	Terminology
1 The arrangement of books according to subject matter	_____ circulation division
2 Responsible for books that are taken out	_____ reference division
3 A type of classification	_____ card catalogue
4 In charge of books that cannot be taken from the library, as encyclopedias	_____ classification
5 Files containing complete record of all the books in that library	_____ Dewey Decimal system

E This matching exercise is based on business letters. Match parts and punctuation with the positions indicated.

Where?	What?
1 In the body of the letter	_____ colon
2 Above the salutation	_____ zone number
3 After the salutation	_____ comma
4 After the complimentary close	_____ clearness, brevity, simplicity
5 Between the city and state	_____ inside address

F Underline the verb in each headline.

1 Savio Club Presents Awards
2 Eagles Trounce Burrs
3 TV Arrives
4 Bishop Confirms 300
5 P.T.A. Meets
6 New Building Tours Begin

G Pretend you are a newspaper reporter. From the notes below write the lead paragraph for a news article. Add a headline that will attract attention.

President Lincoln assassinated
Ford's Theater in Washington
Called the Great Emancipator
Lincoln's lenient theories of reconstruction
John Wilkes Booth, a mentally unbalanced actor

H Rearrange the following sentences in order to obtain a paragraph that will have the quality of clearness. Omit or change any idea or thought that would destroy the unity of the paragraph. After you have revised the order of or omitted sentences, add an appropriate title.

All the work required, all the sacrifices entailed, and all the years of preparation are exciting challenges that I am determined to meet and to conquer. Though mountain climbing always appealed to my imagination, it was not until last summer that it became a burning ambition in my life. Mine is a daring dream, which I hope some day will be realized on the breath-taking summit of a towering mountain. The prospect of attending a training school, where I will learn firsthand the terrors and thrills of scaling fabulous heights, does not discourage me. When my eyes edged up those majestic mountains for the first time, I knew that I would not be satisfied until my heart followed my gaze.

I Answer these questions about the paragraph you revised in Section H.
1 What is the subject of the paragraph?
2 Which is the topic sentence?
3 Where did you put the topic sentence in the revised paragraph? Was it the beginning sentence or in another position?
4 Underline the words that make the paragraph vivid.

J Complete the following statements about social letters.
1 Letters of invitation should be cordial and should contain _____ information.
2 An invitation demands an _____ reply.
3 In a letter of regret the writer gives the _____ for declining.
4 In a letter of acceptance, the _____, the _____, the _____, and the _____ should be repeated.
5 A letter of regret should be just as _____ and _____ as a letter of acceptance.

SELF-CHECK 4

A Select an example of each of the following forms of nouns and verbs in the sentences after the list.

predicate nominative   passive voice, present tense
retained object   active voice, imperative mood
subject as receiver of action compound subject

1 Notice the plants in your backyard.
2 The green coloring matter in plants has been given the name chlorophyll.
3 Green is the color of the food-making substance in plants.
4 Tree buds are made during the summer months.
5 The leaves of all grasses have parallel veins.
6 Brian and I watered the plants every day.

B Use the correct form of the verb shown in parentheses in each sentence and identify the tense you have used.

Sentence	Tense
1 Last Friday the boys _(swim)_ in the pool.	_____
2 John _(sing)_ in the choir for five years.	_____
3 Kevin _(wear)_ his Sunday suit in the procession next Tuesday.	_____
4 Jane _(eat)_ lunch when I called for her.	_____
5 Mother _(bake)_ a cake before they arrive.	_____
6 The sun _(rise)_ long before Father awoke.	_____

C Before each sentence in the second column write the number of the construction that the italicized word or words represents.

Construction	Sentence
1 Indirect object	_____ Johnny Seatiur wrote *Poor Gitchey's Almanac*.
2 Direct object	_____ John was awarded first *prize* in the essay contest.
3 Appositive	_____ The guide showed *us* the geysers in Yellowstone National Park.
4 Object of a preposition	_____ We saw distinct layers of rock, *pages* in the book of the earth.
5 Retained object	_____ Wood is exported by *Finland*.

D Give the gender, number, and case of each pronoun in these sentences. Name each interrogative and each relative pronoun.
1 Was it William Harvey who discovered the truth about the circulation of the blood?
2 Did Atalanta promise to marry any man who outran her?
3 Who defeated Tecumseh at Tippecanoe Creek?
4 Can you imagine the joy with which Washington's troops received the news of French aid?
5 Who was responsible for the Embargo Act of 1807?
6 Which is the greatest commandment?

E Choose the correct degree of comparison in each sentence. The adjective or adverb to be inserted appears in parentheses. Note the part of speech of each.
1 Which coat is (suitable), the green or the tan?
2 Of the three books I have read, I like this one (good).
3 Which is the (sweet) candy, bonbons or licorice?
4 Write this paragraph (carefully) than you wrote the letter.
5 Mother held the baby (gently) than Jane did.
6 Of the three vehicles, the brown auto traveled (rapidly).
7 Where can you find the (large) dinosaur bone?

F Indicate the part of speech of each of the italicized words in these sentences.
1. The Eagles will *rival* the best teams next season.
2. Brian was George's keenest *rival* on the basketball court.
3. The *rival* team cheered loudly.
4. What *average* did you make on that test?
5. I'm sure John will *average* a 90 per cent mark.
6. The *average* size of a dinner plate is nine inches.
7. Richard went *outside* for a minute.
8. *Outside* the compound the refugees were in danger.
9. The *outside* walls were made of clapboard.
10. The paper was an *organ* of the Catholic Action group.
11. The *organ* grinder cranked out a squeaking melody.
12. The doctor prescribed a remedy for the ear *discharge*.
13. *Discharge* the plumber when the work has been completed.
14. The soldier viewed his *discharge* papers with interest.
15. The *club* sandwich appealed to the hungry boy.
16. The *club* required an identification card from each member.
17. Did the trainer *club* the animal before he left the cage?
18. Dennis and Michael *air* their views frequently.
19. Iron rusts when it is exposed to the *air* for a long period of time.
20. A familiar voice came over the *air* waves.

G Insert the proper punctuation marks when copying each of the following sentences.
1. In the pamphlet *Common Sense*, Thomas Paine cried Oh ye that love mankind! Ye that dare oppose not only tyranny but the tyrant, stand forth
2. The Union replied Calhoun next to our liberty, the most dear
3. Was it Daniel Webster who said Liberty and Union, now and forever, one and inseparable! asked Catherine
4. John Greenleaf Whittier wrote The Barefoot Boy
5. It was Horace Greeley founder of the *New York Tribune* who wrote Turn your face to the great West, and there build up a home and fortune

H Select the correct form of the verb in each sentence and explain the agreement.
1. The director and choreographer (meets, meet) with the cast each morning.
2. The composer and the lyricist (was, were) present for the first performance of the musical comedy.
3. The halfback and the captain (work, works) for the good of the team.
4. The president and the dean (are, is) members of the board of trustees of the university.
5. The secretary and treasurer (hand, hands) in a report each Thursday afternoon.
6. The explanation and cause of the economic recession (was, were) developed in the president's speech.

JANUARY REVIEW

Extra Duty
Spelling Workshop

Good spelling indicates that a person takes pride in his work and is interested in improving himself. Seek at all times to increase your ability to spell correctly.

The rules given here concerning words ending in the letter *y* will undoubtedly be applied on many occasions in your writing. Learn them now.

1. A word ending in *y* preceded by a consonant changes the *y* to *i* before adding a suffix.

   ninety + eth = ninetieth   lazy + ness = laziness

   Exception: The *y* does not change when adding *ing*.

   hurry + ing = hurrying   carry + ing = carrying

2. A word ending in *y* preceded by a vowel usually retains the *y* when adding a suffix.

   enjoy + ing = enjoying   relay + ed = relayed

Number your paper 1 to 20 and prepare to take words from dictation. Correctly spell each of the following combinations and indicate by number the rule you apply in each case.

1. candy + ed =
2. cozy + ly =
3. funny + er =
4. library + an =
5. friendly + ness =
6. buy + er =
7. trolley + s =
8. mystery + ous =
9. hurry + ed =
10. drowsy + ly =
11. forty + eth =
12. obey + ing =
13. biography + es =
14. necessary + ly =
15. play + ful =
16. alloy + ed =
17. easy + ness =
18. worry + ing =
19. likely + hood =
20. beauty + ful =

SELF-CHECK 5

A Complete the following statements by inserting the correct word or words.

1. The various sounds used during a radio broadcast are called _____ _____.
2. "America the Beautiful" is a _____ poem.
3. Dictionaries, encyclopedias, and atlases are classified as _____ books.
4. Detailed information about a word is found in an _____ dictionary.
5. Words that have the same general meaning are called _____.
6. An _____ contains brief summaries of events that take place during a year and includes various statistics.
7. Short articles on a variety of topics are found in an _____.
8. A book of maps is called an _____.

B Substitute a synonym for each of the italicized words. Notice how the paragraph is improved.

GUARDIAN OF LIBERTY

On a *little* island in New York harbor stands the *wonderful* Statue of Liberty. This *sign* of freedom is made of copper. Although hollow, the *big* statue weighs over two hundred tons. The torch held *up* beams a *greeting* to all who come to the *great* country of the United States.

SELF-CHECK 6

A Select the word that fits each explanation.

EXPLANATION	WORD
1 Refers to distance or mileage	_____ fewer
2 Denotes place; an expletive	_____ less
3 Denotes possession	_____ farther
4 Used when number is indicated	_____ further
5 Implies an addition in extent or degree	_____ there
6 Used in indicating quantity	_____ their

B Give the syntax of each italicized word in the following sentences. For nouns and pronouns indicate the case and reason for the case; for adjectives name the type and the word modified; include the tense, voice, and mood of verbs.

1. The boys *elected* Richard *president* of the Savio Club.
2. Every seventh grader was *happy* about the *election* results because each pupil considered Richard *reliable* and *trustworthy*.
3. Richard appeared *overjoyed* at the confidence placed in *him*.
4. The new *president* announced that the club would meet every *Thursday* after school.
5. At the first meeting the officers *will appoint* Joseph *chairman* of the clothing drive.

C Point out all the prepositional phrases in the following sentences. Make four columns on a piece of paper with these headings: Preposition; Object (of preposition); Use (in sentence); and Word (or words) modified.

EXAMPLE: The marbles were divided among us.

Preposition	Object	Use	Word modified
among	us	adverbial	were divided

1. Michigan is located near the Great Lakes.
2. The Mississippi River divides the United States into two parts.
3. Members of the seventh grade of Saint Aloysius School are interested in the Savio Club.
4. The Atacama Desert, rich in nitrates, lies in northern Chile.
5. The largest group of islands in the entire world is that of the East Indies.

FEBRUARY-MARCH

Extra Duty
Dictionary Duty

An unabridged dictionary differs from an abridged dictionary in size and content. *Abridged* means "shortened"; hence, *unabridged* means "not shortened." Any dictionary contains almost all the words in the English language now in current usage. However, the unabridged dictionary gives more detailed information about words. In addition, the larger dictionary contains additional sections; such as translations of foreign words and phrases, biographical data concerning famous people, a geographical section or gazeteer, abbreviations and equivalents, explanation of signs and symbols, and new words.

In addition to the formal words in the English language, some words in the dictionary bear one of the follow labels: *colloquial* (colloq.), *archaic* (arch.), *obsolete* (obs.), and *slang*. Each of these labels designates a particular level of speech and language.

COLLOQUIAL	language accepted in ordinary familiar conversation and writing; unsuitable in formal speech and writing
ARCHAIC	language of an earlier period; retained only in poetry or special contexts
OBSOLETE	language no longer in use because it is out of date
SLANG	language comprising terms that have a forced, fantastic, or grotesque meaning

Learn to read these symbols and to avoid the use of such words in compositions, test papers, and all schoolwork.

A Consult a reliable dictionary to find the answers to the following questions.
1. What is the pronunciation of *coliseum*?
2. What symbol represents perpendicular lines?
3. Who was Kipling? What is his full name?
4. What does the abbreviation A.M.A. signify?
5. What does the word *apartheid* mean? How is it pronounced?

B Consult a reliable dictionary to secure the general information indicated in each question.
1. What is delftware? Why is it so named?
2. What is the volume of a cord of wood?
3. For what reason would a captain issue an order to jettison the cargo?
4. What is a lady's-slipper?
5. Explain the abbreviation B.C.
6. What is a karakul? Where is it found?
7. When was James Madison president of the United States?
8. What is a letterhead?
9. What nationality was Johann Gutenberg and for what work was he famous?
10. What part of a boat is the gunwale? Give another term for this part.
11. What is a hansom and how did its name originate?
12. How many fathoms are in 300 feet?
13. What is the boiling point of water according to the Fahrenheit scale? Is it the same on the Centigrade scale?
14. Is a freeway free?
15. Why is the Parthenon famous? Describe it to the class, giving as much information as possible.

C Consult a reliable dictionary; give a synonym to indicate the meaning of each word and attach the correct label—*colloquial, archaic, obsolete,* or *slang*.

1 quoth	5 rumpus	9 kirtle	13 affright
2 sashay	6 jiffy	10 nifty	14 bruit
3 hokum	7 flunk	11 flivver	15 jitters
4 mayhap	8 shoon	12 methinks	16 stuck-up

SELF-CHECK 7

A Match each of the sounds in the first column with a suitable situation from the second column.

Sound effect	Situation
1 The indistinguishable babble	_____ of an old Ford panting up a long hill
2 Staccato peeps	_____ of bees in the meadow
3 The sing-song chant	_____ of a moving porch rocker
4 The spasmodic chugging	_____ of baby chicks
5 The monotonous hum	_____ of children's voices
6 An irritating chirp	_____ of a rake combing the lawn
7 The angry protest	_____ of children's games
8 The rhythmic scraping	_____ of crickets tuning up on a sultry day
9 The contented creak	_____ of a blizzard working itself into a fury
10 That icy whistle	_____ of a tire stuck in a snowdrift

B Choose a suitable adjective describing each of the following.
1 The face of a mother whose child is very ill
2 The face of a child who has just opened a birthday gift
3 The face of a seventh grader who is trying to solve a difficult arithmetic problem
4 The hair of a girl who was caught hatless in the rain
5 The hair of a little boy dressed for a party
6 The eyes of a sickly child
7 The eyes of an insulted young man
8 The lips of a small child being punished
9 The lips of a frightened young woman
10 The figure of an old man laboring up a hill
11 The figure of a soldier on sentry duty
12 The voice of an umpire as he calls a strike
13 The voice of a mother as she sings to her baby
14 The clothes of an organ grinder
15 The clothes of a gentleman dressed for business

C Rewrite the following phrases, taken from the poem "The Legend of the Robes," pages 421–23, in your own words.
1 the spouse/Of Louis of Thuringia
2 her latticed room
3 the ancient casement
4 The chaste decorum of her simple robe
5 russet cloak
6 A step pulsed through the hall
7 all the pomp of ducal dignity/Sunk in obscure retreat
8 raiment comelier than a queen's attire
9 Burning to bruit what gossips burn to hear
10 communing with her words
11 Her soft, slow step is herald to her coming
12 silence chains the lords who grace the feast

D In the following paragraph supply suitable sound words in the blank spaces.

Without its accompanying sound effects a basketball game would not be half the fun! Once the contest begins the insistent _____ of the buzzer and the dull _____ of the ball, as it passes from referee to player, replace the noisy pre-game _____ of the spectators. Then crowd reaction quickens to an excited _____ as a darting forward dribbles the ball in a rapid-fire _____ toward the basket. Muffled _____ from one side of the bleachers and triumphant _____ from the other side frequently tell the story of the ball's fate even before the scoreboard does. At other times the tense silence is punctuated only by the _____ of sneakers as a player turns deftly on the court or by the _____ of a whistle as the referee calls a foul. Hoarse _____ of encouragement and disgusted _____ of disapproval occasionally drift from the stands to the court. At the game's end the excited _____ of winners, losers, players, and rooters merge into a _____ medley. What a lifeless experience a basketball game without sound would be!

E Complete the following statements.
1. An _____ is an interesting incident, sometimes amusing, associated with the life of some person.
2. The poem "O Captain! My Captain!" by Walt Whitman, which mourns the death of Abraham Lincoln, is an example of a _____.
3. A book report gives a brief _____ of a story.
4. A letter of _____ is written to someone who has suffered some sorrow, such as illness or the death of a relative.
5. A day-by-day record you keep of personal experiences in your life is called a _____.

SELF-CHECK 8

A Complete each of the following statements by writing the correct word in the blank space.
1. A _____ adjective is an adjective that points out a definite person, place, or thing.
2. A _____ adjective is an adjective that denotes ownership.
3. A _____ adjective is an adjective that refers to each person, place, or thing separately.
4. An _____ adjective is an adjective that points out no particular person, place, or thing.
5. An _____ adjective is an adjective that may be used in asking a question.

B Tell whether the clauses in the following sentences are restrictive or nonrestrictive. Punctuate accordingly.
1. Abraham Lincoln who emancipated the slaves labored unceasingly to keep our country united.
2. Pope Pius XII was a man whose great love for people of all nationalities became evident during World War II.
3. I prefer students who are enthusiastic and willing.
4. In France the pilgrims visited the house where the Little Flower spent her childhood.
5. Independence Hall which is located in Philadelphia houses the renowned Liberty Bell.

C Make a complex sentence from each pair of simple sentences.
1 World War II ended in Europe on May 7, 1945. On this day the Allies formally accepted the surrender of all forces under German control.
2 Noah Webster wrote the first great American dictionary. He could trace his ancestry back to Governor William Bradford of Plymouth.
3 Angel Falls, in Venezuela, reigns as the highest waterfall in the world. It is about twenty times higher than Niagara Falls.
4 The *Hindenburg* was a huge zeppelin. It exploded just as it completed a flight from Germany to the United States.
5 In the ocean near Florida lives the great barracuda. Fishermen call it the tiger of the sea.

D Complete the following statements by choosing the correct word or words. Give the reason for your choice.
1 You cannot be an outstanding athlete (unless, without) you practice regularly.
2 The missionaries look (like, as, as if) they had suffered many hardships in life.
3 The troops prepared to attack (like, as, as if) the sun rose.
4 (Unless, Without) baptism, you cannot enter the kingdom of heaven.
5 The young Indian bravely swam (like, as, as if) a fish.

E Encircle the introductory word in each adjectival clause and indicate whether it is a relative pronoun or a relative adverb.
1 Hiroshima is the city where the atomic bomb fell for the first time in 1945.
2 The class visited Washington, D.C., which is famous for its historic monuments.
3 Balboa, who discovered the Pacific Ocean, explored the New World in the name of Spain.
4 April is the month when baseball tryouts take place.
5 Pearl Harbor, where the Japanese attacked the United States Fleet on December 7, 1941, is on the south coast of the island of Oahu.

F Tell whether each italicized word is used as an adjective or as a pronoun. Classify it as demonstrative, indefinite, distributive, possessive, or interrogative.
1. Chinese children have great respect for *their* elders.
2. The Romans waged *many* wars against the Gauls.
3. Father Damien treated *everyone* on the island of Molokai with kindness.
4. *That* reservoir provides water for the Great Basin.
5. *What* do you think about the reconstruction period that followed the Civil War?
6. *All* in the senior class made the retreat.
7. Lafayette volunteered *his* services to the American cause in 1777.
8. *Each* member of the United Nations must strive for world peace.
9. In 1930 *few* men believed that Adolf Hitler would rise to great power.
10. The young graduate firmly stated, "*Ours* is the future."

G Tell whether the italicized word in each sentence is an interrogative adverb, a relative adverb, or a conjunctive adverb.
1. *When* did the Civil War begin?
2. Call me *when* you have finished your homework.
3. Peter told his teacher the reason *why* he was late.
4. *Why* did King Saul want to kill David?

H Copy this paragraph, using the correct forms of verbs.

The safety patrol (performs, perform) a very important service for the school. Members of the squad (watches, watch) over boys and girls on their way to and from school. A white safety belt and a silver badge (distinguishes, distinguish) these boys from the other students. One of the boys (wears, wear) a maroon belt, which signifies outstanding performance of duty. The captain, together with the lieutenant, (see, sees) that all members carry out their assigned tasks. Every boy (anticipate, anticipates) the day when he will be privileged to be on the school safety patrol.

APRIL-MAY

Extra Duty
Appreciating Poetry

Writers, especially poets, often present vivid word pictures by using comparisons. One form of comparison, personification, treats a lifeless object as if it had human qualities.

> The tree waved its arms
> As the wind rushed by.

Another way of making a comparison is by means of a metaphor. This is a figure of speech in which two objects are compared by speaking of one as if it were the other.

> The stream was an eel
> Shivering down the mountainside.

The reader, of course, knows that the stream is not an eel. However, if he understands what an eel is—a slippery, wiggling creature—he applies this to the stream and develops a vivid mental picture. Many times an intriguing comparison says much more in a few words than a drab paragraph of many words.

A Explain the similarity between the things compared in these two verses.

1 Fireflies are
  Flickering candles
  On the table
  Of night.

2 The sky
  Was a blue counterpane
  With white cloud tufts
  For decoration.

B Write original metaphors about each of the following objects or persons. Indicate the points of similarity.

rustling leaves   a bouquet of violets   a brave soldier
a beautiful baby   a dedicated priest   a thunderstorm

A limerick is a form of nonsense poem with a definite pattern of rhyme and rhythm. Read the following limerick aloud and tap out the rhythm with your finger.

> There once was a pig that was thinner
> Than the rest, so he thought, "What a winner!"
> "They'll let me go free."
> But mistaken was he,
> This pig was the first to be dinner!

Note that the first, second, and fifth lines have three feet or accented syllables; the third and fourth lines have two feet. What conclusions do you draw concerning the rhyming pattern?

It is customary to mark the first line of poetry and all other lines that have the same end sound with the letter *a*. When a new sound is introduced, the next letter of the alphabet, in this case *b*, is used. What lines of this poem would be marked *a* and what lines would receive the letter *b*? Is the rhyming pattern a-a-b-b-a?

A limerick always contains five lines; the first, second, and fifth lines rhyme and have the same number of accented syllables. The third and fourth lines also rhyme and have the same number of accented syllables. Note, however, that there are not so many syllables in the third and fourth lines as in the first group of rhyming lines that were designated *a*.

C Finish the following limerick. Make sure you adhere to the rhythm and the rhyme scheme.

> Marie and her friends swam in doubles
> But that was before she had troubles,
> For the whistle was blown
> _____
> _____.

28

SELF-CHECK 9

A Answer the following questions about the poem entitled "The West Wind."
1 Who is the author of "The West Wind"?
2 What mood does the poem express?
3 About what country is the poem written?
4 What is the rhyme scheme of each stanza?
5 What objects in the poem are green? White? Brown?
6 What month does the author describe?

B Select the phrase that completes each statement correctly.
1 It is not good form to use the telephone to—1 express congratulations   2 offer sympathy to a friend on a relative's death   3 extend an invitation.
2 Ann Shields should answer the telephone by saying—1 "Hello"   2 "Who is it?"   3 "Shields' residence, Ann speaking."
3 If you witness an accident, first call—1 a priest and a doctor   2 a doctor and a hospital   3 a priest and a policeman.
4 To order articles from a store you would make—1 a business call   2 a social call   3 an emergency call.
5 A social call would include—1 a call to your father's office to report that he was ill   2 a call to your cousin to wish him a happy birthday   3 a call to the Western Union office requesting that wedding congratulations be sent to a relative.

C What type of letter would you write in each situation?
1 Ann Burns invites you to a party, which will take place the day after you go to the country for the summer.
2 For your birthday you received a leather wallet from your Aunt Jane and Uncle John.
3 One of your classmates is in the hospital; you hear he has a broken leg.
4 You wish to write to Sears Roebuck and Company to order softball equipment.
5 Your mother will allow you to have a friend from Chicago spend a week end with you.

D To check your knowledge of longer compositions, answer the following questions.

1. How do you identify the topic of each separate paragraph in an outline?
2. How do you identify each important subdivision within each paragraph in the outline?
3. How many paragraphs must a composition have?
4. What is one method of attaining unity in the composition?
5. When is it necessary to introduce a new paragraph?

E Think of an original composition that you might develop from the six disconnected sentences listed here. Would you need one paragraph or more than one to develop the topic? Prepare an outline in which you indicate topic and the principal points to be developed. If you wish, include details.

My mother wants my father to buy a ranch house.
John, a friend of mine, wants to become a priest.
The odor of pine needles has always intrigued me.
John intends to buy a houseboat and establish a parish for fishermen along Snake River.
She is tired of climbing stairs.
If I had my way, I'd like to live in a cabin in the Sierras.

SELF-CHECK 10

A Read the following paragraph; then follow the directions after it. The sentences are numbered for ease of reference.

[1]Among the snow-capped peaks of the Andes Mountains, which separate Argentina from Chile, stands a huge bronze statue of Christ holding upright a large cross. [2]After a war threat had endangered peace in 1902, the two countries erected the statue so that war between them would be averted forever. [3]Both nations melted old cannons left by the Spaniards to make the statue. [4]On its base is the inscription that the mountains must crumble before Argentina and Chile fight. [5]Since that time the cross in the sky has provided a peaceful solution to the differences between these peoples.

1 List the verbs in the present tense.
2 Give the attributes of the pronoun *them* (sentence 2).
3 Which sentence in the paragraph is simple in form?
4 Give the attributes of the verbs *had endangered* (sentence 2), *is* (sentence 4), *has provided* (sentence 5).
5 Select the verbs in the potential form of the indicative mood. Give the tense of each.
6 Select the adverbial clauses from the paragraph.
7 The words *forever* (sentence 2), *both* (sentence 3), *its* (sentence 4), *since* (sentence 5), *peaceful* (sentence 5), *these* (sentence 5) are what parts of speech?
8 Give the attributes of the nouns *Andes Mountains* (sentence 1), *statue* (sentence 1), *solution* (sentence 5).
9 Choose the noun clause from this selection. Give its use.
10 Give the syntax of the subordinate clause in the first sentence.

B Indicate, by placing either S or P beside the number, whether each word or word group is singular or plural. Use each as a subject in an original sentence.

1 mathematics
2 clothes
3 each book
4 neither of the boys
5 ashes
6 no one
7 everybody
8 athletics
9 each of the men
10 a book of short stories
11 scissors
12 either Jane or Alice

C Choose the correct verb forms to complete each of the following sentences.

1 The class (have, has) completed their reports.
2 The citizens' committee (has, have) voted unanimously to improve the city parks.
3 A group of workers (take, takes) the bus at the corner.
4 The jury (is, are) disagreeing about the verdict.
5 (Do, Does) the team intend to go to San Francisco?
6 A herd of cattle (was, were) sent to the Chicago market.
7 The school orchestra (entertain, entertains) the orphans once a month.
8 The Pacific fleet (has, have) been alerted for action.

D Give the reason for the indicated mark of punctuation in each of the sentences.

1. The Gold Rush of '49 helped to populate the western part of our country. (apostrophe)
2. A citizen reaches the age of majority at twenty-one. (hyphen)
3. At the time of the Civil War the North was to a great extent industrialized; the South was predominantly agricultural. (semicolon)
4. Father, forgive them for they know not what they do. (comma)
5. In his second inaugural address Lincoln urged the nation: "Let us strive on to finish the work we are in; to bind up the nation's wounds; . . . to do all which may achieve and cherish a just and lasting peace among ourselves, and with all nations." (colon)

Made in the USA
Columbia, SC
13 June 2024

013ab44b-9ab0-42eb-9d69-e5fd81ea151eR02